HARVARD ECONOMIC STUDIES

VOLUME XII

THE STUDIES IN THIS SERIES ARE PUBLISHED BY THE DEPARTMENT OF ECONOMICS OF HARVARD UNIVERSITY, WHICH, HOWEVER, ASSUMES NO RESPONSIBILITY FOR THE VIEWS EXPRESSED

LONDON : HUMPHREY MILFORD
OXFORD UNIVERSITY PRESS

SOME ASPECTS OF THE TARIFF QUESTION

AN EXAMINATION OF THE DEVELOPMENT OF AMERICAN INDUSTRIES UNDER PROTECTION

BY

FRANK WILLIAM TAUSSIG

HENRY LEE PROFESSOR OF ECONOMICS IN HARVARD UNIVERSITY

THIRD ENLARGED EDITION CONTINUED TO 1930

WITH THE COÖPERATION OF

HARRY DEXTER WHITE

PROFESSOR OF ECONOMICS IN LAWRENCE COLLEGE

CAMBRIDGE

HARVARD UNIVERSITY PRESS

1934

Second Impression

PRINTED AT THE HARVARD UNIVERSITY PRESS
CAMBRIDGE, MASS., U. S. A.

PREFACE

THE main purpose of the present volume is to consider and illustrate some questions of principle in the controversy on free trade and protection. The three chapters which constitute Part I state these questions and summarize the main conclusions. The succeeding Parts give illustrations and verifications drawn from the history of several industries, — sugar, iron and steel, and textiles. Something is thereby done, I trust, to make more precise and complete the theory of the subject, and to vivify it through illustrations from experience; and some contribution is offered also on the general economic history of the United States.

The inquiries whose results are here given have extended over more than a quarter of a century, and I have utilized in this book portions of various papers published at intervals during the period. In the *Quarterly Journal of Economics* for April, 1889, I printed an article on " Some Aspects of the Tariff Question " which contained the germ of much that is now more fully elaborated. It gives me satisfaction to be able to say that, great as have been the changes during the past twenty-five years in the industries considered then and now, the main reasoning of this early article is not impugned. The extraordinary and in many ways unexpected industrial developments serve to confirm its conclusions rather than modify them. Later articles in the same *Journal* I have used in a more literal sense, by the incorporation of some passages verbatim; two articles on the iron and steel industry, published in February and August, 1900, and another on the beet-sugar industry, published in February, 1912. I have also used parts of an article in the *Atlantic Monthly* for March, 1908, on sugar and reciprocity. Chapter II was printed almost as it stands in the *Atlantic Monthly* for May, 1913. The substance of some of the later chapters was given in lectures delivered at the Lowell Institute in Boston, in 1912.

Valuable aid has come from students who have worked with me on these topics in Harvard University. I have to acknowledge more particularly the aid of Mr. D. F. Dunbar, on the tin plate industry; of Mr. H. L. Perrin, on some aspects of the sugar trade; and of Mr. E. P. Coleman, on copper. Among my colleagues in the University, Dr. M. T. Copeland has given information and helpful suggestions on the fourth Part, dealing with textiles; and Mr. A. H. Cole has kindly read all the proofs and given me the benefit of his helpful criticism.

F. W. Taussig.

Harvard University
March, 1915.

PREFACE TO THE THIRD EDITION

The first edition of this book appeared in 1915; a second in 1918. The four Parts which made up the book in these editions are here printed again without changes of moment. The volume is much enlarged by the addition of Part V, which is entirely new, and brings the narrative and analysis to the date of writing (1930). In it an account is given of the development of the several industries during the two decades from 1910 to 1930.

In preparing the present edition we have had the benefit of a grant from the Harvard Committee on Economic Research. Without that grant, the task could hardly have been undertaken. Dr. White has carried much the largest part of the labor of tracing in detail the changes described in Part V.

CONTENTS

PART I. INTRODUCTORY — SOME PRINCIPLES

CHAPTER I

CHAPTER II

CHAPTER III

PART II. SUGAR

CHAPTER IV

CHAPTER V

CHAPTER VI

CHAPTER VII

CHAPTER VIII

PART III. IRON AND STEEL

CHAPTER IX

CHAPTER X

CHAPTER XI

CHAPTER XII

CHAPTER XIII

PART IV. TEXTILES

CHAPTER XIV

PART V. 1910–1930

CHAPTER XXII

CHAPTER XXIII

CHAPTER XXIV

CHAPTER XXVII

CHAPTER XXVIII

PART I

INTRODUCTORY—SOME PRINCIPLES

SOME ASPECTS OF THE TARIFF QUESTION

INTRODUCTORY — SOME PRINCIPLES

CHAPTER I

DUTIES, IMPORTS, PRICES

IN this introductory chapter I shall consider, even at the risk of repeating elementary matter, the way in which duties work, the significance of the continuation of imports after duties have been imposed, and the possibility of measuring the charge which they lay on the community.

A common notion is that any duty operates automatically as a price-raising cause, bringing at once and permanently a tax up to its full rate. Not a little speechifying of a very effective kind has consisted in an enumeration of extreme rates, with the implication that they bring burdens no less extreme.[1] Even more remarkable is the eagerness with which protected producers have themselves schemed and labored for high duties as if it were certain that they would get the full benefit, in a corresponding rise in the price of their wares. The burden which our protective system imposed on the community has been much exaggerated by its opponents; but the protected producers and their spokesmen have countenanced the exaggeration by virtually endorsing the indictment against themselves. They ask for advances in duties and protest against reductions as if a corresponding effect on domestic prices were certain to appear.

[1] One of the familiar methods of enumeration is to describe the taxes which follow the consumer from the cradle to the grave; a modern use of this tactical device is in the speech of Mr. Underwood, when introducing the tariff bill of 1912–13 in the House of Representatives, August 13, 1912.

The truth is that the levy of a duty may have no influence at all on domestic price; or it may raise the price of the dutiable commodity by its full amount; or it may have an effect intermediate between these extremes.[1]

(1) The first case is the simplest. A duty on a commodity which is produced within the country as cheaply as without, and sold as cheaply, ordinarily has no effect whatever. Of such levies there has been a plenty in our tariff history. Those on the staple agricultural products are the most familiar and conspicuous. In the log-rolling which is an almost universal concomitant of protective tariffs, the notion that a duty will surely be of benefit to domestic producers has caused our farming sections to insist on " their share " of the going favors, and to accept, nay demand, duties on wheat, corn, meat and meat products, which yet have been quite without industrial effect. There has been no more striking illustration of the average farmer's naïve state of mind on this subject than the bitter opposition aroused by the reciprocity treaty with Canada which the Taft administration proposed in 1910–11. The free admission of wheat contemplated by that treaty was supposed to portend disaster to the wheat growers of the northwest; though it was known to all the world that wheat was exported both from the United States and from Canada, and that it was the same in price (allowing for cost of transportation) in these two countries and in England. The range of commodities subjected to duties yet not at all affected by them, has been very wide, including not only agricultural staples, but many manufactured articles.

(2) The second case — that in which the price of the commodity rises by the full amount of the duty — is found when imports continue after its imposition. Nevertheless it is not so easy as may seem at first sight, to determine just how conclusive is the evidence from the fact of importation. It will appear, as we proceed in the discussion, that qualifications of various sorts need to be borne in mind.

[1] In this analysis I follow the method of Albert Gallatin, in his Free Trade Memorial of 1831; reprinted in the collection which I have edited, *State Papers and Speeches on the Tariff*, pp. 122–123.

Under the ordinary conditions of trade, — those of competitive dealings, — the continuation of imports after a duty has been levied shows that the price of the commodity is higher within the country than without by the full amount of the duty. This is not the same as to say that the price is raised to the purchaser or consumer by that full amount; a consequence which no doubt commonly ensues, but by no means ensues under all conditions. It is conceivable that the divergence between foreign and domestic price will come about through a fall in the foreign price, not through a rise in the domestic; or through a partial fall in the one, a partial rise in the other. Of this possibility, more will be said presently. The only thing which is shown by the inflow of imports over a tariff barrier is that the level of price is higher on one side than on the other by the height of the barrier. The reason is obvious: no trader will import goods, and pay the duty on them, unless he can sell them at an advance over the foreign price which will recoup him for the duty paid.

This holds, to repeat, under the ordinary conditions of trade. But it does not hold necessarily in case of goods produced in the foreign country under monopoly conditions. Under monopoly, there is a possibility of difference in charge to different purchasers, and hence a possibility that a duty will not affect price as it would under the conditions of a free market.

That the incidence of a tax on monopoly products is different from that of a tax on competitive products is a commonplace in economics. Whether the tax be in the form of an excise or a tariff duty, the monopolist may find it expedient to bear part of the charge, in an extreme case even to bear the whole of it. He may be confronted by such inelasticity of demand as to make it most profitable to sell at an advance in price less than the tax, perhaps very much less than the tax. Now, the peculiarity of a customs duty is that it makes divided markets. It is imposed not on the whole of the monopolist's output, but only on that part which is exported to the country levying the duty. In the duty-levying country, the monopolist may not raise his price by the full amount of the duty, — *i. e.*, may lower his net price, what is left to him after the tax is paid by himself or others, —

and yet maintain the full previous charge in his home market. Then the divergence between the two markets after the duty has been imposed will be less than the amount of the duty. The foreign producer then will "pay" some part of the tax; not in the sense that he lowers his price all around, but that he lowers it on the quota exported to the duty-levying country.

An analogous case is that of "dumping" in its typical form, — that is, the steady sale of a commodity to a foreigner at a lower price than to domestic consumers. The divergence of prices is here also explicable, as a rule, on the ground of monopoly. Of dumping in its various forms, more is said elsewhere;[1] it is enough at this stage to note that it presents theoretical problems very similar to those of the imports of a monopolized article continuing after the imposition of a duty.

Complete monopoly is rare at best; and this particular consequence of full monopoly seems to be even more rare. I know of no case, either in American or in foreign experience, where one having a complete monopoly has in fact continued steadily to send to a foreign country a product on which a duty has been levied, and then has sold the product at an advance in price less than the duty.

But imperfect monopolies,— those where the product is sold for a considerable time at a price above the strictly competitive rate,— are by no means rare. Competition works out its effects slowly and irregularly. For long periods there are quasi-monopolies due to established reputation, trademark, or brand. No doubt these require for their maintenance, as well as for their first establishment, a considerable degree of business ability; but they are susceptible of being held in a position of advantage for a surprisingly long time. As in the case of complete monopoly, though to a less extent, the returns are so high as to make it possible to make some reduction in price and yet retain enough to make sales worth while. The imposition of a duty may lead to such a concession. Thus, a particular kind of steel tape used by engineers, made in England and widely exported, has a long-established name and a quasi-monopoly position. "Specialties" of

[1] See chapter xiii, pp. 202–212.

various kinds are brought from Europe to the United States under similar conditions, and indeed account for the continued importation of many classes of goods subject to high duties. On such articles the reduction in price which may follow the imposition of a duty is not likely to be great; the divergence between foreign and domestic price will after all not be far from the amount of the duty. But the cases are frequent enough, and divergence sufficiently noticeable, to cause the man of affairs who encounters them to be skeptical about the general proposition that price rises by the full extent of the duty even when imports continue; and they lead the protectionist to jeer once more at the "theoretical" free trader who says that the foreign producer bears no part of the tariff burden.

The case is different with commodities produced under strictly competitive conditions. Here there is a free market, and a market price the same for all purchasers. Here it would seem that there is no possibility of divergence between prices to different purchasers, such as appears in case of monopoly. It would seem, therefore, that the continuance of imports proves at the least that price in the duty-laying country is higher than in the exporting country by the full amount of the duty. Here, too, it would seem clear that in the long run this full amount constitutes a charge on the domestic consumer, not on the foreign producer. These consequences do in fact appear; yet with temporary divergences which again puzzle the ardent free trader and are made much of by the ardent protectionist.

A manufacturer or set of manufacturers whose operations have been developed and adjusted for a large export trade may be "caught" by the sudden levy of a duty. In order to hold their own in a market on which they have relied for disposing of a large output, they may sell in the duty-laying country at a less price than elsewhere. One would suppose that, under competitive conditions, the concession in price would not be confined to the exported quota. Each of the producers, — so the economist would reason, — is desirous of avoiding the fall in price; each will prefer to sell in the home market at full price rather than in the foreign market (now subjected to duty) at a reduced price.

Competition between them will cause the decline to be distributed over all the output. But in fact things often work out, at least for some time, differently from what the close-reasoning economist expects. The producers, it is true, are desirous of staving off the fall in price; but this desire often leads them, without any express agreement or combination among themselves, to maintain their price on ordinary sales, yet cut it perforce on the sales to the protecting country. They do not wish to "spoil" the general market [1] or upset the going price which has come to be regarded as "fair." Thus for a time the consequence may be similar to that of monopoly; there may be a reduction from the going price, for the purchasers in the duty-laying country. But all this is for a time only. Such special sales at reduced prices are unwelcome; they will be dropped as soon as possible. Each producer will prefer to sell all he can in the general market where concessions in price have been avoided. In this general market, too, he will be tempted to push his sales; very probably by concessions other than overt reduction of price, — such as longer credit, ready allowance for alleged damage or shortage, assumption of freight charges. The mercantile world has plenty of devices by which rates are cut in fact, even though nominally maintained. The differences between the prices in sales to the duty-laying country and to other markets will gradually disappear; and then, if imports into the former go on, the normal inference from continued imports can be drawn: price is higher within such a country than without by the full amount of the duty.

Further, that difference will ultimately appear as a charge on the domestic consumers, not on the foreign producers. Only for a time will the latter sell in the duty-laying country at a less (net) price than they have been previously getting, — assuming that this previous price was the strict competitive price. Sooner or later they will withdraw from the business thus made unprofitable or less profitable. If this cannot be done without an appreciable reduction in total output, the process will require time;

[1] Cf. the remarks on a similar situation in Marshall's *Principles of Economics*, Book V, chapter v, § 6 (6th ed.).

most of all, if it cannot be done without allowing large plant to wear out.[1] But in the end special sales to foreign countries and general reductions in price due to the cutting off of the foreign markets, will cease. Exports which may be sent thereafter to the duty-laying country will go under normal conditions, and the normal consequences of duties will appear. Prices of the dutiable commodities will be higher by the full amount of the duty; not only higher within the protecting country than without, but higher by that full amount when measured from the previous level. In the long run, the continuance of imports of staple goods, after a duty has been imposed, proves that the domestic consumer pays an enhanced price, or tax, to the full extent of the duty.

In the present volume, it happens, the discussion of imports, duties, prices will have to do chiefly with staple goods made under competitive conditions; moreover, goods not mainly dependent on the American market, so that even a temporary divergence from normal conditions will rarely need to be considered.[2] As regards the tariff schedules to be considered in the following pages, the general proposition holds, with little need of allowance for the qualifications and exceptions: if imports continue, we may be sure that the domestic purchaser pays a tax of the full amount of the duty.

If now imported goods, steadily sent in over a tariff barrier, are raised in price by the amount of the duty, it follows that any similar goods that may be produced within the country are also raised in price by the same amount. Not only the imported

[1] A case of a different kind, yet analogous to those considered above in that it rests on abnormal conditions, is adduced by Professor Brentano. The Russian state, being under obligation to make heavy remittances to foreign countries on interest account, reduced its railway rates on rye when Germany raised duties on that grain; thus virtually shouldering the duty. The stolidity, lack of resource, and general immobility of the Russian peasantry are also said by Brentano to have contributed, for a considerable time, to the same result. L. Brentano, *Die deutschen Getreidezölle*, p. 22.

[2] An exception to this statement appears in the case of tin plate. There the foreign (British) production had been largely for the American market, and the duty of 1890 did serve for some to depress the British price. See below, chapter xii, p. 176.

supply, but the total supply, sells at a price higher by so much within the country than without. This is the first article, and an essential one, in the free traders' indictment of protective duties: they tax the consumer without bringing a corresponding revenue to the government. They thus cause *prima facie* a net loss to the community. The higher price paid for the imported portion is not open to this charge; what the consumer so pays in taxes is offset by the revenue yielded to the public treasury. It is the higher price of the domestic product which has no offset. All this is a commonplace in economics, and there is no occasion for repeating here what has been so often set forth.

(3) Next we have to consider the third case, intermediate between the two just discussed, — that in which a duty causes a rise in price, but one not up to its full amount. Here the duty is prohibitory, yet has its effects. It is so high as to cause the cessation of imports which would otherwise come in. The case is one in which there is "need" of protection; the commodity could be got more cheaply from abroad; but the duty is greater than is needed to offset the difference between domestic and foreign cost. There is then no overt evidence on the quantitative effect of the duty. The tax on the domestic consumer may be nearly equal to the full amount of the duty; it may be considerably less. So far as the evidence from imports goes, there is nothing to prove there is any tax at all, — the case might be that mentioned first in our analysis.

The intermediate case is the most frequent of all as regards manufactured goods. It is not often that a duty is imposed on these precisely so high as to cause a division of the market between foreign and domestic producers. Such a result was aimed at in our tariff act of 1913, in which the rates were supposed to be adjusted on a "competitive" basis.[1] In fact, a rate that is really "competitive" is difficult to fix, and was arrived at in very few of the duties of 1913. A duty on a manufactured product commonly is either so high as to keep out all imports, or so low as to admit all and thus to be in effect merely a revenue duty. True,

[1] See my *Tariff History of the United States*, p. 418 (edition of 1914).

imports often appear to continue, and a division of the supply between domestic and foreign quotas often appears to be brought about. But the appearance is deceptive; the two sets of goods on examination prove to differ in quality, or to be for other reasons not in reality competitive. Of the need of discrimination in interpreting the evidence from continued imports of manufactured goods, more will be said in the ensuing paragraphs, and still more in the later chapters of the volume.

A duty on the so-called raw materials is more likely to be really competitive; the probability is greater that some part of the supply of such goods will be brought in over the barrier of a duty. The reason for this difference between manufactured goods and extractive products is not far to seek. The latter are likely to be produced not at uniform cost, but higher cost for some parts of the domestic output than for others. When a duty has brought about a rise in domestic price, there will be some increase of domestic production, but not an indefinite increase. Diminishing returns, *i. e.*, increasing cost, will set in, and will bring a limit to the extension of the domestic quota. Imports will continue, even though on a less scale than they would without a duty. Of this situation there have been some striking illustrations in modern tariff history. One was in the continuing imports of wool into the United States during the period from the close of the civil war until wool was admitted free in 1913; a case which will be followed in detail in this volume.[1] Another was in our imports of raw sugar, of which also a full consideration will follow. Still another, the occasion of a vehement political and economic controversy in Germany, is in the sustained imports of wheat into that country after the imposition of the wheat duty in 1879 and its gradual increase in the years thereafter.[2] In all these cases the fact that imports came in steadily after the imposition of the duty proved beyond question that the price of the whole supply, domestic as well as foreign, was raised by the full amount of the levy.

[1] See chapter xix.

[2] On this episode full figures are given in Brentano, *Die deutschen Getreidezölle.*

But, to repeat, in the case of manufactured goods, of which an increased supply can be produced in the long run without rising cost per unit, the division of the market between foreign and domestic producers is not so likely to take place. It may be fairly described as a lucky hit when a duty is adjusted at the exact point which brings about this result. In the tariff experience of the United States at large, and particularly as regards the schedules whose effects will be examined in this volume, the rates have usually been much above the point of prohibition. Imports have ceased. To ascertain then what effect the duties have had, above all to measure their quantitative effects, proves extremely difficult. Statistics of the prices of the goods are not easy to get, and are even less easy to compare with due allowance for differences in quality. In some instances, as with ordinary grades of cotton cloths, it is tolerably certain that domestic prices have been no higher than foreign; the case is in reality our first. With the ordinary grades of woolens, on the other hand, it is clear that domestic prices have been higher than foreign, yet by an amount much less than the duty; the case is the intermediate one. And for another great class of textiles, silk fabrics, the evidence is conflicting and the outcome difficult to state with any precision; there is a conglomerate made up of the two extreme cases, and of various degrees of the intermediate case.

Returning now to a topic touched in passing a moment ago, we have to note some further cautions and qualifications to be observed when drawing inferences from the fact of continued imports. There are not a few cases where imports seem to prove the full rise in price, but in fact do not prove anything of the kind.

In the first place, it must be ascertained whether the goods imported are in reality comparable to those made within the country. Textiles of all sorts have been steadily imported into the United States during the period covered in the present volume, — cottons, woolens, silks. But the imports have been almost exclusively of the finer and more expensive qualities. The less expensive goods, those which are most largely used, have been made exclusively within the country. The consumers have been served by two streams of heterogeneous supplies, not by one of homogeneous supply. Though the custom house statistics register considerable imports of silks and woolens, these have been of grades and qualities different from the domestic goods.

A striking case is that of pig-iron. Of this article also the customs returns show imports in considerable quantities for each year during the last half-century. But for the greater part of the period they were of special qualities only; classed as "pig-iron" in the tariff schedules and in the Treasury statistics, yet in fact without significance in the general iron market. Almost all of the imports were of spiegel-eisen and ferro-manganese, used in comparatively small amounts for mixing with other iron in the Bessemer process. This continued importation proved something about the relation between foreign and domestic price for that particular grade, but nothing about the prices of the enormously greater quantity of pig-iron proper.[1]

Again, exceptional transportation conditions may cause an imported commodity to find its way into some part of the domestic market over a duty which yet is prohibitory as regards the general market. Steel rails may be carried from Great Britain to Galveston, by steamers which are glad to get a return freight for cotton, at very low transportation charges; and it may then be to the purchaser's advantage to import them and pay the duty (*i. e.*, a price raised by the amount of the duty) rather than meet the comparatively high land freights from the American mills, — at Pittsburgh or Birmingham (Ala.). Yet steel rails may be as cheap in Pittsburgh as in Great Britain, and American prices for them in general not higher than British. So economical is water transportation that steel rails have been transported from Europe around Cape Horn to Puget Sound, and have paid a considerable duty, even though rails were in most parts of the United States no dearer than in Europe. Similarly, pig-iron might come from Glasgow to New England and other places on the Atlantic coast, though charged with a duty and though no higher in price at Pittsburgh than at Glasgow. Transportation

[1] Cf. what is said below, chapter x, pp. 144 *seq.*

conditions of this kind explain some continuing imports which have puzzled those who make inferences from the bare statistics of foreign trade.

Lastly, we have to consider another qualification and distinction. It is one thing to say that the continuance of imports proves domestic price to be higher than foreign price by the full amount of the duty; it is another thing to say that the domestic consumer pays a tax to that full amount. The latter proposition, usually stated without qualification by the free traders, is often denied by protectionists of the extreme type. These are likely to maintain that duties operate as taxes on the foreign producer, not on the domestic consumer. To say that duties always tax the foreign producer is absurd. Yet there are conditions, — quite apart from monopoly, or temporary conditions of readjustment, — under which the unqualified free trade statement is not completely true, and the extreme protectionist statement not completely false; conditions under which imports continue, price is higher by the full extent of the duty, yet the domestic consumer is not taxed to that full extent. And conversely there are conditions under which a remission of duty will not lower price by the full amount.

These are the conditions, familiar in economic theory, where production is carried on under varying cost or diminishing returns. The ordinary free trade reasoning, like most of the reasoning of those British economists by whom the theory of international trade was worked out, assumed constant returns, — one uniform cost of production, irrespective of the volume of output. This at least was assumed as regards the foreign supply. The influence of varying cost or diminishing returns on domestic supply, and the consequent special effects of import duties on domestic cost and on the rent of land, were conspicuous in the reasoning of those who attacked the British corn laws. But these same conditions may exist for the imported supply. Suppose that the imports are of agricultural products or raw materials, and that they come from a country whose natural resources are not superabundant. An increase in the output of a commodity so produced will cause its normal price to go up, if the additional increments of supply can be got only at higher cost. A decrease in output, conversely, will cause normal price to go down, if the sources of supply which are abandoned are comparatively poor, and if those which continue to be utilized are comparatively good. The margin of cultivation will rise in the former case, will fall in the latter; and normal price will shape itself correspondingly. The particular case which is to be considered in the present discussion is where an import duty causes part of the foreign supply to be supplanted by domestic supply, and where the abandoned foreign quota had been produced at high cost. The recession of the margin of cultivation will then cause normal price to fall in the foreign country; and though imports continue, and though domestic price be higher by the amount of the duty, it will not be raised by that full amount above the level which prevailed before the duty was imposed. It cannot be said that in this case the foreigner bears any part of the tax; but, also, it cannot be said that the domestic consumer pays a tax of the full amount of the duty. The converse case arises where a duty which had long been imposed and had shut out a foreign supply, is repealed, letting in the foreign article. If the consequent pressure on foreign sources of supply causes resort to poorer grades of land or other natural agents, — if the margin of cultivation goes up, — the normal foreign prices will rise. Then, in the country where the duty has been remitted, price will go down by less than the amount of the duty. Some part of the possible gain to consumers will be offset by the higher cost of the additional foreign supplies.

This sort of general reasoning, however, is in fact less likely to be applicable to imported supply than to domestic supply. The British economists who made much of it in condemning the corn laws, but neglected to consider its applicability to the countries from which corn might be imported, were substantially in the right, even though their theoretic reasoning was not carried far enough. It is much more *probable* that the conditions of diminishing returns will be found for a domestic supply than for a foreign supply. The reason is obvious. The available area in any one country is more likely to be limited, and, therefore, more likely to exhibit considerable variations in cost. A foreign supply is likely to come, actually or potentially, from several countries. Within wide limits, it will probably be produced under conditions not of varying cost but of constant cost. Any considerable increase in the supply of wheat grown in Germany or in England, for example, will probably cause resort to inferior soils, or disadvantageous pressure on all the available soils. But the same increase of supply from foreign countries, — distributed over Canada, Argentina, the United States, India, Russia, Roumania, — will cause no pressure at all. If indeed a single country or area were the sole source of supply for the article subjected to duty, there would be some probability of increasing cost and rising price after the removal of the duty. But this must be a rare case; at all events I know of none in the tariff experience of the United States. More nearly within the bounds of possibility is the case where, though several countries contribute to the imports, all of them have pushed production to the point where additional output is not certainly to be had on the same terms. This possibility exists, for example, in the case of wool; and it has been alleged to exist, though with less plausibility, in that of sugar. As will appear later, it deserves at least to be considered whether a greater demand for foreign wool, due to the abolition of the United States duty, will cause some permanent rise in foreign cost and price, and so fail to bring for the domestic consumer the full expected gain from the remission. Even in this case the answer seems to be in the negative: the conditions of foreign supply are sufficiently flexible to prevent an outcome so disappointing to the free traders.[1]

So much for the details, qualifications, exceptions, which must be borne in mind when interpreting statistics of imports or reasoning about the effect of duties on domestic price. Under the ordinary conditions of trade, if imports continue, the effect of a duty on prices is plain. The nature of the effect is equally plain, though its extent is not so easy to measure with exactness, if imports are stopped by the duty, yet would come in were the duty removed. Quite a different question is whether these conse-

[1] See below, chapter xix, p. 318.

quences from the imposition of a duty are permanent; whether the price of the dutiable article, raised at first by the tariff, may not be lowered eventually in consequence of changes in the conditions of domestic production. This is the question raised by the doctrine of protection to young industries, to which we turn in the next chapter.[1]

[1] The reader will note that I speak in this chapter merely of the difference between price with the duty and price without the duty, not committing myself on the question whether this difference constitutes or measures a national loss. The presumption is that a national loss occurs, and is measured by the enhanced price which the consumer pays on the goods produced at home (not on those imported, since here the consumer's burden is offset by the government's revenue). Those conversant with the theory of international trade need not be told that there is the further possibility that duties will disturb the equilibrium of international demand and supply, and lead to a readjustment by which the duty-levying country will gain. See the classic passage in Mill, *Political Economy*, Book V, chapter iv, § 6. Cf. Marshall's *Memorandum* (of 1908) *on the Fiscal Policy of International Trade*, §§ 7–9; Taussig, *Principles of Economics*, chapter xxxvii, § 1. The possibility has been questioned, but not in my opinion on solid grounds, in a note by H. H. O'Farrell in *Quarterly Journal of Economics*, August, 1912. Some further theoretical aspects of the problem seem to me to deserve attention; but this is not the place for examining them.

CHAPTER II

PROTECTION TO YOUNG INDUSTRIES

THE argument for protection to young industries cannot be stated better than in the terms used long ago by a staunch adherent to the principle of tree trade, John Stuart Mill.

"The only case in which, on mere principles of political economy, protecting duties can be defensible, is when they are imposed temporarily (especially in a young and rising nation) in hopes of naturalizing a foreign industry, in itself perfectly suitable to the circumstances of the country. The superiority of one country over another in a branch of production often arises only from having begun it sooner. There may be no inherent advantage on one part, or disadvantage on the other, but only a present superiority of acquired skill and experience. A country which has this skill and experience yet to acquire, may in other respects be better adapted to the production than those which were earlier in the field; and besides, it is a just remark of Mr. Rae, that nothing has a greater tendency to promote improvements in any branch of production, than its trial under a new set of conditions. But it cannot be expected that individuals should, at their own risk, or rather to their certain loss, introduce a new manufacture, and bear the burden of carrying it on, until the producers have been educated up to the level of those with whom the processes are traditional. A protecting duty, continued for a reasonable time, will sometimes be the least inconvenient mode in which the nation can tax itself for the support of such an experiment. But the protection should be confined to cases in which there is good ground of assurance that the industry which it fosters will after a time be able to dispense with it; nor should the domestic producers ever be allowed to expect that it will be continued to them beyond the time necessary for a fair trial of what they are capable of accomplishing."[1]

[1] J. S. Mill, *Principles of Political Economy*, Book V, chapter x, § 1.

Simple as the general course of the argument is, something more is to be said concerning the form in which it has been most often urged in recent times and the tests by which to judge of success in attaining the desired result.

The form in which the argument most commonly appears in connection with our recent industrial development is the statement that protection ultimately lowers prices. It is admitted (grudgingly perhaps, — and sometimes questioned or even denied) that the first effect of the imposition of a duty is to raise the price of the dutiable article. But domestic competition ensues, it is said, and eventually price goes down. And when it is asked why the domestic producer, if he can bring his commodity to market after all at the lowered price, really needs a protecting duty, the answer is that he needs it *at first*, — during the early stages. He needs to learn; he needs time to develop the full possibilities. All this, it is obvious, is simply the young industries argument. But during the last generation our American protectionists have been chary of using that phrase. The United States is no longer a young country. Its industries are on a great scale, often on a gigantic scale. To call them "infant" invites ridicule. Hence falling prices, alleged to be due to domestic competition, and eventual benefit to consumers, are the pleas dangled before the public. Yet this is the same reasoning, merely put in other words; the question is simply whether there has been successful application of protection to nascent industries.

One familiar misapplication of the argument deserves attention. In the hearings before congressional committees on tariff bills during the last thirty years, there are countless statements, often fortified by more or less accurate statistics, to the effect that the price of one article or another within the country fell after the imposition of a duty on it. All such evidence is beside the point. The question is not whether domestic price falls, but whether it falls relatively to foreign price; whether eventually it comes to be as low as the latter. If both fall together, the domestic price always remaining higher than the foreign, nothing is shown in support of the young industries argument; or rather, it is shown that the facts adduced fail to support the argument.

The circumstance that both sets of prices go down indicates that some other causes, — such as improvements and inventions or new resources, — have been at work to bring a reduction in price the world over. Persistence of the gap between the domestic and foreign price indicates that no special cheapening influence has been at work in the protecting country. Only if the domestic price falls to the foreign level, does the question present itself whether protection to a young industry has been successfully applied. This is so obvious to one trained in the elements of economic reasoning that an apology is almost needed for explaining it. The repeated triumphant parading of a bare fall in prices as evidence of success in the working of protection is perhaps only a part of the general shallowness of the stock presentation of the protectionist case. Yet this sort of presentation is often made by earnest and intelligent men, convinced of the goodness of their case; one more instance, among many that are sadly familiar, to show that the most elementary economic propositions are little understood, and the simplest economic reasoning needs to be stated and illustrated again and again.

A different question, and one not so simple, is whether there is any prospect of gain from protecting young industries in a country as fully developed as the United States has been since 1860; whether, for so robust and full grown a social body as this has become, ridicule is not a sufficient answer, whatever the terms in which the argument is stated. In that earlier formulation of the argument which won a respectful hearing from the fair-minded, stress was laid on the general conditions of the country imposing protective duties. It was a young country that was spoken of by Mill, rather than one having young industries. List's well-known plea rested on his doctrine of stages in economic evolution, — on the inevitableness of the transition from the agricultural and extractive stage to the manufacturing stage, and on the advantages of protective duties for furthering and easing this transition. He found the United States in this stage of development when he was sojourning here during the period of our early protective movement. On his return to Germany, he found his own country in a similar stage, and agitated for nurturing protection there also. The possibility of good results from protective duties under such conditions is now denied by few. But does the same possibility exist when this particular period of transition is past, when the manufacturing stage has been fairly entered, when the question no longer is whether manufacturing industries shall be established at all, but whether some particular kinds of manufactures shall be added to others already flourishing?

Notwithstanding early prepossessions to the contrary, I am disposed to admit that there is scope for protection to young industries even in such a later stage of development. Any period of transition and of great industrial change may present the opportunity. No doubt the obstacles to new ventures were greater during the first half of the nineteenth century than they have come to be in the modern period. The general diffusion of technical knowledge and technical training, the lessening of secrecy in trade processes which is the inevitable result of large-scale operations, the cessation of regulations like the early British prohibition of the export of machinery, the greater plenty of expert mechanics and machinists, — all these factors tend to facilitate the establishment of industries whose difficulties are no more than temporary and transitional. None the less the early stage of any new industry remains difficult. In every direction economists have come to recognize the immense force of custom and routine, even in the countries where mobility and enterprise are at the highest. Departure from the habitual paths of industry brings unexpected problems and difficulties, false starts and initial losses, often a fruitless imitation of familiar processes before new and better ones are devised. All this is made more trying when a young competitor is striving to enter the market against a producer who is established and well equipped. The obstacles in the way of promising industries, though doubtless not so great as they were a century ago, remain great. The experiences of the United States during the last fifty years, some of which will be described in the following pages, indicate that there remains in modern times at least the possibility of acquiring a self-sustaining industry by aid during the early stages.

The most striking cases in which success of this sort may be fairly alleged to have been secured are those of industries quite new, — not existing at all at the time when the protective duty was imposed. Where an industry is already started, or where there exist others closely related, further extension may be expected to take place, if the conditions are really favorable, without any legislative stimulus. If a silk manufacture already is established, the development of new branches of silk making is not likely to meet with the special obstacles to young industries. And if, none the less, protection has been applied, and if thereafter a self-sustaining additional branch of the manufacture has grown up, the question at once presents itself, would not the same growth have ensued in any case ? and was the protection needed ? Such skepticism, however, would be hardly justified if there had been no silk manufacture of any sort before the protection was applied. Precisely this outcome, — the establishment of an industry entirely new, — has appeared under our duties on silks during the last half-century. Without the duties, it is doubtful whether there would have been any silk manufacture at all. And if in course of time that manufacture proved capable of supplying the country with its products more cheaply than those imported, or at least as cheaply, the presumption would be strong that a young industry has been successfully nurtured. It remains to be examined, in the following pages, whether this latter condition has been met; but the other condition, — that an industry completely new was brought into being, — certainly is found in the case of the silk manufacture. In the case of worsteds also, there was virtually no industry at all before the civil war; it has grown up under the barrier of protection. The same thing has happened with plate glass, and with many another commodity. In such cases, — *if* eventual independence has been achieved, — it may be fairly said that protection was applied to an industry really young.

Further: the length of time to be allowed for the experiment should not be too brief. Ten years are not enough; twenty years may be reasonably extended; thirty years are not necessarily unreasonable. When writing of the earlier stages of United

States tariff history, I intimated that the first sharp break, in 1810–20, from the established ways of industry, and the very first ventures in new paths, were sufficient to give the needed impetus, and that thereafter protection might have been withdrawn.[1] An opinion of this sort I should not now support. What has already been said of the tenacity of old habits and the difficulties of new enterprises justifies the contention that a generation, more or less, may elapse before it is clear whether success has been really attained.

Nevertheless, in the end the final test must be applied, — can the industry, after a period not unreasonably long, maintain itself unaided? The gist of the young industries argument is that the community bears an initial charge for the sake of an eventual gain. That gain is secured only if the community is finally supplied with its goods as cheaply as the displaced foreigner could supply it. The young industry must mature so fully as to sustain itself. The final test would seem to be indifference to the continuance of the duty and willingness to meet foreign competition on even terms. If the industry continues to need protection indefinitely, and never succeeds in offering its products as cheaply as they could be got by importation, then its protection cannot be defended on this plea. There may be good pleas on political or social or military grounds; or the stock arguments about home labor and home markets and the "acquisition" of valuable industries may be repeated; but there can be no pretense that a young industry has been nurtured with success.

It happens, however, that there is always the most violent opposition to the application of this, the sole decisive test. In the same breath we are told that prices have been brought down and a flourishing industry has been brought to maturity, — and also that the duties must by no means be touched. It might seem reasonable to infer from this invariable unwillingness to submit to the real test that real success was never attained, — that the talk about domestic progress and lowered prices was empty froth. And yet, with all the obvious inconsistency on the part of the protectionists, it can be fairly argued that their case is not

[1] See my *Tariff History*, pp. 34, 45.

necessarily vitiated. The persistent clinging to the accustomed props, even though these were never designed to be permanent, is often due to mere ignorance or nervousness. Most business men know singularly little beyond the range of their daily routine. When customs duties have kept foreign competitors out of the market for twenty or thirty years; when a trade has habituated itself to domestic supply only; when there is a great din about pauper labor, designing foreigners, ruinous flooding of the market and what not, — there will be opposition to the removal of duties, even though in fact the removal would make no difference. All business men, and all workmen likewise, are uneasy about intruders. They prefer to be on the safe side, and to avoid the slightest chance of having to face competition from new quarters. It will often happen, too, that some special phase of an industry will in fact be damaged by foreign competition, even though the industries as a whole be independent of it. Then there will be as much overt opposition to a reduction or removal of duties as if the whole were at stake.[1]

Under these circumstances it will not be easy for the searcher after truth to interpret the situation rightly and to reach a just conclusion. The facts which he will be able to make sure of, after examining an episode in our tariff history, will often be something like the following. Duties have been imposed that proved prohibitory, and imports have ceased; the simplest test of the working of the duties, — continuance of imports, — is thus not applicable. A domestic industry has grown up and has assumed a character of its own, very probably turning out commodities of grades and qualities different from the foreign. The domestic goods have been cheapened; but so have the foreign. Direct competition has long ceased; the two sets of competitors have gone their diverging ways, each indifferent to the other.

[1] Thus, in 1912, there was opposition to a proposed reduction in duty on sewing machines, even though they had long been exported in great quantities; because some special kinds might still be imported from Germany. The same opposition, under similar conditions, was made to proposed reductions on saws, machine tools, electrical machinery, — all of them articles of which there could be at most sporadic importations. See *Hearings before the Senate Finance Committee*, 1912, on Metal Duties, pp. 172, 342, 1143, 1151.

The American producers allege that they have achieved all sorts of wonderful things, and the evidence may be strong that in fact improvements have been made by them. Their contentions rest, though without their saying it or even being aware of it, on the young industries argument. But they protest vociferously against the slightest reduction of duties, asserting in the same breath that they have distanced the foreigner and that they are in mortal fear of him. Much of their talk is obviously exaggerated. Experts who are competent to compare domestic wares and prices with foreign are not easy to find, and when found are not always unbiased. How has the experiment of protection to young industries really worked? The test of abolishing the duties has not been applied; under the political conditions, very probably it is out of the question that it should be applied. To reach a clear and certain conclusion is impossible. The best that can be done, after interpreting the evidence in the most judicial spirit, is to arrive at some qualified or provisional verdict.

Not infrequently those protectionists who put forward, more or less consciously, the young industries argument, contend that even after the stage of independence is reached a duty should be retained in order to prevent occasional disastrous importation.[1] It is said that even though the domestic industry can supply the market as cheaply as it could be supplied by importation and need not fear competition in ordinary times, protection is still called for because in times of depression abroad the foreigner pours in goods regardless of cost, and subjects the domestic industry to an unfair competition. This is not the demand for support against dumping in the strict sense, — that is, the systematic and continuous disposal of goods at less than cost or less than the normal price; it rests on a fear of spasmodic importations resulting from "overproduction" and the slaughtering of prices. Yet it would seem that precisely this same sort of disastrous competition must be faced at home also. Trade cycles and re-

[1] See for example the passage from Samuel Batchelder's writings quoted in my *Tariff History*, p. 143 note. Cf. a similar utterance by Posadowsky, a conspicuous figure among German protectionists, quoted by Goldstein, *Der deutsche Eisenzoll* (Volksw. Zeitfragen, no. 268), p. 33.

curring periods of depression are peculiar to no one country. Overproduction may take place within the country; every industry must face this possibility, and be prepared to take the lean as well as the fat. The special fear of the price-cutting foreigner doubtless reflects a protectionist feeling which goes far beyond the limits of the young industries argument, — a feeling of suspicion and dislike against foreign supply at any time and under any conditions. The truth would seem to be that the consequences of overproduction, — that is, of miscalculations, mistakes, unforeseen changes in demand, — are less likely to be severe in proportion as the sources of supply are larger and the markets which they reach are wider. An international market is less exposed to fluctuations than a narrower domestic one. What is obviously true of such commodities as wheat, wool, sugar, — that their price fluctuations are less the larger the area over which the general market extends, — presumably holds of manufactured goods also. Considerations of this sort cannot be expected to appeal to the root-and-branch protectionist, for whom the young industries is only one among many arguments, and perhaps not a vital one. Those who have no general terrors about foreign supplies, and are unwilling that the young industries argument in favor of home supply should be pushed beyond its strict limits, will consider the talk about foreign overproduction as mere subterfuge, as a retirement to an entirely different and weaker line of defense after the first and strong line has been given up.

There remains at the very end a most troublesome question. That question remains even if it be proved, either by the conclusive test of abolished duties or by other evidence, that the protected industry has finally succeeded in offering the commodity as cheaply as it could be supplied by the foreigner. Would not this same result have come in any event, protection or no protection? Do not other causes, perhaps changes in the general industrial conditions of the country, explain the growth of the particular industry? To answer this question, a careful examination of the history of all the circumstances is necessary, and a reasonable interpretation of the course of events. And here again the best that can be done is often to reach a qualified and hesitating conclusion. But the presumption, at this stage of the debate, may be said to be against the staunch free trader. If indeed the industry has failed to meet its obligations, so to speak; if it clings to protection indefinitely and refuses ever to meet the foreigner on even terms, — then the presumption is the other way; it is against the advocate of protection to the young industry. But if the industry does accept the challenge, or is clearly able to do so without danger of defeat, then the free trader who maintains that all the protection was unnecessary, and that the same development would have taken place in any case, is fairly called on to show just how and why it would have taken place. He can no longer rest his case on general reasoning. He must consider and explain the actual course of events.

Enough has been said to show that this phase of economic inquiry demands in especial degree investigation of the concrete facts. Most of the economists' reasoning about international trade is deductive. The advantages of the geographical division of labor; the relation of imports to exports, and the flow of specie from country to country; the equilibrium of international payments; the doctrine of comparative costs (presently to be considered in some detail); the nature of the gain from international trade; the fallaciousness of the vulgar arguments for protection,— all this rests mainly on reasoning from general principles. There may be illustration and verification from the facts, and indeed such can be found in abundance; but the core of the reasoning is not statistical or historical or realistic. This holds good also of the very first stage in the reasoning about protection to young industries. When it is laid down that protection in its first stage involves a burden to consumers, and a loss to the community because of a diversion of labor and capital into channels less advantageous, the proposition rests on no specific evidence. The ordinary protectionist would deny it at once; he would not admit that there is any initial loss at all; he would talk about the intrinsic and immediate benefits from acquiring a new industry, about increased demand for labor, about the home market, and so on. The only way to deal with him is to go back to first principles, and alas! to repeat the most elementary analysis. But after passing the elementary stage, and securing (if we can) an admission that the question in this case is whether an initial loss is balanced by an ultimate gain, we can no longer reason in the same general way. Is it probable, or is it not, that eventually the gain will come? Is domestic progress likely to be quickened? Are the conditions in the protecting country really favorable? These are not questions to be answered through deductive reasoning in terms of yes or no; they are to be answered, if at all, through laborious research and in terms of probabilities.

It has often been contended by free traders that the effect of protection is to retard progress, not to promote it. Foreign competition we have been told, quickens the domestic producer. In its absence he is likely to stagnate. Only by opening the field to every rival, whether within the country or without, can we secure the most rapid spread of improvements. On the other hand, the young industries advocates say that the planting of an industry in a new country, under novel conditions, pulls it out of its routine and stimulates improvement. General reasoning might perhaps incline us to the former view. *A priori* the most effective way of promoting progress would seem to be to make the way free and open for the best producer, wherever he may be. But then we are reminded of the difficulties of new ventures, and so on; and our attention is called to the analogy of the patent system. The analogy is not perfect, since the protection of a patent is not granted until the applicant has proved in advance that he really has evolved something new. To make the case of protection to young industries strictly analogous, one would have to require from the applicant proof in advance, not after the event, that he really had planned distinct improvements. None the less, the analogy suggests that an initial privilege to a producer, and a consequent initial burden on the consumer, may be balanced by ultimate gain. The question becomes one of probabilities, not of reasoning straight from premise to conclusion.

Illustrations of either consequence, — of the retardation of improvement as well as of its acceleration, — have been adduced from industrial history. The protective system of France before

1860, which was carried for many articles to the point of complete prohibition of imports, is said to have caused some staple manufactures in France to lag behind the English.[1] The protective system in Germany is said, on the other hand, to have caused one of the staple manufactures — that of iron — to progress.[2] It is certain that since the adoption of the protective system by the German Empire in 1879 there has been an extraordinary advance in all the technique and organization of manufacturing industry. In the United States it has been declared that protection of the woolen manufacture after the civil war caused old plants and antiquated machinery to be retained.[3] Yet in general it is as certain in the case of the United States as in that of Germany that the march of technical improvement has been extraordinarily rapid during the period of the maintenance of a high protective system. What may be the cause of this progress, — what part protection has played, — is doubtless a problem extremely difficult of solution; but at least it calls for careful inquiry into the particular cases. All the general indications from the economic history of the United States are that protective duties in the great majority of cases have not served to bolster up antiquated establishments or to retard improvements; though it may not be so clear that they have so often actually stimulated improvement in the way and to the extent contemplated by the young industries argument. At all events one of the chief objects of the following pages is to consider with care the history of some important protected industries, and reach such conclusion as can be derived by the only method applicable to this sort of economic inquiry, — by direct investigation of the particular cases.

[1] See Amé, *Les Tarifs de douanes*, vol. i, pp. 318, 338, 399.
[2] Compare what is said below, pp. 153 *seq.*
[3] Compare what is said below, chapter xxi, p. 353.

CHAPTER III

THE TARIFF AND WAGES; THE PRINCIPLE OF COMPARATIVE ADVANTAGE

THE doctrine of comparative advantage, — or, in the phrase more commonly used by the older school, of comparative cost, — has underlain almost the entire discussion of international trade at the hands of the British school. It has received singularly little attention from the economists of the Continent, and sometimes has been discussed by them as one of those subtleties that have little bearing on the facts of industry. I believe that it has not only theoretical consistency, but direct application to the facts; and that in particular it is indispensable for explaining the international trade of the United States and the working of our tariff policy. Neither the familiar arguments heard in our controversy nor the course of our industrial history can be understood unless the principle of comparative advantage is clearly understood and kept steadily in view.

Briefly stated, the doctrine is that a country tends under conditions of freedom to devote its labor and capital to those industries in which they work to greatest effect. It will be found unprofitable to turn to industries in which, though labor and capital may be employed with effect, they are applied with less effect than in the more advantageous industries. The principle is simple enough, nor is it applicable solely to international trade. The conversant reader does not need to be told that it bears on the division of labor between individuals as well as on that between nations. The lawyer finds it advantageous to turn over to his clerk that work which he could do as well as the clerk, or even better, confining himself to the tasks in the profession for which he has by training or inborn gift still greater capacity. The able business leader delegates to foremen and superintendents routine work of administration that he could doubtless do better than they; he reserves himself for the larger problems of business management for which he has special aptitude. The skilled mechanic often has a helper to whom he delegates the simpler parts of his trade, giving his own attention to those more difficult parts in which he has marked superiority.

In international trade, however, the principle, if not most important, needs most attention; because it is obscured by the extraordinary persistence of prejudice and of shallow reasoning in this part of economics. Simple as it is in its statement and in its more obvious applications, it extends to some complex and difficult problems, and more particularly to those concerning the varying ranges of prices and wages in different countries. There is perhaps no topic in economics on which there is more of popular confusion than on this; nor can it be said that there is always careful and consistent thinking on it among economists who contemn the popular superficialities. Though fallacies of much the same sort are prevalent in all countries, the United States is above all that for which the principle is most important and for which there is most need of explaining the connection between prices, wages, and the currents of international trade.

Whatever the differences of opinion among economists on the theory of wages, — and those differences are less in reality than in appearance, — there is agreement that a high general rate of wages rests upon general high product, on high effectiveness of industry. It is not necessary here to enter on the question whether, in speaking of the effectiveness of industry, we should consider precisely in what way it can be said to be based on the several factors in production, or caused by them. Some economists regard capital and natural resources (land) as distinct factors, contributing each its specific share to the total product of industry. Others regard them simply as means or conditions for enabling labor to work with effect and so to turn out a large product. The latter seems to me the better way of stating the case, — that labor is the fundamental agent in production; but for the present purpose it is not material which form of statement is preferred. It is agreed among the careful thinkers on economics that high general wages and a high degree of material prosperity can result only from the productive application of labor; good tools or good natural resources, or both, being indispensable to high productivity. And when " labor " is spoken of, it must be remembered that not only manual labor is meant, but the equally important labor of organizing and directing the rank and file. In the United States more particularly, the general effectiveness of labor depends in great degree on the work of the industrial leaders.

Now when there prevails a general high range of wages, due to generally productive application of labor, this high rate comes to be considered a difficulty, — an obstacle. The business point of view is commonly taken in these matters not only by the business men themselves, but by the rest of the community. To have to pay high wages is a discouraging thing in business; does it not obviously make expenses high, and competition difficult? People do not reflect that wages are not high as a matter of course. If they are in general high, there must be some general cause. Once established, they are taken in a country like the United States as part of the inevitable order of things. The ordinary man does not stop to consider why they should exist at all. He regards them as something he must face, and too often as something that constitutes a drawback in industry.

When speaking of wages as high, we may have in mind either money wages or commodity wages (" real " wages, in the older phrase). It is familiar to all that money wages are higher in the United States than in Europe; and it is almost as familiar that the greater money wages are by no means completely offset by higher prices, and that there remains a large advantage in real or commodity wages. Let us center attention for the moment on this latter and more substantial advantage, — the higher commodity wages.

It is obvious that higher commodity wages cannot be handed over to workmen by employers unless the workmen (as guided by the employers and aided by tools and machines) turn out a large product, — unless there is greater *effectiveness* of industry. I say effectiveness, not efficiency, because the latter word has come to be used so often to denote one particular factor that bears on the quantity of product, — the immediate efficiency of the manual workers; by no means the sole or even the commanding factor. In current discussions on the tariff and wages, it has often been alleged that in one industry or another the efficiency or skill of the workmen is no greater in the United States than in England or Germany; that the tools and machines are no better, the raw materials no cheaper. How then, it is asked, can the Americans get higher wages unless protected against the competition of the Europeans? But, it may be asked in turn: suppose *all* the Americans were not a whit more skilful and productive than the Europeans, — perhaps quite as skilful, but not more so; suppose the plane of effectiveness to be precisely the same throughout the realm of industry in the countries compared; how *could* wages be higher in the United States? The source of all the income of a community obviously is in the output of its industry. If its industry is no more effective, if its labor produces no more, than in another community, how can its material prosperity be greater and how can wages be higher? A high general rate of real wages could not possibly be maintained unless there were in its industries at large a high general productiveness.

But when once these two concomitant phenomena have come to exist, — a high effectiveness of industry and a high general rate of wages, — it follows that any industry in which labor is *not* effective, in which the plane of effectiveness is below that in most industries, finds itself from the business point of view at a disadvantage. It must meet the general scale of wages in order to attract workmen; yet the workmen do not produce enough to enable that general scale to be met and a profit still secured. Such an industry, in the terms of the principle now under discussion, is *ipso facto* working at a comparative disadvantage. In other industries, product is high; that is, labor cost per unit is low. In this industry, product is low; labor cost is high. The industry does not measure up to the country's standard, and finds in that standard an obstacle to its prosecution.

Consider the same problem, — the relation between wages, costs, prices, — from the point of view of money wages. Here again we are beset by everyday fallacies and superficialities. High money wages, it is commonly alleged, cannot be paid unless there be high prices for the goods made. A dear man is supposed to mean a dear coat, and a cheap man a cheap coat. Yet it is beyond dispute that in the United States, while money wages are higher than in European countries, the prices of things bought are on the whole *not* higher. Though some things cost more, and higher money wages therefore do not mean commodity wages higher in the same degree, real wages remain higher by a substantial amount. The dear man may perhaps mean a dear coat, — of this we shall learn more when we come to consider the domestic conditions of production for clothing; but the dear man certainly does not mean dear food, and probably does not mean a dear house. The explanation is simple: though wages in money are high, the effectiveness of the dear man's labor on the whole is also high, and therefore goods on the whole are *not* dear. Where a man who is paid high wages turns out a larger number of pieces, each piece can be sold at a low price, and the employer still can afford to pay the high wages. With reference to individuals, the business world is constantly accepting this principle. A good man, we are told, is cheap, even at high wages. To use the same phrase, a good industry is cheap even though high wages are paid in it. Where labor is effective, high wages and low prices go together.

None the less, an established high rate of wages always presents itself to the individual employer as a difficulty that has to be overcome. And to the employee it presents itself as a thing in danger, — something that must always be jealously guarded. Yet it is a real difficulty for the employer only where the effectiveness of labor is not great; and for the employees also it needs no protection, so far as the competition of foreign products is concerned, where this same essential condition is found. If, indeed, such effectiveness does not exist, then the American employer cannot pay the prevailing high rate of wages, and hold his own in free competition with producers in countries of lower wages. In other words, he cannot hold his own unless there is the comparative advantage in his particular industry. The prevalence of a general high rate of wages is due to the fact that in the dominating parts of the country's industrial activity the comparative advantage exists. These dominating industries set the pace; in them we find the basis of the high scale of remuneration; it is they which establish a standard which others must meet, and which to the others presents itself as an obstacle.

Some further explanation of these general statements is necessary before they can be made to fit all the facts. What has just been said of dominating industries holds only as regards those industries and those commodities which play a part in international trade.

For sundry reasons, many articles do not come within the range of international dealings. It is out of the question that they should be exported or imported. Such are bulky articles, not readily transportable for any distance, like bricks; these are necessarily produced near the spot where they are used. Such again are articles greatly affected by national habit, like furniture or household utensils; and, — to mention a highly important class, — such are houses and house-room, which must be provided once for all by domestic labor. Things of this sort may or may not be higher in price than they are in foreign countries. They are made by labor which is paid the current high rates of money wages. If that labor is more effective than in foreign countries, the commodities will yet be lower in price than abroad. But if that labor is not effective as compared with similar labor in foreign countries, the commodities will be higher in price. Domestic commodities, therefore, — meaning by that phrase the commodities which are necessarily produced within the country, — may be higher in price than they are in foreign countries, or the same in price, or even lower in price, according to the effectiveness of the labor engaged in producing them. If by some change in the underlying conditions, — say, an extraordinary cheapening of transportation, — their importation were to become feasible, the employer would find it impossible to compete with foreigners *unless* there was the same effectiveness of industry in producing them as there was in the dominant industries.[1]

[1] So far as money wages are concerned, the dominating industries are those which export. I have considered this problem fully in a paper in the *Quarterly Journal of Economics* (vol. xx), from which I quote the following paragraphs (pp. 510–511): —

" Those countries have high money wages whose labor is efficient in producing exported commodities, and whose exported commodities command a good price

As regards commodities potentially within the range of international trade, — and with these alone the tariff controversy is concerned, — the principle of comparative advantage applies more fully and unequivocally to the United States than to any country whose conditions are known to me. The difference in money wages between the United States and European countries is marked; the difference in commodity wages, though not so great, none the less is also marked. Notwithstanding these high wages, constituting an apparent obstacle or handicap for the domestic producer, the United States steadily exports all sorts of commodities; not only agricultural products, but manufactures of various kinds. Evidently they could not be exported unless they were sold abroad as cheaply as foreign goods of the same sort are

in the world's markets. The general range of money incomes depends fundamentally on the conditions of international trade, and on those conditions only. The range of domestic prices then follows: it is high so far as the efficiency of labor in domestic commodities is small, low so far as the efficiency of labor in domestic commodities is great.

"The situation is simplest in the case, — difficult to find in the real world, but instructive for illustration of the principle, — of a country having a monopoly of a given article of export or set of exported articles. By monopoly, I mean here not that the producers within the country fail to compete effectively among themselves, but that the producers of no other country compete with them. The price of such exported articles would depend, in the manner with which the reader may be supposed familiar, on the equation of international demand. The more the consumers in other countries care for them, the higher will their prices be pushed. The less the labor with which these articles are produced at home, the higher will be the money wages resulting from these high prices. The higher money wages in the exporting industries will set the standard for money wages in the country at large; and the general high wages may or may not be accompanied, as already explained, by high domestic prices.

"Where a country exports in competition with other countries, — the well-nigh universal case, — the same forces are at work. The prices at which the exports are sold depend on the world demand for the commodity. In that world demand, or, to speak more carefully, interplay of demand, the extent to which the consumers in the several countries care for the articles imported into them determines which countries shall sell their exports on advantageous terms. Those countries whose exports are in most urgent demand will have the greatest possibility of high money incomes. Whether they will have high incomes in fact, depends on the labor cost of their exports. The wheat which is exported both by the United States and by Russia sells at the same price; but that price means large money returns in the country of machinery, efficient labor, and cheap internal transportation, and low money returns in the country which lacks these advantages."

there sold. That these products of highly paid labor are exported and are sold cheap, is proof that American industry has in them a comparative advantage. There are other goods which, though not exported, are also not imported; goods where the balance of advantage is even, so to speak. They are not such as are ruled out of the sphere of international trade once for all, because of great bulk or necessity of production *in situ;* they might conceivably be imported; yet in fact they are not imported. These are the products of industries in which American labor is effective, yet not effective to the highest pitch; effective in proportion to the higher range of money wages in the country, but barely in that proportion. And finally there are the goods whose importation continues, even though there is no obvious obstacle to their domestic production from soil or climate. These are things which, it would seem, could be produced to as good advantage at home as abroad. They *could* be produced to as good advantage; but they lack the comparative advantage. They do not measure up to the standard set by the dominant industries. The obstacle to their successful prosecution within the country is not physical but economic. It is they which find in high wages an insuperable difficulty. In this class belong the industries which are protected, and which would not hold their own without protection. They are in a position analogous to that of the strictly domestic industries in which labor is not effective, but which, being carried on of necessity within the country, have high prices made necessary by high money wages. The obvious difference between the two cases is that the force which causes the strictly domestic industries to be carried on is an unalterable one, such as the difficulty or impossibility of transportation; while that which causes the protected industry to become domesticated is the artificial one of a legislative barrier.

What, now, are the causes of industrial effectiveness and comparative advantage ? To put the question in other words, what are the industries in which a comparative advantage is likely to appear ? and, more particularly, in what directions is the labor of the people of the United States likely to be applied with special effectiveness ?

The more common answer has been, in agriculture. A new country, with abundance of fertile land, finds its labor most effective in the extractive industries. Hence the United States long were steady exporters of wheat, meat products, cotton. Hence Canada is now a heavy exporter of wheat. Wheat is specially adapted to extensive culture, and is easily transportable; it is the commodity for which nature gives to a new country in the temperate zone a clear comparative advantage. The international trade of the United States was long determined chiefly by the country's special advantages for the production of wheat and similar agricultural staples.

It should be noted, however, that not only the natural resources told, but the manner in which they were used. From the first, inventiveness and ingenuity were shown. The United States early became the great country of agricultural machinery. Especially during the second half of the nineteenth century, the skill of the makers of agricultural implements and the intelligence of the farmers who used the implements were factors not less important than the great stretches of new land. Still another factor of importance was the cheapening of transportation. From the very beginning, the Americans have been energetic and successful in overcoming the vast distances of their country. Our railroads have cheapened long hauls as nowhere else. The most striking improvements of this sort were made in the last third of the nineteenth century; then new lands were opened, and agricultural products exported, on a scale not before thought possible. When the effectiveness of labor is spoken of, the effectiveness of *all* the labor needed to bring an article to market is meant; not merely that of the labor immediately and obviously applied (like that of the farmer), but that of the inventor and maker of threshing-machines and gangplows, and that of the manager and worker on the railways and ships. In other industries even more markedly than in agriculture, the labor of the directing heads, of the planners and designers, tells in high degree for the final effectiveness of the labor which is applied through all the successive stages.

That the situation began to change with the opening of the twentieth century does not need to be explained at length. The period of limitless free land was then passed, and with it the possibility of increasing agricultural production under the specially advantageous conditions of new countries. For one great agricultural article — cotton — the comparative advantage of the country indeed maintained itself, and its exports continued to play a great part in international trade. The exports of other agricultural products, — wheat, corn, barley, meat products, — have by no means ceased, nor will they cease for some time. But they tend to decline, absolutely and even more relatively. Other articles grow in importance, such as copper, petroleum, iron and steel products, various manufactures. For some of these, — copper, for example, — the richness of our natural resources is doubtless of controlling importance. But the manner in which those natural resources are turned to account is in all cases important; and in many cases the comparative advantage of which the exports are proof rests not on the favor of nature at all, but solely on the better application of labor under conditions inherently no more promising than those of other countries. What are the causes of advantage under these less simple conditions?

The same question may be asked regarding a closely-allied phenomenon, referred to a moment ago. A considerable range of manufactured articles, though not exported, are yet not imported. The domestic manufacturer holds the domestic market with ease, while paying higher wages than his foreign competitor. The range of such industries is wider than is commonly supposed. It is obscured by the fact that our tariff system imposes needless and inoperative duties on a quantity of things which would not be imported even in the absence of duties. On the other hand there is a considerable range of articles on which the duties do have substantial effect, — articles which would be imported but for the tariff. Some of these continue to be imported notwithstanding high duties; they pour in over the tariff wall. Why the difference between the two sets of cases: those in which the domestic manufacturer holds his own irrespective of duties, and those in which he needs the duties or even is beaten notwithstanding the tariff support?

The answer commonly given is that American producers can hold their own more easily when much machinery is used. Then, it is said, the wages bill forms a smaller proportion of the expenses of production, and the higher wages of the United States are a less serious obstacle. But it requires no great economic insight to see that this only pushes the question back a step. Why is not the machinery itself more expensive? The machinery was made by labor. It is a commonplace that a commodity made with much use of machinery is the combined product of two sets of laborers, — those who make the instruments and those who operate them. If *all* those whose labor is combined for producing the final result are paid higher wages than in foreign countries, why cannot the foreigners undersell where much machinery is used as well as where little is used?

The real reason why Americans are more likely to hold their own where machinery is much used, and where hand labor plays a comparatively small part in the expenses of production, is that Americans make and use machinery *better*. They turn to labor-saving devices more quickly, and they use devices that save more labor. Where Americans can apply machinery, they do so; and not only do so, but do so better, on the whole, than their foreign competitors. The question remains one of comparative effectiveness. Their machinery is not necessarily cheaper; absolutely often it is dearer; but it is cheap relatively to its effectiveness. It is better machinery, and the labor that operates it turns out in the end a product that costs not more, but less, than the same product costs in countries using no such devices, or using devices not so good.

In general, it may be laid down that this sort of comparative advantage is most likely to appear in the United States in two classes of industries, — those that turn out large quantities of staple homogeneous commodities and those that themselves make tools and machinery. Only where many identical things are turned out, does it pay to construct an elaborate and expensive plant. A machine-using people directs its energies to best advantage where thousands of goods of the same pattern are to be produced. Hence the repeated experience that, notwithstanding high duties, there is a tendency to import specialties and goods salable in small quantities only. Goods used by the masses in large quantities, as distinguished from luxuries bought by the comparatively few who are rich, are likely to be produced at home, without danger of being pushed by competing imports. If specialties, such as goods made to order, *must* be supplied by domestic producers, they are likely to be what the customer thinks inordinately dear; because they are made preponderantly, or at least in greater degree, by hand labor which is paid high wages and which by the very conditions of the case cannot use labor-saving machinery. Again, implements themselves, big and little, are likely to be well made in a country where people are constantly turning to machinery; from kitchen utensils and household hardware to machine tools, electric apparatus, and huge printing presses. These are things in which the success of American industry is familiar; which are exported, not imported; in which it is proverbial that the Yankee has a peculiar knack, — another way of saying that he has a comparative advantage.

The relation between high wages and the use of machinery calls for a word more of explanation. It is usually said that high wages are a cause of the adoption of machinery, and that we find here the explanation of the greater use of machinery in the United States. I believe that the relation is the reverse; high wages are the effect, not the cause. To the individual manufacturer it may seem a cause; he schemes to save in the wages bill by adopting a labor-saving device. But the reason why he is induced to scheme is that labor-saving devices are in common use and that the effectiveness of industry at large is therefore great, — hence high wages. No doubt the general situation has its reflex influence on the individual. Every one is put to his trumps; every one feels the need of playing the industrial game at its best. The abundant resources which so long contributed greatly, and indeed still contribute, to making labor productive and wages high, thereby stimulated the introduction of labor-saving methods in industries not so directly affected by the favor of nature. But the fundamental cause of the prevalent use of machinery was in the intelligence and inventiveness of the people; these being promoted again by the breath of freedom and competition in all their affairs. What are the ultimate causes of industrial progress and industrial effectiveness is not easily stated; complex historical, political, perhaps ethnographic forces must be reckoned with. But these causes work out their results in modern times largely by prompting men to improve their implements and to use unhesitatingly new and better implements. Thence flows a high rate of return for their labor; it is not the high rate of return that leads them to use the better tools.

In creating and maintaining the comparative advantage which comes from the better application of the machine processes, the business man — the industrial leader — has become in recent times a more and more important factor. The efficiency of the individual workman has been much dwelt on in discussion of the rivalries of different countries: aptitude, skill, intelligence, alertness, perhaps inherited traits. No doubt qualities of this sort have counted in the international trade of the United States, and still count. The American mechanic is a handy fellow, — it is from his ranks that the inventors and business leaders have been largely recruited, — and he can run a machine so as to make it work at its best. But there is a steady tendency to make machinery automatic, and largely independent of the skill of the operative who runs it. The mechanics who construct the machines and keep them in repair must indeed be highly skilled. Once, however, the elaborate machine is constructed and kept in perfect running order, the operative simply needs to be assiduous. Under such circumstances the essential basis of a comparative advantage in the machine-using industries is found in management, — in invention, rapid adoption of the best devices, organization.

The business leader has been throughout a person of greater consequence in the United States than elsewhere. He has loomed up large in social consequence because he has been of the first economic consequence. He has constructed the railway, and opened up the country; he has contributed immensely to the utilization of the great agricultural resources; he has led and guided the inventor and mechanic. I am far from being disposed to sing his praises; there are sins enough to be laid to his account. But he has played an enormously effective part in giving American industry its special characteristics. His part is no less decisive now than it was in former times, — nay, more so. The labor conditions brought about by the enormous immigration of recent decades have put at his disposal a vast supply of docile, assiduous, untrained workmen. He has adapted his methods of production to the new situation. His own energy, and the ingenuity and attention of his engineers and inventors and mechanics, have been directed to devising machinery that will almost run itself. Here the newly-arrived immigrant can be used. So far as the American can do this sort of machinery making to peculiar advantage, so far can he pay wages to the immigrants on the higher American scale and yet hold his own against the European competitor who pays lower wages to the immigrant's stay-at-home fellow. But it is on this condition only that he can afford to pay the green hand wages on the American scale, or on some approach to it: he must make the total labor more effective. The main cause of greater effectiveness in the dominating industries is to be found, under the economic conditions of recent times, not so much in the industrial quality of the rank and file as in that of the technical and business leaders.

Similar reasoning is applicable to another cause of effectiveness in industry which has been much discussed of late, — "scientific management." Some persons believe that here is a panacea of universal application; any and every industry can be made more effective by systematic observation and experiment on each of its steps and management based thereon. With reference to the protective system it was maintained, for example, after the reduction of duties in the tariff act of 1913, that scientific management, if generally adopted, would enable all American industries to meet the new and sharp competition of foreigners. The truth is that here also the question is one of comparative advantage. Scientific management is likely to tell more in some industries than in others. Apparently it tells most in industries of the standardized type, — precisely those in which industrial leadership already has proved of cardinal importance and in which Americans have already shown the greatest aptitude for leadership. It implies large-scale operation; since the heavy expense of preliminary investigation and the enlarged supervisory staff are worth while only if the expense is spread over a large output. It is adapted not to industries which produce specialties or small lots of numerous and varied articles, but to those in which the steady repetition of the same operations makes it profitable to work out an elaborate system. The indications are that it will not radically change the character of American manufacturing industry or modify the division between domestic and foreign sources of supply. Rather is it likely to accentuate existing relations; to strengthen American industry where it is already strong. Not all industries equally will feel its influence, but those in which this special form of industrial leadership tells with special effectiveness.

Returning now to the invention and operation of machinery, we have to consider a further possibility, — one which has played a considerable part in recent tariff discussions. The more machinery becomes automatic, the more readily can it be transplanted. Is there not a likelihood that apparatus which is almost self-acting will be carried off to countries of low wages, and there used for producing articles at lower price than is possible in the country of high wages where the apparatus has originated? In hearings before our congressional committees a fear is often expressed that American inventors and tool-makers will find themselves in such a plight. An American firm, it is said, will devise a new machine, and an export of the machine itself or of its products will set in. Then some German will buy a specimen and reproduce the machine in his own country (the Germans have been usually complained of as the arch plagiarists; very recently, the Japanese also are held up *in terrorem*). Soon not only will the exports cease, but the machine itself will be operated in Germany by low-paid labor, and the articles made by its aid will be sent back to the United States. Shoe machinery and knitting machinery have been cited in illustration. The identical apparatus which has been brought in the United States to extraordinary perfection is sent to Europe (perhaps even made in Europe by the American manufacturer), and is there worked by cheaper labor. The automatic looms, again, which have so strikingly influenced the textile industry of the United States, and so much increased its effectiveness,[1] are making their way to Europe, — here again being pushed into use by the American loom makers themselves. Is it not to be expected that they will be operated by cheaper English and German and French labor, and that their products will be shipped back to the United States, to the destruction of the very American industry which they had first made strong and independent?

This possibility is subject to exaggeration. It is not so easy as might be supposed to transplant an improved system of production and all that hangs thereby. However automatic a machine may be, intelligence and knack in operating it are always called for; though less, perhaps, among the ordinary hands than among the machine tenders and foremen. It is a common experience that the same machinery will produce in the country of its invention and manufacture better results than when transplanted. Those very automatic looms, just referred to, are making their way very slowly into Europe. They do not fit into the traditional industrial practices, and do not accomplish what they accomplish in the United States. The difficulties which impede the transfer of machinery and methods, however perfected and however available for every applicant, are most strikingly illustrated in the rivalry of the Orient. We hear frequently of the menace of the cheap labor of China, India, Japan. Will not these countries deluge us with the products of cheap factory labor, when once they have equipped themselves with the latest machinery? The truth is that they will in all probability never thus equip themselves. To do so, would require more than the mere shipment of the machinery and the directions for working it. A completely different industrial environment would need to be transplanted. The yellow peril has been as much exaggerated in its economic possibilities as in its military.

[1] See below, pp. 273 *seq.*

None the less, some possibility of this sort does exist, especially in the rivalry between those countries of advanced civilization which are more nearly on the same industrial level. It is by no means out of the question that shoe machinery or automatic looms shall be worked as well in Germany as in the United States. Supposing this to be done, cannot the German employer who gets his operatives at low wages undersell the American employer who must pay high wages? Is not the comparative advantage which the United States possesses in its ingenious machinery necessarily an elusive one, sure to slip away in time? An advantage may indeed be retained indefinitely where skill or intelligence on the part of the individual workmen are necessary. Even here there is a doubt whether it will persist, in view of the spread of education and technical training the world over. At all events, in the widening range of industries where the workman merely tends semi-automatic machinery, the manufacturing industries of the country having high wages would seem to be in a perilous situation.

The only answer which can be given to questioning of this sort is that the leading country *must retain its lead*. As fast as other countries adopt the known and tried improvements, it must introduce new improvements. Unrelaxed progress is essential to sustained superiority; he who stands still inevitably loses first place. Such was in the main the relation between England and the other western countries during the first three-quarters of the nineteenth century. English machinery was exported and English methods were copied throughout the world, but the lead of the British was none the less maintained. As fast as the other countries adopted the devices which originated in England, that country advanced with new inventions or with goods of new grades. A similar relation seems to exist at the present time between Germany and the other countries which follow her lead in some of the chemical industries.[1] It appears also in the position of the United States in those manufacturing industries which contribute to our exports. As fast as the American devices are copied elsewhere, still other improvements must be introduced.

[1] See a passage quoted in my *Tariff History*, p. 393, note.

This will seem to the American manufacturer a harsh sentence, and a heartless or unpatriotic one to the ordinary protectionist. What? To be deprived of the fruits of our own enterprise and ingenuity, without protection from a paternal government against the interlopers? Yet I see no other answer consistent with the general reasoning of economics on international trade and the geographical division of labor. The gain which a country secures from its labor is largest when that labor is applied in the most effective way; and labor is applied with the greatest effectiveness only when it proves this effectiveness by sustained ability to hold the field constantly against all rivals.

This train of reasoning, however, can be carried further. It is conceivable that improvements and inventions will be so completely adopted by all the advanced countries as to bring about an equalization in their industrial conditions; which of necessity would lessen the volume and the importance of trade between them. Where an invention is introduced in a single country, it gives that country at the outset a comparative advantage, leads to exports, and swells the volume of international trade. When the invention comes into international use, however, the industry which it serves may drift toward the countries of low wages; and these then may export the products. *May* export them, be it observed; for this tendency is greatly checked by those obstacles to imitation and transplanting which have just been referred to. But suppose the tendency not to be checked: suppose that each and every new device comes to be adopted in all countries, and used in all with equal effectiveness. Then the ultimate consequences will be different from those that nowadays follow the introduction of improvements. No one country will then possess advantages in manufactures over others; no one will be able to export to another; trade between them in manufactured goods,— if the assumed conditions hold absolutely, — will cease. All countries will secure in the same degree the benefit of the universalized inventions.

Such would be the inevitable outcome of complete equalization of the effectiveness of labor. The total income of a community is the product of its industry, — in the last analysis, of its labor. If labor is equally productive everywhere, differences in prosperity will cease. Then there will be no room for comparative advantages based on invention, peculiar effectiveness, better machinery, more skilful organization. The only trade between countries will be that based on unalterable climatic or physical advantages; such trade, for instance, as arises between tropical and temperate regions and between temperate regions having markedly different natural resources.

This consummation will not be reached for an indefinite period; nay, probably it will never be reached. Certainly it is beyond the range of possibility in any future which we can now foresee. But some approach to it is likely to come in the relations between the more advanced countries. There is a tendency toward equalization in their use of machinery, and so in their general industrial conditions. For the United States especially, the twentieth century will be different from the nineteenth. The period of free land has been virtually passed. That great basis of high material prosperity and of high general wages no longer exists as broadly and strongly as it did during the first century of our national life. The continued maintenance of a prosperity greater than that of England and Germany and France must rest on other causes. Now that fresh land can no longer be resorted to by the expanding population, a higher effectiveness of labor must depend almost exclusively on better implements and higher skill, — on labor better led and better applied. It may be reasonably hoped that the United States will long remain the land of promise, in the van of material progress; but the degree of difference may be less than it was. This lessening difference will come about, probably, not because the United States will fall back but because other countries will gain on her. Such has been the nature of the changed relation between England and the countries of the Continent during the last generation; and such, — to go back earlier, — was the change in the relative positions of Holland and England in the course of the seventeenth and eighteenth centuries. England no longer retains the unmistakable leadership which she had over the Continent during the greater part of the nineteenth century. But she has not retrograded; the countries of the Continent have progressed. Such is likely to be the nature of the coming race between the United States and other advanced countries. And the outcome is one which every friend of humanity must welcome. It means diffused prosperity, economic and social progress.

For an indefinite time, however, differences in general industrial effectiveness will remain. They will obviously remain, so far as they rest upon natural causes, — differences in soil, in mineral wealth, in climate. They will remain also in many manufacturing industries in which physical causes are not decisive. Some countries, — the United States among them, we may hope and expect, — will use machinery better, will apply labor-saving appliances more freely. The people of the United States will direct their labor with greatest advantage to those industries in which their abilities tell to the utmost. The development of the different industries will unquestionably continue to be affected by the accidents of invention and of progress, by dominant personalities in this country and in that, by the historical development of aptitudes and tastes, by some causes of variations in industrial leadership that seem inscrutable. But a general trend is likely to persist; in the United States labor-saving devices will be adopted more quickly and more widely. It will be shown in the following pages how this tendency has appeared in the great development that has taken place since the civil war, and how the effects of tariff legislation have been themselves influenced by the general tendency. In the industries where machinery can be used to most effect, this country will continue to have a comparative advantage.

PART II

SUGAR

CHAPTER IV

INTRODUCTORY — LOUISIANA

The duties on sugar as they stood for the half-century after the close of the civil war illustrate several questions of principle. They present a clear case of the continuance of imports in face of duties; and yet a case which, as regards the imports of the later years of the period, needs to be interpreted with caution. During these later years, moreover, the imports came chiefly from regions with which the United States had special trade relations; either because of political control, as with Hawaii, Porto Rico, and the Philippines, or because of reciprocity treaties, as with Cuba. The relaxations of duty for the regions thus favored caused this schedule of the tariff to stand by itself. The domestic production of sugar, and especially of beet sugar, increased fast, under conditions which can be understood only in the light of the doctrine of comparative advantage. The refining of sugar, again, came to be during the half-century a great-scale industry, and was dominated by one of the earliest of the trusts. This was a conspicuous case in which the protective system might be charged with having nurtured or at least strengthened a monopoly. Lastly, the revenue from sugar was large; its fiscal yield throughout was important for the federal budget. Varied questions hence present themselves, ramifying into phases of economic inquiry that seem at first sight to stand in no connection with the sugar duties.

The duty on sugar during the greater part of the period was not far from two cents a pound. Under the tariff acts of 1870 and 1883, it was a little more than two cents (2.25 under the act of 1883). Under the tariff of 1890, the so-called McKinley bill, sugar was admitted free. But a bounty was then given on sugar of domestic production, at the rate of two cents a pound; so that protection was retained at this rate. In the tariff act of 1894, the "Wilson bill," a new system was adopted, bringing a lowered rate. The duty was made *ad valorem* instead of specific; the rate was made forty per cent, which, at the low prices of that period, was equivalent to little more than one cent a pound. Shortly after, however, the act of 1897 (Dingley) restored the duty very nearly to the level which had prevailed before 1890; it was fixed, on the grades chiefly imported, at about $1\frac{2}{3}$ cents per pound. In the act of 1909 (Payne-Aldrich) this figure was not changed.

The tariff act of 1913 reduced the duty to $1\frac{1}{4}$ cents a pound.[1] A much more incisive change was contemplated in the act, but never came to pass. In 1916 and thereafter sugar was to have been admitted free, the interval from 1913 to 1916 being allowed in order to give the protected industry time for readjustment. But when 1916 came the expected repeal was indefinitely postponed. The duty therefore remained, at the lower rate set for what had been expected to be merely a transition period.

The duties above stated were on raw sugar. On refined sugar there were additional duties, so-called "differentials," designed to give protection to the refiners. The effects of the two sets of charges — on raw and on refined — are quite distinct, though often confounded in popular discussion. For the present, attention will be confined to the duties on raw sugar, by far the most important in quantitative effect and presenting also the problems of most interest to the economist.[2]

Until about the year 1880, the effects of the sugar duty were of the simplest sort. The imports were large, the domestic production comparatively small. The imported supply was from eighty to ninety per cent of the total. Hence the duty in the main was not protective. It was chiefly a revenue duty: by far

[1] This duty was subject to a reduction of 20% on sugar from Cuba, whence come almost all the imports. The duty on Cuban sugar was one cent. On the Cuban rebate and its effect see below, pp. 75–79.

[2] For the details of the sugar duties, and the causes which led to the changes in the several tariff acts, I refer the reader to my *Tariff History of the United States*. The duties were usually arranged by gradations according to the quality (saccharine content) of the raw sugar, and sundry complicated questions arose because of the tariff gradations. These, however, though troublesome for the customs administrators, have but little bearing on the protective controversy.

the greater part of what the consumers paid in the way of enhanced price, or tax, went as revenue to the federal Treasury.

The domestic production was confined to Louisiana. There it had suffered during the civil war, and at the period with which we begin was less important, both absolutely and in proportion to the imports, than it had been before 1860. During the decade 1870–80 the Louisiana output, fluctuating with the seasons, ranged from 100 to 200 million pounds a year. The imports ranged from 1000 to 2000 million pounds. Not only was the Louisiana supply thus small in comparison with the total, but it was produced under conditions not dissimilar from those in the competing foreign countries. The question of the effects of protection was presented without complexity. The Louisiana sugar, like that imported, was made from cane, and by substantially the same methods and with labor of very much the same character. The climate, however, is less favorable for sugar cane in Louisiana than in Cuba, Java, and the other regions whence cane sugar is imported. The duty was "needed" for protection, because the Louisiana sugar was produced under physical conditions less favorable. The effect of the duty, considered from any but the mercantilist point of view, was obviously disadvantageous. But the national loss, assessed according to the orthodox reasoning, was not quantitatively considerable, since the supply came preponderantly by importation.

The later course of development in Louisiana brought some considerable changes. The Louisiana supply increased very much beyond what it was in 1870–80; yet it remained about the same proportion of the total, — not far from 10 per cent of the country's consumption. The increase was irregular, fluctuating with the Louisiana crops, which are peculiarly subject to variation from year to year because of the possibility of frost, — the serious natural drawback in this region. After 1890 there was a substantial gain, no doubt due in part to the effect on men's imagination of the bounty given by the McKinley tariff act. It is true that the bounty was intended to do no more, and in fact did no more, than make up for the abolition of the duty. But a bounty seems to make a greater impression than a duty, — not only on the general public, but also, strange as it may seem, on the producers whose affairs are directly concerned.[1]

Possibly there was in some degree a really greater benefit to the Louisiana sugar planters from the bounty than there had been from the previous duty; since some small fraction of the latter had probably been intercepted by the refiners.[2] At all events the Louisiana sugar output grew very rapidly during the bounty period (1891–95), and reached, toward its close, dimensions which at no later date were much exceeded.

After the bounty episode there were important changes in the internal organization of the industry in Louisiana. Sugar prices the world over were low during the closing years of the nineteenth century and the opening years of the twentieth, chiefly because of the pressure on the market of the bounty-fed sugar from Continental Europe. The Louisiana industry necessarily felt the pressure, and thereby was forced, as is so often the case when profits are threatened by adverse conditions, to put its best foot foremost. Plantation methods and sugar-house methods were improved. Many plantations passed out of the hands of the old easy-going families, and were managed more efficiently by new men. The previous system of having a sugar-mill on every plantation was superseded by one of independent central sugar-mills, each grinding the cane and extracting the sugar for a dozen plantations, and each equipped with expensive and well-planned machinery.[3] A necessary part of the new method was a network of light railways for carrying the cane to the grinding centers. The transition to this more capitalistic system, it may be noted, was not peculiar to Louisiana, nor first undertaken there. It took place in the other cane-sugar regions also, at about the same time and because of the same pressure from low prices of sugar. At all events, with the improvements, sugar

[1] Compare the similar case with beet-sugar production; below, p. 80.

[2] For the consideration of this aspect of the situation, see below, p. 110.

[3] See the testimony before the Senate Committee of 1911 on Sugar Refining (Hardwick Committee), pp. 1760–1797. The new system seems to have originated in Java among the Dutch, then to have been copied in Cuba, and adopted last in Louisiana. See the testimony of a well-informed observer, Mr. Rionda, in the suit of U. S. Govt. *v.* Am. Sug. Ref. Co., Transcript of Record, p. 7914.

making in Louisiana held its own and even showed some increase during the years 1900–10.

The changes in duty provided for in the tariff act of 1913 were strenuously resisted by the Louisiana planters and their representatives in Congress. The complete repeal of the duty then contemplated was alleged to threaten ruin to their industry; and it was these protests which were most effective in bringing about in 1916 the retention for an indefinite period of the lowered rate which had been expected to endure for the transition period only. The indications are that in fact free sugar would have caused most of the Louisiana planters, perhaps all of them, to give up sugar and turn to something else. Their industry seems to be, in the main, unable to hold its own without protection; it cannot put sugar on the market as cheaply as competitors in Cuba and Java, or as those in the better-situated beet regions. The case is the comparatively simple one of a domestic industry dependent on an import duty. More complex are the consequences of the sugar duty in other regions, to which attention is given in the chapters which follow.[1]

[1] Since the first edition of this book appeared (1915) additional information on the cane sugar industry in Louisiana and elsewhere has been supplied in a report on *The Cane Sugar Industry* published by the Bureau of Foreign and Domestic Commerce of the Department of Commerce. The report, issued in 1917, gives data for an earlier period, the fiscal year 1913–14. For that year, it covers not only Louisiana but most of the other cane-growing regions described in this book, — Cuba, Hawaii, Porto Rico, — and gives figures in detail on cost of production in each of them. As regards Louisiana, costs, while they vary surprisingly for the several plantations and mills, are in general markedly higher than in any other region; so much higher as to indicate that little sugar would continue to be produced in the state under free trade. Cf. the footnote to p. 79, below.

CHAPTER V

HAWAII

THE first important modification of the comparatively simple situation which continued so long as Louisiana alone was favored against the importing countries came from the reciprocity treaty with Hawaii in 1876. The islands of the Hawaiian group went through several industrial stages after their first contact with white men during Cook's memorable voyage (1778). At the outset sandal wood was the dominant article of commerce; next they became a center for the whaling trade of the Pacific; last came the stage of sugar planting. The treaty of 1876 provided for the reciprocal free admission into the United States and the Hawaiian islands of certain commodities, among which sugar was the only considerable article of commerce. The free admission of sugar into the United States proved to be of signal importance. Not only did it transform the internal conditions of the islands; it altered their relations with the rest of the world, and eventually led to their incorporation into the United States.[1]

At the time when the reciprocity arrangement was concluded, there was no expectation of any such considerable economic consequences. Political motives, in the main, led to the treaty. It was feared that Great Britain would acquire the islands; much was said of their desirability as a coaling station. The treaty seems to have been due chiefly to the persistent prepossession for

[1] The treaty, concluded in 1875, went into effect in 1876. It was to remain in force for seven years, then to be terminable on a year's notice. In 1884 a convention renewed the treaty for seven years from the date of ratification; thereafter it was to be again terminable on a year's notice. Ratification did not take place until 1887; seven years after that date, *i. e.*, in 1894, the arrangement once more became terminable.

It was provided in 1884 that the United States might maintain a coaling and repair station at Pearl Harbor, a magnificent bay not far from Honolulu; and Hawaii engaged to give no other power a lien or lease on any of its harbors. Nothing was done by the United States at Pearl Harbor during the treaty period, but in later years (1907–13) much work was done for improving the channel, constructing a huge dry dock and erecting fortifications.

owning or controlling foreign lands, — as if a nation by that one stroke secured additional riches, — and to the general jingo-mercantilist fear of being got the better of by another country. Something was due to the fact that American missionaries were established in the islands, and had great and growing influence among the natives. Though it was pointed out, in the debates, that sugar planting, already carried on in the islands, would become more profitable under the treaty, no great extension of the industry was anticipated.

The effect, however, was immediate; and it has proved to be cumulative. Before the treaty the imports of sugar had never risen to 20 million pounds. They touched that figure in the very first year (1876). Thereafter the rate of increase was extraordinary, each year showing a sharp advance above its predecessor. By 1882, the imports exceeded 100 million pounds; by 1887, 200 millions. There was some relaxation during the period of the McKinley tariff, 1890–94, for reasons presently to be explained. After 1895 the upward movement was resumed. The Hawaiian supply so grew that it finally exceeded that from Louisiana, large as the latter had become. By 1908 the quantity of sugar from the islands was more than 1000 million pounds; and it remained above that figure thereafter. From an insignificant item, it became an important one; in recent years (1908–13) about one-seventh of the total supply has come from this source.

Who got the benefit of this remission of duty? The United States Treasury lost very considerable amounts; so much sugar came in free that otherwise would have been taxed. The consumers in the United States did not get the benefit. The price of sugar did not fall; nor could it be expected to fall. By far the larger portion of the sugar consumed continued to be imported from non-favored regions and remained subject to duty. The Hawaiian planters did not sell their sugar at a price below that current in the United States, — a price necessarily higher by the full amount of the duty of two cents a pound. Clearly it was the planters whom one would expect to be the beneficiaries from the remission. And so it proved. The Hawaiian sugar naturally found its way to the Pacific coast, and there was sold at the full

American duty-paid price.[1] It soon supplied the whole of California and the other coast states, and, as the imports from the islands grew, made its way eastward toward the Missouri river. It was a main factor in the contest which went on for a while between the eastern refiners and those of the Pacific coast, — an episode of which more will be said in due course.[2] But in all this the purchasers of the Hawaiian sugar found no advantage. They paid at least as much for their sugar as the people of New York or Massachusetts, who consumed dutiable sugar. The effect of the reciprocity treaty was to include the Hawaiian planters within the pale of the protective system. They were put in the same position as the planters of Louisiana. Or, to state the outcome in other terms, the United States gave a bounty of two cents a pound to the sugar growers of Hawaii.

This is the normal effect of a remission of tax on part of the supply. So long as some fraction of the supply continues to be steadily taxed, — so long as dutiable imports persist, — the whole is raised in price by the full amount of the tax or duty. The producer, domestic or foreign as the case may be, gets the benefit of the remission, not the consumer. The effect is the same in kind, only less in degree, if there is a partial remission, — if part of the supply is subjected, say, to only half tax or half duty. If a portion of the supply continues to pay the full tax regularly, the half which is remitted follows the same course as would the whole: it goes into the pockets of the producers.

Hence the extraordinary growth of sugar planting in Hawaii, and the extraordinary increase of the imports into the United States. The growth in the islands, however, took place under circumstances in many respects peculiar, and with unexpected political and social consequences. At the risk of some digression from our main topic, attention may be given to some of these consequences.

The planters who reaped the high profits were chiefly Americans, or of American extraction. Some were descendants of the

[1] Subject to a slight reduction, however, which enured to the advantage of the sugar refiners; see below, p. 108.

[2] See below, pp. 104, 105.

American missionaries who during the preceding half-century had had such remarkable success in converting and guiding the natives. Some were new arrivals, who hastened to exploit the rich opportunity. Among the latter was the astute Spreckels, who combined the profits of Hawaiian planting with those of refining in California, built up a great fortune, and became an important figure in the islands. But the planters of the "old" American families remained the dominant element. Sugar growing, under any conditions a large-scale industry, was the more readily concentrated in comparatively few hands through their control, by lease from the government or by ownership, of the best available land. The great planters became an oligarchy, succeeding the missionaries as the real power behind the Hawaiian throne. The swarthy monarchs, King Kalakaua and his sister and successor Queen Liliuokalani, were little disturbed in their sham royalty so long as they confined themselves to dissipation and petty plunder. But both in turn were deposed when they undertook really to rule. There never was a more pasteboard throne than that of the latter-day Hawaiian kings and queens.

The enviable situation of the planters, — increasing output of sugar, high dividends on plantation shares, and high prices of sugar land, — received a rude shock in 1890. In that year the McKinley tariff act admitted sugar into the United States free of duty. Consistently with the protective principle, the Louisiana sugar growers were placated by a direct bounty of two cents a pound. But the Hawaiian planters, not yet within the American pale, received no bounty. They had now to accept for their sugar the price of the open market, like the planters of Cuba and Java and Brazil. The price of sugar went down sharply in the islands; it is said to have fallen in a single day after the passage of the tariff act from $100 to $60 a ton.[1] Hence great depression and much soreness of heart. The hard times that ensued meant, to be sure, not that all profits had disappeared, but in the main that the extravagances of the past had to be given up. As the heavily-watered sugar company stocks shrank, planters' expenditures could no longer be on a recklessly generous scale. More-

[1] C. Whitney, *The Hawaiian Islands*, p. 194.

over, the pressure of need caused the methods of growing cane and extracting sugar to be greatly improved, — the same result that ensued a few years later under similar conditions in Louisiana. The hard times of 1891–94 proved a blessing in disguise; they led to improvements which were extraordinarily profitable under the favorable conditions which soon were restored.

The uneasiness and discontent bred by the pressure of 1891–94 led to the Hawaiian revolution of 1892, and to the treaty which the administration of President Harrison made for the annexation of the islands to the United States. It would not be just to say that sugar and reciprocity, and a desire to get once more under profitable cover, were the sole motives for the upsetting of the frail monarchy. The queen Liliuokalani and her predecessor Kalakaua had not been creditable specimens of royalty, and doubtless were a good riddance. Among the planters themselves there was some division of opinion on the expediency of annexation. None the less it is clear that the root of the movement was in the sugar situation, — in the wish to get back somehow into the golden relations with the American market. This was certainly the case when annexation was finally accomplished. It will be recalled that the Cleveland administration, on coming into power in March, 1893, withdrew from the Senate the annexation treaty concluded by its predecessor, and caused the collapse for the time being of the whole movement. But the Hawaiian monarchy was gone for good, and the Hawaiian Republic (with a carefully guarded suffrage!) took its place. Very soon after, in 1894, the United States again imposed, in the Wilson Tariff Act, a duty on sugar; not quite so high a duty as that before 1890, but high enough, — Hawaiian sugar being throughout admitted free, — to restore a handsome bounty for the island planters. Good times returned in the islands, and were rendered more secure by their final annexation in 1898. As soon as President Cleveland went out, the McKinley administration emphasized its adoption of directly opposite policies by renewing the negotiations for annexation. A treaty for annexation was concluded as early as June, 1897; but ratification by the Senate did not come until 1898, when the Spanish War and the Philippine conquest brought an added pressure. The favored position of Hawaiian sugar rested thereafter not on the basis of a revocable treaty (the treaty had become, after 1894, terminable at twelve months' notice), but on the solid foundation of a complete incorporation in the American dominions. Sugar growing, which had barely held its own from 1890 to 1894, now resumed its upward march. New plantations were opened, old ones enlarged their output, more and more sugar was poured into the United States, and the islands again boomed.

The increase of the Hawaiian sugar crop during the later years took place in a way that serves to illustrate still other economic principles. The tendency to diminishing returns in agriculture showed itself as the sugar growing resources of the island were pushed further. The best plantation lands had now been in use for many years. As more sugar was got from the soil it became necessary,— even for the maintenance of output at the existing rate,— to resort to high cultivation. The Hawaiian plantations hence became large importers and users of fertilizers. Therein they were in contrast with Cuba, where sugar land was abundant, and where, as one patch showed signs of exhaustion, the planter simply moved on to another virgin plot. Not only was there this pressure on the good sites in Hawaii: there was the natural tendency to descend in the scale of cultivation, and to use poorer and poorer sites. Sugar cane depends on abundant precipitation. This is supplied on the windward slopes of the islands by the moisture laden winds from the Pacific. But on the leeward slopes, and on inland areas shut off from the ocean by mountain barriers, the rainfall is insufficient. Here great irrigation works were set up, largely by pumping from artesian wells, and sometimes with an admirable technical equipment.[1] In other words, under the bait of the artificially high price of sugar, capital and labor were turned to the utilization of natural resources not in themselves of the best. It is part of the same pressure on the land that

[1] On one great plantation, separated by mountains 6,000 feet high from the water-soaked side of the island of Kauai, electric power was developed on the mountain streams on that side, transmitted over the mountains to the drier area, and there utilized in pumping water for irrigation from artesian wells. See the *American Sugar Industry and Beet-Sugar Gazette*, April 5, 1906. Cf. Whitney, *The Hawaiian Islands*, p. 194; *Bulletin Bureau of Labor, 1903*, pp. 725, 726, 733.

sugar cultivation in Hawaii was intensive; the yield per acre is said to have been higher than in any other cane growing country;[1] fertilizers, as has just been noted, were imported in large quantity. As is often the case in descriptions and discussions of intensive cultivation, these refined methods and high acreage yields were spoken of as meritorious, proving that the industry was doing well. In fact they proved that the land was being forced, that the tendency to diminishing returns had set in, and that strenuous exertions were being made to overcome the difficulties.

Hence there must be some qualification to the statement or implication in the preceding paragraphs, that the bounty or protection on Hawaiian sugar enured to the special profit of the sugar planters. It did, so far as they produced the sugar on the more favorable sites or under the more favorable conditions. So far as they had to turn to poorer sources of supply, or pushed their plantations to extra yield by high cultivation, they were led to make that disadvantageous application of labor and capital which is the more ordinary consequence of a protective duty. The higher price of sugar enabled the planters to carry on some sugar growing which they could not have carried on without the bonus. It is impossible to determine how large a part of the sugar planting of the islands was in this sense wasteful. The circumstance that during the years of free sugar (1890–94) their output, though it failed to increase, did not shrink (it remained not far from 300 million pounds), would indicate that up to this amount cultivation had not been pushed to the point of slackening returns. On the other hand, the output, after a steady growth from 1894 to 1908, remained after the latter year virtually stationary (at about 1,000 million pounds); apparently showing that with this

[1] Whitney, p. 198. Cf. R. S. Baker, in the *American Magazine*, Nov., 1911: "I have seen great fields plowed nearly three feet deep with huge steam plows; and the stories of the use of fertilizers are almost unbelievable to a person accustomed to the ordinary farming methods of the middle West." The statistics of Hawaiian trade given in the U. S. Reports on Commerce and Navigation show that the islands imported annually (*e. g.*, in 1910 and 1911) a million dollars' worth of fertilizers, chiefly phosphate.

amount the margin of profitableness, even though it may not have been quite reached, was being approached.

One further illustration of general economic principles may be noted. The bonus has caused in the islands a rearrangement of industry which has conformed to the principle of comparative advantage. It made sugar production a peculiarly advantageous industry, — advantageous, that is, from the profit-making point of view. Sundry commodities were imported into the islands for which they seem to be well adapted and which had formerly been made within their own limits. Though possessed of a temperate climate, and apparently capable of producing at moderate cost wheat, Indian corn, meat, they imported these staples.[1] Sugar had been made the more profitable industry, and to this all the energies of the inhabitants were turned. Possibly the same result would have ensued in any case; sugar may have a comparative advantage even without a bonus; but the devotion of practically all the land and labor and capital of the islands to this one industry was settled once for all by the special advantage which was given it by favored treatment on the part of the United States.

Still another aspect of the Hawaiian experience is significant: its labor problem. The light-hearted easy-going native — the Kanaka — proved unwilling to do the unremitting hard labor of the cane fields and sugar mills. He had proved an excellent sea-

[1] "Hawaii, with a climate unexcelled, and a soil capable of producing the majority of both temperate and tropical products, nevertheless imports the bulk of its food. Although in the fifties, and a bit later, Hawaii supplied the Pacific coast with wheat and potatoes, it now spends abroad over one million dollars annually for food deficits of man and beast, the greater portion of which could be and should be raised on the islands. Of this amount nearly $300,000 goes for hay and grain, and $80,000 for dried fish, although the waters surrounding the islands teem with fish! . . . Hawaii could greatly increase both the quality and quantity of its cattle-raising by pursuing the industry more intelligently and less extravagantly. Corn is necessary to put the stock on the market in prime condition; but although there is scarcely a cattle range where corn would not flourish at a very small outlay of either time or money, the cattle men get their corn from California and pay two cents a pound for it!" Whitney, *Hawaiian America*, pp. 159, 173.

In 1911 the islands imported from the United States,

Meat and Dairy Products	$897,000
Breadstuffs (including flour)	1,950,000
Fish (chiefly canned)	390,000

man, and could be induced to serve as teamster or cowboy. But for plantation work others had to be sought. Indeed, the Hawaiian race was disappearing; it could not resist the vices and diseases of civilization. The natives had been declining in numbers from their very first contact with the white race, and before long became a minor part of the population. Other labor had to be resorted to, more hardy in the fields and more willing to labor long and steadily. The Chinese were brought into the islands by the thousand. They came under a "penal labor contract," devised in the early days (the act authorizing it was passed in 1850): a contract under which the laborer bound himself for service at fixed wages for a period of years, and could be apprehended and delivered to his employer if he ran away.[1] As an agent of the United States Department of Labor remarked, this arrangement had "all the advantages of slavery without its disadvantages."[2] The Chinese coolies were a semi-servile labor force, absolutely at the planter's disposal for the stipulated term (usually five years), while yet he suffered no loss if they should die. That the coolies were not an entirely wholesome constituent in the population was obvious enough from the outset, and an attempt was made (in 1878–86) to secure Portuguese laborers from the Azores. A few thousand Portuguese were brought in under labor contracts and placed on the plantations. But though tough and hard-working, they proved, like the Kanakas, unwilling to remain permanently on the sugar fields. As soon as the stipulated term of service expired, they took a bit of land for their own cultivation or became artisans.[3] The planters found

[1] See Professor Katherine Coman's *History of Contract Labor in the Hawaiian Islands*, Publ. Amer. Econ. Assoc., 3d series, vol. iv (1903).

[2] *Report on Hawaii*, Bulletin Department of Labor, no. 66 (Sept., 1906).

[3] Some 10,000 Portuguese in all were brought in under contract, most of them between 1880 and 1885. "The Portuguese were brought in for the purpose of supplying plantation laborers, but most of them are engaged in skilled or semi-skilled occupations and even when the demand for field labor was most pressing, the second generation of Portuguese were leaving the islands. . . . While many Portuguese remain on the plantations till old age, they do not care to remain field laborers all their life." *Report on Hawaii*, *Ibid.*, pp. 423, 429.

The Portuguese have tended in more recent years (1904–12) to drift to California; see note by V. S. Clark, in Publ. Amer. Statist. Assoc., June, 1913, p. 466.

it necessary to fall back on Asiatic labor, partly Chinese, partly Japanese.

After the annexation of the islands to the United States, in 1898, the labor problem entered on still a new phase. The prohibition of the immigration of Chinese laborers applied to Hawaii; moreover, the contract labor system was made illegal by the act of Congress providing for the government of the new territory. The planters were compelled to turn to the Japanese. These entered thereafter by the thousand, and became the largest single element in the population of the islands. They were not so docile as the Chinese, especially in view of their being "free,"—no longer contract laborers. They were able to ask for higher wages, and even to strike. They "made trouble" in various ways. But the planters, compactly organized, came to an agreement for uniformity in their rates of wages; [1] they would not overbid each other; and the Japanese were satisfied with a moderate increase of pay. There was and is a constant movement to and fro between Hawaii and Japan; for the plantation laborer remains a bird of passage, as he always has been. For a time there was a movement also between Hawaii and California. The tension between the United States and Japan concerning the immigration of Japanese laborers was due in no small part to the fact that the islands became a stepping stone toward the land of high wages and real freedom. The agreement of 1908 by which Japanese immigration to the United States proper has been controlled by Japan itself put an end to this cause of friction; but in Hawaii the Japanese remain, and constitute the bulk of the laborers in the sugar fields.[2]

The political and social conditions resulting from this unexpected industrial development are obviously not consonant with the ideals of democracy. A great mongrel mass of sugar-plantation laborers,—Chinese, Japanese, the wasting Hawaiians, a very few Portuguese; above them an oligarchy of rich planters,

[1] Coman, p. 48.

[2] The following tabular statement shows what striking changes have taken place in the population of the islands. The total population is supposed to have declined enormously since their discovery; and beyond doubt it declined very rapidly until the date of reciprocity (1876). It is estimated to have been 300,000 in the

with their bankers and shipping agents and other associates, and a few hangers-on; all dependent on a single industry puffed to unnatural dimensions by legislative favor, — this is not a welcome addition to the American commonwealths.

Most people think of an addition to a nation's dominions as they do of an addition to an individual's possessions. John Smith is more prosperous if he acquires more real estate; and the United States are supposed to be more prosperous if they acquire more territory. Hence we were willing to pay twenty millions for the Philippines, and think we did well to get Hawaii of its own offering and Porto Rico by right of conquest. In truth, they have been doubtful boons. If indeed new acquisitions serve to open, for settlement and utilization by a vigorous race, territory that otherwise would have lain fallow, there is a real gain. Such was the result of the Louisiana purchase, and of the acquisition of Texas and of the Pacific coast. These expansions, too, made possible a great extension of the geographical division of labor. But no such gains have come from our newly acquired dependencies. It is difficult to find in the whole Hawaiian episode anything but

eighteenth century. In 1832, when the first census was taken, 130,000 were enumerated (Coman, p. 7). For some later years these are the census figures:

	1853	1872	1884	1896	1900	1910
Total Population	73,138	56,897	80,578	109,020	154,001	191,909
Pure Hawaiian	70,036	49,044	40,014	31,019	29,799	26,041
Part-Hawaiian	983	1,487	4,218	8,485	7,857	12,506
Foreign born Chinese	361	1,938	17,937	19,382	21,746	21,674
Foreign born Japanese	....	....	116	22,329	56,230	84,207*
All other	1,755	4,428	18,293	27,805	38,369	47,481

* Including Koreans.

It will be seen that the total population declined until the reciprocity period was reached; that the native born Hawaiians (including all born in the islands, whether or no of the original stock) declined in numbers steadily, both before reciprocity and after; and that the marked growth in the total since reciprocity has come chiefly from the appearance, successively, of the Chinese and Japanese. — The figures are taken from Bulletin of the Department of Labor, 1903, p. 369, and from the 13th Census Bulletin on the Population of Hawaii.

Since 1910 a new element has appeared in Hawaii, — the Philippinos; these constituted in 1910–12 the most numerous Asiatic immigrants to the islands. Publ. Amer. Statist. Assoc., June, 1913, p. 466.

one long course of error. The American consumer paid for thirty years (barring the brief respite while the McKinley Tariff was in force) a tidy sum annually to the Hawaiian planters. In the later years of the period this tribute amounted to twelve or fifteen millions of dollars a year. For this there has been nothing of any real value to show, — unless it be a stepping-stone to the Philippines, another dependency hardly less unprofitable.[1]

[1] I have left this chapter unchanged as it stood in the first edition, published in 1915. The report on Cane Sugar made by the Department of Commerce in 1917 and referred to above (p. 57 note) gives a wealth of added detail on the Hawaiian sugar industry as it stood in 1914, and more particularly brings out the great divergences in costs of production between different plantations in the islands. So far as concerns the questions of principle and their application to the Hawaiian situation, as discussed in the text, no modification was called for by this added evidence.

CHAPTER VI

PORTO RICO; THE PHILIPPINES; CUBA

THE war with Spain brought new complications of every sort, and among them none more striking than those in the sugar situation. In addition to Hawaii, Porto Rico and the Philippines became territory of the United States. Cuba was attached to this country by political and industrial ties. These three, as well as Hawaii, were producers of sugar. With regard to all, essentially the same problems arose.

The case of Porto Rico was almost precisely like that of Hawaii. The consequence of our acquisition of Porto Rico was that after 1901, this island was treated as an integral part of the United States. Its sugar, as well as its other products, became exempted from duty. Porto Rico was from the very outset in the position which Hawaii obtained through its annexation in 1898. Even more promptly and unconditionally than the other dependency, it was brought within the pale of the protective system.

It need not be explained again why sugar from Porto Rico, like that from Hawaii, was sold in the United States at the duty-paid price, though itself free of duty. The imports from the island (or supplies, — since in the view of the law they are not "imports") had not been considerable before 1900, having ranged not far from 100 million pounds a year. After the date when the favored treatment began, they rose fast. They doubled within three years, increased to nearly 500 millions in 1909, and were (in round numbers) 765 millions in 1913. Call it subsidy, bonus, protection, whatever name you will: the obvious fact was that the American consumer paid the full tax, which went, however, not to the federal Treasury but to the Porto Rican planters.

Whether the planters made unusual profits depended, as in the case of Hawaii and Louisiana, on their facilities for production. According as these were more or less good, the bonus operated either to put extra gains into their pockets or to sustain them with no exceptional profit in an industry carried on under unfavorable conditions. The rapid and continuous increase of the sugar output seemed to indicate that the conditions were favorable and that the planters profited handsomely. When an industry doubles its output every five years (such was roughly the rate at which Porto Rican sugar increased during the decade 1900–1910) it is reasonable to infer that the profits are more than generous. On the other hand, well-informed persons state that the land readily available for sugar growing is limited. Though some parts of the island have land equal to the best in Cuba, there is not enough for indefinite extension. Porto Rico is everywhere mountainous; the flat areas along the coast and in the valleys, alone available for sugar culture, are not large. Hence the prediction was made that even with the bonus from the sugar duty the output, while it might approach 1,000 millions, could not exceed that quantity.[1]

In Porto Rico, as in Hawaii, the situation led to attempts to extend cultivation and push the yield. Sugar growing was made profitable under conditions that would not have allowed a profit without the bonus. Rainfall and water supply again were of the first importance. The island is divided from east to west by a mountainous ridge, which causes the precipitation (here chiefly borne by northeast winds) to be heavy on the northern side, but on the southern side insufficient for the cane's need of abundant moisture.[2] The insular government undertook great irrigation works, involving the expenditure of millions of borrowed money,[3] all for promoting sugar cane culture; with

[1] Statements to this effect have been made to me by persons conversant with sugar planting and with the natural conditions in Porto Rico.

[2] "The average annual rainfall throughout the dry [southern] zone is forty-six inches, varying between twenty and sixty inches. The average amount is insufficient for the cultivation of cane, and a rainfall approaching the minimum is a destructive drought." *Report of the Governor of Porto Rico* (Commissioner of Interior's report), 1911, p. 139. Cf. *Report for 1909*, p. 84, for an account of the physical geography of the island.

[3] By 1911, bonds to the amount of $4,000,000 had been authorized for irrigation works. A map of the proposed systems is in the *Report of the Governor of Porto Rico for 1911*.

the expectation, of course, that payments by the planters for the water would make the investment remunerative. From the engineer's point of view, even from that of the zealous colonial administrator, these were most excellent projects. But the economist must question whether they represented a fruitful investment, resting as they did on the unstable foundation of prices raised by the effect of duties.

In Porto Rico, as in Hawaii, it has been the enterprising and money-making American who has chiefly profited. "The lands suited to cane culture are rapidly passing under the control of wealthy corporations, by purchase or by contracting for a term of years the cane of the 'colonos' or farmers."[1] This is doubtless inevitable. The same transition has taken place as in Louisiana and indeed in Cuba. Cane sugar making has come to be a large-scale industry, with great central mills to which the cane is brought by light railways for crushing. Only those who have large capital can embark in such an industry with success, and it is they who are likely to reap the larger share of any unusual profits. As an American official remarks, "it is the opinion of many close observers that the colonos and the peons who do the field work are not getting their share of the product."[2]

Turn now to the Philippines. They were long treated with less generosity than Porto Rico and Hawaii. Imports from the Philippines were admitted for many years at three-quarters of the ordinary rates of duty. The sugar duty after 1897, it will be remembered, was 1.62 cents per pound on the grades of sugar usually imported.[3] Philippine sugar got a remission of one-quarter, about two-fifths cent per pound. This arrangement continued until 1909.

[1] *Report of the Governor of Porto Rico* (Treasurer's Report), p. 85.

[2] *Ibid.*

[3] Philippine sugar was and is of lower grade (*i. e.*, less saccharine content) than that usually imported; hence the duty collected on it was less than the figure stated in the text, and the remission of one-quarter was less. These differences, however, affected simply the method by which the duty per pound of raw sugar was adjusted to the content of pure sugar.

The difference between remission of the whole duty and of a part of the duty, as has already been noted, is one of degree only. In neither case does the consumer benefit. The favored producer simply gets in the former case a bonus or protection of the whole of the duty, in the latter of a part of it. So with regard to the Philippines: during the period from 1901 to 1909, their producers sold the sugar at the full duty-paid price, and were able to keep for themselves the fraction of a cent which the United States remitted from the duties.

So moderate a degree of favor had no considerable influence on the imports from the archipelago. These imports had never been large; and they showed no tendency to increase during the period of partial remission. Under the Spanish régime, sugar planting had been carried on, as had most other industries, in lazy and slipshod fashion. American rule, for the time being at least, seemed to bring no change in this regard. The bonus previous to 1909 was not sufficiently large to lead to any change of moment.

In the tariff act of 1909, however, a new policy was adopted. Philippine products were admitted free, and among them sugar. This remission of duty, however, was not unqualified. Only 300,000 gross tons of sugar (674 million pounds) were to come in free; any amounts beyond this limit were to be subject to duty.[1] The restriction was due to a fear on the part of the domestic producers that imports might increase indefinitely: a fear justified by the course of events in Hawaii and Porto Rico. For the time being the amount allowed was generous enough,— far in excess of the then existing sugar output in the Philippines. The effect on that output, none the less, was immediate and marked; so much so as to suggest that the limit might have been reached within a few years. The imports of sugar from the Philippines, which had been 80 millions of pounds in 1909, rose to not less than 435 millions by 1912. The remission of duty

[1] The same policy was adopted in the tariff of 1909 as regards tobacco and cigars from the Philippines: free admission of a limited quantity. In general, Philippine products "which do not contain foreign materials to the value of more than twenty per cent of their total value" were made free of duty. Rice, however, remained on the dutiable list.

on this considerable quantity, as need hardly be repeated, had the same effect as in the other cases: a loss of revenue to the United States Treasury, no gain to consumers, a bonus to the Philippine sugar producers.

The tariff act of 1913 caused this situation to be altered. The restriction on the amount of sugar which might come in free was removed; it was provided that sugar, like other Philippine products, should be admitted without limit of quantity. But the duty was designed to be completely removed at an early date (1916) from all sugar. As matters turned out, when 1916 came around, it was retained. Had its retention been seriously contemplated in 1913, the unlimited free admission of Philippine sugar would hardly have been granted. Somewhat unexpectedly, the Philippine producers secured for an indefinite period and without limit of quantity the same bonus as the producers in the other favored districts, — about one a cent pound.

The liberal treatment of the Philippines had long been urged by President Taft, whose own experience in the government of the islands led him to regard with perhaps sentimental favor all measures for their benefit. It was largely through his influence that the free admission of their sugar was brought about in 1909. In view of the way in which Hawaii and Porto Rico had been dealt with, the argument for extension of the same favors to the Philippines was wellnigh unanswerable. It was strengthened by the general tenor of the current protectionist reasoning, — the notion that duties are aimed at foreign producers and are borne by them.[1] In fact, the duties had not been taxes on the Philippine producers at all; they had simply served, through their previous partial remission, to give a partial bounty; they now

[1] This same notion appears in the legislation which regulated the financial relations between Porto Rico and the United States during the transitional years immediately after the conquest of that island, 1898–1901. The revenue from duties collected on imports from Porto Rico was put into a "trust fund" to be used for the benefit of the island, and in due time was so used, for roads, schoolhouses, and the like. (W. F. Willoughby, *Territories and Dependencies of the United States*, pp. 113, 114.) The assumption evidently was that the duties had brought a burden, not on American consumers, but on the islanders, and was no longer to be left on them once they became a part of us.

served, through their complete remission, to give a complete bounty.

Last in the list of dependencies and quasi-dependencies comes Cuba.

The sugar supplies from Cuba were, throughout the period under discussion, by far the largest constituent in the total, ranging from one-third to nearly one-half of the amount consumed in the United States. They fell off, inevitably, at the time of the insurrection against Spain and the consequent disordered state of the island; but after the restoration of peace the normal large amounts were again sent to the United States. Until 1903 they were subject to full duty. But in the course of the new arrangements which came after the Spanish war, Cuba, like the Philippines, was given a favored position. When the independence of the island was finally settled, and the United States troops withdrew, a reciprocity treaty was concluded by which Cuba made certain reductions of duty on American products imported into Cuba, and the United States made a general reduction of twenty per cent on Cuban products imported in the United States. Sugar was by far the largest article of import from Cuba, and the significance of the reduction on sugar was shown by some special stipulations regarding this commodity. The treaty went into effect in 1903. Cuban sugar thereafter was admitted at a reduction of about one-third cent from the full duty.[1]

[1] It was particularly provided that " no sugar imported from Cuba . . . shall be admitted into the United States at a reduction of duty greater than twenty per cent [of the rates of 1897] . . . and no sugar, the product of any other foreign country, shall be admitted by treaty or convention into the United States, while this convention is in force, at a lower rate than that provided by the tariff act . . . of 1897." In the tariff act of 1913 provision was made for putting an end to this restriction on the tariff legislation of the United States.

Cuba admitted a large list of United States articles at reductions of 25, 30, and 40 per cent; the most important being in the schedule which granted a reduction of 30 per cent. The treaty was to remain in force for five years, thereafter terminable on a year's notice.

Most Cuban sugar is of the grade (testing 95°) which was dutiable under the tariff acts of 1897 and 1909 at 1.65 cents; 20 per cent of this is .33 cent; the net duty on Cuban sugar was thus 1.32 cents.

So long as imports paying full duty came in from other sources, this reduction must be expected to enure to the benefit of the Cuban producer, not of the American consumer. The case would seem to differ from that of the Philippines (until 1909) in degree only. Though the sugar imports from Cuba had always been large, and became even larger under the influence of the favored treatment, they were in no year sufficient to displace entirely the full-duty sugar from other countries. These full-duty imports became, it is true, small in proportion to the total. They diminished to less than ten per cent of the total consumption, and in some years to hardly more than five per cent. But this small percentage still meant imports that were large absolutely: hundreds of millions of pounds came in each year, and they paid duties amounting at the full rate to several millions of dollars. These continuing imports, by no means small or sporadic, would seem to prove that the price of *all* the sugar consumed was raised by the full amount of the duty, that the American consumer got no benefit from the Cuban remission, and that the Cuban producer got a gratuity of one-third cent on each pound.

This conclusion, however, is subject to a qualification of the kind considered in the first chapter of this book:[1] a qualification which shows once again the need of watchfulness in drawing inferences from the bare statistics.

The Cuban sugar supply was so large, and the proportion of full-duty sugar so small, that the situation began to approach that which would appear if full-duty sugar had been completely pushed out of the United States market. Had this result been reached, — had importation from non-favored regions ceased, — the relaxed duty on Cuban sugar would have been the only one in fact collected, and the price of sugar in the United States would have been raised not by the amount of the nominal duty, but by that of the Cuban duty, — not by 1.65 cents, but by 1.33 cents. All the other preferences to sugar producers, both those in the United States proper and those in the several dependencies, would have been reduced to the same extent. The rapid exten-

[1] See p. 16 above.

sion of production in the various favored regions threatened to bring about this result, — surely one to be welcomed by the American consumer. Though this consummation was not quite reached in the later years of our period, say in 1906–1913, the approach to it caused an appreciable relaxation of the burden from the full duty and some diminution of the gratuity to the privileged producers.

Raw sugar has come on the American market in recent times by instalments distributed unevenly through the year. The domestic beet sugar (of which more will be said presently) is marketed during the autumn months; but this supply reaches chiefly the western region, beyond the Missouri river. Toward the end of the year, the Louisiana crop appears, followed in January by that from Cuba and Porto Rico. During the first quarter of each year, from January until April and May, these West Indian supplies are virtually the only ones available. Then follows a comparatively lean period, in summer, when imports from Java come in; these are (or were) the main full-duty imports. The Hawaiian crop also arrives between the early spring and December. Of all the several supplies, that from Cuba is by far the largest; so much so, that during the early months of the year, it dominates the market. Virtually no other duties were paid at this season than those at the reduced rate on Cuban sugar. Under such circumstances it might happen that for the time being the domestic price was settled solely by the Cuban rate, — *i. e.*, the outside price plus the duty on Cuban sugar; or that some Cuban producers held back a considerable part of their sugar, waiting for the later months when the price would again rise to the full-duty level, and maintaining the price for the time being at a point somewhere between full duty and Cuban duty. Conceivably, so much of the supply might be thus held back as to keep the price throughout at the full-duty level. In fact, it was the intermediate stage which seems to have been settled by the higgling of the market, with variations in different years and in different months of any one year. The Cuban planter did not get the whole of his differential tariff advantage; but neither did the domestic purchaser. The case shows the need of caution in inferring once for all, from the continuance of imports, that every part of the supply is necessarily raised in price by the maximum duty imposed on any part of the imports. Here, as in other parts of the economic world, there are eddies and cross-currents which must be watched and understood.[1]

Needless to say, such a transition period could not last indefinitely. The steady increase from the various favored sources of supply, — Hawaii, Porto Rico, the Philippines, Cuba, and the domestic beet-sugar region, — was sure in time to drive out completely the full-duty sugar, and to leave sugar from Cuba alone dutiable. Then this alone would affect the domestic price, and the differential advantage to the Cuban planter would cease.

During the transition period, though the Cuban planter failed to keep for himself the reduction in duty, the domestic consumer did not necessarily secure it. Such a seasonal and intermittent concession in price as the Cuban sellers were forced to make was likely to be absorbed by one or another of the various intermediaries who intervene before the sugar finally passes over the retailer's counter. It would appear that the refiners, who stand first in the chain of middlemen, kept some slice of the concession for themselves. It is quite possible that the wholesale and retail dealers kept the rest. It may be that the consumer got a fraction of it, either directly, or indirectly in the form of "bargains" in other articles, made possible by a shading of the terms on which the dealer secured his sugar.[2] The connection between wholesale prices and retail is a loose one; all that can be laid down is that a long-continued decline in wholesale prices has its effect ultimately in lowering retail prices also, and that this is

[1] Until about 1909 the planters seem to have got the full benefit of the "differential" on Cuban sugar. Thereafter, as their increased output pressed on the American market during the spring months, the American purchasers began to get part of it. By 1912 and 1913 the Cubans seem to have lost even the whole, at least during part of the season; this is to be inferred from the fact that considerable quantities of Cuban sugar then were sold in England. See the Record in the suit of U. S. Govt. *v.* Am. Sug. Ref. Co., pp. 7926, 7929.

[2] The head of the well-known firm of sugar brokers, Willett and Gray, estimated that for the years from 1903 to 1911 the amount remitted on Cuban sugar was

likely to be the case even if the wholesale fall is not large. Spasmodic and irregular changes, on the other hand, even though considerable, are more likely to dissipate their effects before the retail purchaser is reached.

divided between Cuban planter, American refiner, and American purchaser in these proportions:

Total remission (on the basis of 96° sugar)		$0.337
Received by the Cuban planter	$0.097	
" " " refiner	.063	
" " " consumer	.177	
		$0.337

"Consumer" here signifies the purchaser from the refiner (wholesale dealer). *Hardwick Committee Report* (1911), p. 3551.

No essential changes in the conditions of competition between the different producing regions took place after the first edition of this book was published (1915). Cuban sugar, however, displaced more and more completely the full-duty sugar; and the Cuban duty came to be with less and less modification the effective rate borne by the consumer. The great war led soon to a sharp rise in the price of sugar throughout the regions that supplied the United States and the Allies, and all engaged in the industry made most handsome profits. These extraordinary changes, however, did not alter the relative conditions of the different producers supplying the United States. The analysis made in the text remains applicable to the later conditions; the general range of sugar prices went up, but the differentials and bonuses remained in essentials unchanged.

As regards Cuba as well as the other cane regions from which sugar supplies came to the United States, detailed and accurate information is given in the Department of Commerce report on cane sugar (see p. 57, above), published after the appearance of the first edition of this book. The figures on cost of production given in this document show strikingly how more favorable are the natural conditions in Cuba than elsewhere. The average cost of production (made up, to be sure, from greatly varying costs in the individual plantations and mills) was found to be, in the year considered (1913–14),

in Cuba	$28.92 per ton, or	1.446	cents per pound.
" Hawaii	$44.59 " " "	2.229	" " "
" Hawaii	$44.59 " " "	2.229	" " "
" Porto Rico	$52.29 " " "	2.614	" " "
" Louisiana	$79.50 " " "	3.975	" " "

CHAPTER VII

Beet Sugar

The beet-sugar industry presents questions essentially different from those considered in the preceding chapters. The sugar beet is grown in the temperate zone, and its cultivation is one among many possible forms of agriculture. In view of its peculiar position and significance, it deserves careful and detailed consideration.

Chronologically, the beet-sugar supply is among the later additions to the total for the United States. Barring a slight amount from one or two California enterprises, no beet sugar at all was produced in the country before 1890. The bounty given by the tariff act of that year (1890) is often referred to in the literature on the subject, especially that put forth by protectionists, as having had a stimulating effect on the industry. Though this bounty was no more than an equivalent for the duty then remitted, it may have given some impetus, for the same psychological reasons as in the case of the Louisiana planters.[1] Several states also gave bounties for the production of beet sugar, usually moderate in amount and limited in time; these constituting, so far as they went, a substantial bonus.[2] Probably no less effective than the bounties at the start, and more effective as time went on, was the propaganda of the Department of Agriculture. That Department preached beet sugar in season and out of season; spread broadcast pamphlets dilating on the ad-

1 "It is certain that it [the tariff act of 1890] gave new hope to both operators and growers, and between the time this act went into effect, in October, 1890, and the following June, some $6,000,000 had been invested in beet-sugar factories in this country. . . . This small bounty, even for a brief time, was a wonderful stimulus to the struggling industry." G. W. Shaw, in Bulletin no. 149 (*The California Sugar Industry*) of the University of California, 1903, p. 17. Cf. p. 55 above, on the Louisiana situation.

2 On the bounties which several states have given, see a note by Mr. P. T. Cherington, in the *Quarterly Journal of Economics*, February, 1912, p. 381.

vantages of beet growing for the farmer and giving minute directions on methods of cultivation; maintained a special agent, who kept in touch with the manufacturers and farmers, and annually reported on the progress of the industry. The result was familiarity with the possibilities throughout the country, the removal of all obstacles from inertia and ignorance, and a rapid development in all regions where there was a promise of profits.[1]

At all events, the beet-sugar product increased rapidly after 1890. It quadrupled between 1890 and 1900, and more than quadrupled between 1900 and 1910, — a remarkable rate of growth. Far from remaining insignificant and quite negligible, its contribution to the country's sugar supply became more and more important. It surpassed that of Louisiana cane sugar, equalled that from Hawaii, and itself was surpassed only by the supply from Cuba. In round numbers, over one billion pounds of beet sugar were produced in each of the four years, 1908–12. The years 1912–13 and 1913–14 still showed a marked increase.

Equally significant and striking was the geographical distribution of the industry. The tabular statement on the next page shows what that distribution was.

One fact is obvious on a cursory inspection of these figures. The beet-sugar industry is in the main massed in the far west, — in California, Utah, Colorado, and the adjacent region. The agricultural belt of the central states has a very slender share. Only one state in this part of the country, Michigan, makes a considerable contribution to the supply. Wisconsin, and Ohio (not separately given in the table) each adds a little. No other state in this region has more than one beet-sugar factory. Barring Michigan, the production of beet sugar may be said to be confined to the Rocky mountain and Pacific states.

The explanation of this geographical concentration does not lie in any obstacles from climate or soil in other parts of the country. The beet flourishes over a very wide area. An in-

[1] A series of *Special Reports on the Progress of the Beet-Sugar Industry* was issued by the Department, and from these I shall quote freely in the following pages. The "Special Agent," though by no means a scientific person, acquired and diffused much information.

structive pamphlet issued by the Department of Agriculture shows the zone in which the sugar beet may be expected to "attain its highest perfection."[1] This zone or belt, two hundred miles wide, starts at the Hudson, and sweeps across the country to the Dakotas; turns southward through Colorado,

BEET-SUGAR PRODUCT IN THE UNITED STATES
(IN MILLION POUNDS)

	Total	California	Utah	Colorado	Michigan	Wisconsin	Other States
1899–00	163	85	19	2	33	..	24
1900–01	172	57	17	13	55	..	30
1901–02	365	140	28	45	105	6	41
1902–03	438	159	38	78	109	8	46
1903–04	466	136	46	89	128	11	56
1904–05	470	93	57	111	104	22	83
1905–06	635	144	48	209	122	27	85
1906–07	970	178	82	343	177	36	154
1907–08	852	180	93	245	171	37	126
1908–09	1,025	255	98	299	212	34	127
1909–10	1,120	280	77	206	278	36	243
1910–11	1,019	291	76	206	260	38	148
1911–12	1,199	323	115	250	251	57	203
1912–13	1,385	318	119	432	190	46	139
1913–14	1,467	342	114	448	244	25	140

New Mexico, and Arizona; and then, turning again, proceeds west and northwest through California, Utah, Idaho, and the Columbia valley. It includes a great part of the north central region. Yet in the last mentioned, the most important and productive agricultural region of the country, there is virtually

[1] H. W. Wiley, *The Sugar Beet*, p. 5. This pamphlet has been published in several editions by the Department of Agriculture; my references are to the edition of 1908 (*Farmers' Bulletin 52*).

In the Department's *Report on the Sugar-Beet Industry for 1910 and 1911*, at p. 29, a statistical statement is given of the millions of acres in the country (including such states as Illinois, Indiana, Iowa, Kansas, Ohio) adapted to sugar-beet raising; and the complaint is made that " if one farmer in four of these states were to plant a three-acre patch and give it the care that could readily be bestowed on so small a plot, it would be unnecessary for us to buy foreign sugar," — a mercantilist utterance of the sort often found in the Department's publications.

no beet growing or sugar making, except, as just mentioned, in Michigan. The climatic and agricultural possibilities are not turned to account until the far west is reached.

The reason for the absence of beet growing and hence of sugar-beet production in the north central region is to be found in the principle of comparative advantage: agriculture is applied with *greater* effectiveness in other directions. It is not that the climate or soil or even the men make it more difficult to grow beets here than in Europe. It is simply that other ways of using the land are found more advantageous.

An excellent investigator in the agricultural aspects of the beet-sugar industry has said:[1] "The growing of beets is not agriculture, but horticulture." All the manuals and pamphlets insist on the need of elaborate preparation, minute care, much labor directly in the fields. The planting of the seed does indeed take place by drills, the plants coming up in continuous rows. But after this first operation, painstaking manual labor is called for. When the young shoots come up, they need first to be blocked, then thinned. "Blocking" means that most of the beets in the rows are cut out by a hoe, only small bunches being left, about ten inches apart. These bunches are then "thinned"; every plant is pulled out by hand except one, the largest and healthiest. "Great care should be exercised in this work, and by careful selection all the inferior plants should be removed. . . . When thinning, it is a good plan to give the ground a thorough hand hoeing."[2] Throughout the growing period the beets must be cultivated, partly with a horse cultivator, partly with the hand hoe. "The cultivator and the hoe should be used alternately until the beets are too large for horse cultivation without injuring them. Hand laborers should continue to go over the beet field, pulling the weeds and grass that may have persisted."[3]

[1] Professor G. W. Shaw, of the University of California; among his various writings see the pamphlet on *Sugar Beets in the San Joaquin Valley*, p. 6; *Bulletin*, no. 176, Agricultural Experiment Station, University of California.

[2] *The Sugar Beet*, p. 20.

[3] *Report on Progress . . . 1909*, p. 19. The same story appears in all the accounts of beet-sugar growing. See for example the statements of Mr. Hatha-

Essentially the same situation appears when harvesting is reached. The beets may be first loosened by a plow and by a lifter; but each individual beet must be pulled out by hand. Then they are knocked together gently to remove the adhering dirt. Finally, they are " topped "; that is, the neck and leaves are cut off with a large knife. " The removal of the tops of the beets is a tedious process, which in Europe is performed by women and children. . . . Constant supervision is necessary in this work." [1]

No machinery has been devised that serves to dispense with the large amount of hand labor called for. " Several attempts have been made to construct a mechanical device by which the beets can be topped, thus saving a large expense, and perhaps a successful device of this kind may some day be invented. So far as is known at the present time [1908], however, this process has not been successfully accomplished by machinery, and the topping must still be done by hand." [2] " Inventive ingenuity in Europe and especially in America," said the Special Agent of the Department of Agriculture in 1906, " has been directed to planning a harvester which will do away, as far as possible, with this expensive hand work. . . . It cannot be said that any of these newly-devised implements works successfully in all soils." [3] In 1912 the Department's report again had to confess that " a really successful beet topping and harvesting machine " was yet to be devised, and that " at present all the operations of pulling, topping and loading are done by hand." [4]

It follows that the successful growing of the sugar beet calls for a large amount of monotonous unskilled labor. No small part of it is labor that can be done by women and children and tempts to their utilization. Not only does the typical American farm and farm community lack the number of laborers required; the labor itself is of a kind distasteful to the farmers. " Thinning

way, of the Michigan Beet-Sugar Company, before the Committee on Ways and Means in 1909; *Tariff Hearings of 1909*, p. 3311.

[1] *The Sugar Beet*, pp. 21, 22.

[2] *Ibid.*, p. 22 (1908).

[3] *Report on Progress* . . . 1906, p. 38.

[4] *Report for 1910 and 1911*, p. 64.

and weeding by hand while on one's knees is not a work or posture agreeable to the average American farmer. Bending over the rows and crawling along them on one's hands and knees all day long are things that the contracting farmer is sure to object to as drudgery. . . . Our farmers ride on their stirring plows, cultivators, and many implements." [1] As was remarked by a witness at a tariff hearing: "the thinning and the topping of the beets it is pretty hard to get our American fellows to do, and they prefer to hire the labor and pay for it." [2]

Anticipating for a moment what will be said in the following paragraphs of the beet-sugar industry of the Mountain and Pacific regions, it may be pointed out how this need of extra labor has been met. The labor situation is instructive not only as regards the beet-sugar industry itself, but also as regards the general trend in the United States during the last generation.

Almost everywhere in the beet-sugar districts we find laborers who are employed or contracted for in gangs; an inferior class which is utilized, perhaps exploited, by a superior. The agricultural laborers in the beet fields are usually a very different set from the farmers. On the Pacific coast they are Chinese or Japanese. Except in Southern California, where the Mexicans are near at hand, most of the work is done by Japanese, under contract; there being usually a head contractor, a sort of sweater, who undertakes to furnish the men. In very recent years Hindus (brought down from British Columbia) also have appeared in the beet fields of California. In Colorado "immigrants from Old Mexico compete with New Mexicans (*i. e.*, born in New Mexico), Russians, and Japanese." [3] Indians from the reservations have been employed in Colorado. At one time, convict labor was used in Nebraska. In some parts of Colorado, in Montana, and

[1] *Report on Progress . . . 1906*, p. 24. A correspondent writes me from California (1912): "Otherwise than in the performance of such labor as can be done with teams, very few Americans undertake hand labor in the beet fields."

[2] *Tariff Hearings of 1909*, p. 3418. "Americans will not do that work; not one in fifty," said a Colorado beet grower, testifying (in 1911) before the House Committee to investigate the American Sugar Refining Co.; *Hearings*, p. 3192. Compare a similar passage in *Report of Kansas State Board of Agriculture for September, 1906* (a special report on sugar beets), p. 20.

[3] V. Clark, in *Bulletin Department of Labor*, September, 1908, p. 483.

at the beet fields of the single factory in Kansas, refugees from German colonies established long ago in Russia are employed. In Michigan, the main labor supply comes from the Polish and Bohemian population of Cleveland, Buffalo, Pittsburgh. The circulars issued by the Department of Agriculture and by the state boards and bureaus repeatedly call the attention of the beet farmers to the possibility of employing cheap immigrants. The troublesome labor problems, it is said, need not cause worry: here is a large supply of just the persons wanted. "Living in cities there is a class of foreigners, — Germans, French, Russians, Hollanders, Austrians, Bohemians, — who have had more or less experience in beet growing in their native countries. . . . Every spring sees large colonies of this class of workmen moving out from our cities into the beet fields."[1]

The sugar manufacturers, who buy the beets and make the sugar in their factories, play a large part in bringing this labor to the fields. Indeed, they play a large part in every phase of the industry, — on its agricultural side as well as on its manufacturing side. They supply seed; give the farmers elaborate directions on methods of cultivation; employ supervisors to visit and inspect the farms, and to spur the farmers to the needed minute care; of necessity they test the beets at the factory, and pay according to sugar content; and they often undertake to provide the labor. Sometimes the factories contract to attend to the field labor themselves, receiving from the farmers a specified price, — so much for bunching and thinning, so much for each hoeing, so much for topping. The farmers then have nothing to do but supply "reasonable" living accommodations.[2] More

[1] *Report on Progress . . . 1904,* p. 37. Compare the *Report of the Kansas State Board of Agriculture,* cited above, p. 19. A correspondent writes me from Bay City, Michigan: "We secure the laborers in such centers as Cleveland, Detroit, Chicago, and Pittsburgh, and these laborers when brought to Michigan make a contract with the farmer to take care of his beets at a certain sum per acre, averaging about $20 per acre. . . . It is safe to say that about two-thirds of the beets are taken care of by outside labor. In our own case [a large sugar company] we probably brought in about 1800 laborers." On some smaller beet tracts in Michigan, the farmers and their families do the work themselves, employing no "outside" labor.

[2] The form of contract used by the Great Western Sugar Co. of Colorado is

often farmers not thus provided for secure their laborers through contractors, at a fixed price of so much (varying from $15 to $20) per acre for all the work; these middlemen being hunted up or selected for the farmers by the factory managers. Such "sweaters" make a profit from their sub-contract with the field hands; the system being open to the possibilities of overreaching which are too familiar under such arrangements.

All this is part of the transformation which has been wrought in so many parts of our social and economic structure during the last quarter of a century by the great inflow of immigrants. Agriculture as well as manufacturing industry is feeling the influence of the new conditions. Laborers from the congested foreign districts of the cities — Italians, Bohemians, "Huns," "Polacks," Russians — make their way to the market gardens surrounding the cities, to vegetable districts such as that of the Chesapeake peninsula, to the cranberry fields of New Jersey; these do the hard work for the shrewd Yankee farmers. Some of them may be on the way to the acquisition of land through their savings. But certainly for the time being the conditions are socially and industrially unwelcome. They are not dissimilar to those of the *Sachsengängerei*, of ill repute in eastern Germany. They are very different from the conditions which we think of as typical of agriculture in the United States. As in these analogous cases, so in the beet fields, there is an agricultural proletariat.

As yet, however, the main agricultural region of the United States, — the great central region in which are the wheat and corn belts, — has been little affected. Here we still find extensive cultivation, agricultural machinery, the one-family farm. It is true that during the harvest season there is a heavy demand for agricultural laborers, and that this is satisfied by laborers who may be said also to constitute an agricultural proletariat. It is true, further, that the stage of pioneer farming has been passed or is rapidly being passed, that rotation is becoming more sys-

printed in the *Hearings of the Committee to investigate the American Sugar Refining Co.* (1911), p. 3186.

tematic and skilful, the land more valuable, cultivation more intensive. Nevertheless this remains the region of the one-family farm. The farmers " ride on their stirring plows and cultivators " and in this way are able to do most of the work on their lands for themselves.

Throughout the corn belt, more particularly, there is no sugar-beet industry of any moment. It pays better to raise corn; there is a clear comparative advantage in corn growing. This grain is peculiarly adapted to extensive agriculture. It also lends itself readily to the use of machinery; corn can be " cultivated " between the rows by horse power. It is a substitute for root crops, and can be rotated steadily with small-grain crops.[1] It is a direct competitor with the sugar beet for cattle fattening. The advocates of beet raising always lay stress on the value of the beet pulp, the residue at the factory after the juice has been extracted, for cattle feeding. But corn is at least equally valuable for the purpose, and the typical American farmer raises it by agricultural methods which he finds both profitable and congenial. One man can grow forty acres of corn. He can plant only twenty acres of beets; and these he cannot possibly thin and top.[2] In Iowa " the farmers are progressive, successful, and satisfied. In fact, this has been the main obstacle to installing the sugar industry there. The farmers have not shown a disposition to grow the beets. When the farmers are advised that beet culture is accompanied with considerable hard work, factory propositions usually succumb to the inevitable. The farming class of the state is accustomed to the use of labor-saving implements in the fields." [3]

It is not an accident that the states of the Great Lakes region in which the sugar-beet industry has shown some development,—

[1] See the excellent analysis by Professor H. C. Taylor, in *Annals of the American Academy of Political and Social Sciences*, xxii, p. 179 (1903). Cf. the same writer's *Agricultural Economics*, pp. 65 *seq.*, and Carver's *Rural Economics*, p. 100. Professor Taylor, in a recent paper (*The Place of Economics in Agricultural Education and Research*, p. 96; published by University of Wisconsin, 1911) states more explicitly his conclusion that " it is hardly probable that the sugar beet will ever be able to compete with corn on even terms in the corn belt of the United States."

[2] *Tariff Hearings of 1909*, p. 3417.

[3] *Report on Progress . . . 1904*, p. 56.

Michigan, and in much less degree, Ohio and Wisconsin, — are outside the corn belt. Except along the southern edge of these states, the grain does not ordinarily mature. Yet even here corn remains a formidable competitor of the sugar beet, in its use through ensilage.[1] It is cut green, stored in the silos, and so is available for cattle feeding. It continues to be available in rotation with other grain and with grass. During the last two decades Wisconsin has become a great dairy state. "The pasture, hay, and corn lands of the state form the basis of the livestock industry."[2] Here there is a profitable system of agriculture in which there is no need of the minute attention, the elaborate cultivation, the wearisome labor, which are required for the sugar beet. As compared with the far west, Michigan and Wisconsin, as will presently appear, lack some climatic advantages. A tariff subsidy may make it worth while for their farmers to grow the beets; but without the subsidy this use of the land cannot compete with others more advantageous.

When the tariff legislation of 1913 was under consideration the beet-sugar makers of Michigan pleaded strenuously for the maintenance of protection on the ground of consideration for vested interests. It must be admitted that the plea was in one regard of exceptional force. Not only had the general policy of protection been long maintained by Congress, and investment in accord with it encouraged; but, as one of the witnesses before the Ways and Means Committee said in 1909, "the investment which our company made in the sugar business was made on the invitation and urgent advice of the United States Government through its Department of Agriculture."[3] It was a serious responsibility which the Department thus took on itself. Its zeal too often was indiscriminate. Its propaganda rested, in part at least, on

[1] My colleague, Professor T. N. Carver, states to me: "Corn silage will furnish fifty per cent more feed, acre per acre, than any root crop. Moreover it costs half as much, or less than half, to grow an acre of silage and feed it as it does to grow an acre of any root crop and feed it. The only chance for beet-root cake is to sell it as a by-product, the balance being covered by the profits on sugar."

[2] *Progress of the Dairy Industry in Wisconsin*, by H. C. Taylor and C. E. Lee, p. 7; *Bulletin* no. 210 of the Agricultural Experiment Station, University of Wisconsin (1911).

[3] Mr. C. N. Smith, in the *Tariff Hearings of 1909*, p. 3317.

a crudely mercantilist principle; on the assumption that it is desirable to produce within our own borders anything and everything that can possibly be produced there, and that a tariff policy based on this assumption will be maintained indefinitely.

Turn now to the far west, where most of the beet sugar is made. Two conditions are favorable to beet growing in this western region: the climate, and the special advantages of irrigation.

The variety of the beet suitable for sugar making flourishes in a cool climate; but it needs plenty of sun. "Abundance of sunshine is essential to the highest development of sugar in the beet. Other things being equal, it may be said that the richness of the beet will be proportional to the amount — not intensity — of the sunshine."[1] Evidently the cool region of cloudless sky in the arid west meets this condition perfectly.

Again: "in respect to moisture, the sugar beet is peculiar in some respects. . . . There are three periods in the life history of the sugar beet which demand entirely different treatment so far as moisture is concerned: (1) the germinating or plantlet period; (2) the growing period; (3) the sugar-storing period." During the first "the beet needs sufficient moisture and warmth to germinate and start it, but never an excess." During the second, "the beet needs little if any moisture." During the third, or sugar-storing period, "the plant should be given no water. The conditions desirable at this period are plenty of light and dry cool weather. If the beet is given moisture to any considerable extent, it will be at the expense of both sugar and purity."[2]

The irrigated regions of Colorado, Utah, Idaho, Montana supply just the right combination of climate and moisture: cool temperature, abundant sunshine, moisture as needed, absence of moisture when harmful. Hence Colorado and Utah are described as the ideal beet-sugar states. "Considering everything, Utah is the ideal beet-sugar State. . . . Its natural conditions

[1] Professor G. W. Shaw of the University of California, in the pamphlet already referred to, p. 6.

[2] I quote again from Professor Shaw's instructive pamphlet, at pp. 16, 17.

are quite similar to those of Colorado." [1] In Colorado 12 to 25 tons of beets to the acre are readily secured; even in the early days 15 to 17½ tons were got on the average; whereas in European countries not only is the tonnage per acre less, but the sugar content smaller.[2] California, where the industry first was undertaken on any considerable scale, and where it has grown steadily, has some special advantages. A good part of its beet district has just the required combination of climate and precipitation.[3]

Contrast such exceptionally favorable climatic conditions with those of the Great Lakes region. The successive reports of the Department of Agriculture dwell on the uncertainty of the beet-sugar crop in this zone because of the irregularity of rain and sunshine. The Michigan farmer, unlike the grower in the irrigated region, cannot count with certainty on abundant sunshine and cannot apply moisture exactly when needed: difficulties which threaten not only the quantity of the crop but also its saccharine content.[4]

[1] *Report on Progress . . . 1909*, p. 37.

[2] *Report on Progress . . . 1904*, p. 46.

[3] "The exceptional soil and climatological conditions in California seem peculiarly adapted to the production of beets with a high sugar content. While their reported yield per acre is not so great as that of some other states, the sugar content is decidedly in excess of any other, so that with an acreage considerably less than that of Michigan the total yield of sugar is much more. The calculated yield per acre for the past season was very nearly 3,310 pounds. Many of the California soils are very retentive of moisture, so that with an annual rainfall far below that of the central and eastern part of the country beets can be grown successfully without irrigation. The little rain which they have is usually so nicely distributed through the early and middle seasons of growth as to leave almost ideal conditions for the period of ripening, with its accompanying storage of sugar in the cells. This ripening process is also materially assisted by the alternation of cool nights and warm days, a condition which seems best suited to the formation and storage of sugar in this plant." *Report on Beet-Sugar Industry in 1910 and 1911*, p. 19.

I take some satisfaction in recalling that, when discussing the beet-sugar situation as early as 1889, I referred to the unusual possibilities of California. "It is not impossible," I wrote then, "that the extraordinary combination of soil and climate in California may bring about a development which could not be attained in other parts of the country." *Quarterly Journal of Economics*, iii, p. 266, note.

[4] References to the vicissitudes of the weather, similar to that quoted in the text, abound in the Department of Agriculture's *Reports on Progress, e. g.*, Report

The same climatic difficulties are encountered in the European countries where sugar beets are grown. There also the beet harvest and the sugar output are greatly affected by the weather during the growing and harvesting season. The north central states of our own country are not in this respect at a disadvantage. But they possess no climatic superiority for beet growing; whereas they do possess agricultural and industrial superiority for other crops. Beet growing, in other words, suffers from a *comparative* disadvantage. The far western region, on the other hand, does have unusual natural advantages for the sugar beet. Whether these natural advantages are so great as to enable the industry to hold its own, in free competition with cane sugar and with beet sugar made in the European regions of permanently cheap labor supply, is another question. But they explain why, under the stimulus of protection, the industry grew fast in that region, and in widely distributed parts of it; while yet under the same stimulus it made little progress in the typical agricultural states.

It is constantly said, with reference both to the mountain states and to those of the central region, that the culture of the sugar beet brings special agricultural benefits. The high cultivation, it is said, improves the quality of the land; general fertility is enhanced; a better rotation is established; the by-products, especially the beet cake, are valuable for cattle feeding, and this in turn provides manure and maintains fertility; the factory makes a market for local coal and lime; it "stimulates banking and almost all kinds of mercantile business." These advantages have been dwelt on almost *ad nauseam* in the

for 1903, p. 139; for 1904, p. 113; for 1909, p. 46. Concerning the effect on the quality of the beets, see Report for 1903, p. 140; for 1904, p. 57.

A typical statement is that of a recent report: "Normally, the length of the growing season is sufficient and the rainfall is ample and suitably distributed throughout spring and summer, with dry, increasingly cool, fall weather to afford conditions needed for maturing sugar. It is to be noted, however, that in the case of the last crop (1911) this normal condition of affairs was seriously altered. A fine growing season was followed by an unusually rainy ripening and harvesting period, so that what had given promise of being the greatest crop ever produced turned out very poor in quality, although of fair tonnage." *Report on Beet-Sugar Industry in 1910 and 1911*, p. 22.

publications of the Department of Agriculture.[1] So far as the tariff question is concerned, they prove altogether too much. If beet culture is so very advantageous for the farmer, why does he need a bonus or protective tariff to be induced to engage in it? The American farmer is not an ignorant or stolid person; he has access to a multitude of educational and propagandist agencies, and is even beset by them; he is a shrewd observer, a ready innovator. With the transition from pioneer farming, the agricultural methods of the central region have been revolutionized during the past generation. If beet culture were really so advantageous a part of the general change, we might expect its speedy and wide-spread adoption. The advocates of beet growing have simply accepted the common and fallacious notion that the highest cultivation is necessarily the most advantageous cultivation. The agricultural expert is apt to be intent on the gross product, on the largest yield per acre. But the best agriculture is that which secures the largest yield not per unit of area but per unit of labor. Minute cultivation means a large product per acre but by no means necessarily a large product per man.

The only solid ground for maintaining that protection for beet sugar has been of advantage to agriculture is that of the young industries argument. Ignorance, settled habits and prejudices, unaccustomed methods, the inevitable failures in first trials, all these obstacles may have stood in the way of the beet-sugar industry in its first stages. It is true that the argument for protection to young industries was not supposed to apply to agriculture by List and his followers, since unalterable conditions of soil and climate were thought to determine once for all the geographical distribution of the extractive industries. It would, perhaps, be hazardous to lay down an unqualified proposition of this sort. The course of industry may conceivably be guided and diverted to advantage in agriculture as well as in manufactures. The difference between the two cases would seem to be simply one of probability, of degree. None the less, an important difference in degree remains. It is more *likely* that industry will pursue

[1] See for instance *Report on Progress . . . 1901*, pp. 132 *seq.*

its "natural" course in agriculture than in manufactures; since agriculture is affected much more by the physical factors of soil and climate and much less by acquired skill.

There are still other grounds for questioning the applicability to agriculture of the young industries argument. There is not in agriculture that close contact between different producers or that stress of competition between them which is most likely to lead to improvements; and a stimulus to improvement is the essence of the argument. In the contemporary German controversy, considerations of this sort have been advanced in support of the duties on grain; but there is quite as much weight in the counter argument that agricultural improvement is most effectively spurred by adversity. It comes not from high prices and easy gains, but low prices and the need of facing a difficult situation.[1] The low prices of sugar which prevailed for a considerable period (especially in the decade 1890–1900) proved a blessing in disguise to the Louisiana sugar planters; their methods of cultivation and sugar extraction were improved in the effort to meet conditions of depression. The same seems to have been the case with the Hawaiian planters during the period (1890–94) of free sugar.[2] It has already been pointed out how difficult it is to say whether protection tends on the whole to promote technical improvement or to retard it.[3] A general proposition one way or the other would be as hard to prove conclusively with reference to agriculture as with reference to manufactures. But it seems clear that acquired skill and established advantages count for more in manufactures than in agriculture; and that tariff protection is therefore an even less promising device for promoting better use of the soil. Education, experiment stations, diffusion of the right sort of information, are much more promising. But education and the spread of information, to be really effective, must be adapted to the economic conditions. In this regard our Department of Agriculture for many years showed no discrimination. Under the Republican régime

[1] See Ballod, in *Verhandlungen d. Vereins f. Sozialpolitik, 1909*, p. 143, and Esslen, *Das Gesetz des abnehmenden Bodenertrags*, pp. 226, 237.

[2] Cf. above, p. 62.

[3] See chapter ii, p. 28, above.

of 1897–1913 its publications were pervaded by a crude mercantilism. Its propaganda for beet sugar rested not on the young industry and eventual independence principle, but on the crude protectionist doctrine that any and every increase of domestic supply was necessarily to the country's advantage.

Questions in some respects different arise concerning the beet-sugar factory, which buys the beets from the farmers and makes the sugar. Here there is what the business world calls "a straight manufacturing proposition." Whether the manufacturing of sugar can be done to advantage in the United States depends on the same conditions as in other manufactures. It is much affected by the opportunities for using machinery and for the exercise of American inventive and engineering capacity in improving machinery. Such evidence as I can get indicates that so far as this branch of the industry is concerned, the conditions are not unfavorable to its sustained prosecution with little need, if any, of tariff support. When the first factories were built in California the machinery was imported from Germany. "The Yankee inventive genius of machinery men at once took hold of the matter, making so valuable improvements that both the above mentioned factories [at Watsonville and at Chino] were shortly refitted with machines of American make, and every factory in this country in the last few years has purchased American machines."[1] So in the Department of Agriculture's pamphlet on the industry, it is stated that "in the early days of the beet-sugar industry in this country, Europe was called on to furnish all machinery. Now very little is imported, and in fact some of the foreign factories are using American-made machinery."[2] The breaking loose from European tutelage and the introduction of technical improvements are significant indications of the successful adaptation of a new industry to American conditions and of the ability to meet foreign competition unaided. It

[1] Shaw, *The California Sugar Industry* (1903), p. 17.

[2] *The Sugar Beet* (1908), p. 38. Similar statements have been made to me in conversation by persons engaged in beet-sugar making. Others, however, no less well informed, have expressed to me a doubt whether any appreciable improvements have been made by the American makers, especially when compared with what the Germans have done.

should be borne in mind, moreover, that the factory managers take an active part in directing and supervising the agricultural operations. In this regard there seems to be abundant and successful enterprise. The managers of the beet-sugar factories have been chiefly instrumental in bringing the indispensable labor supply to the farms. Through traction engines and the like they have grappled with the difficulties of transporting the beets from the field to the factory. They have selected the seeds, and have assiduously spread information among the farmers on the best ways of getting a large tonnage of beets and a large content of sugar. In the far west especially, all this activity has been carried on with industrial and pecuniary success. Neither in the factory itself nor in the problems of organization arising from the interdependence of farm and factory has there been a lack of skill or energy.[1]

It is probably another sign of successful adaptation to new conditions that the American beet-sugar factory carries its operations a stage further than do the factories of Europe. The latter usually produce raw sugar only, which is sent to refineries for the last stage of preparation; precisely as our cane sugar is imported in the "raw" form, and goes through the refineries before being marketed for consumption. The American beet-sugar factories, on the other hand, make refined (granulated) sugar, which is sold at once to the grocers. In Europe the greater geographical concentration of beet growing and sugar making, and the consequent ease of transportation to refineries near by, probably account for the practice there prevailing. The different American practice doubtless took its start because refining was controlled, during the earlier years of beet sugar, by the Sugar Trust and its affiliated concerns; but it persisted because it fitted the geographical and industrial conditions of the industry. Another reason is that in continental Europe beet

[1] There was and is bickering, inevitably, between the farmers who grow the beets and the sugar manufacturers; the farmers maintaining that the manufacturers beat down the growers and pocketed the bulk of the profits for themselves. Very likely this was the case; but the growers got quite enough to make beet culture worth while, as is proved by its rapid extension. See *Hearings on the American Sugar Refining Co.* (Hardwick Committee) 1911, pp. 3313 and *passim.*

farming and sugar making constitute commonly one integrated enterprise, and are associated either with estate farming on a large scale or with direct coöperation between large-scale agriculturists and the factory owners. A different sort of coöperation between farm and factory was necessary under our conditions of land ownership, and this has been worked out successfully by the American manufacturers. Neither in the technical aspects of the manufacturing industry, nor in its appropriate organization, is there indication of disadvantage in the United States.

This brings us to the close of our examination of the sources of sugar supply, and their relation to the tariff. Let us now, by way of summary, proceed to a quantitative estimate of the consequences of the duty on raw sugar; postponing for the moment the consideration of the effect (comparatively slight, as will shortly be shown) of the additional duty on refined sugar.

The burden of the sugar duty can be measured with greater exactness than is often possible. We know that the price of sugar was raised by the duty throughout the area of consumption. In this case, we have no reason to question the significance of continued imports. The only serious qualification which needs to be made is that which arises for the later years from the uneven and irregular effect of the partial remission on Cuban sugar.[1] Except for this, we could say with confidence that from 1897 to 1913 the price of sugar was raised, the country over, by the full amount of the duty, — one and two-thirds cents a pound. Allowing for the modifying influence of the Cuban remission, we may make our calculations on the assumption that the effect of the duty during the years immediately preceding 1913 was to raise the price of all sugar by one and one-half cents. The figure may not be accurate to the last dot; but the economist is fortunate when he can measure his results with so close an approach to exactness as this.

Of the tax paid by consumers in the form of enhanced price, a little less than one-half went to the government treasury; the rest, — more than half, — was handed over to the various

[1] Considered in the preceding chapter, pp. 76 *seq.*

favored sugar producers. Let us imagine the United States government to present an account, rendering to its wards, the sugar consumers, a statement of what had become of the sums collected from them. The government would properly enter on the debit side the total which it had taken from the consumers, on the credit side an enumeration of the various ways in which it had distributed the total. The fiscal year 1909–10 may be taken as representative. For that year the account would stand thus:[1]

United States Government in Account with Sugar Consumers,
for the fiscal year 1909–10

Dr.	Cr.	Paid over (mill. dollars) to	
		U. S. Treasury	Sugar Producers
Taxes collected on 7,400 mill. lbs. of sugar @ $1\frac{1}{2}$ c.	On 300 mill. lbs. of full-duty sugar	$5.3	...
	" 3,500 " " " Cuban "	45.6	$5.2
	" 1,100 " " " Hawaiian "	...	16.6
	" 570 " " " Porto Rico "	...	8.5
	" 175 " " " Philippine "	...	2.6
	" 750 " " " Domestic Cane Sugar	...	11.2
	" 1,025 " " " Domestic Beet Sugar	...	15.4
		$50.9	$59.5
$111.0		$110.4	

It appears that in 1909–10 the government collected 111 millions of dollars from the sugar consumers. It put about 50 millions into its own treasury, using that sum for meeting public expenses; and handed over about 60 millions to the various sugar producers. The proportion going to the sugar producers tended to grow greater during the whole of our period, — from the close of the civil war until 1913. During the early years

[1] Figures of this sort are not so easy to compile as one might suppose. They must be put together from scattered statements in the Treasury Department *Report on Commerce and Navigation* and in the *Statistical Abstract*.

Domestic production is reckoned by seasons, not by fiscal years, and some adjustment is necessary for comparison with the imported (non-domestic) supply.

In any year it will be found that there are slight discrepancies between the figures given in the various sources. For the present purpose, the discrepancies signify nothing. The figures, which I have intentionally given in round numbers, state the outcome without any substantial deviation from statistical accuracy.

of the period, the sugar duty had been mainly a revenue tax. By its close, the characteristic features of a protective duty had emerged: the treasury received less in revenue than the favored producers secured in largess or bounty.

With the passage of the tariff act of 1913, the situation changed. The steady increase of the domestic supply, and of that from Cuba also, served to shut out completely the full-duty importations; only sporadic supplies came from other than the favored regions. The duty on Cuban sugar, — one cent a pound, — thus became the effective rate. The following account, made up for the year 1916 on the same plan as the preceding one for 1909–10,

THE UNITED STATES GOVERNMENT IN ACCOUNT WITH SUGAR CONSUMERS
for the calendar year 1916

DR.	(Mill. dollars)	CR.	Paid over (mill. dollars) to U. S. Treasury	Paid over (mill. dollars) to Sugar Producers
Taxes collected on 8,161 mill. lbs. sugar @ 1 c.	$81.6	On 35 mill. lbs. of full-duty sugar.....	$ .4	...
Taxes collected on 35 mill. pounds full duty sugar @ $1\frac{1}{4}$ c.	.4	" 3,731 " " " Cuban " ...	37.3	...
		" 505 mill. lbs. of Louisiana sugar...	...	$ 5.0
		" 1,566 " " " U. S. beet " ...	...	15.7
		" 1,196 " " " Hawaiian " ...	...	12.0
		" 880 " " " Porto Rico " ...	...	8.8
		" 250 " " " Philippine " ...	...	2.5
			$38.0	$44.0
	$82.0		$82.0	

shows the trend. The total sugar tax became less, in consequence of the lower rate of duty; but of the total paid by consumers a smaller proportion went to the Treasury as revenue, a larger proportion to the sugar producers as bonus or protection.[1]

[1] Apparent discrepancies in the figures are due to the omission of some petty items, *e.g.* Treasury receipts from molasses imports.

On the beet sugar industry valuable information was supplied after the appearance of the first edition of this book in a *Report on the Beet Sugar Industry*, issued in 1917 by the Federal Trade Commission, at the same time with the report from the Department of Commerce on cane sugar (see p. 57, note), and covering the same year, — 1914. The data given in this document indicated that most makers of beet sugar in the arid and semiarid regions could hold their own even if the duty were removed; while those in the less favorable regions, notably in Michigan, would eventually succumb under free trade.

CHAPTER VIII

REFINED SUGAR AND THE SUGAR TRUST

The sugar refining industry has always been protected by duties higher than those on raw sugar. In early times,— before the civil war, — one factor that contributed to high duties on refined sugar was the circumstance that it was considered a luxury. Most persons used "brown" sugar; only the rich used refined. Partly for this reason, partly because of the disposition to protect sugar refining like other industries, the difference between the rates on raw and refined, — the so-called "differential" of recent years, — was so considerable that all refining was carried on within the country.[1] The imports were mainly in the form of raw sugar. In this regard the situation remained unchanged from 1789 to the present time.

The mode of assessing the sugar duties and of fixing the differential has given rise to legislative and administrative difficulties. Until 1883 the duties were graded according to the "Dutch standard," — the method of grading universally used in earlier times. Cane sugar as it comes from the sugar houses or sugar mills of the plantations is not pure, and is more or less discolored; it may contain anywhere from 3 per cent to 25 per cent of impurities. Under the "Dutch standard" its sugar content is supposed to be indicated by color. Dark or dirty sugar has low numbers; as the sugar becomes lighter, it is designated by the high numbers. The number 16 indicates approximately the line of division between raw sugar and refined. Sugar up to no. 13 is

[1] Thus, to give some typical figures, the duties on sugar were:

	On raw	On refined	Differential
1789	1 cent	3 cents	2 cents
1802	2½ cents	7 "	4½ "
1816	3 "	10 @ 12 "	7 to 9 "
1842	2½ "	6 "	3½ "
1861 (March)	¾ "	2 "	1¼ "

On some of the early problems of legislation and administration, see C. S. Griffin, "The Taxation of Sugar, 1789–1861," in *Quarterly Journal of Economics*, xi, p. 296.

dark and presumably impure; sugar of no. 16 is very light gray in color; number 20 is white. Under the tariff acts before 1883 the "Dutch standard" alone was used in grading the duties; sugars of low number had lower duties, those of high number higher duties. Serious embarrassment ensued, however, because of artificial coloration of sugars having high saccharine content; and in 1883 the polariscope test was adopted for grading the sugar duties.[1] This optical test, — one of the striking applications of science to industry, — determines the saccharine content of sugars without regard to color and with perfect accuracy. It had been in familiar trade use for some time before 1883, and its belated adoption by the government is but one of the many examples of the tendency of public management of business to lag behind private. Some relic of the "Dutch standard" system, however, remained in the tariff acts of 1883 and subsequent years, in that the dividing line between raw and refined sugar was still fixed on the old basis, that is, according to color. All dark sugar was dealt with as raw sugar, and was subjected to duties varying according to saccharine content as indicated by the polariscope test.[2] All white sugar was treated as refined sugar, and subjected

[1] In the years preceding 1883, sugars having high saccharine content were artificially colored dark in order to bring them in at a lower rate of duty. Long contests in the courts ensued, the government trying to collect higher duties, while the importers contended that under the language of the statute color alone, irrespective of saccharine content, settled the rate of duty. The importers finally won their case; hence the final application of the polariscope tests in the act of 1883. On this episode see D. A. Wells, *Report on the Assessment and Collection of Duties on Imported Sugars* (New York, 1878); "How Congress and the Public deal with a Great Revenue Problem," *Princeton Review*, November, 1880.

[2] Thus in the tariff acts of 1897 and 1909, all sugar below 16 Dutch standard was assessed for duty as raw sugar, on a scale graduated by the polariscope test. Sugar testing 75° (75 per cent of saccharine content) paid 95/100 of a cent. For each additional degree, the duty became 35/1000 of a cent higher. Hence sugar testing 96° (which is the grade most largely imported) paid 1.685 cents per pound. *If* there were such a thing as raw sugar testing 100°, the duty on it would be 1.825 cents per pound. The duty on refined sugar, *i. e.*, "all sugar above number 16, Dutch standard, or which has gone through a process of refining" was 1.95 cents in 1897, and 1.90 cents in 1909; leaving a differential (as stated in the text) of 0.125 cents in 1897, and of 0.075 in 1909.

The word "differential" is sometimes used in discussions of the sugar situation to designate not the additional duty on refined sugar, but the difference in price

to an additional duty, — the so-called "differential." Under the act of 1883 this differential, serving as protection to the sugar refiner, was about one cent a pound. In later tariff acts it was much reduced, being

in 1890,	1/2	cent	per	pound	(0.5 cent)
1894,	1/8	"	"	"	(0.125 ")
1897,	1/8	"	"	"	(0.125 ")
1909,	3/40	"	"	"	(0.075 ")

The significance both of the earlier high differential and of its later reduction can be understood only in view of the technical and financial development of the industry. The period from 1870 to 1890 saw two great changes, closely connected. Large-scale production developed with surprising rapidity; combination among refiners promptly ensued. The essential process of sugar refining did not indeed undergo great changes. As before, refining was accomplished by passing the raw sugar through ground boneblack. But machinery was applied much more effectively; the scale of operations was enormously enlarged; the capacity of the individual establishment became immensely greater.[1] In no modern industry have the economies of the great establishment been more pronounced. A single refinery can turn out daily 5,000, 10,000 even 15,000 barrels of refined sugar. Were it not for the limitation imposed by the expense of distributing the output over a wide area, it would seem that one vast plant could refine the sugar of the whole United States. As it is, there were in 1914 but two refineries on the Pacific coast, three or four on the Gulf coast, half-a-dozen or thereabouts on the eastern seaboard; and among these were a few older ones of comparatively small size, and some newer and larger ones that may be truthfully said

between raw sugar and refined. To avoid confusion, I shall use "margin" to designate this latter amount, reserving "differential" to indicate the refiner's protection under the several tariff acts.

[1] An official in a refining company has given me the following figures showing the capacity of a refinery under his charge (not one of the largest) at the following dates:

in 1870,	250,000	lbs.	(about	700	barrels) daily
1880,	450,000	"	("	1,300	") "
1890,	700,000	"	("	2,000	") "
1900,	1,250,000	"	("	3,600	") "

to illustrate the wastes of competition. A refinery on the modern scale costs millions of dollars; when ready, and operating to full capacity, it does its work with extraordinary economy; to get it ready, however, in competition with established rivals, is a formidable task.

These would seem to be conditions almost ideally favorable for cut-throat competition and for the eventual emergence of some sort of combination. As they gradually developed, there came in fact the successive stages of the sharpest sort of competition; reduction in the cost of refining, and in the margin of price between raw and refined sugar; struggles and failures for the smaller refiners, sustained profits and dominance for the larger concerns; finally in 1887 the sugar trust, a "trust" in the older and more accurate sense of the word. The refusal of the courts to sustain this first form of combination led shortly (1891) to the formation, under strict corporate organization, of the American Sugar Refining Company. This great combination remained the conspicuous figure in the industry, and though no longer in any strict sense a trust, continued so to be called. With the year 1887 the combination problem emerged full-fledged.[1]

It has already been noted that under the act of 1883 (from 1883 to 1890) the differential on refined sugar was about one cent a pound. This meant a high rate of protection. The improvements in refining had reduced the cost of converting the raw sugar into refined to a figure considerably less than the differential. It seems to have been brought down even then to the figure at which it has been maintained ever since, — not far from $\frac{5}{8}$ cent a pound. The differential duty under the act of 1883, in other

[1] For brevity, I shall hereafter follow popular usage in designating the American Sugar Refining Company, as "the trust."

On the history of the trust, see a monograph by Vogt, "The Sugar Refining Industry" (University of Pennsylvania), 1908; and on the earlier phase, up to 1900, J. W. Jenks, *The Trust Problem*, pp. 130 *seq.* Much information is to be got from the *Report of the Industrial Commission of 1898 on Trusts and Industrial Combinations* (1900); in the evidence before the Senate Committee of 1894; in the *Hearings before the Committee on the Investigation of the American Sugar Refining Co.*, usually spoken of as the Hardwick Committee (1911–12); and in the voluminous testimony given in the suit instituted by the Government (in 1912–15) for the dissolution of the trust.

words, was much more than 100 per cent upon the cost of refining. It was virtually prohibitory of the importation of refined sugar. This high protection was not due to any deliberate intent. As in so many other cases, it was simply a legacy from older days, entailing consequences quite unexpected on the part of the legislators who had put it on the statute book.

The immediate effect of the prohibitory duty unquestionably was to promote the formation of the trust, and to enable it during its first years to reap large profits. The trust was formed in 1887. The price of refined sugar was at once raised, — that is, the margin between the price of refined sugar and raw sugar. No doubt competition during the years preceding had brought the margin below the line of normal profit; but it was promptly raised above that line. The chart on page 105 has been prepared to show the relation between the price of raw and refined sugar. A glance at it will show that for two years after 1887 the margin was high, and the profits of refining were then great. It is no wonder that the head of the combination, when testifying before the Industrial Commission in 1899, made the remark, destined to become notorious, "the mother of all trusts is the customs tariff bill." [1]

The subsequent course of events showed, however, that this dictum needed qualification. One of the unsettled questions with regard to combinations concerns the extent to which they are held in check by real or potential competition. The history of competition in this particular case has been so often rehearsed that the briefest review will here suffice. At a comparatively early date, in 1889, the trust became at loggerheads with the great sugar refiner of the Pacific Coast, Spreckels, of whose peculiar position in that region more will be said presently. The Trust established a rival refinery in California; the Californian, in retaliation, built one at Philadelphia. There was also other competition on the eastern seaboard. As the chart shows, the margin between refined sugar and raw, and hence the profits of refining,

[1] *Report of the Industrial Commission* (of 1900), i, p. 101. On this earlier period, see the excellent account in Jenks, *The Trust Problem* (1900), pp. 133 *seq.*, where is also a chart showing in much detail the fluctuations in the prices of raw and refined sugar.

were sharply reduced during this first period of competition (1890–91). But the warring factions soon united. Spreckels was taken into the combination on favorable terms. The more considerable eastern competitors were also absorbed. For five or six

CHART I[1]

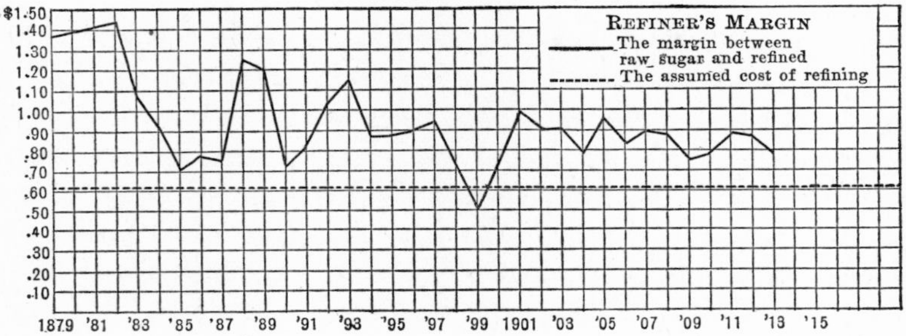

[1] The cost of refining is usually stated to be $\frac{5}{8}$ cent a pound, or $62\frac{1}{2}$ cents per cwt. This is "cost" in the accountant's sense; including all direct and indirect outlays, but not including anything for return on the investment in the way of interest or profit. The amount by which the margin exceeds this "cost" is the source of profit for the refiner. The figure commonly given for cost ($\frac{5}{8}$ cent) is, of course, a rough and approximate one. It is much affected by the refinery's "running full": the more complete and steady is the utilization of the great plant, the lower is the cost per unit. I suspect that $\frac{5}{8}$ cent is a liberal estimate of cost for a large refinery well managed and utilized to full capacity. But it seems to be impossible, under existing trade conditions, to run a refinery continuously to its full capacity.

Looking at the figures given for prices of raw and refined sugar, it will be seen that the margin varied from maxima of 1.42 in 1882 and 1.26 cents in 1888 to a minimum of .5 cent in 1899. The former figures meant a very large margin for profit; the latter meant no profit at all. During the later years (1902–10) the margin varied from .75 to .90 cent; or, in round numbers it exceeded cost, and contributed to interest and profits, by an amount varying from $\frac{1}{8}$ to $\frac{3}{10}$ cent per pound. I doubt whether it could be proved that, allowing for interest and "reasonable" business profits, this brought a price in excess of total normal cost. Compare what is said below, chapter xii, p. 210, on "cost."

The figures given are averages for the successive years. Such figures might be misleading, since there might be variations within each year, concealed in the averages, that would affect the significance of the table and chart. But in this case more minute and detailed tabulations lead to no changes in the results. A chart showing the price figures month by month has been made for me by Mr. H. L. Perrin of Boston University, who has carried on an investigation of the trust's history under my guidance, and no deviations were found that would modify the conclusions stated in the text. I am glad to acknowledge my indebtedness to Mr. Perrin.

years after 1892, the trust was again in almost sole control, and its profits again were high. Under the act of 1890, the tariff differential on refined sugar was such as to make competition by foreign refiners impossible, and so sustained the position of the trust. As the chart shows, the refiner's margin was profitably high in 1892 and 1893. The tariff act of 1894 reduced the differential (from $\frac{1}{2}$ to $\frac{1}{8}$ cent a pound), and the margin, though still comfortably high, became less excessive. The Trust was in virtual control of the domestic situation for several years after 1892, but after 1894 was held in check in some degree by a possibility of foreign competition under the lowered differential of 1894.[1]

Beginning with 1897, however, a new period of domestic competition set in, and there was a sharp decline in the margin and in the profits of refining. Competition ensued between the trust and the Arbuckles, — a large coffee firm which refused to accept the Trust's terms for sugar and proceeded to build a refinery of its own. The competition was so bitter that for a year or two the profits of refining seem to have entirely disappeared. This cut-throat contest was followed by a truce. After the opening of the twentieth century the situation in the sugar refining trade might be not inaccurately described as one of armed neutrality. The trust retained a strong position, yet not a controlling one. The Arbuckles remained as competitors; and on the eastern seaboard there were other competitors also. The margin became comparatively moderate. The profits of refining do not seem to have been excessive.

That tariff protection did not in itself have a determining effect on the gains of the refiners was shown by the absence of any visible influence on these gains from the Cuban reciprocity arrangement.

[1] It is not easy to make out precisely what was the situation of the refiner (*i. e.*, the trust) during the period when the tariff act of 1894 was in force. The sugar duties of that act were regarded as a surrender to the trust; see my *Tariff History of the United States*, p. 308. It has been said that the *ad valorem* duty of forty per cent then imposed on raw sugar worked to its advantage. For some figures on the profits of refining under the several tariff acts of 1890, 1894, 1897, see the testimony of Mr. W. P. Willett before the Hardwick Committee (1912), pp. 3548–3549.

The Cuban treaty went into effect in 1903. It has already been shown[1] that within a short time it caused the price of Cuban sugar to fall in the United States, during a considerable part of each year; not indeed to fall by the full amount of the Cuban remission (20 per cent of the general duty), but by a substantial part of the remission. The refiners, in other words, were able to buy Cuban raw sugar at a substantial reduction below the full-duty price. The protection to them as refiners was thereby vastly increased. For the duty on refined sugar was not affected by the Cuban treaty; this remained throughout at the full rate of the tariffs of 1897 and 1909. Obviously the foreign refiner could not compete with the American refiner who got his Cuban sugar at less than the full-duty price of raw sugar. Except during those few months of the year in which full-duty sugar was imported from Java and other non-favored regions, the American refiners were in the position of having a protection that amounted virtually to prohibition.[2] Yet the price of refined sugar was not maintained at all at the full-duty rate; it followed in the main the oscillations in the (reduced) price of Cuban raw sugar.

Surveying the whole course of events, it may be thus fairly said that the history of the sugar trust, so far as its refining operations are concerned, supports the view that protection, though it may stimulate the formation of a combination and for a time swell its profits, does not enable monopoly gains to be maintained permanently. After a few years of high profits, competition has set in. The strictly manufacturing profit in the long run was kept within competitive limits.

One further aspect of the case may be disposed of at this point. The refining industry, whether or no it needed protection in earlier days, ceased to need it by the close of the nineteenth century. The industry is one in which great plant and large-scale production tell to the utmost. It is of the kind in which American en-

[1] See p. 77, above.

[2] The Cuban remission was not in terms limited to raw sugar; it would have applied to any refined sugar imported from Cuba; but in fact none came thence to the United States.

It is this situation which probably accounted for the indifference with which the refiners acceded to the reduction of the differential in the tariff act of 1909.

terprise finds a congenial field, and in which this country has a comparative advantage. The indications are that refining is done as cheaply in the United States as in foreign countries, and that it does not need the prop of protection. Even with no protection at all, — that is, with no duty at all, or with such a duty only on refined sugar as would offset that on raw sugar, — the industry would maintain itself.

There were other parts of the trust's operations, however, which were influenced by the tariff. The strictly refining profit, which alone has been considered hitherto, was supplemented, for a time at least, by some other sources of gain. These were connected with the peculiar raw sugar situation described in the preceding pages.

Typical of these supplementary pickings were the extra profits secured on Hawaiian sugar. It has already been intimated that although the Hawaiian planters secured almost the entire amount of the remission of duty on their sugar, some fraction went elsewhere.[1] Hawaiian sugar was sold in the United States, from the beginnings of reciprocity in 1876, on the basis of the New York price of raw sugar. But the planters never received quite the full New York price; they sold their sugar at that price *less* a fraction of a cent. The Hawaiian sugar naturally went to San Francisco, the nearest port. There it was sold at the New York price, less a sum which roughly represented the difference between the cost of carrying the sugar to San Francisco and that of carrying it to New York. This arrangement began in the days before the formation of the trust, and was then due to the circumstance that on the Pacific Coast refining was in the hands of monopoly. The same extraordinary growth of large-scale operations had taken place in California as in the eastern region, and had led to the disappearance of all refineries except one (that of the well-known Spreckels). If there had been effective competition among refiners in California, the Hawaiian planters doubtless would have secured the full benefit of the remission of duty on their sugar, without the loss even of this small slice. But as there was but one purchaser for their sugar in California, he could confront

[1] See above, p. 60.

them with the alternative of either accepting from him a slightly lower price or transporting their sugar to the more distant market of New York. Hence the arrangement by which Hawaiian sugars were regularly sold in California at a fraction below the New York price. Needless to say, no benefit arose to the consumer from this reduction. The Californian refiner, so far from selling his product at a lower price than that of the east, sold it on the Pacific coast at a price higher by the cost of transportation from the eastern refiners across the country. The refiner pocketed an extra profit in both directions. He bought the raw sugar at a price below the New York quotation, and sold his refined sugar at a price above the New York quotation. It is not surprising that one of the great fortunes of the country was accumulated.

As has already been noted, a struggle set in between the Californian refiner and the trust in 1889, and came to an end in 1892; and after that time the trust, associated with Spreckels, dominated the field on the Pacific Coast even more completely than elsewhere.[1] The arrangement with the Hawaiian planters remained as before. They sold their sugar at a fraction less than the New York price. From time to time there were variations in the terms of the contracts between them and the refiners. At one period the trust became what is described in the pleasant phraseology of business as "hoggish," and insisted upon too great a reduction from the New York price. The Hawaiian planters thereupon threatened to build a refinery of their own in California and in fact proceeded to do so; though before the stage of real competition was reached, a truce between the contestants seems to have been patched up.[2]

[1] In the holding company (The Western Sugar Refining Company) which took over the California refinery operated by the trust and the Spreckels refinery, each party held one-half of the stock. The refinery which had been operated by the trust was immediately closed, and was ultimately destroyed by the San Francisco earthquake. The Spreckels plant sufficed to refine all the sugar consumed on the coast. See *Hardwick Committee Hearings* (1911), pp. 927–932.

In 1911 the trust sold its stock in the Western Sugar Refining Co. (to the Spreckels interests); this being part of the policy of conformity to law adopted by the later managers.

[2] In the earlier period, until about 1890, the Hawaiian planters were not united, and accepted varying prices for their sugar. Later they combined, and made

To many persons the process by which the Californian refiner, — at first Spreckels, later the trust, — secured a slice of the profits of the Hawaiian planters will seem iniquitous. To the dispassionate observer, it will appear simply as a quarrel over booty, in which neither party could claim virtue or be deemed guilty of sin. So far as the consumers of sugar were concerned, it made no difference how the contestants haggled over the division of the spoil. No doubt the refiners for a while secured substantial pickings; but had they not done so, the Hawaiian planters would simply have secured so much more.

An extra profit of the same sort was secured by the trust in its purchases of Louisiana sugar. Here too the commanding position of the refiner enabled the purchase of raw sugar to be made at prices below those which would have prevailed under a competitive régime. The trust was virtually the sole purchaser of raw sugar in Louisiana; for here also the march of large-scale production eliminated the small refiner, and left the one huge concern alone in the field. The planter of Louisiana, like the Hawaiian planter, was confronted by the alternative of paying for the transportation of the sugar to a more or less competitive market in New York, or of selling it to the trust in Louisiana at a price slightly below that of New York. It was simplest for him to accept the second alternative. Louisiana raw sugar was regularly sold at a fraction below the New York price. The refined sugar, on the other hand, was disposed of in the Mississippi Valley with no corresponding reduction. Here again the operations of

contracts for a year or series of years with the trust, stipulating that all planters should get the same price, — a fraction below the New York price. In 1912 the reduction from the New York price was $\frac{1}{4}$ cent for sugar delivered at San Francisco, $\frac{1}{10}$ cent for sugar delivered at Atlantic ports. The trust contended that its obligation to take at once all the Hawaiian sugar offered made some such reduction reasonable; and the willingness of the Hawaiians to enter on the arrangement for sugar delivered at the eastern ports ($\frac{1}{10}$ cent reduction) doubtless rests on this circumstance. It is not clear that during the later years of the period the arrangement was such that the Hawaiian planters had ground for complaint. See on this subject, the statement of Willett, in the record of the suit of the U. S. Gov't *v.* Amer. Sug. Refining Co., i, p. 83 (1912); testimony before the Hardwick Committee (1911), pp. 89–90, and 3610; and the pamphlet by F. C. Lowry, *Our High Tariff on Sugar* (published in various editions, 1909–1912; see the edition of 1909, p. 4).

the trust were regarded by staunch protectionists as thoroughly iniquitous; and so needless to say, they were regarded by the Louisiana planters. And no doubt there was one point of difference between the case of Louisiana and that of the Hawaiian planters: the planters of the former could plead that the trust deprived them of some part of the protection which Congress intended to give. The bonus to the Hawaiians arose through no deliberate intent; but Louisiana sugar was doubtless meant to have protection, through an enhancement of the price of raw sugar, by the full amount of the duty. A fraction of this protection was intercepted by the trust. And this fraction, like the other gains, tended to dwindle during the later years, as competition from various quarters deprived the trust of its position of control.[1]

It was often intimated that the trust secured in other directions additional profits. Thus it was alleged that extra gains were made through ownership of sugar lands and production of raw sugar in Cuba, Porto Rico, even in the Philippines. But the combination seems to have entered on no operations of this sort. Individuals owning shares in it no doubt were also investors in sugar plantations; but it seems to be strictly true that in so doing they acted simply as individuals. Americans were not slow to see the opportunities for profit created by the various exemptions from the sugar duty, and they took advantage of them in Cuba and in Porto Rico, as they did in Hawaii.[2] In view of the popular hatred of trusts and trust methods, and the special obloquy under which the sugar combination fell, it is not sur-

[1] Whether the Louisiana planters were "oppressed" by the trust during the later years is not easy to make out. Their spokesmen naturally thought so; see the testimony before the Hardwick committee (*Hardwick Report*, p. 1841). The representatives of the trust pointed out (*ibid.*, p. 133) that they engaged to take the whole amount offered by any planter, at the stipulated reduction from the New York price, and to hold it and assume the risk of depreciation; all of which served to make the arrangement a reasonable one. See also the testimony of Mr. Atkins in the suit of U. S. *v.* Am. Sug. Ref. Co., Transcript of Record, p. 6318. — It must be remembered that during the later period the price of refined sugar in the Mississippi valley could no longer be kept up, being subject to the competition of other refiners and also to that of the beet-sugar makers of the west.

[2] Cf. p. 60, *supra*.

prising that anything unwelcome or objectionable in the situation should be fastened on it, and that there should be suspicion of activity on its part in the sugar growing dependencies. Coolly considered, however, all this is seen to have nothing to do with the refining situation or the trust. It made no difference to the consumer what sort of plantation owner in Hawaii or Porto Rico, — native or American, trust stockholder or unaffiliated planter, — was benefited by the sugar tax. Even if the trust had owned all the plantations, the causes of its profit from raw sugar would have been distinct from those of its profit on refining. As it happened, the two problems were distinct not only in their economic significance but as regards the persons involved. The trust itself owned no sugar lands and made no raw sugar; and such of its shareholders as invested in plantations played no dominant or even considerable part in the raw sugar situation.

A different phase of the trust's activity, and one which again was connected more with the duty on raw sugar than with the differential on refined, appeared in its endeavor to control the beet-sugar factories. The astute and unscrupulous head of the combination seems to have concluded, about 1900, that beet-sugar production would be profitable so long as the duty on sugar remained high; that the duty in fact was likely to remain high; and that the trust might secure a share of the beet-sugar profits as well as those from buying and refining cane sugar.

Accordingly large purchases were made of shares in various beet-sugar companies, from California to Michigan; and additional factories were erected by subsidiary companies. Here again the popular view was that the transactions were particularly objectionable because undertaken by a trust. It is probably true that the prices of refined sugar in the Rocky Mountain and Pacific regions were stiffened; since it was here that beet sugar was most largely produced, and here also that the combination profited most from a high margin on its refined sugar. In the main, however, it made little difference to the consumer whether the beet-sugar enterprises were owned by the trust or by "independents." Each benefited to the full by the import duty on raw sugar; and each based the price for refined sugar on the New

York quotation. Nor was it of consequence to the farmer who sold the beets to the factories: he received the same price from both, and was suspicious of oppressive dealings by both, though doubtless with an added tinge of suspicion when aware of selling to a trust-controlled factory. The manufacture of beet sugar was at the least as well managed by the combination; it seems to have been better managed. So far as I am able to judge, combination in this case conduced to industrial efficiency. In the selection of seed, the conduct of agricultural experiments, the instruction of farmers, the agents of the trust were active and capable. Factory operations proper were also carried on at least as well as by independent makers. All this, however, had but little connection with tariff problems. These remained essentially the same, whoever owned and managed the beet-sugar enterprises. What might have been the consequences of control of beet sugar by the trust, if extended to the full and continued for a long time, is no easy problem. But the enforcement of the Sherman law, and a change in the personnel of the trust's management, led about 1910 to a policy of gradually divesting itself of the beet-sugar properties and investments. The same policy, of giving up the various arrangements for combination and control, was followed in other directions. The episodes described in the preceding pages belong to the history of the past.

It is obvious that the differential on refined sugar and the possible gains of the refining combination were quantitatively of vastly less importance than the duty on raw sugar. The latter meant a tax, in the form of higher prices of sugar, of a hundred millions a year or more; the former could make a difference at the most of a few millions. The effective duty on raw sugar I have reckoned at $1\frac{1}{2}$ cents a pound. The differential on refined, after 1894 was only $\frac{1}{8}$ cent a pound. The utmost additional profit made possible (not necessarily gathered in) by the trust because of the tariff was a matter of a small fraction of a cent, — perhaps $\frac{1}{10}$ cent or at most $\frac{1}{5}$. In the popular mind, the entire sugar duty was usually associated with trust control and trust robbery. Yet this part of it, — the differential on refined, — bears chiefly on another set of problems, — the significance of a very small fraction of profit on a huge volume of transactions, and the possible gain to be secured by something much short of iron-clad monopoly. An additional profit of $\frac{1}{10}$ cent per pound meant several millions a year for the refining combination, but was of negligible effect on the price of sugar for the retail purchaser.[1]

[1] In this sketch of the Sugar Trust, I have confined myself to those operations which had to do directly with the protective tariff. The furious speculation in sugar stock and its manipulation by insiders, the political corruption or semi-corruption practised by the early managers, the trust's methods of competition, the much-discussed episode of the capture of the Philadelphia (Segal) refinery, — all belong to the history of the trust problem, in which this particular combination could be the subject of a veritably sensational chapter. The frauds on the revenue through underweighing are also outside the scope of the present volume. They are connected with the administrative side of customs duties, and with the unsavory political conditions of the closing years of the nineteenth century. On the death in 1907 of H. O. Havemeyer, who had maintained through his life a curious despotic control of the trust, its management came into other and better hands, and a new phase began.

PART III

IRON AND STEEL

CHAPTER IX

A SURVEY OF GROWTH

THE present Part will consider the iron and steel industry, its extraordinary advance since 1870, and the influence of the tariff on that growth. No phase of the country's economic development shows changes so striking. None raises questions more difficult to answer concerning the effects of protective duties. To understand the complexity of the factors which have been at work, and the nature of the special problems that arise, a survey must first be made of the growth of the industry and of the various influences which have affected it.

In 1870 Great Britain was still the world's commanding producer of iron and steel. Notwithstanding half a century or more of almost continuous protection, the United States held but a distant second place. The output of pig-iron in the old country in 1870 was very nearly six millions of tons; that in the new country was but little over a million and a half. But, as the appended figures show,[1] the United States gained rapidly and surely on its rival. During each of the three decades from 1860 to 1890, the annual production of American pig-iron doubled. The figure for 1870 was twice that of 1860; 1880 doubled 1870; and 1890 again doubled 1880. The British output increased considerably during the same period, but could not meet the pace of its astounding

[1] The figures of production, at quinquennial intervals, are (in 1,000 tons of 2,240 lbs.):

	Great Britain	United States	Germany
1860	....	....	545
1865	....	....	988
1870	5,963	1,665	1,391
1875	6,365	2,024	2,029
1880	7,749	3,835	2,729
1885	7,415	4,044	3,687
1890	7,904	9,203	4,658
1895	7,703	9,446	5,464
1900	8,960	13,789	8,384
1905	9,608	22,992	10,700
1910	10,012	27,304	14,556

rival. By 1890 the United States passed Great Britain and established her position as the leading iron making country of the world. In the decade from 1890 to 1900 the United States failed to maintain the remarkable geometric progression; yet the output of 1900 was again doubled in 1910. Germany alone showed an advance at all comparable; Great Britain did no more than maintain a steady plodding pace. In 1910 the United States production of pig-iron exceeded twenty-seven million of tons, a total larger than that of Great Britain and Germany combined, and nearly twenty times as large as the American product of forty years previous. If, as the extreme protectionists contend, the growth of domestic industry is in itself proof of the success of their policy, a degree of success was attained in this case that could admit of no cavil.

This enormous increase, however, was by no means evenly distributed over the United States. Within the country a revolution took place, which was part and parcel of the changed relation to other countries, and which must be followed before the new situation can be understood.

The first great impulse to the production of crude iron on a large scale came in the United States with the successful use of anthracite coal as fuel. During the twenty years preceding the civil war (1840–60) the site of the industry and its growth were governed by this fuel.[1] Hence eastern Pennsylvania was the main producing district. The supplies of ore near this region were smelted with its anthracite coal, and Philadelphia was the central market. Proximity to the seaboard made foreign competition easy, except so far as it was hampered by the tariff duties; and the very existence of the iron industry was felt to depend on the maintenance of protection. For some time after the close of the civil war this dominant position of anthracite iron was maintained. In 1872, when the systematic collection of detailed statistics began, out of a total production of 2,500,000 tons, one-half was smelted with anthracite coal, a third with bituminous coal or coke, the remainder with wood (charcoal). The use of

[1] For an account of the industry during this period I refer to my *Tariff History of the United States*, pp. 123–125.

soft coal, which had begun before 1860, became rapidly greater. Already in 1872 it was important; and from year to year it grew. In the periodic oscillations between activity and depression which mark the iron trade more than any other industry, anthracite iron shrank in the slack periods, and barely regained its own in the succeeding periods of expansion. Bituminous or coke iron, on the other hand, held its own during the hard times, and advanced by leaps and bounds with each revival of activity.[1] In 1875 for the first time its output exceeded that of the rival eastern fuel; after that date the huge advance in the iron product of the United States was dependent on the use of coke. Indeed, the use of anthracite alone began to shrink at a comparatively early date. It soon ceased to be used on any large scale as the sole fuel, coke being mixed with it for use in the blast-furnace. What is classed as " anthracite iron " is smelted with a mixture of coke and hard coal; and even with the aid of the coke, this means of reducing the ore came to be of less and less importance. Anthracite coal was completely displaced as an iron making fuel.[2]

[1] During the earlier years, bituminous coal was much used in the blast-furnaces without being first coked. But soon this crude procedure was given up, and the coal was used in the form of coke.

[2] The production of pig-iron by fuel at quinquennial intervals is given below. By way of illustrating the trend over a long period, the year 1855 has been taken as the starting-point. The figures, as in the previous table, indicate thousands of gross tons:

	Pig-Iron smelted with			
	Anthracite		Bituminous	Charcoal
1855	341		56	303
1860	464		109	248
1865	428		169	234
1870	830		508	326
1875	811		846	367
1880	1,614		1,741	480
	Anthracite alone	Anthracite and Coke		
1885	250	1,059	2,389	357
1890	249	1,937	6,388	628
1895	56	1,214	7,950	225
1900	40	1,677	11,727	384
1905	...	1,674	20,965	352
1910	20	629	26,528	396

Charcoal iron has qualities that make it advantageous for certain uses, and hence it continues to be produced in small quantities.

This change is easy of explanation. It was the inevitable result of the greater plenty and effectiveness of coke; and it was powerfully promoted by the rapid development of the United States west of the Appalachian chain, and the nearness of the coke region to this growing market. Anthracite, at best, is an obdurate fuel. At the same time its strictly limited supply, and the cleanliness and freedom from smoke which make it an ideal domestic fuel, maintained its price at a comparatively high level. On the other hand, the vast supplies of bituminous coal and the feverish competition in opening coal lands and marketing their product caused an almost uninterrupted fall in its price. Coke proved, ton for ton, a better fuel than anthracite; and the supplies of bituminous coal available for coking proved almost limitless.

Pittsburgh, whose destiny as a great iron center was perceived long ago, is situated in the heart of the region where coking coal is plentiful. To this point the iron industry converged, attracted first by cheap fuel, and soon by other geographical advantages of the region, — its easy access to the growing western country, and the added opportunities of securing super-abundant quantities of the best ore. Pennsylvania has remained the greatest iron-producing state in the Union; but since 1880 it has been western Pennsylvania, and no longer eastern, which has secured to the state its leading position. After 1890 this district alone yielded steadily forty per cent of the enormous iron product in the country; and it is here, and in the other western districts in which the same industrial forces have been at work, that we have to study the conditions on which the growth of the iron industry depended.

The westward movement was determined not only by the geographical distribution of the fuel. It was no less affected by the distribution of the ore supply; and the effect of this in turn rested for many years on the revolution wrought in the iron trade by the Bessemer process.

The first inventions which made iron plentiful were Cort's processes for puddling and rolling. Through three-quarters of the nineteenth century this was the mode in which the world got its supply of the metal in tough form, usable where heavy strain must come on it. The processes involved at once a considerable plant, complex machinery, and strenuous exertion by skilled and powerful laborers, — conditions which during this period promoted the supremacy of the British iron trade. In the decade 1860–70 the process devised by Sir Henry Bessemer, to which his name attaches, began a second revolution in the iron trade. That process involved a still larger plant and still more elaborate machinery; and it applied machinery more fully to the elimination and subsequent replacing of the carbon on which the toughness of the iron depends. By the new methods the production of mild steel — that is, tough iron — became possible on a vastly greater scale. Bessemer steel displaced puddled iron in most of its uses. Not only this: the cheap and abundant supply, besides filling needs previously existing, made possible a much greater use of iron and steel for plant, machinery, durable instruments of all sorts. One of the first applications of the method was to rails, where the elastic and impact-sustaining steel enabled railway engines and cars to be doubled and quadrupled in size, and to become more efficient in even greater ratio. Gradually and steadily, new and wider uses were found for the cheap steel. From great ships down to the smallest nails, almost every instrument became cheaper and better. Wood was supplanted by steel for a variety of uses, and the slow-growing and easily exhausted stores of timber were re-enforced by the well-nigh limitless deposits of iron ore in the earth's crust. A new domain in nature's forces was opened to man.

But the Bessemer process depended for its availability on special kinds of ore and pig-iron, — such as are nearly free from certain admixtures and especially from phosphorus. Ores adapted to it hence became doubly valuable, and the accessible parts of the earth were scoured to find them. The deposits of Great Britain in Cumberland and Lancashire contained important supplies, yet not in quantity adequate to the new demand; and the Spanish fields of Bilboa, on the Bay of Biscay, became an indispensable supplement for the British iron masters. In the United States, also, some of the sources previously used in the region east of the Appalachian chain proved to be available, — such as the famed deposits, once unique in their ease of working, in the Cornwall hills of eastern Pennsylvania. But the greater part of the eastern ores were too highly charged with phosphorus, or for other reasons unavailable. Here, as in Great Britain, a distant source of supply was turned to. The Lake Superior iron region, long known to explorers and geologists, suddenly sprang into commanding place. Here were abundant and super-abundant supplies of rich and properly constituted ore. These and the equally abundant coal of Pennsylvania were brought together, the iron made from them was converted into steel by the Bessemer process; and thus became possible the astounding growth in the production of iron and steel in the United States.

The iron mines of the Lake Superior region stretch in widely separated fields along the lake, from the middle of its southern shore to its farthest northwestern end. At the extreme eastern end is the Menominee iron field, usually described in connection with the other Lake Superior fields, yet differing from them in important respects. The ore of the Menominee district is easily mined; and it is easily shipped, finding an outlet by the port of Escanaba on Lake Michigan, and thus traversing a much shorter journey to its eastern markets than that from the Lake Superior mines proper. But it is usually of non-Bessemer quality, and hence played no considerable part in the most characteristic effects of the new developments. The great Bessemer ore fields of Lake Superior are four in number: in geographical order from east to west, the Marquette, the Gogebic, and the neighboring Vermilion and Mesabi. As it happens, the geographical order has been also, in the main, the order of exploitation. The easternmost, the Marquette, finding its outlet by the port of that name, was the first to be worked on a great scale. Even before the civil war, mining and smelting had begun; and, as the Bessemer process was more and more largely used, especially after 1873, it was exploited on a larger and larger scale. Here began the digging of Bessemer ore on a great scale, and its transportation to a great distance. After a considerable interval the second field, the Gogebic, began to be worked, in 1884. Lying some two hundred miles further west, along the boundary line between Wisconsin and Michigan, and finding its outlet by Ashland, on the southern shore of Lake Superior, here was found perhaps the richest and purest Bessemer ore. At about the same time, in 1884, began the development of the most distant of the fields, the Vermilion, lying to the north of the extreme end of Lake Superior, in the state of Minnesota, close to the Canada frontier. Here, too, were great stores of rich Bessemer ore, shipped by the port of Two Harbors, on the northern shore of the lake.

In all these fields the ore was secured by what we commonly think of as "mining," — by digging far into the earth, and bringing the material up from a greater or less depth. But the latest and now the most important of the fields gave opportunity for the simplest and cheapest form of mining. Great bodies of ore are lying close under the ground, and, when once the surface glacial drift has been removed, are obtainable by simple digging and shovelling, as from a clay pit.[1] Along the Mesabi [2] range of hills, lying about one hundred miles northwest of the end of Lake Superior, distant not many miles from the Vermilion range, vast tracts of rich iron ore, finely comminuted and easily worked, lie close to the surface. Here a new source of supply was added, offering unique opportunities for exploitation on a great scale. These opportunities were availed of with astounding quickness. The Mesabi field at once sprang into the front rank among the Lake Superior fields, and, indeed, among all the iron ore fields of the world. In 1890 the region was a trackless waste. In 1892 it was opened by railway. Towns sprang up, huge steam-shovels attacked the precious ore, and long trains carried it to the newly constructed docks at the port of Duluth. Even during the depression that followed the crisis of 1893 the output from this field mounted year by year. In 1893, virtually the first year of operation, 600,000 tons were shipped from it; in 1894, thrice that amount; and in 1895 it became, what it has since remained, the

[1] It should be noted that in the Marquette region, also, iron ore was secured at the first working and for many years thereafter by open cuts. But the extraction of ore on a great scale has proceeded by underground operations.

[2] Variously spelled: Mesabi, Mesaba, Messabi, Messaba.

most productive of the iron mining districts. A little less than half of the ore is of Bessemer grade. Its physical constitution, moreover, is such that, for advantageous use in the furnace, other ore needs to be mixed with it. Were it all of Bessemer quality, and in the best form, the other fields might have been entirely displaced. With the limitations in the quality of the Mesabi ore, the other fields still found themselves able to hold their own in the market, though their supremacy was ended by the favored rival.

For many years the Lake Superior mines have been the main sources of supply for the iron ore of the American iron industry. A steadily increasing share of a steadily increasing total has come from them. In 1910 the total iron ore product of the country exceeded 50 million tons; and over four-fifths of this enormous mass came from the Lake Superior region.[1]

In this brief description of the Lake Superior iron region, reference has been made to the ports by which the ore is shipped, — Escanaba, Marquette, Ashland, Duluth, Two Harbors. To each of these the ore must be carried by rail from the mines, — sometimes a few miles, sometimes, as with a large part of the Minnesota supplies, a hundred miles and more. And, with this first movement, only the beginning is made on a long journey. From the shipping port the ore is carried eastward by water to meet the coal. Some goes down Lake Michigan to Chicago and Gary,

[1] The United States Geological Survey, in its successive admirable *Reports on the Mineral Resources of the United States*, has followed the history of the iron fields of Lake Superior, as, indeed, of all the mineral resources of the country. In the issue for 1895–96 (forming vol. iii of the *Seventeenth Annual Report* of the Survey) a summary description is given, with convenient sketch maps showing the location of the several fields.

The relative importance of the fields, the order in which they were developed, and their relation to the iron ore production of the whole country, are shown by the following figures:

Iron Ore Production (*in millions of gross tons*)

	1880	1890	1900	1910
Menominee	.6	2.3	3.3	4.2
Marquette	1.4	3.0	3.5	4.4
Gogebic	..	2.8	2.9	4.3
Vermilion	..	.9	1.6	1.2
Mesabi	..	..	7.8	29.2
Total Lake Superior	2.0	2.5	19.1	43.4
Total United States	7.1	7.6	27.6	51.2

where it meets the Pennsylvania coal about half-way. Some goes farther, through Lakes Huron and Erie, and meets the coal at Toledo, Ashtabula, Cleveland, and other ports on Lake Erie. The largest part is unloaded from the vessels at lake ports, and carried by rail to the heart of the Pittsburgh coal district, there to be smelted by the coal on its own ground. No small amount goes even beyond, — to the eastward in Pennsylvania, beyond the Pittsburgh district, even into New Jersey and New York, almost to the seaboard itself. Hence the cities of Erie and Buffalo have become important ore-receiving ports on Lake Erie; the ore, if not smelted there, going thence by rail on its journey to the smelter. This last and farthest invasion of distant regions by the Lake Superior ore was promoted for many years by the import duty on the competing foreign ore which sought to find an entrance by the Atlantic seaboard, — an aspect of the iron trade of which more will be said presently.

The iron producing region which depends on the Lake Superior ores thus stretches over a wide district, the extreme ends being separated more than a thousand miles. Close by the iron mines are a number of charcoal-using furnaces in Wisconsin and Michigan. The still unexhausted forests of these states supply this fuel in abundance; and charcoal iron, though long supplanted for most uses by its coke-smelted rival, has qualities which enable a limited supply to find a market, even at a relatively high price. Next in order come Chicago (South Chicago) and its suburb (this it virtually is) the new-created city of Gary; with which must be classed some neighboring cities, such as Milwaukee in Wisconsin and Joliet in Illinois. It is one of the surprises of American industry that iron manufacturing on a huge scale should be undertaken at such points, distant alike from ore and from coal. The coke is moved hundreds of miles by rail from Pennsylvania, and meets the ore which has travelled no less a distance from Lake Superior. Ease of access to the western market gives these sites an advantage, or at least goes to offset the disadvantage of the longer railway haul of the fuel. Other iron producing points of the same sort are scattered along Lake Erie. At each of the ports of Toledo, Lorain, Ashtabula, Erie, Buffalo, especially Cleveland, ore is smelted, and iron and steel making is carried on. But the coal region itself — Pittsburgh and its environs — remains the heart and center of the iron industry. Hither most of the ore is carried; and here the operations of smelting, converting into steel, fashioning the steel into rails, bridges, plates, wire, nails, structural forms for building, are performed on the greatest scale. For some years the natural gas of this region added to its advantages and aided in its exceptionally rapid growth. But each supply of gas exhausted itself before long, and new discoveries did not maintain the inflowing volume at its first level. It was the abundant and excellent coal which formed the sure basis of the manufacturing industries, and the permanent foundation of iron and steel making.

Whether the ore goes to the coal or the coal meets the ore halfway, one or both must travel a long journey, by land as well as by water. One or both must be laden and unladen several times. A carriage of 800, 900, over 1,000 miles must be achieved, with two separate hauls by rail. Fifty years ago, even thirty years ago, it would have seemed impossible to accomplish this on a great scale and with great cheapness. The geographical conditions on which a large iron industry must rest were supposed by Jevons in 1866 to be the contiguity of iron and coal.[1] But here are supplies of the two minerals separated by a thousand miles of land and water, and combined for iron making on the largest scale known in the world's history. One of the most sagacious of American students of economics, Albert Gallatin, early predicted that the coal area of western Pennsylvania would become the foundation of a great iron industry, and that only with its development would the American iron manufacture attain a large independent growth.[2] But he could not dream that his prophecy

[1] Jevons, *The Coal Question*, second edition, chap. xv. Jevons in that chapter looked for important changes in the United States, chiefly from the wider use of anthracite in iron making. The fact that "the Americans are, of all people in the world, the most forward in driving canals, river navigations, and railways," was noted by him as sure to affect the American iron trade; but even his keen imagination and wide knowledge could not foresee how much and in what directions this "driving" would operate.

[2] "A happy application of anthracite coal to the manufacture of iron, the dis-

would be fulfilled by the utilization of ores distant fifteen hundred miles from the seaboard, transported from a region which was in his day, and remained for half a centurv after his day, an unexplored wilderness.

For the iron trade the most important section of the Pittsburgh coal district is the famed Connellsville coke region, lying some fifty miles south of Pittsburgh, along the banks of the Youghiogheny river. Here is a level and uniform outcrop of the best coking coal; and from this has come most of the coke used in smelting Lake Superior ores, and, indeed, the greater part of that used in the United States. Considerable supplies have come also from other near-by regions in Pennsylvania and West Virginia; and Alabama has made from her own coal the coke for smelting her iron. But the Connellsville coke is by far the most important as regards both quantity and quality, and it alone has steadily furnished more than half of the total. Whether used near the mines, in the Pittsburgh district, or carried hundreds of miles to meet the ore, this unexampled supply of the best fuel has been the basis of the whole iron and steel manufacture.[1]

covery of new beds of bituminous coal, the erection of iron works in the vicinity of the most easterly beds now existing, and the improved means of transportation which may bring this at a reasonable rate to the sea-border, may hereafter enable the American iron master to compete in cheapness with the foreign rolled iron in the Atlantic district. . . . The ultimate reduction of the price of American to that of British rolled iron can only, and ultimately will, be accomplished in that western region which abounds with ore, and in which is found the most extensive formation of bituminous coal that has yet been discovered in any part of the globe, and this also lying so near the surface of the earth as to render the extraction of the mineral less expensive than anywhere else." Albert Gallatin, "Memorial to the Free Trade Convention" (1832), as reprinted in *State Papers and Speeches on the Tariff*, pp. 179, 180.

[1] The production of coke was (in tons of 2,000 lbs.):

	United States	Connellsville region
1880	3.3 millions	2.2 millions
1890	11.5 "	6.5 "
1900	20.5 "	10.4 "
1910	41.7 "	19.7 "

In the second column I have combined in a single figure the production of the older Connellsville region and that of the "lower district" which came to be of importance after 1900. See *Mineral Resources of the United States*, 1911, Part II, pp. 215, 256, 259.

The price of coke to the iron masters went down during the period here under consideration (1870–1910), partly because of cheaper production at the mines, partly because of cheaper carriage from mines to works. In the earlier years (about 1870) coke at the ovens was sold for $3.00 a ton. Its price, while fluctuating greatly, was usually below $2.00 in later years, even falling as low as $1.00 in periods of depression. On the whole, fuel was provided for the American iron master at prices less than those paid by his rivals in any part of the world; while low rates of transportation enabled it to be carried to the furnaces without sacrifice of this cardinal advantage.

The history of the American iron trade after 1870 thus came to be in no small part a history of transportation. The cheap carriage of the ore and coal was the indispensable condition of the smelting of the one by the other.[1] Clearly, this factor was not peculiar to the iron industry. The perfecting of transportation has been almost the most remarkable of the mechanical triumphs of the United States. Great as have been the evils of our railway methods, disheartening as have been some of the results of unfettered competition, the efficiency of the railways has been brought to a point not approached elsewhere, largely in consequence of that very competition whose ill effects have been so often and so justly dwelt on. In the carriage of iron ore and of coal the methods of railway transportation which had been de-

[1] "Few people who have not actually run a blast-furnace realize what it means to fill the capacious maw of one of these monsters with raw material. A stack of 200 tons' daily capacity, running on 50 per cent ore, must have delivered to it each day something more than 400 tons of ore, 250 to 300 tons of coke, according to the character of the metal required, and over 100 tons of limestone, — say 900 tons of raw materials. Add the 200 tons of pig-iron shipped out, and we have a daily freight movement of 1,100 tons, taking no note of the disposition of the slag. This is 55 carloads of 20 tons each [A modern ore car will carry 50 to 60 tons; and coal cars have been introduced carrying 90 tons. — F. W. T.]. . . . Starting up a furnace of ordinary capacity calls immediately for the labor, from first to last, of nearly a thousand men; for the use of at least a thousand railway cars, and many locomotives; for perhaps several steamers and vessels on the lakes." A. Brown. "The Outlook in the American Iron Industry," in the *Engineering Magazine*, October, 1899, p. 88. — By 1910, the daily capacity of a "modern" iron furnace had again been doubled, reaching 400 tons a day, and bringing a corresponding increase in the ore and fuel required.

veloped under the stress of eager competition were utilized to the utmost; and the same was true of the transfer from rail to ship and from ship to rail again, of the carriage in the ship itself, and of the handling of accumulated piles of the two materials. The ore is loaded on cars at the mines by mechanical appliances. At the Mesabi mines the very steam-shovel that digs the ore from the ground deposits it in the adjacent car. At the lake, high ore-docks protrude hundreds of yards into the water. On top of them run the trains, the ore dropping by gravity from openings in the car-bottoms into the pockets of the docks. Thence it drops again through long ducts into the waiting vessels, ranged below alongside the dock. At every step direct manual labor is avoided, and machines and machine-like devices enable huge quantities of ore to be moved at a cost astonishingly low.[1] The vessels themselves, constructed for the service, carry the maximum of cargo for the minimum of expense; while the machinery for rapid loading and unloading reduces to the shortest the non-earning time of lying at the docks. At the other end of the water carriage, especially on Lake Erie, similar highly developed mechanical appliances transfer from boat to railway car again, or, at will, to the piles where stocks are accumulated for the winter months of closed navigation. At either end the railway has been raised to the maximum of efficiency for the rapid and economical carriage of bulky freight. What has been done for grain, for cotton, for lumber, for all the great staples, has been done here also, and here perhaps more effectively than anywhere else: the plant has been made larger and stronger, the paying weight increased in proportion to the dead weight, the ton-mile expense lessened by heavier rails, larger engines, longer trains, and easier grades, the mechanism for loading, unloading, transhipping perfected to the last

[1] "Every extra handling means more cost. . . . Formerly it was necessary to trim the cargoes; and this had to be done by hand, and gave employment to a great many men at exceedingly high wages. The work, however, was killing while it lasted. Now trimming is in most cases done away with, because the immense size of the freighters renders them stable in any weather; and, if there is any great inequality in the trim of the boat, it is rectified by shifting the water ballast from one compartment to another." Peter White, *The Mining Industry of Northern Michigan,* in Publ. Mich. Pol. Sci. Assoc., iii, p. 153.

degree, or to what seems the last degree until yet another stage towards perfection is invented. And evidently here, as elsewhere, the process has been powerfully promoted by unhampered trade over a vast territory, and the consequent certainty that costly apparatus for lengthened transportation will never be shorn of its effectiveness by a restriction in the distant market.

Still another factor has been at work in the iron trade, as in other great industries, — the march of production to a greater and greater scale, and the combination of connected industries into great single-managed systems. The iron trade showed more markedly than any of the great industries the manifestations of the new conditions. Both vertical and horizontal combination proceeded apace.

Of these two forms of combination, the former — single management of successive stages in production, the "integration" of industry, — developed first, and contributed most surely and most largely to the effectiveness of production. Iron mines, coal mines, coke ovens, railways, steamers, docks, smelting works, converting works, rolling mills, steel works, machine shops, — these were combined into imposing complexes. The great iron and steel companies operated iron mines on Lake Superior, coal mines and coke establishments in Pennsylvania, docks and railways, as well as iron and steel works proper. The largest of them, the Carnegie Company, built as early as 1897 a railway of its own, specially equipped for the massive and cheap carriage of ore and fuel, from the shore of Lake Erie to the Pittsburgh coal district. At its terminus on Lake Erie (Conneaut) a new harbor and a new city were created. The economy in production from such widely ramifying organizations is not merely or chiefly in dispensing with the services and saving the gains of so many independent middlemen: it arises mainly from consistent planning of every stage, the nice intercalation of operations, the sweeping introduction from end to end of expensive and rapid-working machinery, continuously supplied under homogeneous administration with the huge quantities of material which alone make possible the effective and economical utilization of the great plant.

The horizontal form of combination, — what has come to be known as the trust, — appeared later; and the extent of its contribution to industrial effectiveness is not so certain. The extraordinary burst of consolidation and combination at the opening of the present century is familiar. The most momentous and conspicuous single episode was the formation of the United States Steel Corporation in 1901. Sundry other horizontal combinations in the iron industry had preceded it, such as the steel and wire combination, and others for steel hoop and tin plate. The giant Steel Corporation gathered them into one fold. Not that the whole of the iron and steel trade was absorbed: perhaps one-half of the output of the crude materials (coal, ore, and pig-iron) came under its control, with a larger share for some of the finished products. A considerable number of enterprises remained independent. Each of these was on a large scale, compared with the units of the previous generation. Each carried on vertical combination, operating its own mines of ore and coal, and carrying the iron to the stage of steel and its semi-finished products. The Steel Corporation itself carried this form of industrial organization to a greater degree than any, more particularly in its conduct of transportation by land and water. It has never been doubted that well-managed vertical combination conduced to efficiency in the iron trade. Whether the other form, — single management of all the establishments doing the like things, — conduced also to efficiency, is more open to question. The motive for it was beyond question double: in part an expectation that consolidation would lead to economies; but, no less, a wish to put an end to competition, to secure gains from monopoly or quasi-monopoly, or at all events to avoid the paring of profits under competition. That the huge iron and steel enterprises produce more cheaply than their smaller predecessors is beyond question; but how far that cheapening has been further promoted by the combination of parallel and competing enterprises is among the economic problems still unsolved.[1]

[1] Of the enterprises merged in the Steel Corporation, the two largest, before 1900, were the Carnegie Company, and the Federal Steel Company, the latter dominated by the firm of J. P. Morgan & Co. Both carried on vertical combination on a great scale, — mining the coal and ore, transporting them on railways

While the Lake Superior ores, utilized under the conditions just described, constituted by far the most important source of supply for the iron industry, a large contribution came from another source, also, — from the southern states.

In the region where the states of Tennessee, Alabama, and Georgia adjoin, the conditions once thought indispensable for a flourishing iron industry exist in perfection. Here are great deposits of ore, easy of working; and close by them great deposits of coking coal, no less easily worked. Before the civil war, these natural advantages were not utilized: the régime of slavery and the lack of means of transportation prevented any resort to them. But with the quickening of the industrial life of the south when once the civil war and reconstruction were passed, the mineral resources of this region were developed on a rapidly enlarging scale. Alabama, where the best deposits of coal occur, became a great iron producing state: here again, though for a less distance and on a smaller scale, the ore made its journey to the coal. The rate of growth was most rapid between 1880 and 1890: the pig-iron output of Alabama rose from 69,000 tons in 1880 to 915,000 in 1890. In 1900, it was 1,200,000 tons; in 1910, near 2,000,000 tons. The large supply of labor at low wages contributed to the easy and profitable utilization of this source of supply. The free negro turned miner, and proved not only a docile laborer but also, — paid, as miners are, according to the tonnage brought to the pit's mouth, — on the whole an efficient one.

The southern ore contains phosphorus in too large amounts to make it available for the Bessemer process; and this for some time

and vessels of their own, and operating great iron and steel works. The Carnegie works centered about Pittsburgh, the Federal about Chicago. The American Steel & Wire Co. illustrated both vertical and horizontal combination. The same was the case with the so-called "Moore properties": the National Steel Company with its affiliations, the Sheet Steel, Tin Plate, and Steel Hoop companies. The Bridge (structural steel) and Tube companies had no raw-material supplies of their own, and so represented horizontal combination only.

The history of the great consolidation has often been told. The authoritative account is in the *Report of the Commission of Corporations on the Steel Industry*, Part I (1911). An excellent summary is in Berglund, *The United States Steel Corporation*, in Columbia University Studies (1907).

gave it a place somewhat apart in the iron industry of the country. The iron made from it did not compete with that from the Lake Superior ore, and was used chiefly for general foundry purposes. Marketed at a very low price, the increasing supplies made their way to places farther and farther removed. Pittsburgh itself soon used Alabama iron for foundry purposes; the western states and the eastern alike were supplied; in New England it displaced Scotch pig, previously imported in considerable quantity.

With the opening of the twentieth century, the technical development of the industry took in some respects a new direction; but the changes were of no considerable significance for the tariff problems. Bessemer ore and Bessemer steel, which had dominated before 1900, were in part supplanted. For some time (since about 1880) Germany had been making steel from phosphoric ores by the basic (Thomas-Gilchrist) process; indeed, that process had influenced the growth of the German iron industry as profoundly as did the Bessemer process the growth in the United States. Bessemer ores, though the deposits were by no means exhausted in the United States, became less plentiful, and hence somewhat higher in price; a growing proportion of steel came to be made from basic ore and iron. In addition, a steadily increasing amount of steel was made by the open-hearth process, which is available both for Bessemer and non-Bessemer iron. Open-hearth steel is supposed to be tougher than Bessemer steel, and has been in demand for rails and other purposes. By 1910 the output of open-hearth steel (preponderantly from basic iron) exceeded that of Bessemer steel. One consequence was a facilitation of competition, since control of the Bessemer ores, so greatly prized before, was of lessened importance. These changes, however, had no appreciable effect on the geographical distribution of the industry or on its relation to possible imports. Lake ore and Pittsburgh iron remained the dominant factors, and the industry continued to be unaffected by foreign competition both because of its technical strength and because its main seats were far inland.

The outcome of the great changes in the geographical distribution of the iron industry is shown in the following tabular statement: —

PRODUCTION OF PIG-IRON IN THE UNITED STATES [1]
(*In thousands of gross tons: 1,217 = 1,217,000 tons*)

	1872	1880	1890	1900	1910
Eastern District (eastern Pennsylvania, New York, New Jersey)	1,217	1,610	2,342	1,903	2,868 [2]
Western Pennsylvania alone	387	772	2,561	4,922	10,621
Central District (western Pennsylvania, Ohio, Indiana, Illinois)	849	1,502	4,517	8,756	20,301
Southern District (Alabama, Tennessee, Virginia, Maryland)	127	238	1,554	2,356	3,107
Total for United States	2,549	3,835	9,203	13,789	27,303

In the eastern district proper the output barely held its own. The total production in 1910 was not greater than in 1872. On the other hand, the central district increased its production steadily and enormously, whether in western Pennsylvania itself or in the neighboring states of Ohio, Indiana, Illinois. This is the region where Lake Superior ore is smelted with Pittsburgh coal: in and about Pittsburgh itself, in the immediately adjacent parts of Ohio, and at the various lake cities where the ore meets the coal, Chicago, Cleveland, Toledo, and the rest. Almost as

[1] In this table the figure for eastern Pennsylvania is for the iron smelted in the state with anthracite, or anthracite and coke mixed, while that for western Pennsylvania is for the bituminous (coke) iron. The separation by fuels, it is true, does not indicate with complete accuracy the geographical distribution. But the iron smelted in Pennsylvania east of the Appalachian chain was formerly smelted almost entirely with anthracite, and is still smelted mainly with a mixture of anthracite and coke; and, at all events, this was the only mode in which the statistics at hand made it possible to separate the eastern and western parts of Pennsylvania.

In the southern district, Virginia and Maryland are near the seaboard, and might be constituted a group apart from the other states there included. But the iron industry in them, as in the others, is of recent growth, and depends both for ore and fuel on different sources of supply from those of the northern seaboard region. By far the most important iron producing state in the southern district of the table is Alabama.

[2] The increase in this district is due entirely to the development of great steel plants in Buffalo, N. Y., using Lake ore and Pennsylvania coal, and therefore belonging industrially rather to the central district than to the eastern.

striking is the rate of growth in the southern district, of which Alabama is the most important state. While the total production here was far outweighed by that in the central district, it exceeded after the opening of the present century that of the eastern district.

Another aspect of the subject appears in the labor situation. The power of the labor unions among the iron workers has been less in the United States than in Great Britain. The Amalgamated Association of Iron and Steel Workers had been in 1870–90 a powerful organization, modelled on the British unions and strong in its bargaining with the employers. But the Carnegie Company cut loose from it a decade before the formation of the Steel Corporation. The great Homestead strike of 1892, almost a pitched battle, resulted in the defeat of the Amalgamated Association. Shortly after the great consolidation, the Steel Corporation itself faced (in 1902) a strike from the Association. Again the union suffered a defeat. The Carnegie works had been put on a non-union basis after the Homestead strike; most of the other works of the Steel Corporation were similarly made non-union after the strike of 1902. The Amalgamated Association retained a hold in a few of the Steel Corporation's works, and in some independent establishments. But it was shorn of its former considerable power, and the course of the iron industry was little affected by trade union complications.

In consequence the American iron and steel master was free to push on with new processes, to remodel and improve organization, to readjust his labor force. In this respect he had an advantage over his British rival. Whatever be one's sympathy with labor organizations, it is not to be denied that a well-entrenched union tends to oppose the introduction of labor saving devices. This attitude is the inevitable consequence of the dependence of laborers on hire by capitalist employers. The first effect of a new machine or a better rearrangement is to displace some laborers or to lower their pay. Moreover, the belief in "making work" is too deep-rooted to permit the installation of improved processes without strong even though silent opposition. The mere existence of a powerful union, — one not to be fought without heavy loss, — has a benumbing influence, checking the very consideration of radical changes and tending to keep industry in its established grooves. Such was and is the influence of the strong organization of the British iron workers (the engineers); it led to struggles and strikes, in which the union, though sometimes beaten, retained a strong position. The American iron makers, themselves men of overmastering temperament, and engaged in an industry where changes were rapid, shook loose from this sort of control. Beyond doubt, they were also induced to adopt a drastic non-union policy by another circumstance; infraction of discipline by the union men and their opposition to discharge of the insubordinate and incompetent. This phase of unionism has shown itself in the United States more than in other countries, the impulse to domination among the employers being matched by the same propensity among their employees. The most friendly observer of the trade-union movement in the American iron trade was compelled to confess the faults of the unionists in this regard.[1] All in all, the defeat of the union movement served to make the iron industry more free and more vigorous, so far as concerns the advance of productive power and the cheapening of the products.

It need not be said that this by no means tells the whole story, or makes a conclusive case for the policy of the iron masters on unionism. The bargaining of the unorganized workmen with a powerful employer resulted in evil conditions, or at least delayed the abolition of evil conditions, more especially as regards the long hours of work. The twelve-hour day and the seven-day week — ugly blots on any industry — were more easily maintained than could have been the case if a strong union had been in the field. No doubt the much-attacked Steel Corporation was not the worst offender. As regards wages, hours, safety, sanitary conditions, it was not usually behind its competitors; more often it was in advance of them; but it set the example of trying to stamp out unionism, and so preventing the men from pressing their claims.

[1] See Fitch, *The Steel Workers*, pp. 102–103.

Even more dubious in its social consequences was another phase of the labor situation, — the condition of the unskilled workers. The very great numbers of these employed in the iron industry were recruited almost exclusively from the newly arrived immigrants. The same is the case in the coal mines and at the coke ovens. Such nationalities as the Italians, the Bohemians, the so-called Huns and Polaks from the Slavonian parts of Austro-Hungary, supplied the men for heavy and dirty work. Needless to say, the iron industry was not peculiar in this regard. All manufacturing industries were profoundly affected by the abundant supply of unskilled laborers willing to work at comparatively low rates of pay.

Nowhere was this influence of a cheap labor force more striking than in the fuel supply. The nature of the operations caused cheapness to be attained at the coal mines and coke ovens, partly indeed by machinery and organization, but largely by cheap labor. The mining of coal is mainly pick-and-shovel work, requiring little handicraft skill or trained intelligence; and this is still more true of the work at the coke ovens. The coal mines of the United States drew to themselves the lowest and poorest kinds of manual labor; except, indeed, where machines for cutting the coal proved applicable, and skilled and intelligent mechanics were consequently called on to work them. The miners in England seem to have maintained a better relative position. Their trade organization has been strong, the standard of living and of efficiency comparatively high. In the United States multitudes of newly arrived immigrants have been drawn to the mines, partly through deliberate arrangement by the employers, partly through the silent adjustment of supply to demand. There they have huddled, — inert, stolid, half-enslaved. The nationalities that have contributed of late years so heavily to our immigration have here found employment such as they could at once turn to. In times of activity their condition is passable. In the periods of depression which recur in the iron trade, the price of coke sinks, production is restricted, wages fall, and the barest living is all that the miners and coke workers can secure, — sometimes not even this. The American or Americanized laborers met a disheartening situation and tried in vain to stem the tide of falling wages and half-employment, with its attendant misery, strikes, bloodshed.

So far as concerns the relation of domestic producers to foreign, the effect of this cheapness of unskilled labor was the same as if labor-saving devices had been introduced for cheapening the heavy work. Not a few mechanical devices were introduced, in the iron trade and elsewhere, for work of this kind, such as steam-shovels, and loading and unloading machinery for vessels. But an immense amount of brute muscular work remained. This would normally be dear in a country of high wages and free opportunities. In such a country one would not expect men to turn to it unless attracted by good pay; and to the employer, as has been already set forth, good pay always presents itself as an obstacle. It might be expected, therefore, that industries in which coarse manual labor is called for would be at a comparative disadvantage in the United States. But the anomalous labor conditions resulting from the influx of immigrants largely removed the employers' obstacle: the labor was and is cheap. Not that it has been as cheap, in terms of money, as in European countries. Humanitarian persons who are shocked by the low wages and evil conditions of our congested immigrant districts sometimes declare that these people are no more prosperous than at home. This is going too far: the fact that they continue to pour in by the hundred thousand, still more that those on the ground steadily send for their relatives and friends, proves that some gain is secured. But only a sort of half-way position is attained, — higher than the European, not so high as the normal American. Whether the well-being of the American people as a whole, or that of humanity as a whole, has been promoted by this social and industrial revolution, is a most intricate question, which need not here be considered. It suffices for the purposes of the present inquiry to point out that common labor has been cheap, measured by American standards, and that the employer needing much of it has not been compelled to bid very high. The result is the same for him, to repeat, as if he had devised effective machinery for doing the work and had in this way secured a comparative advantage.

CHAPTER X

HOW FAR GROWTH WAS DUE TO PROTECTION

AFTER this survey of the growth of the iron industry and of the main factors that have been at work, we are prepared to consider what has been the influence of the protective system.

It will be of service to note at the outset the duties on two typical articles. On pig-iron the rate was, in round numbers, $7.00 per ton from 1870 to 1894; it was $4.00 per ton from 1894 to 1909. On steel rails, the rate was $28.00 per ton from 1870 to 1883; $17.00 from 1883 to 1890; $13.44 from 1890 to 1894; and $7.84 from 1894 to 1909. The duties in force from 1909 to 1913 are of no importance for the present inquiry. Indeed, those imposed in the tariff act of 1897 are not of consequence; for, as will presently appear, the great industrial changes significant for our problems occurred in the period from 1870 to 1897. Throughout that period the duties on both of the articles mentioned, and on all the cruder forms of iron and steel, were specific (by weight), and were highly protective. The duty on steel rails was particularly high, being equivalent to one hundred per cent on the foreign price during most of the time from 1870 to 1883, and from 1883 to 1894 still equivalent to between fifty and eighty per cent.[1]

[1] DUTIES ON PIG-IRON AND ON STEEL RAILS, 1870–1913
(*Per gross ton of 2,240 lbs.*)

	Pig-Iron	Steel Rails
Act of July 14, 1870	$7.00	$28.00
" June 6, 1872	6.30	25.20
" March 3, 1875	7.00	28.00
" March 3, 1883	6.72	17.00
" October 1, 1890 ("McKinley")	6.72	13.44
" August 27, 1894 ("Wilson")	4.00	7.84
" July 24, 1907 ("Dingley")	4.00	7.84
" August 5, 1909 ("Payne-Aldrich")	2.50	3.92
" " 1913	free	free

The war duty on pig-iron had been $9.00 a ton; it was reduced to $7.00 in 1870. Steel rails as a separate item appeared for the first time in 1870. The reductions of duties in 1872 were part of the "horizontal" 10 per cent reduction

The extraordinary growth of the domestic industry has already been described. So far as the increase of domestic production is concerned, the protectionist may well point with pride. If the justification of his policy is to be determined by this test, there can be no question that the history of the American iron trade gives superabundant proof of success. The record indicated by the mounting production of pig-iron is matched in almost every

CHART II

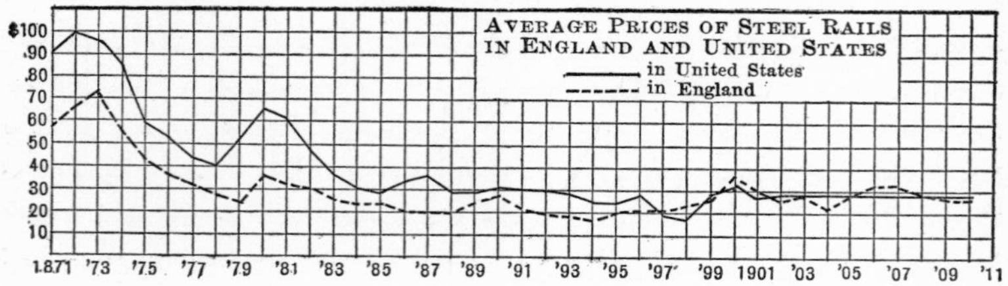

branch of the industry. For steel rails, the other article referred to in the preceding paragraph as typical, we find a growth from no production at all in 1870 to an output of 1,000,000 tons by 1880, of nearly 2,000,000 tons by 1890, and after that one regulated solely by the requirements of the railways. The increase in the domestic product has been enormous.

But not only this: the fall in domestic prices has been unmistakable.

Let the reader glance at the appended chart. It shows the price of steel rails, in Great Britain and in the United States, year by year from 1870 to 1910. For the first twenty-five years of this period, until about 1895, the American price ranged higher than the British. The gap between the two lines is great, and it persists. Prices could not have differed so greatly but for the high duty. Some excess of price in the United States would no doubt have appeared even under free trade, — enough to cover transportation charges. But this very marked excess could not have continued but for the duty. During many of the years between

made on most manufactured articles in that year, repealed in 1875.— For the history of the various tariff acts and the way in which the iron and steel duties were dealt with in them, the reader is referred to my *Tariff History of the United States*.

1870 and 1895 imports of steel rails were considerable, showing that the domestic price was higher than the foreign price by the full amount of the duty. During other years of this period imports ceased; but domestic prices, though not higher by the full amount of the duty, were still considerably higher. Throughout the quarter century the protective duty raised the price of the total supply, whether imported or domestic. The railways were compelled to pay more for their rails, and the public presumably more in rates for the carriage of passengers and freight. Presumably, be it said, for the relation between the cost of constructing railways and the rates charged for railway service is a loose and uncertain one. Steel rails were a cardinal factor, during precisely these years, in enabling railway traffic to be conducted more effectively and charges to be lowered. Probably rates would have been reduced even more had rails been cheaper; but it would be hazardous to reckon how far the tariff system, in keeping up their price, brought a burden on the general public, how far it simply lessened the profits or increased the losses of railway promoters and investors. But this doubt regarding the ultimate incidence of such a tax does not affect the conclusions pertinent for the tariff controversy. For a long time, the purchasers of all rails, domestic or foreign, paid a tax because of the duty on the foreign article.

With the decade 1890–1900, however, and more particularly with the years 1895 and 1896, a change set in. The lines on the chart came together. The American price fell to the level of the British. For a time it even fell appreciably below the British level. In no year since 1895 has it been appreciably above it. Taking the period since 1895 as a whole, the American price has been virtually the same as the British. It has been very steady, — so steady as to point to an agreement of some sort for the maintenance of a price. But, though there may thus be evidence of a combination or trust, the price situation no longer shows any influence of the tariff. Here again the protectionist will point with pride, and this time with pride more clearly justified. The object of protection to young industries, — the ultimate fall in price to the foreign level, — seems to have been attained.

The same general trend would appear on a chart showing the course of pig-iron prices during the same forty years. Such a chart would be less simple, and would need more explanation, than that for steel rails. Grades of pig-iron differ in the two countries; continuous price figures for the significant grades are not easily secured for the entire period; and allowance has to be made for differences of quality. For these reasons, the graphic presentation is most striking in the case of steel rails, whose quality is as homogeneous as can be the case with any commodity and whose prices are on record from the first year of the period to the last. The course of events which thus is sharply defined for rails is typical of what has happened with almost all the cruder forms of iron and steel: extraordinary increase of domestic production; domestic prices at first higher than the foreign; continuance of imports for a while, then their cessation; reduction of the domestic price; finally, equality of price for the foreign and the American products. To repeat, the outcome seems to have been precisely that predicted by the advocates of protection to young industries. True, the term " young industries " is rarely applied to such a giant as the American iron industry. But, as has been pointed out, the contention that protection operates in the end to lower prices is simply the young industries argument in a different turn of phrase.[1] Substantially it is this argument which has been advanced, and which seems to be verified by the actual course of events.

Further details of the changes in the iron trade are shown in the appended tables, giving year by year the domestic product, the imports, the prices of some important grades of iron in the United States and Great Britain. It will be of service to consider not only the general sweep, but some of the details.

The iron industry is peculiarly liable to the periodic fluctuations of modern industry. Indeed, it reflects in the extreme the alternations of activity and depression between which intervene the recurring commercial crises. The explanation of this special sensitiveness is not far to seek. The periodicity of crises is closely associated with the variations in the spirit of investment.

[1] See chapter ii, p. 19, above.

In so-called good times, new enterprises of all sorts are freely launched. In the succeeding periods of dulness, few are undertaken. But investment and fresh ventures in our modern days mean the erection of plant, tools, and machines; and these mean iron and steel. When new and ever new railways formed the main outlet for the investment of the rapidly growing accumulations of savings, it was inevitable that their construction, — rapid in the days of activity, slow and halting in those of depression, — should cause periods now of urgent demand for iron, then of glutted markets. Within the last decade or two the railway has become relatively less important in new investments; but the ever-growing use of iron and steel in buildings, ships, tools and machinery of all kinds, has caused the oscillations in the iron trade to persist. Naturally, these phenomena are accentuated in the United States, where material progress is rapid beyond comparison and where the investment of capital proceeds fast and feverishly. Hence we find that with every rising wave of enterprise and investment the price of iron rises, and its production mounts with sudden rapidity. Then comes the crisis: prices fall, production halts, and a period of depression follows, more or less long according as the conditions for revival appear later or sooner. Not infrequently, the iron industry feels a chill before the commercial storm breaks. A slackening in the launching of new enterprises naturally appears as some among the enterprises already set up begin to weaken under the test of active operation. Hence the maximum production of iron and the highest range of prices for the cycle sometimes come in the year immediately preceding the crash. In 1872–73, it is true, the largest production and the highest price came in the year of the crisis itself, in 1873. Before the disturbances of 1884 and of 1893, however, a relaxation in the rate of output and the beginning of a fall in prices are seen in advance of the general overturn. During the first decade of the present century, no such premonitory symptoms seem to have appeared. The output of pig-iron rose without a check until the crisis of 1903 set in, and even more steadily up to the great crisis of 1907.

A glance at the tables will show, again, that during the earlier part of the period under consideration, — until about 1890, — the imports of pig-iron responded regularly to the increasing demands of the active periods, and fell as regularly during the dull times that followed. Throughout the greater part of the nineteenth century the domestic supply of iron needed to be regularly supplemented by imports; and in the years 1871–72 there was simply a somewhat increased resort to a regular foreign supply. But, as the domestic product became larger, the imports became less and less important, and, except in the years of rising speculation and investment, virtually ceased. It is true that the custom-house returns show continuous and considerable imports throughout the period. But the case is one of those where special qualities continue to be imported, giving no indication of the relation between foreign and domestic prices for the grades chiefly used. Thus in the decade 1870–80, and even later, Scotch pig-iron was imported in considerable quantities, being thought specially adapted for certain kinds of smooth castings, and so bought abroad in the face of a duty which advanced its price beyond that of domestic iron. In later years southern iron was found available for these purposes, and the importation of the Scotch brand ceased. Similarly, spiegel-eisen and ferro-manganese, — classed with the ordinary kinds of pig-iron in the custom-house returns, — continued throughout to be imported in varying quantities. These are used, in comparatively small amounts, solely for mixture with ordinary iron in the last stages of conversion into steel.[1] Setting aside such special cases, imports practically ceased in the dull periods of 1875–78, and again in 1884–85. On the other hand, they revived, and became of considerable volume in the active years 1879–82, and again in the year 1886–87. After this latter period, however, they ceased to come in, even during the periods of activity. The year 1890, when first the American iron product exceeded that of Great Britain, marks also the end of this spasmodic competition. With

[1] The production of these special brands varies greatly, within the country and without, apparently from the sporadic and easily exhausted pockets of the peculiar ore. But the domestic production, on the whole, has been rapidly increasing. See the *Report of the American Iron and Steel Association for 1898*, p. 40.

that year the revolution in the iron trade of the United States was virtually accomplished, and the new stage was entered on.

During the years of activity preceding 1890 — 1872–73, 1879–82, 1886–87 — the price of iron in the United States was at the seaboard higher than the price in Great Britain by the full amount of the duty. This much the fact of importation suffices to prove. At other times iron did not come in, — that is, only certain special qualities came in; and the American price, while higher than the foreign, was not higher by the full amount of the duty. The tables of prices amply verify these statements. In the busy years the difference between American and British prices was large enough to offset duty, freight, and other charges; and imports flowed in. In dull years the margin shrank; and imports ceased, except for the special qualities. Until 1893 the American public had to pay roundly, sometimes the full amount of the duty, sometimes less, but always a very substantial added price, for the eventual gains which might be credited to the protective system.

A precise measurement of this burden has sometimes been attempted. Following the simplest lines of reasoning, it has been argued that the total domestic production, multiplied by the rate of duty, would gauge accurately the added charge on the community.[1] The dangers of the hasty application of deductive reasoning could not be better illustrated than by the comparison of this version of the situation with the facts. Had there been no duty on iron, the price at the seaboard would unquestionably have been lower than it was, — at times by the full amount of the duty, at other times by less. The price in the interior, say at Pittsburgh, also would probably have had a somewhat lower range; but how much lower it is impossible to say. The freight charges from the seaboard would have impeded competition from imported iron, raising the price at which it could then be supplied. The iron output west of the Alleghanies was being made more and more cheaply and sold more and more cheaply, as the years went on; and the free admission of iron, while it might have caused prices to be lower, would at no time after 1882 or 1883 have

[1] See the Appendix to D. A. Wells's *Recent Economic Changes*, pp. 469, 470.

caused a decline in the heart of the country by the full amount of the duty in force. Indeed, in the latter part of this decade — 1888 or 1889 — the price in this region was little higher, if at all, than that at which foreign iron could have been supplied, duty free. And, further, even admitting that domestic prices were much higher than foreign, it is probable that the removal of the duty and the consequent demand on Great Britain for iron would have caused the price of British iron to go up. The level of prices would indeed have been the same in the two countries (allowing for freight and the like); but it would have been higher than the foreign level which in fact prevailed. A great increase in the demand on the British iron masters for iron, consequent on the absence of the American duty and the lessening of American product, might have raised the price in Great Britain, not only temporarily, but over the whole period. During the first decade of the period, say until the year 1880, it is not unlikely that Great Britain could have sent to the United States all the iron that would have been imported there, if free of duty, without such pressure on the British coal and iron mines as to have caused enhanced cost and permanently enhanced prices. But with the extraordinary increase in the American demand after 1880, the additional quantity could not have been supplied from Great Britain except on harder terms. The price of iron in Great Britain would have risen in face of so great an addition to the annual demand, and the common international level would have been somewhat higher than the British price was in the absence of this demand.

A different question concerns the effect of the tariff system, — still during this earlier period, until about 1890, — on the range of the periodic fluctuations. The sources of supply were narrowed. The differences between highest and lowest prices were greater than they would have been without a duty or with lower duties. When a " boom " came, the domestic iron which was on hand, or was obtainable promptly from furnaces in blast, soared in price to the importing level. The abrupt and great rise in price tempted equally abrupt and great increase in the building of new iron furnaces, with the consequence that, when the boom collapsed and the demand fell, a large supply from the increased number of furnaces was on the market, and caused prices to fall as sharply as they had been before sharply raised. This is but an illustration of a simple principle: the wider the range of the sources of supply, the greater the steadiness of prices. Fluctuations of the same general sort there would have been in any case: the price of iron in all the great countries rises and falls in sympathy with general industrial conditions. But interplay between the markets of different countries, under a system of free exchange, would have mitigated in some degree the extent of the oscillations.[1] The extremes were made wider apart in the United States by the protective régime; and so another count is added to the indictment which its opponents may fairly bring against it.

But, to repeat, the protectionist may point with pride to the final outcome. In the end his object was attained: the industry became self-sufficing, needed no further props, eventually supplied its product as cheaply as could be done by the now fairly beaten foreigner.

The uncompromising advocate of free trade has but one reply to make: that the same result would have come about in any case. He may maintain that it is a case of *post hoc ergo propter.* The protectionist assumes that his policy was necessary to bring the iron industry to maturity. No: it would have grown as fast and as far without protection. And this rejoinder is not without show of reason. To weigh its probative force, we must consider again the main factors that have led to the victorious progress of the industry.

The mode in which the great iron ore deposits of Lake Superior were utilized has already been described. The main factor which promoted their development was improved transportation, mak-

[1] That such an interplay would have lessened the fluctuations in prices is made more probable by the fact that the ups and downs of industrial activity are not precisely synchronous in the international sphere. The speculative revival in 1870–73 began in England and on the Continent earlier than in the United States. The American revival in 1879–80, on the other hand, preceded the European, as did also that of 1886–87. In 1889–90 — certainly so far as iron went — the European demand again showed renewed strength earlier than the American; and the same was true in the period 1897–99.

ing rich natural resources available that would have been thought, a generation before, too distant for use. The cheapening in the carriage of ore and coal, however, was simply one phase, — an important one, but by no means a dominant one, — in the general cheapening of carriage by rail and water. The immense area over which free trade was permanently assured, the mechanical genius and commercial enterprise of the people, the possibilities of fortune-building through the exploitation of the great western country, — such were the impelling forces by which the means of transportation were driven to their high stage of efficiency. The protective system can claim no credit for this result. The advance appeared in the apparatus for international trade as well as in that for domestic, and in domestic trade such as would have existed without protection as well as in that fostered by protection. And this was probably the one factor which, acting in conjunction with the great natural resources, counted for most in promoting the growth of the iron industry. Through it that industry in the United States, so far from having to deal with ores of no special excellence and obdurate and limited fuel, was able to bring together unlimited supplies of both materials on easy terms and in perfect quality. How much such easy command of proper materials tells is shown by the growth of the iron manufacture in Alabama and the adjoining southern region. Here the close contiguity of coal and iron caused a great industry to develop in the face of difficult social conditions and of the competition of the strong and comparatively old industry in Pennsylvania. The cheapening of transportation gave Pennsylvania herself the equivalent of contiguous ore and coal, and was the main element in promoting the advance of her iron industry also.

Yet it must be admitted that other causes also had their effect, such as improvements at the mines and at the furnaces and iron works. At the mines, whether deep-worked or open-cut, the organization, the engineering, the machinery became better and better. The ores were systematically sampled and analyzed, their chemical and physical constitution ascertained, and the various kinds carefully assorted for different uses or mixed in the most advantageous combinations. At the iron and steel works the discoveries of applied science were before long systematically turned to account. Forty years ago the blast furnaces and iron works of the United States were behind those of Great Britain in their technology. Matters went much by rule of thumb. The ore and coal and flux were dumped into the furnace, and the product marketed as it chanced to turn out.[1] As time went on, the American works were no longer backward in the application of the best scientific processes. The economies from production on a large scale, — these being partly from the better organization of labor, partly from better technical appliances, — probably were secured more fully in the American establishments than in European. These were improvements in the iron industry itself, such as might be with some reason ascribed to the stimulus given by protective legislation.

Here again, however, we are dealing with causes whose operation was not confined to the iron industry or the protected industries in general. In part, they were of world-wide effect. All countries shared in the advances of the arts and the triumphs of applied science. True, in our own country special industrial excellence was achieved in many directions; but not solely or peculiarly in the protected industries. American mining engineers pushed their art with signal success in coal mines and in mines for the precious metals, as well as in copper and iron mines. No more remarkable achievements were made than in electrical engineering, where a nurturing shelter from foreign competition cannot possibly be supposed to have played a part. An important cause throughout the industrial field was unquestionably the wonderful growth of technical and scientific education. The supply of intelligent and highly trained experts, to whom the management of departments and separate establishments could be intrusted with confidence, facilitated the process of consolidation and the organization on a grand scale of widely ramifying enterprises. It may be a question how far our scientific schools

[1] See an instructive article by J. S. Newberry in the *International Review* for November, 1874, i, especially pp. 778–780, where it is pointed out that at that date " the ingenious, enterprising, and energetic Americans " were still " far outdone by their English relatives."

and institutes of technology have been successful in stirring invention and developing initiative talent. The prime essential for leadership seems to be here, as elsewhere in the intellectual world, inborn capacity. But the rapid spread and complete utilization of the best processes were greatly promoted by them. They were largely instrumental in enabling advantage to be taken of chemical, metallurgical, and mechanical improvements in the iron and steel works. Their influence showed itself no less in the railways, the great commercial and manufacturing plants, the textile works, manufacturing establishments at large. Their influence in permeating all industry with the leaven of scientific training was strengthened by the social conditions which enabled them to attract from all classes the plentiful supply of mechanical talent. Hence American industry showed not only the inventiveness and elasticity characteristic of the Yankee from early days, but that orderly and systematic utilization of applied science in which the Germans have hitherto been — perhaps still are — most successful. The rapid accumulation of ample capital still further facilitated the ready trial and bold adoption of new and better processes.

On such grounds as these it might be alleged that the iron industry would have advanced during the forty years in much the same way, protection or no protection. And yet the unbiased inquirer must hesitate before committing himself to such an unqualified statement of what would have been. Rich natural resources, business skill, improvements in transportation, widespread training in applied science, abundant and manageable labor supply, — these perhaps suffice to account for the phenomena. But would these forces have turned *in this direction* so strongly and unerringly but for the shelter from foreign competition? Beyond question the protective system caused high profits to be reaped in the iron and steel establishments of the central district; and the stimulus from great gains promoted the unhesitating investment of capital on a large scale. During the decade 1880–90 the iron output in the Pittsburgh district and the rest of the central region served by the Lake Superior ores grew from comparatively modest dimensions to independent greatness.

Profits were good in all these years, and were enormous during the periods of active demand in 1880–82 and 1886–87. They continued high in the large and well-provided establishments until the crash of 1893. The mounting output was the unmistakable evidence of profitable investment. Thereafter the community began to get its dividend. Prices fell in the manner already described, and the iron industry entered on its new stage. The same sort of growth would doubtless have taken place eventually, tariff or no tariff; but not so soon or on so great a scale. With a lower scale of iron prices, profits would have been lower; and possibly the progress of investment, the exploitation of the natural resources, even the advance of the technical arts, would have been less keen and unremitting.

No one can say with certainty what would have been; and the bias of the individual observer will have an effect on his estimate of probabilities. The free trader, impatient with the fallacies and superficialities of current protectionist talk, will be slow to admit that there are any kernels of truth under all this chaff. What gain has come, will seem to him a part of the ordinary course of progress. On the other hand, the firm protectionist will find in the history of the iron trade conclusive proof of brilliant success. And very possibly those economists who, being in principle neither protectionists nor free traders, seek to be guided only by the outcome in the ascertained facts of concrete industry, would render a verdict here not unfavorable to the policy of fostering "national industry." Few persons, whether convinced protectionists or thinkers of would-be judicial spirit or plain every-day business men, will be able to resist the appeal to national pride. Mere achievement of the leading place among the world's producers stirs a sense of triumph; just as a victory on the battlefield, even in a dubious cause, kindles the joy of conquest.

The history of the iron industry in Germany during the same period shows similar phenomena and raises almost the same questions. In 1879, when Germany turned from a system not far from complete free trade to one of protection both for manufactures and for agriculture, the iron industry was the center of attention among the manufactures. The duty on pig-iron, previously admitted free, was made 10 marks per ton, with corresponding duties on other forms of iron and steel; not a high rate of protection as things have gone in the United States, yet substantial. During the twenty years after that date, the iron industry of Germany developed in much the same way as the American: rapid increase of domestic production, virtual cessation of imports, decline of domestic prices. By the opening of the twentieth century the German industry, as has already been noted, passed that of England, so far as quantity of output goes; imports became sporadic and comparatively insignificant; exports became large and steady. The decline in prices, it is true, was checked in Germany by the Kartells in the iron trade, and showed itself to the full only during the years when these combinations were not in command of the situation. But there can be no reasonable doubt that domestic cost and competitive domestic price were brought down to a level as low as the British. Moreover, in Germany as in the United States, these results came about in unexpected ways and in consequence of technical improvements whose effect had not been foreseen. What the Bessemer process proved to be for the iron trade of the United States, the Thomas-Gilchrist (or basic) process proved for that of Germany. It made possible the utilization for steel making of the enormous iron ore deposits of Luxemburg-Lorraine, whose high phosphorus content had prevented them from being available for the Bessemer method. The basic process had just been perfected at the time when the protective tariff of 1879 was enacted; but the leading German iron master then declared that it would prove of no advantage to his country's industry. In fact, it proved the making of that industry. Because of it, the Luxemburg ores could be carried in vast quantities, largely by water (the Wesel and Rhine), to the great coal region of the lower Rhine, which became an iron making district comparable in size and influence to that of Pittsburgh. Technical advance in the strictly converting and manufacturing processes took place in Germany at least as rapidly and effectively as in other countries. There, as in the United States, the wide application of exact scientific methods was promoted by the diffusion of technological training; while originating and inventive science progressed in a manner to command the admiration of the world. The German iron industry grew from youth to robust and energetic manhood.[1]

The argument for protection to young industries was put forward more unequivocally in Germany than in the United States. For both countries, it might indeed have been contended that the stage for nurturing protection had been of earlier date and had already been passed by 1870–80; for in both the transition from the comparatively primitive methods of charcoal iron making to the methods of the modern iron trade had been accomplished long before.[2] None the less, there is a *prima facie* case for the protectionist, — again an apparent confirmation of the validity of the young industries argument,— from the nature and extent of the industrial development during the last two decades of the nineteenth century. And yet, for Germany as well as for the United States, the same doubt may be expressed: would not all this growth have taken place in any case? Would not the basic process in Germany (perfected as it was before the duty was put on) have solved in any case the problem how to use the Luxemburg ores? In some respects the question seems to call for an affirmative answer in Germany even more than in the United States; since in Germany not only the great coal supplies but those of ore also were familiarly known, and no exploration for new resources could play a part, as in the case of our own ore

[1] A careful and detailed survey of the development of the German iron industry is given by G. Goldstein, in a series of articles published in the *Verhandlungen des Vereins zur Beförderung des Gewerbefleisses*, Berlin, 1908–09. An excellent brief account, with extracts from the speeches of those who advocated protection to the iron industry because "young," is in the same author's paper, *Der deutsche Eisenzoll; Ein Erziehungszoll, Volkwirtschaftliche Zeitfragen*, Berlin, 1912. On later developments, among them the growing importation of ore, see an article by E. Günther, in Schmoller's *Jahrbuch*, Heft 3, 1914.

[2] Professor M. Sering in his *Geschichte der Preussisch-Deutschen Eisenzölle von 1818 zur Gegenwart* (Schmoller's *Forschungen*, iv) traces the history of protection to iron, with special regard to the period 1840–70, and concludes that in this earlier period there was successful application of protection to young industries; intimating also that the German iron industry was well on its feet when he wrote (1882) and that there was no good ground for duties as high as those enacted in 1879. Compare, for the United States before the civil war, what I have said in my *Tariff History of the United States*, pp. 123 *seq.*

deposits on Lake Superior. And would not German science, and German methodical application of science, have pursued the same forward course; would not the same spirit of victorious enterprise have led to the upbuilding of great manufacturing industries?

To such questions no certain answers can be given. It is impossible to prove which is the right solution of the economic problem. To reach anything like a well grounded conclusion would call for a consideration of all the causes of economic progress; and this in turn for a consideration of progress of every kind, intellectual, moral, political. What has brought about the extraordinary industrial advance of Germany since the war of 1870? the no less extraordinary advance of the United States since our civil war? Those whose attention is centered on the protective controversy invariably ascribe too much to this one factor. They fail to perceive that the phenomena are large and complex. I am disposed, for myself, to believe that other factors were much more important than the protective tariffs of either country; not only the other economic factors which have been described in the preceding pages as regards the United States, but all the influences of the social environment. In both countries, and especially in Germany, the spirit of industrialism and capitalism permeated the community as never before. The spirit of boldness engendered by great victorious wars may be fairly supposed to have had its part in stimulating boldness in the conquests of peace also.[1] If it is difficult in the highest degree to

[1] I venture to reprint here some passages from my presidential address of 1904 before the American Economic Association, on the "Present Position of the Doctrine of Free Trade," *Papers and Proceedings of the Seventeenth Annual Meeting*, pp. 54 *seq.*

"Not only the spirit of freedom and enterprise within the community has its effect, but that spirit with reference to other communities also. The political position of a country and its martial success seem to have a reflex effect on the industrial success of its citizens in time of peace.

"Here the recent development of Germany is apposite. Her industrial advance during the last thirty years [1870–1900] is one of the striking phenomena of our time, and leads naturally to speculation as to its causes. No doubt these causes are varied, as in all such cases. The thorough organization of popular education and of scientific education is one cause. The stimulating effect of free trade within the country, as established by the Zollverein since 1834, is another: though

measure with precision the effects of the strictly economic factors, such as the protective tariff, how much more difficult is it to gauge those of the great underlying social and spiritual forces !

Discussions like these bear on still another general topic, one which has much engaged the attention of economists: the method of investigation appropriate for their subject, and more particularly the extent to which historical and statistical inquiry can contribute to the elucidation of principles. The economists of Ricardo's school were wont to say that a conclusion as to the effects of protection could be reached only by deductive reasoning, such as was commonly used by them. John Stuart Mill, in his statement of the method proper in the social sciences, treated this

this gain had been enjoyed by France throughout the nineteenth century, and by England for centuries before. Much is due to the whole change in the political and social atmosphere which came with the crumbling of petty absolutism, and which was consummated with the foundation of the German Empire. But to all this must be added the new spirit which came over the country after the war of 1870. Germany emerged from the conflict with a new sense of strength and confidence. The new feeling communicated itself to the field of peaceful industry. Vigor, enterprise, and boldness showed themselves. Large enterprises in new fields were launched and successfully conducted, and great captains of industry came to the fore. A spirit of conquest in all directions seems to have spread through the people, bred or at least nurtured by the great military conquest of the Franco-German war.

" Is it fanciful to suppose that consequences of the same sort have appeared in other countries also after victorious wars ? England emerged from the Napoleonic wars with a great feeling of pride and power. She alone had never yielded to the great conqueror. The period which followed was that of her most sure and rapid economic advance. She then established the hegemony in the industry of the civilized world which she maintained through the century. The northern part of the United States, after the civil war, felt a similar impulse. That struggle had been on a greater scale than was dreamed of at the outset, and its outcome proved the existence of unexpected power and resource. It is probably no accident that the ensuing years showed a spirit of daring in industry, and sudden and successful activity in commercial enterprises.

" No one is more opposed than I am to all that goes with war and militarism. It is with reluctance that I bring myself to admit that the same spirit which leads to success in war, may also lead to success in the arts of peace. Yet so it seems to be. Men being what they are, nothing rouses them so thoroughly as fighting. The temper which then pervades a community, communicates itself by imitation and emulation, and shows itself in all the manifestations of its activity. A great war lifts the minds of men to large undertakings, and takes its place with other factors in stimulating the full exercise of the powers of every individual."

problem as a typical one, and set forth the difficulties of disentangling the effects of tariff policy from those of other forces operating on a country's prosperity.[1] But in our own time, Professor Schmoller has questioned the validity alike of the general theorem and of the particular example. Attentive examination of the industrial policy and history of this or that country, he maintains, may show whether or no protective duties serve to promote prosperity.[2] Is any aid on the question of method to be got from the present inquiry as to the duties on iron in the United States?

Certainly the statistical and historical material is here as complete as it could possibly be made. The elaborate reports of the British and American Iron Associations, the publications of the Geological Survey, the detailed customs statistics, the extensive technical literature, supply information as full and detailed as the economist can hope to secure. If ever the inductive method is applicable, here is an opportunity.

The argument for protection to young industries has been considered in this volume on the assumption that the immediate effect of protection is to cause a national loss, — one measured, in the simplest case, by the volume of domestic production multiplied by the rate of duty. That loss, it has been argued, may be offset by gain at a later stage; at the outset, however, a loss there is. But as has already been noted,[3] the stanch protectionist will deny this *in toto*. There never is a loss. The community is richer from the start. True, the prices of the articles taxed may

[1] J. S. Mill, *Essays on some Unsettled Questions of Political Economy*, p. 148; see also his *System of Logic*, Book VI, ch. vii, §§ 2, 3, 4.

[2] In the article "Volkswirthschaft" in the *Handwörterbuch der Staatswissenschaften*, reprinted in the volume *Ueber einige Grundfragen* (1898), Mill is referred to as trying to prove his theorem "with the inept example [*groben Beispiele*] that the general inquiry, whether a system of protection makes a country rich, can lead to no result. He fails to see that he puts his question wrongly; *i. e.*, in terms too general. Specialized investigations, such as Sering's on the German iron duties, Sombart's on the tariff policy of Italy, and others of recent times, show that inquiries which examine properly the facts in detail may prove, with reasonable certainty, when protective duties operate to promote prosperity." *Ueber einige Grundfragen*, p. 296. Cf. what Schmoller says in his *Grundriss*, ii, Book IV, especially pp. 647 *seq.* (1st edition).

[3] Chapter ii, p. 27.

for a while be higher. But a home market springs into being at once, capital previously idle finds employment, a demand for labor is created, the rate of wages is maintained at a high level. No doubt, all such familiar disquisition will be set aside summarily by the person severely trained in economics. It belongs to the A B C of the subject; and the proper place for its discussion is the elementary class-room. No doubt, too, the reasoning on which we conclude that there is a national loss is in its essence very simple. It is but a common-sense application of the principle of the division of labor, a simple corollary from an analysis of the gains from the geographical distribution of industry, and perhaps a platitude not to be dignified as "deductive reasoning." And yet, when we meet the protectionist on his own ground, this platitude leads to some reasoning by no means of the simplest sort. Is an additional market really created by protection ? Is there employment for idle capital, or only transfer of capital previously employed ? Is the rate of wages made high or kept high ? The reader who has followed the voluminous economic literature which German scholarship has piled up in recent years meets not infrequently the contention in favor of *Schutz der nationalen Arbeit.* Yet often he is left in doubt just how and why national labor is to be shielded by protection, — whether for preventing sudden shifts in the historically rooted industries of a slow-moving people, or for elevating the condition of labor in the whole country. Or, to take another example, it is often set forth, in the same quarters, that the burdens which the great social legislation of Germany imposes on her employers must be offset by duties on the products of competing foreign employers, — a proposition to which the stanch protectionist would unhesitatingly assent. But, if this be a good ground for compensating duties, why is not a general higher range of wages also a good ground, or any other condition unfavorable to the employer, — *e. g.*, high income or property taxes, or poorer natural advantages ? To answer these questions, some severe reasoning is called for: plain common-sense, unsupported by sustained argument from principle, does not suffice. The most exhaustive statistical and historical inquiries, on the extent of the home market, the situation of domestic labor, the amount of the burdens on the employer, can lead us to no secure result until we have not only grasped, but followed into all its ramifications, the main conclusions concerning the effects on national prosperity of the new direction of the productive forces brought about by tariff restrictions.

Similarly, our statistical inquiry on the American iron industry can lead us directly to no conclusion on the old and perhaps stale dispute on protection and free trade. The initial question — is there a national loss because of the higher price of the dutiable article ? — cannot be answered from facts and figures. So far Mill and his associates were right. The effects of protection on national prosperity cannot be discerned by examining, however laboriously and critically, the facts either as to the prosperity of the community at large or as to the growth of protected industries.

If, indeed, this much be settled, — if the conclusion here assumed with regard to the general principle be accepted, — then the next stage in the inquiry assumes a different form. Professor Schmoller has remarked that inductive and deductive reasoning are as indispensable each to the other as the right foot in walking is to the left.[1] For the particular sort of economic problem here under consideration the analogy holds perfectly. A long step forward must first be taken by deduction alone, — that is, by reasoning from premises established through very simple observation. But thereafter both laborious digging at the facts and their critical interpretation in the light of familiar premises must proceed side by side. Even so, as has just been remarked, there may be almost insuperable difficulty in the way of reaching a firmly-grounded result. And in any case, for the settlement of the underlying questions of principle we are still compelled to rely mainly on general reasoning from simple premises.

[1] *Grundfragen*, p. 293.

TABLE I

PRODUCTION, IMPORTS, EXPORTS OF PIG-IRON, 1870–1912[1]

Calendar Year	Production	Imports	Exports
1870	1,665,179		
1871	1,706,793	219,228	2,097
1872	2,548,713	264,256	1,329
1873	2,560,963	138,132	9,092
1874	2,401,262	54,612	14,320
1875	2,023,733	74,939	7,864
1876	1,868,961	74,171	3,424
1877	2,066,594	59,697	6,918
1878	2,301,215	66,504	2,957
1879	2,741,853	304,171	1,153
1880	3,835,191	700,864	1,886
1881	4,144,254	465,031	6,207
1882	4,623,323	540,159	5,620
1883	4,595,510	322,648	3,798
1884	4,097,868	184,269	3,870
1885	4,044,526	146,740	6,277
1886	5,683,329	361,768	8,919
1887	6,417,148	467,522	6,850
1888	6,489,738	197,237	14,489
1889	7,603,642	148,759	13,681
1890	9,202,703	134,955	16,471
1891	8,279,870	67,179	14,946
1892	9,157,000	70,125	15,427
1893	7,124,502	54,394	24,587
1894	6,657,388	15,582	24,482
1895	9,446,308	53,232	26,164
1896	8,623,127	56,272	62,071
1897	9,652,680	19,212	262,686
1898	11,773,934	25,152	253,057
1899	13,620,703	40,372	228,678
1900	13,789,242	52,565	286,687
1901	15,878,354	62,930	81,211
1902	17,821,307	619,354	27,487
1903	18,009,252	599,574	20,379
1904	16,497,033	79,500	49,025
1905	22,992,380	212,466	49,221
1906	25,307,191	379,828	83,317
1907	25,781,361	489,475	73,703
1908	15,936,018	92,202	46,696
1909	25,795,471	176,442	62,989
1910	27,303,567	237,233	127,385
1911	23,649,547	148,459	120,799
1912	29,726,937	129,325	272,676

[1] The figures are derived from the American Iron and Steel Association Reports. They are for gross tons (2,240 lbs.) For later figures see p. 404.

TABLE II

PRICES OF PIG-IRON IN THE UNITED STATES AND IN GREAT BRITAIN, 1873-1912[1]

Year	Gray forge Pittsburgh (U. S.)	Cleveland (Great Britain)	Bessemer Pittsburgh (U. S.)	West Coast Bessemer (Great Britain)
1873	$35.80	$27.95		
1874	27.16	18.13		
1875	23.67	14.61		
1876	21.74	12.86		
1877	20.60	11.06		
1878	18.09	10.28		
1879	22.15	10.02		
1880	27.98	12.26		
1881	22.94	9.47		
1882	23.84	10.58		
1883	19.04	9.55		
1884	17.17	8.87		
1885	15.27	7.99		
1886	16.58	7.43	$18.96	$10.60
1887	19.02	8.27	21.37	11.22
1888	15.99	7.93	17.38	10.86
1889	15.37	10.60	18.00	12.68
1890	15.78	11.64	18.85	13.80
1891	14.06	9.76	15.95	11.80
1892	12.81	9.33	14.37	12.04
1893	11.77	8.45	12.87	11.18
1894	9.75	8.67	11.38	11.06
1895	10.94	8.77	12.72	11.30
1896	10.39	9.96	12.14	11.96
1897	9.03	10.52	10.13	12.26
1898	9.18	10.82	10.33	13.24
1899	16.72	14.68	19.03	16.63
1900	16.90	16.70	19.50	19.13
1901	14.20	11.00	15.90	14.25
1902	19.50	11.95	20.65	14.45
1903	17.50	11.25	19.00	13.80
1904	12.90	10.65	13.75	13.00
1905	15.60	12.00	16.35	14.70
1906	18.20	12.90	19.55	16.40
1907	21.50	13.65	22.85	18.05
1908	15.25	12.30	17.10	14.50
1909	15.55	12.00	17.40	14.10
1910	15.25	12.25	17.20	15.90
1911	13.97	11.60	15.70	15.35
1912	14.54	14.20	15.95	17.80

[1] The figures are derived from American Iron and Steel Association Reports. and from British periodicals. They give the prices of two grades of iron which are fairly comparable in the two countries,—foundry iron and Bessemer iron. For later figures see p. 403.

CHAPTER XI

COPPER

The present chapter makes a digression. We leave for the moment the history of the iron industry and turn to copper. Yet there is no digression as regards the sequence of thought. The course of events in the copper trade serves to illustrate further what was said in the preceding chapter concerning the difficulty of proving whether protection has been applied with success to a young industry, and to show the need of discrimination in the interpretation of historical and statistical data.

The duties on copper received little attention during the greater part of the period covered in this volume. But during some of the earlier years they were much discussed. Their history centers about the act of 1869, by which for the first time a considerable protective duty was imposed. Before the civil war copper in bars or pigs was subject to a nominal duty only — 5%; copper ore was free. During the war the duty on copper was raised to two and one-half cents a pound, copper ore being subjected to the nominal duty of 5%. The act of 1869 imposed a duty of five cents a pound on copper, and, what was quite as important, one of three cents a pound on the copper content of imported ores. The measure was frankly protective, and in accord with the general drift of the time. Congress was then extending and stiffening the high duties for which the exigencies of the civil war had given occasion. The copper bill was vetoed by President Johnson, but passed over his veto, being aided in its passage by the bitter contest between the President and the dominant Republicans. The duties then established remained in effect without change until 1883. In that year they were reduced slightly, the rate on copper being fixed at four cents. In the McKinley act of 1890 a sharp reduction was made, — one so considerable as to mark a turning point: the duty on copper was fixed at one and one-quarter cents, that on the copper content of ore at one-half cent. The act of 1894, as might have been expected, went still farther, and admitted copper in all forms free of duty. Thereafter it remained free. The effective protection was thus maintained for about twenty years, from 1869 to 1890. That the process of reduction should have been carried so far in the protectionist act of 1890 indicated that even at this comparatively early date the duty was felt to be of little consequence. Whatever effects, good or bad, are traceable to the copper duty must be searched for in the period before 1890.

Turning now to domestic production, we find a plain and uncheckered situation: rapid and continuous growth. In 1869 the domestic output was 28 millions of pounds; in 1880, about 60 millions; in 1890, after a decade with an unparalleled rate of growth, 265 millions. After 1890 the advance continued year by year; and in 1910, the annual output exceeded 1,000 millions of pounds. The United States had become the greatest copper producing country in the world. So far as concerns the growth of domestic production, the apparent success of the protectionist policy is so extraordinary as to suggest at once the need of cautious interpretation: the figures on their face seem to prove too much.

Not only was there this vast increase in domestic output: exports set in early and soon reached great dimensions. Some slight imports continued for a few years after 1869, insignificant as compared with the home product. About 1880 exports began; fostered for a time (as will presently be explained) by a "dumping" policy on the part of the copper producers, but rapidly passing beyond this semi-artificial stage, and developing as normal exports. By the middle of the decade, 1880–90, they attained each year dimensions considerable in comparison with the output, — 10 per cent and more. After the changes of duty in 1890 and 1894, and especially after the removal of all duties in the latter year, the course of international dealings became radically different from what it had been before. A larger and larger proportion of the mounting domestic product was sold in foreign countries, until by the close of the century the foreign consumption exceeded the domestic. Copper became one of the leading articles of export from the United States. At the same time, with the complete abolition of duties, a large transit trade developed. Copper was imported both in the form of ore and of bars, and then reëxported. The great smelting and refining establishments handled both domestic and imported ore. All in all, the United States became the dominant country in the world's copper markets. In no branch of industry has American progress been more great or rapid, in none has the " American invasion " been more spectacular.

The course of prices was such as must be expected with a development of this sort. The chart on page 164 tells the story at a glance.[1] For the first decade after the imposition of the duty in 1869 the price of copper in New York was higher than the price in London, the difference being usually the amount of the duty, — not far from five cents a pound. In other words, the ordinary effect of a protective duty appeared. During the next decade there was unstable equilibrium: the American price was at times somewhat higher than the British, at times lower, but with no divergence at all equal to the duty (four cents under the act of 1883). And in the next decade, all difference in price ceased. Even before the complete abolition of the duty (1894) domestic and foreign prices became virtually the same. After 1894 they necessarily moved together.

The chart has every feature of what might be called a representative young industries chart. So far as concerns the relation between domestic and foreign prices, it is precisely like the chart showing the course of steel prices abroad and at home.[2] For a few years after the imposition of the copper duty, domestic price is raised by the full amount of the duty. As time goes on, domestic price falls nearer and nearer to the level of the foreign, until finally all difference ceases. The American consumer in the end gets his copper quite as cheaply as if it were imported.

[1] I am indebted for the preparation of this chart to Mr. E. P. Coleman, Jr., who investigated the copper industry under my guidance while an undergraduate in Harvard College.

[2] See p. 140, above.

CHART III

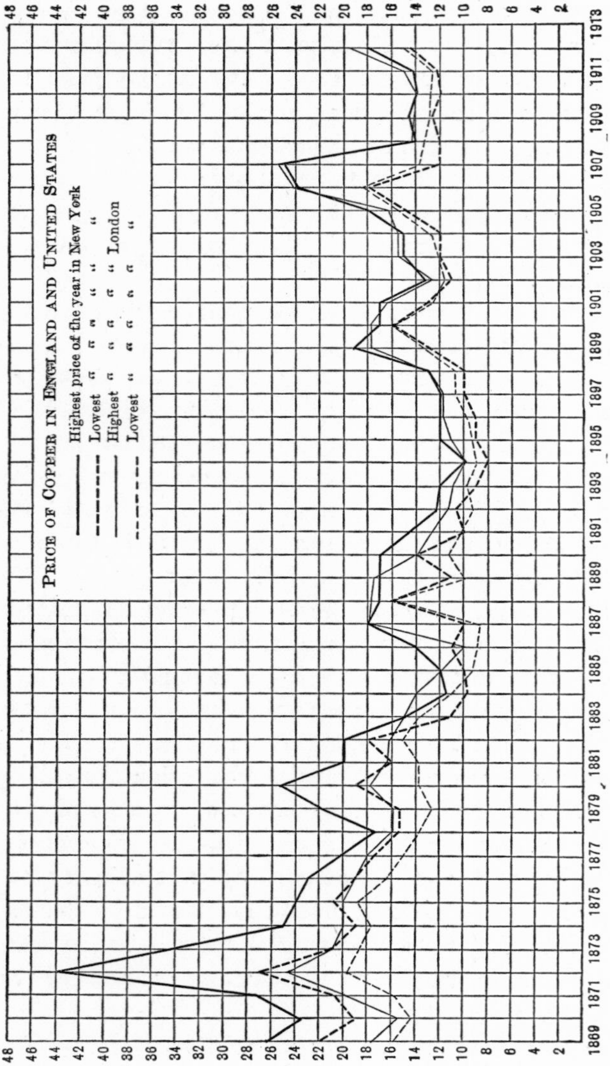
PRICE OF COPPER IN ENGLAND AND UNITED STATES
Highest price of the year in New York
Lowest " " " " " "
Highest " " " " " London
Lowest " " " " " "
48 46 44 42 40 38 36 34 32 30 28 26 24 22 20 18 16 14 12 10 8 6 4 2
1869 1871 1873 1875 1877 1879 1881 1883 1885 1887 1889 1891 1893 1895 1897 1899 1901 1903 1905 1907 1909 1911 1913

Moreover, in this instance the consummation was reached promptly, and the abolition of the protective duty also came promptly. The other data seem to be confirmatory: there is rapid and great increase of production, displacement of imports, complete independence of foreigners. The protectionists may be expected to point with pride to this record.

Yet in fact the case has rarely been cited by the protectionists; partly perhaps because of alleged monopoly and manipulation on the part of the domestic producers, but chiefly because the not unfamiliar history of the industry shows that the tariff in reality was of little consequence. The extraordinary progress of the industry was obviously due to the discovery and exploitation of great natural resources, — resources so rich and so tempting that the same effects on production, prices, and international trade would have come about, whatever the rates of duty.

Three episodes stand out: the development of the copper mines in the Michigan peninsula, the discoveries in Montana, those in Arizona and the southwest. These are significant for the tariff situation in their chronological order. Indeed, the earliest (the Michigan case) is the only one in which some influence from the duties might be sought with any show of plausibility.

That there were rich deposits of copper in the now famous peninsula of Michigan had long been known; the distribution of the "native" copper among distant Indian tribes had early attracted the attention of travelers and ethnologists. Some appreciable production of copper from this source took place before the civil war. Whatever copper was then produced in the country came from the Michigan region; and it remained virtually the only source of supply until the decade 1880–90. The remoteness of the peninsula, its dense primeval forests, the rigorous winter climate, stood in the way of systematic exploitation with large capital outlay.

That stage was reached in the middle of the decade 1860–70. There had been a steady increase in the Michigan output during the first half of that decade; then came a sudden burst. The renowned Calumet & Hecla mine was opened in 1866, and began almost at once to turn out great quantities of copper.

The story of Calumet & Hecla is typical, and not so simple as is implied in most versions and allusions. It was by no means a case of treasure-trove, — a pile of riches uncovered at a stroke and easily turned to account. The mine proved indeed to contain the best deposits in the district; but before this was ascertained, heavy investments had to be made and great risks taken. Many persons refer to copper mining, and especially to a famous mine like the Calumet & Hecla, as if it were a mere matter of digging out of the ground shining lumps of pure vendible copper. The metal in fact is obtained by working over vast quantities of hard copper-bearing rock brought up from great depths; the interior must be carefully explored, developed, preserved from caving in; expensive hoisting apparatus must be installed, with crushing machinery, water supply, a railway for carrying the rock to the water, and so on. The whole calls for heavy investment and for great initial risks. Even in this case, where handsome returns came in at a comparatively early stage, there were several years of uncertainty, of false starts and ill-devised apparatus, of imminent failure. Had it not been for the extraordinary energy, courage, technical and administrative ability, of the younger Agassiz, and the unflinching persistence of his associates — they staked their all — the venture would have been not phenomenally profitable, but utterly disastrous. How far under such circumstances, a fortune, if it finally comes, can be said to be earned, or in what measure successes are offset by failures, prizes in the lottery by blanks, — this is one of the problems of economic principle and economic policy to which it is most difficult to give an answer in precise terms.[1]

But the particular question here under consideration can be answered with ease and certainty. It is not the question whether mining enterprises in general, with their need of great investment and assumption of heavy risks, do or do not come within the scope of the young industries argument. There may be some

[1] See the vivid account of the enterprise in the *Letters and Recollections of Alexander Agassiz*, chapter iv. On the general significance of risk, especially in metalliferous mines, compare Einaudi, *La Rendita Mineraria*, § 13, pp. 47 *seq.*, and Taussig, *Principles of Economics*, chapter xliv, ii, pp. 92 *seq.*

ground for maintaining as a matter of general reasoning that, even though minerals be classed as "raw materials," the essential reasons for giving aid to nascent industries still hold. In this instance, however, it appears that the young industry was started and was being actively prosecuted before protection was applied. The decisive experiments and investments were made in 1867–68; by 1868 success was in sight; dividends on Calumet & Hecla began in 1869 and thereafter were continuous and generous. And it must be remembered that this mine never stood alone. Though the largest and most conspicuous in the Michigan group, it was not the earliest, nor the only one amply profitable. The production of copper in the peninsula was already considerable when the Calumet & Hecla mine began, and continued to grow from various other mines as well. The duty of 1869 clearly was superfluous as a device for encouraging ventures still in the experimental stage.[1]

During the decade 1870–80, as has just been pointed out, the price of copper in the United States was higher than the English price, and during a considerable part of the decade it was higher by the full extent of the duty. There being no ground for giving any credit to protection because of its having given needed aid to a young industry, the free trader can find nothing to balance the loss then caused to the community by the tariff charge. And for a year or two at the close of this period he adds something to his indictment; the charge on the community was made higher by

[1] The following figures, giving in round numbers the production of copper, indicate what was the position of the Michigan mines in 1860–80. For comparison I have given figures for later years also. By 1890 Michigan had lost its dominant position among the copper producing districts; the discoveries in Montana and Arizona (to mention the chief) completely changed the situation.

Copper Produced (*in millions of pounds*)

	Calumet and Hecla	Total in Michigan	Total in United States			
1860	..	12	16			
1870	14	26	28			
1880	32	51	60			
			Montana	Arizona	Utah	Total United States
1890	60	100	112	34	...	260
1900	78	142	270	116	19	606
1910	73	220	283	297	125	1,080

combination among the copper producers. The mining companies of Michigan then produced almost all the American copper; price agreements among them were not difficult to arrange; the increasing output caused prices to fall, especially during the years of depression that followed 1873. In 1879–81 there was a combination, and an abrupt rise in prices, — the latter furthered of course by the revival of industrial activity. To maintain prices at home, the combinations sold for export at lower prices. It was a clear case of dumping, explicable on the theory of monopoly price. As it happened, the combination found itself plagued unexpectedly by the return to the United States of part of the copper which had been sold abroad at the low export price: the domestic price soared so much that it proved profitable to bring back some of this copper and sell it in the United States even after paying duty. The whole train of events serves to illustrate both the ordinary operation of protective duties and those concomitants which appear when the protected producers combine. It has to do with the young industries argument only in showing how completely the domestic copper industry had passed the experimental stage to which this plea for protection is applicable.

The later development of copper production in the United States stands even further apart from any connection with the tariff, and hence may be dismissed briefly. In the decade 1880–90 Montana became an important producer, and very shortly the greatest producer; the Anaconda mine being as conspicuous in this state as Calumet & Hecla was in Michigan. Here again there was economic exploit almost romantic in character: discoveries, risks (including Indian fights), bold investments, great fortunes. Before long a similar course of events set in at another far distant locality, in Arizona, where still further copper resources of vast extent were discovered and developed. They made certain the American command of the industry, and contributed their quota of American fortunes. And in recent years the remarkable development of porphyry mining in the southwest, — Arizona, Utah, Nevada, — has added another chapter of the same sort. There are economic problems in plenty through all this remarkable episode in economic history. As in Michigan, there were great risks, heavy investments, intricate questions of mine management and mine engineering, the dominance of forceful personalities, — conquests almost Napoleonic. Thus the same question of prizes and blanks arises. How far were private enterprise and the prospect of riches indispensable for industrial advance? Other problems are more peculiar to the later western episodes. The speculative character of copper mining led to product gambling and stock gambling, to dubious episodes like the flotation of the Amalgamated Copper Company. Looking over the long-run course of events, one finds a general, even though very irregular, response of supply to demand. The growth of electrical industries has caused an enormous increase in the demand for copper. To this on the whole the supply has responded; so that, notwithstanding occasional violent fluctuations, the trend of prices, if the occasional flare-ups be disregarded, has shown no such marked rise as might have been expected from the changed conditions of demand.

But all this serves to show once more that the main problems, interesting enough to the economist, lie outside the protective controversy. The only direction in which light could be got on the tariff question is in the possible applicability of the argument for aiding young industries. And here the result is simply negative. The case has only a sort of methodological significance. The fact that an industry has developed after protection was applied does not prove that it developed *because* protection was applied. The course of copper prices and copper production is just such as one would expect in an example of successful protection to a young industry; yet it is clear that in this instance the same results would have ensued if there had been no duties at all. The extraordinary richness of the natural resources; the prospect of fortunes in return for daring, persistence, able management; the achievements of American mining engineers, — these quite suffice to explain the great development which has taken place. It follows that one must be cautious in other cases also; in that of the iron and steel industry, for example, considered in the preceding chapter. To eliminate protection as a *vera causa* may not be so easy as in the case of copper. But the evidence must be scanned critically. Only in the rarest instances can the economist prove beyond cavil his conclusions on any concrete question of public policy. He must compare, weigh, discriminate, judge; and the need of discrimination could hardly be better illustrated than by this example from the copper tariff.

CHAPTER XII

PROTECTION AND COMBINATIONS. STEEL RAILS; TIN PLATE

We return now to the iron and steel industry, and take up the question of the connection between the tariff and the trusts. The growth and influence of combination have been no less conspicuous in the iron and steel industry than in sugar refining. Here also it is to be asked whether the protective system promoted combination and monopoly, or increased the profits of combination.

So far as the Steel Corporation itself is concerned, it can hardly be said that combination was promoted by the tariff. In this regard the case is different from sugar refining, where there is tenable ground for maintaining that the very formation of the trust was fostered by the sugar differential. The Steel Corporation was not formed until after the period when the tariff was of vital consequence for the iron and steel industry. It came after the depression of the closing years of the nineteenth century, when prices had fallen almost dramatically and when the independence of the American industry had become an accomplished fact. It was proximately the result of competition, feared to be of ruinous effect, among the domestic producers themselves. The great consolidation was expected not only to obviate such competition, but to carry still further the economies in production which had already been secured by the constituent integrated enterprises. Though the tariff may have been the mother of the sugar trust, it had no such relation to the steel trust.

A different question is whether the tariff increased the profits of the consolidated industry; and still different is the question whether among the constituent corporations united in the Steel Corporation there may not have been incitements to combination, as well as increased profits, from the tariff. Two typical cases will serve to show what answers can be given to these questions: that of steel rails, already considered in its bearing on the young industries argument; and that of tin plate. The latter, as it happens, suggests in its turn the young industries problem: was it nurtured to success through tariff aid?

In the steel rail branch of the industry, pools and price agreements were common during the earlier period, from 1870 to about 1900. They had the same checkered history as pooling arrangements in manufacturing industries at large. They were held intact with comparative ease in years of activity and rising demand, but collapsed in times of depression.

A formal pool (the Steel Rail Association) was established early and was maintained until 1893, though with breaks and with the quarrels over allotments which always appear under such combinations. In 1893 it went to pieces, but was shortly reëstablished, and kept in working effect until 1897. Then, under the cumulative influence of long-continued depression, it broke down completely. A couple of years of fierce cut-throat competition followed, prices collapsing beyond precedent. But in 1899 the pool was again set up, and was maintained until 1901, when the Steel Corporation was formed and the new stage was reached by the iron and steel industry at large.[1]

Hence the decline in the price of steel rails which has been already considered did not take place by gradual steps spread over a considerable period; in other words, did not take place in the manner to be expected in case of a commodity produced under continuously competitive conditions. It came through a series of sudden drops, following the collapses of the successive pools. For years at a time, the price was kept by combination at figures extremely profitable. It is not to be doubted that the retention of a duty heavy enough to keep out foreign competitors invited and aided combination. It thus served to swell the profits of the rail makers, and especially of those among them

[1] Accounts of the steel rail pools of this earlier period are to be found in the *Iron Age*, November 16, 1893; February 11, 1897; January 1, 1901. On the general prevalence of such agreements in the iron and steel trade see Belcher, "Industrial Pooling Agreements," in *Quarterly Journal of Economics*, xix, p. 111 (1904).

who were foremost in organization and technical advance. The decade from 1880 to 1890 was the golden period for the leading iron and steel manufacturers. Profits all around were high; those in rail making were enormous. All this is part of the price which the public had to pay for the gains, real or supposed, from protection to the young industry. The free trader is justified in saying that the initial burden, serious even if tempered by domestic competition (as is implied in the young industries argument), was made needlessly and indefensibly high by monopolistic combination.

With the opening of the twentieth century, however, and the advent of the Steel Corporation, the situation changed. Some effect of combination on the price of steel rails persisted; but did not appear in the same way as before. The influence of the tariff in raising prices and fostering combination virtually ceased.

As our price chart [1] indicates, steel rails were sold after 1902 at the unchanging price of $28.00 a ton. No sensible person will believe that the price could be held at this precise figure, without a variation from month to month or from year to year, except through the abrogation of competitive bidding. For several years after the formation of the Steel Corporation, there was a firmly organized pool, with allotted percentages of output and with money payments to offset variations from those percentages.[2] As time went on, this close-knit form of combination was given up; doubtless in pursuance of the avowed and sincere desire of the Corporation to "be good" and to conform to the federal statute. A loose understanding was substituted, probably not such as to constitute a violation of the Sherman act, but sufficient to maintain the same unvarying price.[3]

[1] See the chart on p. 140.

[2] See for example the testimony in the government suit of 1912–13 against the Steel Corporation, *Transcript of Record*, pp. 1674–1681. There was apparently no written agreement, but all the essentials of a pool. An arbitrary figure ($17 or $18 a ton) was fixed, presumably an approximation to prime cost; everything received above this by each member was paid to a representative of the pool, who divided the money among the members according to fixed allotments. This arrangement was kept up until 1904, possibly even to a later date.

[3] See the testimony in the Steel Corporation suit, pp. 92, 337.

The steady price maintained under these conditions[1] was not, however, higher than the foreign price. So much is shown on the chart: the two series went to virtually the same level, and remained, on the whole, in the same relative positions. British prices of rails were more irregular than American prices, and therein showed the effect of the higgling of the market; but they were, as a rule, no lower. The price in the United States may have been an unduly high one, — high, that is, compared with domestic cost of production and with the price that would have ruled under free competition. On this point there is some evidence, presently to be considered, from the fact that rails were sold for export at lower prices than those paid by domestic consumers.[2] But such discrimination has nothing to do with the immediate tariff question, — the relation between foreign and domestic prices. If the domestic price is as low as the foreign, the tariff has ceased to be an operative cause. The stage where it ceased to be operative was reached, so far as steel rails are concerned, by the opening years of the century.

It is not within the scope of the present volume to consider the problems of combination; but a word may be said on one aspect, suggested by the even course of the steel rail price since 1902. Beyond question the influence of the Steel Corporation was exerted toward maintaining the unvarying price, and beyond question this was part of a large general policy. The guiding spirits of the Corporation endeavored deliberately to lessen the ups and downs of the iron and steel trade; to prevent prices from soaring in times of active demand and from sinking abruptly in the ensuing periods of depression. That policy was sought to be applied to all the forms of crude iron and steel, and showed its

[1] The steadiness of price was not in reality so complete as the chart, based on the "official" quotations, would indicate. During 1903 there was heavy demand for steel rails, and the mills were unable to fill the orders that poured in from the railroads. The contract price remained $28.00, but not for prompt delivery. Premiums were paid for "spot" rails; in other words, the market price went up. Considerable importations took place during this year, chiefly to ports on the Pacific Coast, — the only importations of consequence since 1887. This flurry subsided within a year.

[2] See what is said below on exports and "dumping," pp. 202 *seq.*

effects in a comparative steadiness of the prices of all these articles during the years before and after the crisis of 1907, — a steadiness in sharp contrast with the advance and recession of prices which had been the concomitants of similar industrial cycles during the nineteenth century. It happened that steel rails, being not only produced by a comparatively small knot of large-scale establishments, but usually sold in large blocks to the railways, offered specially favorable conditions for carrying on the policy without deviation. For other products that policy was more difficult to hold; and toward the end of the period of depression its maintenance proved impossible. Prices of steel billets and the like fell sharply in 1911. Nevertheless, looking at this period of expansion and contraction as a whole, a general steadying influence still appears. That it appears as regards prices, does not prove that it is to be found in output and employment also; fluctuations in these continued; yet even here it might be said with some show of reason that a moderating influence was exerted.[1]

These are matters on which, as indeed on so many of the phenomena of concentration and combination, further evidence must be awaited before judgment can be passed. It remains to be seen whether combination, with its almost inevitable concomitant of prices above the competitive rates, tends to mitigate the fluctuations of industry. Such is a common opinion among German investigators. It may be that this gain will prove impossible to secure at all; or, if secured, may be outweighed by the shackling of progress, the accentuated inequality of distribution, and other possible evils of monopoly. But these ulterior questions go quite beyond the range of the protective controversy.

Questions somewhat similar arise in the case of tin plate: a curious episode in tariff history, much debated and much misunderstood.[2]

[1] See an article by E. S. Meade, "Price Policy of the Steel Corporation," *Quarterly Journal of Economics*, May, 1908, xxii, p. 452.

[2] On this topic, I have been greatly aided by the research of one of my students, Mr. D. E. Dunbar, the results of whose work are shortly to be published in book form as one of the Hart Schaffner & Marx prize essays.

Until 1890, tin plate had been left outside the pale of the protective system. The duty was so low that no tin plate was produced within the country, and the total supply was secured by importation. This exceptional treatment was long the cause of protest on the part of the protectionists. It was said to have arisen from a wrong construction by the Treasury Department of a clause in one of the earlier tariff acts, whose language was such as to be held to impose a low *ad valorem* duty, — one much lower than Congress may have intended to levy. At all events the duty, as unequivocally fixed in a series of acts preceding that of 1890, was a moderate one, and operated as a strictly revenue duty; therein being in marked contrast to the highly protective duties on other iron and steel products. This anomaly was put an end to when the McKinley tariff act, with its emphatic protectionist intent, was passed in 1890. The duty was raised to the level of the others in the iron and steel schedule. The increased rate, however, did not remain in effect long; a sharp reduction was made in the Wilson act of 1894. After a slight advance in 1897 (by no means to the figure of 1890), the duty was again lowered in 1909 to the precise rate of 1894. The salient fact in all these changes is that in 1890 a high duty was applied, but was maintained for only four years, the later duties being comparatively moderate.[1]

The development of the industry under this short-lived application of high protection was extraordinary; so extraordinary as to surprise friends no less than foes. The act of 1890 had provided that the duty imposed by it should not remain in effect

[1] The precise duties, with *ad valorem* equivalents (on the basis of foreign prices) for the specific duties of 1875 and 1890, were:

1862	25 per cent *ad valorem*
1872	15 " " " "
1875	1.1 cents per lb. (equivalent to 20 per cent)
1883	1 " " " (" " 30 ")
1890	2.2 " " " (" " 70 ")
1894	1.2 " " "
1897	1.5 " " "
1909	1.2 " " "
1913	15 per cent *ad valorem*

A duty of 2.5 cents a pound had been provided (*i. e.*, probably meant to be imposed) in 1872, but had never gone into effect, because of the Treasury ruling referred to in the text.

after 1897 unless the domestic production in some one year before July 1, 1897, should amount to one-third of the importations. In other words, the maintenance of the high duty had been made contingent on a considerable development in the domestic output, and the legislators evidently were not sure that this development would take place. It happened that not only the amount called for under the act was produced at home, but very much more. The domestic production advanced by leaps and bounds, and within three years [1] the required quota of one-third was supplied. All the provisions of the act of 1890 were of course swept away in 1894, and the duty, as just noted, was almost cut in half. The advance of the domestic tin plate industry, however, went on without a halt, while imports steadily declined. By the close of the decade the domestic product had entirely superseded the foreign. Some imports continued after 1900, but they were only nominal. Almost all the tin plate that continued to be brought in from England was reëxported under drawback, chiefly by the Standard Oil Company, the imported plate being made up into the large square tin cans which this Company's export trade has made ubiquitous in the tropics and the orient. So far as domestic consumption was concerned, imports were completely superseded. The districts in Wales from which tin plate had previously come, and which indeed had previously been almost the sole producers for the whole world, were hard hit, and went through a long and trying period of depression, which was observed by the American protectionists with a satisfaction but little concealed.[2]

Before the decade was completely ended, however, another event occurred, most unwelcome to the protectionists, and received with a jubilant "we told you so" by the other side. In 1898, in the course of the veritable mania for combinations which characterized this era in the United States, the American Tin Plate Company was formed, including virtually all the producers of tin plate. The protective tariff became the mother of a trust,

[1] That is, by 1894. The tin plate duty, though imposed in 1890, did not go into effect until July 1, 1891.

[2] I append at the close of this chapter statistics on the tin plate situation.

and that trust exploited the possibilities of protected monopoly. Not long after, in 1901, the great Steel Corporation absorbed the Tin Plate Company as one of its constituents; the great trust succeeded the smaller trust. The protectionists were put on the defensive when the free traders alleged that this sort of thing was the natural consequence of a protective tariff.

So much on the conspicuous aspects of the case. A more detailed examination, however, is necessary, in order to make clear the effect of protection both on the establishment of the industry within the country and on the development of monopoly conditions.

Tin plates are thin sheets of iron or steel coated with tin (in former times, iron sheets were used, since the revolution in steel making, always steel). Their production involves two distinct operations: the making of the steel sheets or so-called black plates, and their tinning. The former of these operations, the more important, divides itself again into two; the making of the crude steel in the form of suitable bars, and the rolling of these bars into thin sheets suitable for tinning. Of the cost of a given quantity of tin plates, something like two-thirds is the cost of the black plates or steel sheets; and of the cost of the black plates again, 60 per cent is the cost of the steel bars (known in the trade as sheet bars).[1] The making of the fundamental raw material, — crude steel in the form of bars, — has been subject to the general influences described in the preceding survey of the steel industry at large. The production of the black plates by rolling from the bars, and the coating of these sheets with tin, involve operations of a more special kind.

The unexpected growth of the tin plate industry after 1890 was due chiefly to the cheapening of the fundamental raw material, — sheet bars. The decade after 1890, it will be remem-

[1] For example, in the middle of 1913, the constituent elements in the cost of production for a ton of tin plate stood in round numbers as follows:

Sheet bars (including freight, wastage, and the like)	$31.00
Cost of Rolling	20.00
Cost of Tinning	25.00
	$76.00

I derive these figures from information privately given.

bered, was the period in which the American steel industry reached the stage of independence. For some years after the crisis of 1893, crude steel was considerably cheaper in the United States than in England; and though this extreme situation did not endure after the ensuing revival of trade, differences between domestic and foreign prices became negligible and remained so. The American maker of sheets and tin plates was no longer at a disadvantage in the price of his bars. Before 1890 he had been at such a disadvantage; and the continued importation of tin plate was to all intents and purposes the importation of bars in this form. It was the changed situation as regards the raw material which explains the unchecked progress of the tin plate industry in face of the reduction of duty in 1894. A duty on tin plate of 1.2 or 1.5 cents a pound (the rates of 1894 and 1897), was a very different matter according as the material was or was not as cheap as in Great Britain. With that material equally cheap, the duty of 1.2 cents was no less effective for protection in 1894 than the duty of 2.2 cents had been in 1890. The main cause of the rapid growth of the tin plate industry in 1890–1900 was the lowered price of crude steel; it was one among the consequences of the general revolution in the iron and steel industry.

Both for this earlier period, and for the later stage which set in with the formation of the Steel Corporation in 1901, the relation between domestic and foreign prices of tin plate is instructive. The chart on page 180 shows this relation for the entire period 1890–1913. It indicates that immediately after 1890, American prices exceeded foreign by the full amount of the duty. During the years in which the McKinley duty was in effect (1891–94) there was what may be called the normal effect of protection: domestic prices were raised by the full amount of the duty. Toward the middle of the decade, however, imports ceased; prices were not higher in the United States even by the amount of the lowered duty of 1894. Some difference in price remained, chargeable to the duty, but held in check by competition among the domestic producers, and apparently in process of continuous reduction, — a reduction made possible chiefly by the decline in the price of crude steel.

Then came in 1898 the spectacular episode of the American Tin Plate Company, and the exploitation of tariff possibilities by the newly-formed monopoly. Attempts at pooling and price agreement had been made by the scattered tin plate producers in 1896–98, with the usual instability of these looser forms of combination. Finally, one of the arch promoters in this promoting period, Mr. W. H. Moore, was enlisted, and succeeded in bringing

CHART IV

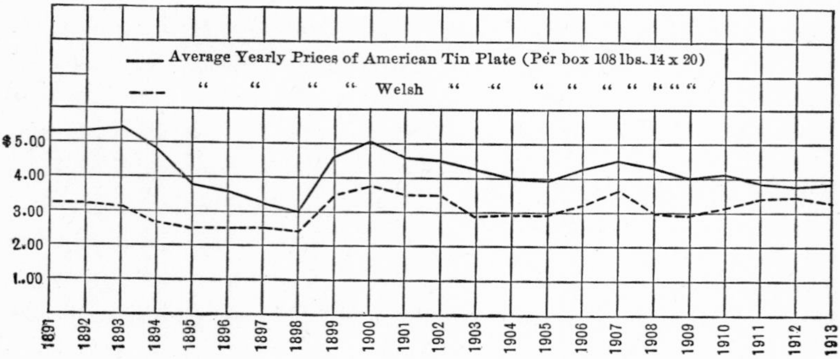

about a tight organization. The Tin Plate Company bought out once for all the various competing concerns, in part with cash, chiefly by the issue of its own common and preferred stock. With the meteoric financial operations that ensued the present inquiry is not concerned. The stock was liberally watered, its par value being four or five times the price in cash which would have sufficed to purchase all the plants; and it became an active speculative stock. This was one of the most profitable among the many profitable speculations of that extraordinary time. So far as the price of tin plate was concerned, the effect was unmistakable. The American price advanced at once, and advanced as compared with the British price. It was raised to the full limit permitted by the tariff (now that of 1897, with a duty of 1.5 cents a pound).[1]

[1] On this earlier stage, see the good account in Jenks, *The Trust Problem* (1900), pp. 157 *seq.*, where is also an elaborate chart showing the course of prices 1888–99.

For two or three years, this situation was maintained with no great modification. The price of tin plate was kept, if not quite up to the foreign price plus duty, much above the price which would have prevailed under competition. The Tin Plate Company paid dividends on its common stock as well as on its preferred. It was a profitable property when absorbed by the Steel Corporation in 1901; and that absorption was doubtless expected to strengthen the command of the tin plate industry by the great combination.[1]

After 1901, however, the situation changed in several respects. In the first place, the Steel Corporation's command of the industry became less, not greater. Some competition had sprung up even before 1901. The Tin Plate Company's operations had been too profitable not to invite competition, notwithstanding endeavors to shut out interlopers by exclusive contracts with the makers of tin plate machinery. When the company was formed, in 1898, it controlled 95 per cent of the country's output. In 1901 its successor, the Steel Corporation, found it still in control of nearly three-quarters of the output. The proportion, however, declined almost steadily after 1901, until by 1911 and 1912 the Steel Corporation produced no more than 60 per cent of the total. The independent manufacturers, some of them large-scale producers, had a very substantial part.

Not only in control of the output, but in the course of prices also, is there evidence of changed conditions. As the chart shows, the domestic price continued for many years to range higher than the foreign; yet with a tendency toward a lessening of the difference. At no time after 1901 was there such an exploitation of the tariff as in the year immediately after the Tin Plate Company was formed. The domestic price, though higher than the foreign, was by no means higher by the full amount of the duty. Imports quite ceased; the duty was prohibitory; but the domestic consumer paid a tribute less than the amount of the

[1] The tin plate stock was exchanged for stock of the Steel Corporation on these terms:

	U. S. Steel Corporation Preferred Stock	
For every $100 of	Preferred Stock	Common Stock
Tin Plate, Preferred Stock	125	...
" " Common "	20	125

duty. Gradually that tribute became still less; the domestic price approached the foreign; until finally, by 1911, almost all difference had disappeared. The price within the country became virtually as low as without. The protectionist, surveying the whole course of development, might maintain, for this branch of the steel trade as for others, that notwithstanding regrettable aberrations there had been ultimate gain from the nurture of the nascent industry.

Considering first the years from 1901 to say 1910, when prices were still higher within the country than without, we may inquire what degree of influence was exerted by the Steel Corporation, and to what extent the prices and the profits can be called monopolistic. Control of 60 or 70 per cent of the output is not complete monopoly, but it gives necessarily a commanding position. The independent manufacturers, though no doubt really independent, were yet in awe of the one great producer. Prices were not fixed by combination or agreement; there was a studious effort to do nothing that would constitute a violation of the anti-trust law; but there were conferences and understandings, and friendly pressure for the maintenance of prices. The fact that most of the independents had to procure their material — the sheet bars — from the Corporation, contributed not a little toward its influence throughout the tin plate trade. Here, as elsewhere, the policy of the Steel Corporation was to maintain steadiness, preventing fluctuations in prices and if possible in output. Though not so eminently successful as in the case of steel rails, its policy did serve to minimize fluctuations. The steadied prices were doubtless somewhat higher than unrestricted competitive prices would have been, and in so far were the source of some quasi-monopolistic gains, — gains shared by the independents, or at least by those among them who could produce as cheaply as the Steel Corporation itself.

One important factor throughout this period, not in the United States only, but the world over, was the constant increase in the demand for tin plate. The total output and the total consumption rose rapidly and without halt. The Steel Corporation's own output, though it fell relatively to the whole, rose absolutely.

The use of prepared food, conserved in tins, spread more and more, and the ever-increasing quantities of tin plate found a ready market. It was this increase of demand which proved the saving of the tin plate makers of Wales. The long stage of depression through which the Welsh industry had to pass came to an end as other markets gradually enlarged, — in South America, the East, and the Continent. The Welsh product rose not only to its former dimensions, but even above. This upward swing led to a stiffening of British prices, which in turn contributed to wiping out the difference between them and American prices. Some technical changes also took place in Wales as well as in the United States; of these, more presently.

A significant phase of the course of events after 1901 was the development of an export trade from the United States: not merely the export under drawback of imported tin plate (in the form of tin cases), but the export of tin plate of domestic manufacture. These exports began, as is shown in the table appended to the present chapter, shortly after the formation of the Steel Corporation, and reached substantial dimensions by 1905. In 1911 and 1912 they increased markedly, and in the latter year were near five million dollars' worth. At first they went almost exclusively to Canada, for whose market the Steel Corporation had geographical advantages. But in the very recent period (1911 and 1912) large quantities were sent to South America and Asia. Virtually all were exported by the Steel Corporation. Not only this; they were "dumped" by the Corporation. Prices to foreigners were steadily lower than to purchasers in the United States. The policy of selling at lower prices abroad was extended also to American buyers who used tin plate in an export trade of canned goods. Such buyers were given a rebate or drawback, similar to that which the government grants on the export of goods in which imported materials have been used.

Systematic dumping of this kind suggests monopoly price, or something closely akin to it. The general reasoning which points to this conclusion is stated below.[1] Suffice it here to say that the

[1] See the next chapter, pp. 208 *seq.*

practice of selling abroad various products at lowered prices, — not tin plate only, but others as well, — adds to the evidence going to show that the prices of many forms of iron and steel were fixed under conditions different from those of unfettered competition. Even though the Steel Corporation possessed no monopoly in any strict sense of that term, and even though its control of prices therefore was restricted and precarious, the general situation was that of a combination price, not a strictly competitive price. A preponderant control of output, — sixty per cent or something of the kind, — suffices to bring about, not indeed complete control of price, but an overshadowing influence. It is possible that, as the advocates of combination assert, the conditions, though somewhat different from those of competition, are not worse, but better. They may be conditions of greater stability, and yet not of prices "unreasonably" high. Without entering on the moot questions thus raised, we may accept this part of the evidence as indicating the continuance under the Steel Corporation of some degree of monopolistic control of the tin plate industry.

But quasi-monopoly and its corollary, discrimination in favor of foreign purchasers, was not the only factor, perhaps not the main factor, in the tin plate exports. After all, there was not complete monopoly, but only some approach to monopolistic conditions; profits doubtless above the competitive rate, but not profits so high as to leave a great margin for reductions in favor of one or another buyer. Though some shaving in price, some acceptance of profits lower than those got at home, might facilitate exports, cost of production and minimum price must have been brought within the neighborhood of the cost and of the prices of those rival producers who must be met in the foreign markets. Tin plate, or anything else, would not be sold abroad at a loss; if it could be sold abroad at low prices, it must be produced at low cost. Such must be the situation if the dumping is continuous, not sporadic. Was the cost of tin plate lowered within the country? Were improvements in production made, of a kind not found elsewhere? Did the American industry progress, not merely in volume, but in technical efficiency as well?

These questions, already considered with regard to the cruder forms of iron and steel, arise also for the two processes by which bars are converted into sheets and then coated with tin, — rolling and tinning. Both had been, through the nineteenth century, largely of a handicraft character. Though the bars were passed through rolls under power, more hand labor seems to have been involved in tending and operating the rolls than in other parts of the iron and steel industry. Tinning was even more distinctly a handicraft operation; the sheets were hand-dipped. When the McKinley Act was passed in 1890, the tin plate mills first established in the United States were copied from the Welsh. Sometimes the whole equipment, — rolls, shears, pots, — was imported, and then was operated by Welshmen also brought over. This sort of literal transmigration of industry has not infrequently taken place after our imposition of heavy import duties. And when it happens, and so long as there is mere transmigration, the need for protection persists. There is then no comparative advantage; the thing is done no better in the United States than abroad; and, wages being higher here, the expenses of production are also higher, and the American manufacturer cannot hold his own without protection. It is the next stage that is of more concern to the economist. The industry feels the influence of new surroundings. Machinery, labor-saving devices, inventions and short cuts, are in the air. Some changes from the old-world methods will not fail to be made. The question is whether these changes will be great enough really to transform the industry, and bring it up to the same level of effectiveness as the dominant American industries. Possibly it too will come to have a comparative advantage; and the object of protection to young industries will then have been attained.

The evidence on this subject is not easily interpreted. It is difficult to make out whether a real transformation followed the transmigration of the tin plate manufacturer. If English writers, technical and non-technical, are to be believed, the Welsh industry had fallen into ruts, and remained so for some time even after the shock from the loss of the American market; whereas the Americans promptly went ahead with new machines, larger plants, better organization of labor. Allowance must be made, when reading all such British jeremiads, for the desire to stir up John Bull, the tendency to overpraise the foreigner as a means of arousing the man at home. It must be admitted, too, that engineers and employers lay stress on all bad things in the labor unions, and sometimes arouse suspicion in their insistence on the opposition of the Welsh workman to labor-saving devices. But there remains a solid basis of fact for these allegations. In the Welsh tin plate industry the union long encouraged, and the workmen maintained, the policy of restricting output; and they opposed labor-saving devices. It would seem clear that the employers also, established as they had long been in apparently secure possession of the tin plate trade, fell into a certain stolid conservatism. Something like stagnation set in.[1]

In interpreting the evidence from the other side, — that of the American manufacturers and engineers, — there is also need of

[1] Thus in 1901, a writer in the (English) *Iron and Coal Trades Review*, May 2, 1901, speaks of "labor-saving appliances thoroughly exploited in America. . . . There is not a single point about the Welsh tin plate trade that can be said to compare favorably with the American." It should be said, however, that an unmistakable bias against the trade unions runs through this paper. A correspondent of the *London Economist* (January 29, 1910) remarks that "the English manufacturers sullenly clung to their old methods" for a considerable period, but "eventually scrapped their worst mills" and regained prosperity. *The Iron and Coal Trades Review* for March 28, 1913, printed an extended paper, read before the South Wales Institute of Engineers, by Mr. H. Spence Thomas, in which the Welsh industry is described and some comparison made with the American. "American practice gives 1,500 to 2,000 boxes per mill per week, whilst the English average is only half of this quantity." "In America all the pots are handled by overhead cranes, . . . by these mechanical means America is a great way ahead of the generality of our English works." In the discussion on this paper (p. 488) there was reference by several speakers to the difficulty of introducing improvements in face of the workmen's opposition. One referred to an episode in his own experience: "he put up an electric crane to do work for annealers that had hitherto been done by themselves; yet not one penny had been got off the annealers' wage bill" [the annealers were paid by the piece]. Still another said that "they were handicapped by the disinclination of the workmen as a whole to coöperate. If this could be secured, he felt they could do as well in the matter of output and economy as was now done in America."

On the restriction of output by the men (to 36 boxes per eight-hour shift), see Jones, *The Tin Plate Industry*, pp. 182 *seq.* This limit, easily within their powers, was slowly and reluctantly given up, in 1900–02. On opposition to labor-saving devices, *ibid.*, p. 185; and on American improvements, p. 132.

caution. These witnesses blow hot and cold. At one moment patriotic pride and a wish to prove how deserving is their industry lead them to descant on the improvements they have introduced and on the superiority of their ways over the foreigners'. In the next breath — when the tariff is mentioned — they will assert that they have no superiority at all, that their machines and processes are quite the same as in Wales, that their wages are twice as high, and that they will infallibly be ruined by a cut in the duties.

It would seem beyond question that some considerable improvements were made by the American tin plate makers. Welsh implements and methods, though copied slavishly at the outset, were not long retained without change. Gradually the tin plate mills were made more efficient. For example, the rolls were increased in size (width) from 18 inches to 28 inches. Overhead cranes operated by electric power were introduced for handling the material. Machine pots (for tinning), with some automatic appliances, took the place of hand pots; though the plates, it is said, still continued to be fed through singly by hand. In charging the annealing furnaces, however, the hand method was superseded by charging machinery. Certain of these changes were in time copied by the Welsh makers; sometimes doubtless with the same labor-saving results as in the United States, but in other cases (and these perhaps typical) with less success than in the originating country.

The spokesmen for the American manufacturers, though they admit the introduction of considerable improvements, maintain that in the main rolling and tinning are still handicraft operations. If this is true; if the industry has not been developed much beyond the handicraft stage; if it is carried on mainly by specially skilled workmen, with comparatively little use of machinery and labor-saving devices, — then it is presumably not up to the American industrial standard. It remains under a comparative disadvantage, and the young industry has not been nurtured with success. The evidence from the general economic situation, however, strengthens the impression that these expert witnesses understate their own case. It seems to be beyond question that the lead has been taken in the United States, at least for parts of the industry, and that American devices and improvements have been copied in Wales; always an indication not only of progress on the part of the Americans, but of probable sustained superiority.[1] There is the evidence, further, from the considerable and growing exports, and the parallel evidence from the approach of the American domestic price to the foreign level. Of this last-named change there is striking corroboration in the circumstance that the Standard Oil Company finally gave up the purchase of imported tin plate, on which it had so long taken the government's drawback when exporting the case-oil. This shrewdly managed concern at last bought its tin plate from the domestic makers, *i. e.*, from the Steel Corporation: proof conclusive that the price was as low as that of the foreign plate.[2]

On the whole, the verdict is not unfavorable to the protectionist. It is so, that is, on the question of real success in bringing the new industry to the stage of complete independence; from which follows the further conclusion, not at all welcome to the protectionists, that the occasion for retaining the duty quite ceased. Ultimate independence was achieved, and achieved through domestic improvements. No doubt other factors coöperated: the cheapening of the raw material and the world-wide increase in the demand for tin plate. The unrelenting free trader may indeed maintain that these factors would have led in any case to the same outcome. American invention and improvement, he may say, exercised their influence in every direction, and would have done so in the tin plate industry under any circumstances. It is no more possible to disprove the free trader's contention than it is to prove beyond cavil that of the protectionist. The

[1] Mr. Jones, in his excellent book on the *Tin Plate Industry* (pp. 99, 100), is disposed to admit that protection to young industries was in this case applied in the United States with success; and adds that "if in spite of the difference in the general level of prices in the two countries, the money costs of production differ so little, it is obvious that the net amount of human energy employed in tin plate manufacture is much lower in America than in Wales."

[2] I have come across nothing to indicate whether the Standard Company got a rebate or "drawback" from the Steel Corporation, such as the latter concern gives to manufacturers who use its products in export business. Presumably it secured the "drawback," like others.

difficulties in the way of exact proof remain for this inquiry, as they do for almost every concrete investigation in the economic field. But the protectionist has a strong case.

On the other question also, that of the development of trusts under protection, the free traders have often overstated their case. Surveying the course of events in the three industries for which the connection between protection and combination has been considered, — steel rails, tin plate, and sugar refining,[1] — the outcome cannot be said to confirm the doctrine that the tariff nurtures monopolies permanently. Protective duties high enough to shut out foreign competition do tempt to the formation of a combination; and they do make it easier for the combination, when formed, to raise prices and secure abnormal profits. This happened conspicuously in the cases of refined sugar and of tin plate; it happened, less conspicuously, in the earlier stages of the steel rail industry. There is here no small charge in the debit account against protection. But in the long run the situation did alter: no one of the combinations was able to maintain indefinitely a price raised by the full extent of the duty. Domestic competition did set in, and brought the profits and prices much below the level which full exploitation of the tariff would have caused. This domestic competition was no doubt a halting and restricted one. A combination price, somewhat akin to a monopoly price, was long maintained. Yet even this price was subject to the influences of domestic cost, and to the indirect action of competition as well as to its direct. Gradually the effect of the protective tariff in supporting combination melted away, and the trust problem presented itself unveiled and bare. Such is likely to be the general drift. The industrial influence of the protective tariff tends to become less and less; but the march of great-scale production proceeds apace. Whether or not the tariff system is radically altered, the economic and political problems of the future will be much the same, — great social problems, that will dominate the public life of the country for generations to come.

[1] On the sugar refining trust, see above, chapter viii, pp. 100–114.

STATISTICS ON TIN PLATE [1]

	Domestic Product (in 1,000 tons)	Imports (1,000 tons)	Exports of Domestic Tin Plate (1,000 tons)	Proportion of Product by Steel Corporation (Per cent)
1890	....	329.0		
1891	1	327.9		
1892	18.8	268.5		
1893	55.2	253.1		
1894	74.3	215.0		
1895	113.7	219.5		
1896	160.4	119.2		
1897	256.6	83.8		
1898	326.9	67.2 [2]		
1899	360.9	58.9		
1900	302.7	60.4		
1901	399.3	77.4	..	73.1
1902	360.0	60.1	1	71.4
1903	480.0	47.4	1	76.4
1904	461.1	70.6	4	71.4
1905	493.5	65.7	11	71.3
1906	577.6	57.0	12	73.5
1907	514.8	57.7	20	72.6
1908	537.1	58.5	17	71.1
1909	612.0	62.6	5	61.9
1910	722.8	66.6	13	61.1
1911	784.0	14.1	35	60.0
1912	963.0	2.0	76	60.0

These figures are for calendar years; they are taken from the Statistical Reports of the American Iron and Steel Association. They include terne plate as well as tin plate proper. The tons are gross tons (2,240 lbs.).

[1] For later figures see p. 404.

[2] In 1898, and thereafter virtually all the imported tin plate was reëxported under drawback.

expenses are lower.[1] But certain special machines, — for embroideries and for factory work, — continue to be imported. The explanation seems to be that few of any particular kind are wanted; the processes of manufacture cannot be standardized; the turning out of interchangeable parts by the thousand is not feasible. Handwork is called for in greater degree. Under such conditions the special advantage of the American producer disappears. The situation is a familiar one. Where ingeniously perfected machinery can be applied in large-scale operations, the American is likely to hold his own; but where handicraft skill is needed for a special article, he cannot compete with a country where such skill is as great and where current wages are lower.[2]

Similarly, knitting machines are both imported and exported. A circular automatic machine has been perfected in the United States, and is widely made here and used for the commoner and cheaper grades of cotton knit goods; it is even exported. But a very elaborate German machine for knitting full-fashioned goods continues to be imported; because the fabrics for which it is used are more expensive, less quantities are bought, and hence fewer of the knitting machines are used. Made as they are in comparatively small quantities, the machines are turned out more cheaply in Germany, and most of them are imported; and yet none of the widely used circular machines are imported.[3]

[1] An American manufacturer of sewing machines, testifying before a tariff committee in 1912, remarked that the Singer Sewing Machine Company had been compelled (by German duties on American machines) to manufacture in Germany, but found it could not do so as cheaply there as in the United States. "The plant may be the same and the machinery the same and the buildings the same, but the conditions in each country are not the same." (*Hearings before the Senate Committee on Finance*, 1912, pp. 352–355.) Similarly the International Harvester Company was induced by German and Russian duties on its American-made agricultural implements to establish factories for making these same implements in Germany and Russia, yet found it impossible to make them as cheaply in these countries of lower wages. I have been assured of this by officials of the Company.

[2] The same manufacturer (just referred to): "I can see, by examining the [German] machine, the handwork, the parts that had been filed, and the fact that they do not go so far with interchangeable construction as we do in this country." *Hearings*, p. 355.

[3] See the testimony of the one American manufacturer of the full-fashioned machine, *Senate Tariff Hearings of 1912*, pp. 919 *seq.*

Illustrations are abundant; at the risk of being tedious, I will mention a few more. Anvils continued to be imported through the period of high protection, notwithstanding a heavy specific duty. The imported anvils, made largely from scrap-iron, are hand-welded. Unless so made, they do not give an easy rebound, and the blacksmith who uses steadily one of a different kind finds his arm stiffening (a "glass arm"). Cast-iron anvils are made in the United States, turned out in quantities from well-designed models. They serve well enough when only occasional use is called for. Wrought anvils are also made in the United States, but of cheaper quality and in the lighter weights. For steady blacksmith's work the imported anvils are preferred; and they have continued to be imported, under high duties as well as under low.[1] Files, on the other hand, are equally good whether turned out by hand in small quantities or by machine in great quantities. The machine-made files have displaced the hand product, except where a few files of special kinds are wanted. Files are not only made with success in the United States, but are exported on a large scale; while a few hand-made files of special sizes or shapes continue to be imported.[2]

Some kinds of cutlery, again, are steadily imported; others are not imported at all. Pocket knives are brought in from England and from Germany, and one of the curious manifestations of extreme protectionist spirit during the period 1890–1909 was in the elaborate duties on this article.[3] Table cutlery, on the other hand, is supplied by the domestic manufacturer without competition from the foreigners; hence there was no attempt to levy particularly high duties on this kind of hardware.

[1] The anvil situation has been thus explained to me by persons engaged in the trade.

[2] Professor Lloyd, writing of the English file industry in his excellent book on *The Cutlery Trade* (1913), remarks at p. 59 that "hand cutting [of files] is likely to survive for small work and miscellaneous orders; but while the older process still claims to produce a superior article, it cannot be maintained that the method possesses any important advantages, whether technological or commercial." An American file manufacturer who exported a quarter of his output to all parts of the world exhibited to a congressional committee a file of which there were considerable imports; and, as might be expected, this was a "high grade file . . . on which there is very much labor." *Senate Hearings of 1912*, pp. 481, 482.

[3] See my *Tariff History of the United States*, pp. 343 *seq.*

The explanation of the difference between the two groups is clear. Table cutlery, and more especially table knives, are made in great quantities of a single pattern. Automatic machinery, interchangeable parts, standard patterns, mass production, — here the Americans can outstrip the foreigners. Pocket knives, on the other hand, are little standardized. There is a bewildering variety of patterns; comparatively small numbers of any one can be put on the market. A similar situation is found in the case of carving knives. The Sheffield manufacturer of these (a petty producer compared to the American table knife concern) can hold his own in the American market even in face of high duties; so can the German "manufacturer," who is in the main a middleman conducting an industry still in the stage of the domestic system. Hence it is that carving knives, unlike table knives, continue to be imported, vying with the protected American article. And for the same reasons, certain kinds of pocket knives and carvers nevertheless have complete command of the domestic market, and were not affected at all by the marked reductions of duty made by the tariff act of 1913, — namely, those of a standardized and staple sort, made in quantities, and affording opportunity for the methods of production in which the American is proficient.[1]

The second group of iron and steel products, — steel rails, pipe, sheet iron, corrugated iron, structural steel, wire, and the like, — have been exported since the decade 1890–1900. It was then that the revolution in the American iron trade was accomplished; and it was during the severe depression of 1893–96, and in consequence of the low prices then ruling in the United States, that the exports of these comparatively heavy products set in. The causes which led to their cheapening and which made it possible to sell them in foreign markets have been sufficiently explained in the preceding chapters, — rich and accessible mines, transportation at low rates, efficient organization of production on a

[1] See Professor Lloyd's book, just referred to, on *The Cutlery Trades*, pp. 55, 208, 387, on the many patterns of pocket knives and the consequent difficulty of applying machine methods. Cf. pp. 40–41, 394, on table knives. Here again I am indebted for confirmatory information to persons engaged in the trade.

great scale, technical advances. They differ in some respects from the causes that explain the exports of machinery and tools. Ingenuity and nicety in the finished product tell less, organization of the processes of production tells more. Yet in both cases the source of the comparative advantage has been chiefly in the human factors, and among these again in the ability and enterprise of the business leaders.

In the second group, however, still another factor has been of influence: persistent and systematic development of the foreign market by the dominant Steel Corporation. In that development, again, dumping has played a large part, — deliberate and continuous sales to the foreigner at lower prices than those charged to the domestic purchaser. Dumping alone would not explain the phenomenon. Even with the special concessions, sales to the foreigner could hardly take place unless the usual price of the article were close to the export level. But the concessions may just make the difference; without them, the exports might not be possible; and they raise the whole question whether a country gains from foreign sales brought about in this way.

The part played by the Steel Corporation has been surprisingly large. Great as is the scale of operations by some of the other iron and steel enterprises, no one of them has undertaken to cultivate the foreign field with the same enterprise and tenacity. Before the Steel Corporation was formed some of its constituent companies, — the Carnegie, the Federal Steel, the American Wire companies, — had established foreign agencies and had begun export sales. In 1903, — a year of depression and low prices in the iron trade, — a special subsidiary company of the Steel Corporation, the United States Steel Products Company, was formed for handling all of its foreign business. The business done by that Company has been by the million. It had (in 1912) some fifty-eight foreign offices, and large warehouses in England, South America, Australia, South Africa; it possessed a line of steamships of its own, and operated others under charter. Its export sales included steel rails, structural steel, pipe, wire, sheet-iron, and in recent years tin plate. Some of these articles were exported by other companies also, such as steel rails and structural steel; but none operated on a scale comparable to that of the Steel Corporation.[1] Some goods were sold abroad at prices no less than those at home, — *i. e.*, were not dumped at all. Among those were fencing wire, especially barbed wire, — a peculiarly American product, comparable to the iron and steel manufactures of our first class. But it seems that ordinarily the sales to foreigners were at reductions from the current domestic rates. One curious form of dumping was that of "allowances" to domestic manufacturers who bought material from the Steel Corporation for use in making articles which those manufacturers later exported, such as machinery, boilers, agricultural implements, or "containers" (*e. g.*, tin plate for canned goods). Such manufacturers, on proof of actual export, — of the sort required by the government before granting a drawback for import duties paid, — were given rebates from the usual domestic prices.

Two sorts of questions present themselves: one, whether a country gains by dumping or loses by being dumped on; the other, how it comes about that dumping takes place at all.

On the first question, the drift of protectionism and mercantilism is naturally in favor of dumping. It is in accord with protectionist reasoning to regard exports and devices for increasing exports with favor. Imports are thought presumably harmful to a country, exports presumably beneficial. The Steel Corporation's representatives, when testifying before Congressional committees and before the courts, have not failed to parade with

[1] The following are the figures for 1904–13 of the exports by the Steel Products Co. (*i. e.*, the Steel Corporation), compared with the total exports of iron and steel.

Iron and Steel Manufactures

Year	Total Exports (Fiscal years)	Exports by Steel Products Co. (Calendar years)	Year	Total Exports (Fiscal years)	Exports by Steel Products Co. (Calendar years)
1904	$111.9 mill.	$31.4 mill.	1909	$144.9 mill.	$41.1 mill.
1905	134.7	32.7	1910	179.1	53.1
1906	161.0	43.9	1911	230.7	69.5
1907	181.5	47.2	1912	268.1	92.0
1908	184.0	33.3	1913	306.0	

See the figures given before the Stanley Committee (*Report*, p. 2749), and those given in the government suit against the Steel Corporation (Defendants' Exhibit, ii, p. 38). The two sets of figures agree, except for 1905, for which I have taken the second-named source of information.

pride this part of their operations, confident that they would be thought herein to have deserved well of the country. The average man beyond question would approve, and so would the average writer on financial and economic topics.

It is part of the same general attitude that, conversely, dumping is resisted by the countries into which the articles are sent, at least when there are in those countries competing industries. The protectionist approves when his own country dumps, but is alarmed and indignant when the foreigner resorts to the same practice. Our government laid a countervailing duty on sugar during the period when the countries of continental Europe gave bounties on the export of sugar. Canada embodied an anti-dumping clause in her tariff legislation of 1904 and 1907.[1] Our own tariff act of 1909 contained a sweeping section levying additional duties equal to any and every export allowance or bounty by foreign countries: and the same provision was made in the act of 1913.

On the principles involved in this first question, I am unable to do better than repeat what I have said elsewhere:[2] —

"'Dumping' I take to mean the disposal of goods in foreign countries at less than normal price. It can take place, as a long-continued state of things, only where there is some diversion of industry from the usual conditions of competition. It may be the result of an export bounty, enabling goods to be sold in foreign countries at a lower price than at home. It may be the result of a monopoly or effective combination, which is trying to keep prices within a country above the competitive point. Such a combination may find that its whole output cannot be disposed of at these prices, and may sell the surplus in a free market at anything it will fetch, — always provided it yields the minimum of what Professor Marshall happily calls 'prime cost.'

"Now, if this sort of thing goes on indefinitely, I confess that I am unable to see why it can be thought a source of loss to the dumped country; unless, indeed we throw over all our accepted reasoning on international trade and take the crude protectionist

[1] For an account of the Canadian legislation see a paper by Professor A. Shortt, *Quarterly Journal of Economics*, vol. xx, p. 250.

[2] I quote again from the paper cited at p. 155, above.

view *in toto*. If one country chooses to present goods to another for less than cost; or lets its industrial organization get into such condition that a monopoly can levy tribute at home, and is then enabled or compelled by its own interests to present foreign consumers with goods for less than cost, — why should the second country object? Is not the consequence precisely the same, so far as that other country is concerned, as if the cost of the goods had been lowered by improvements in production or transportation, or by any method whatever? Unless there is something harmful *per se* in cheap supply from foreign parts, why is this kind of cheap supply to be condemned?

"The answer to this question seems to me to depend on the qualification stated above — *if this sort of thing goes on indefinitely*. Suppose it goes on for a considerable time, and yet is sure to cease sooner or later. There would then be a displacement of industry in the dumped country, with its inevitable difficulties for labor and capital; yet later, when the abnormal conditions ceased, a return of labor and capital to their former occupations, again with all the difficulties of transition. It is the temporary character of dumping that gives valid ground for trying to check it.

"A striking case of this sort has always seemed to me to be that of the European export bounties on sugar which for so long a period caused continental sugar to be dumped in Great Britain. These bounties were not established of set purpose. They grew unexpectedly, in the leading countries, out of a clumsy system of internal taxation. They imposed heavy burdens on the exchequer, as well as on the domestic consumer, in the bounty-giving countries; and they were upheld by a senseless spirit of international jealousy. Repeated attempts to get rid of them by international conferences show that the cheap supply to the British consumer, and the embarrassment of the West Indian planter and the British refiner, rested not on the solid basis of permanently improved production, but on the uncertain support of troublesome legislation. It might well be argued that these conditions would come to an end sooner or later. The longer the end was postponed, the worse was the present dislocation of industry and the more difficult the eventual return to a settled state of things. No doubt these were not the only considerations that in fact led Great Britain, the one great dumping ground, to serve notice that she would impose import duties equal to the bounties, unless these were stopped. Perhaps this decisive step would have been taken even if it had appeared that the bounties were to continue as a permanent factor in the sugar trade. But it is in their probably temporary character that the sober economist finds justification for the policy that led to their abolition. At all events there is tenable ground for arguing that Great Britain, in causing them to be stamped out, acted not only in the interest of the much-abused consumers of sugar on the Continent, but in the permanent interests of her own industrial organization."

These principles should be borne in mind, and at the same time may be subject to qualification, when we turn from the simplest case, — that of dumping in consequence of export bounties or the like, — to the more complicated case where goods are sold abroad at lower prices quite without public subsidy. Here it is not so easy to answer our second question, — how does it happen that sales are made to foreign purchasers at lower prices than to domestic? How explain the phenomenon?

The precise phenomenon now under consideration, it must be remembered, is the disposal of part of a supply at a lower price than is got for the bulk of it. It is quite different from another phenomenon, common enough, and often called "dumping," — throwing the whole of a supply on the market and disposing of it for whatever it will fetch. It is the discrimination in price which calls for explanation, and especially the discrimination in favor of foreigners. This again seems to be of two kinds: sporadic and irregular, or continuous and deliberate. The explanation would seem to be different according as it is of the one kind or the other.

Sporadic dumping commonly takes place by the disposal of part of a supply in some out-of-the-way market, while yet the accustomed price is maintained in the usual markets. It is part of the halting process by which the equilibrium of demand and supply is brought about; one of many instances to show that the results which the economist thinks probable or certain come to pass not smoothly or promptly but by slow and irregular steps. "Fair prices" and "square dealing" play a larger part in every-day transactions than is apt to be admitted by the economist, skeptical as he is about the pseudo-morals of trade. A manufacturer thinks it "fair" to treat his regular customers with equality, and not to sell to one at lower rates than to another; and conversely the customers expect him to treat them "right." Moreover, the prices of many goods, more particularly of specialties and articles having a brand or trade-mark, are much influenced by tradition and custom. The producer of such an article strives with all his might to maintain the traditional price, even though it proves difficult to sell the whole of his output at that price. Hence when there is a hitch in disposing of the entire current supply, he will welcome a chance to "dump" in some unfamiliar market. The temptation to do so comes the more frequently and pressingly under the conditions, usual in modern industry, of large plant and heavy overhead charges. If the prime cost ("direct" or "productive" expense) is got back at these low-price sales, and if total cost or "fair price" can be maintained in the usual sales, there is a net gain from this sort of dumping. It may take place within a country as well as through the export trade; but it seems to be more likely in the latter. Where indeed exports take place regularly and on a considerable scale, there is no greater probability of special concessions to the foreigners than to out-of-the-way domestic purchasers. But where the export is occasional and irregular, it affords a tempting opportunity for sporadic dumping. The market at home — the main one — is not "spoiled." All this will not prevent an eventual collapse of the traditional domestic prices, if the supply is steadily larger than can be sold at those prices; but it staves off the collapse, and if the condition of over-supply is but temporary, may serve to tide over a period of depression without "breaking" the market. Shrewd business men have questioned whether it is good policy;[1] but there seems

[1] Thus a member of Lister & Co., a great British silk manufacturing firm, admitted occasional sales for export at lower than home prices, but said "this class of business has many objectionable sides," "causes irregular work," tends

to be a strong recurrent temptation to relieve the general market in this way.

Continuous and steady dumping is a different matter. And it does take place. Sales at lower prices are made to foreigners, not only sporadically, but for long periods and systematically. This phenomenon would seem to be explicable only on another ground, — that of monopoly. Where there are competing producers, no one of them will steadily accept lower prices than the others. Each will be desirous of selling in the most advantageous market. There will be dumping of the sporadic sort only, by one of the competitors or by several of them, at times when the total output is not easily carried off at remunerative prices. The more effective is competition, the more standardized the article, the less likely is even sporadic dumping. On the other hand, the more removed the conditions are from those of smooth-working competition, — to the degree that there is influence from brands, specialties, quasi-monopoly, complete monopoly, — the more is there likely to be departure from a uniform market price, and the more likely is it that discrimination and dumping will appear.

Dumping due to monopoly is simply one form of the discriminations in price which appear under monopoly conditions, and which are familiar to economic students.[1] The monopolist sells at high prices where he can, and accepts lower prices where he must. If there are protective duties or other factors within the country (such as advantages of location) which prevent competition from foreigners, a higher price may be got by the monopolist at home than is secured in the foreign market where competition operates without restriction.

Such would seem to be the explanation of a large part of the export business of the Steel Corporation. Much of that business

to spoil reputation because quality and costs are cut keenly, and so on. See *Report of the* (Chamberlain) *Tariff Commission*, ii, Part 6, paragraph 3326. Similarly, the President of the U. S. Steel Corporation spoke of this sort of dumping as a "sporadic business," "an uneconomic practice, and one that does not develop continuous business." (*Testimony of the Government suit against the Steel Corporation*, 1913, x, p. 3843.)

[1] See, *e. g.*, Taussig, *Principles of Economics*, ch. 15, §§ 4, 5.

is secured by systematic dumping. Though part of the Corporation's export is similar to that of the strictly competitive iron and steel articles, a substantial part is to be explained on the ground of monopoly. The monopoly is not an iron-clad one, nor is the price secured in the domestic market such as would appear under full monopoly. It is a quasi-monopoly price, not a strict monopoly price. But that price has been a profitable one, somewhat higher than could have been maintained under really effective competition. Much the same seems to be the situation in Germany, under the Stahlwerksverband. There, too, combination has kept the prices of many iron and steel products above the competitive range; though the combination has taken the form of the Kartell, — the strictly-enforced agreement of quasi-independent producers, — not that of the domination of the market by one great consolidated concern. There, too, export prices have been steadily lower than domestic prices. And in both countries the discrimination is approved by the protectionists: high prices within the country, and large exports stimulated by lower prices without, are alike welcome under their philosophy.

It is often maintained that lower prices to foreigners are in no way disadvantageous to the domestic consumers; they enable the business to be carried on continuously, keep the working force intact and employed, lessen the overhead charges per unit, and so on. The reasoning is specious, but not tenable. All these same desirable results would be attained if the reductions in price were made to favored domestic purchasers, not merely to foreigners. Yet if made to a special knot of domestic purchasers, the question would at once be asked, why not equally to all? Why not lower the price for everybody, to the extent needed in order to dispose of the whole output? Then there would also be continuous operation, steady employment of workmen, reduction of overhead charges, and so on. Lurking under the advocacy of this sort of dumping, there is almost always an express or implied premise of a mercantilist character, — that international trade is a thing quite by itself, and that exports cause an advantage of a special sort, not to be secured by any commonplace sales within the country.

The argument that monopoly conditions explain the case may be put in another way. The domestic price (higher than the export price) may or may not be a "fair" or normal price, that is, such a price as would bring the usual rate of profit, and would be maintained under competitive conditions. If it is a fair price, then the foreign price being lower, is less than fair. In the long run, the business as a whole then would prove a losing one; the domestic business just pays, the foreign business does not pay. Then surely the low foreign price would not be indefinitely maintained; such dumping could not go on. Or the foreign price may be not less than "fair," but quite a sufficient one, — enough to bring the normal profit, overhead charges and all being reckoned in. In this case only will the dumping be steady and continuous. But in this case the domestic price, being higher, is necessarily *more* than "fair"; and the permanent maintenance of a domestic price higher than normal indicates that competition is not free, — that there is some approach to monopoly conditions.

In all such discussion, we are confronted with the question, *is* there a "fair" profit or a "normal" price? Is the notion applicable to such industries as the iron and steel manufacture of our day? Is there a representative firm or a representative outfit whose expenses of production can be said to be normal? How much allowance must be made, in an unbiased and careful process of cost measurement (say in an inquiry conducted by a government bureau) for depreciation, risk, obsolescence, the reward of capable management? The striking thing is that those engaged in the industries speak without hesitation about ascertainable cost and reasonable price. They aver, for example, that the price of twenty-eight dollars a ton so long maintained for steel rails was no more and no less than a fair price. The truth seems to be that they have in mind very much what the economist has in mind; not something which is ascertainable with strict accuracy, — even the most refined system of cost accounting gives at best a basis for inferences, — but a rough approximation. The cost figure is of service, so far as concerns matters of public policy, mainly in checking *marked* deviations from a reasonable price. With reference to steel rails, for example, the manufacturer who maintained that under the conditions of the period 1900–1910, $28 was a fair price, would doubtless admit that $27 or $29 might with equal plausibility be considered fair. Who could say in advance how things would turn out in the long run? How much would have to be allowed for depreciation, running at half-time, contingencies of all sorts? What is the normal or reasonable rate of return in a manufacturing industry of this kind? A public body (say a Trade Commission) charged with ascertaining and fixing a fair price could not possibly do more than settle an approximate standard. Our manufacturer would probably admit at once that $35 would be clearly more than fair, and $20 clearly less than fair; and as to the figure of $28, would merely say that it was "about right."

The steel rail situation, as it happens, illustrates in more ways than one the various possible phases of dumping and its concomitants; not only the connection between dumping and monopoly, and the difficulty of gauging the "fair" price, but the shifts in industrial conditions which necessarily affect the approximated reasonable price. That domestic price of $28 a ton, long maintained and unvarying: *was* it "fair"? If so, the foreign price was less than fair; and then rail making as a whole was conducted at a loss. If the foreign price (less than $28) was itself fair, then the domestic price was more than fair, and rail making as a whole was more than sufficiently remunerative. For a large part of the period during which the fixed price was kept up, the latter probably was the case; the industry, though not exorbitantly profitable, yielded more than a normal or competitive return. As the years went on, however, the situation shifted. With the general advance in prices, expenses of production rose, and profit became less. The consequent gradual shaving of the margin of gain appears to have proceeded so far by the close of the decade (about 1910) that the $28 price was but little more than fair, and the foreign perhaps something less than fair. The business as a whole was very likely stripped of any marked monopoly profits; the two sets of prices averaged "about right," and were maintained at their divergent rates largely through inertia. The process by which this outcome was reached was insidious, and alike unexpected and unwelcome to the rail makers. Yet the established policy of a fixed domestic price, the fear of public discussion about a rise in price, the higgling of the market as regards foreign prices, a disposition to go slow and await a possible turn in the tide of rising expenses, — these might explain an acquiescence through a considerable period in a situation quite at variance with what had been expected from the dumping policy.

It must not be supposed that all of the export business done by the Steel Corporation was or is at reduced prices, or is explicable solely on the grounds just stated. Many of the articles are sold abroad because they are cheap at home also. This seems to be the case with wire and especially wire fencing, in which American ingenuity and adaptiveness play the same part as in tools and machines. So it seems to be, in part at least, with structural steel and bridge-work. Structural steel for buildings, for example, is not supplied by the Steel Corporation at lower price than those quoted by its competitors in foreign countries; but it is lighter and better designed, and preferred even at the same or a higher price.[1] A considerable part is played by skill and persistence in merchandizing, — by steady and well-planned cultivation of the foreign market. Not a little is due to the economies from a great and varied business. In many foreign places it is worth while to maintain agencies and to make considerable shipments only where a variety in products enables considerable sales to be rolled up. Here are the advantages of large-scale production; advantages, to be sure, which can be secured not merely by size, but by skilful management. It is not to be denied that ability in management has played a large

[1] The Steel Corporation built the first steel structure in Buenos Ayres in 1905, and from that date until 1913 built every steel structure in the city. The European steel makers offered lower prices per ton, but "we were endeavoring to get a higher ton price by giving a lighter structure that will answer for a greater amount of work." (President Farrell of the Steel Corporation, testifying in the Government Suit against the Corporation, *Evidence*, x, p. 3795.) This is the sort of steel work which has been most skilfully developed by American engineers and steel makers; in other words, in which they manifest a comparative advantage.

part in the development of this part of the Steel Corporation's business. Here, as elsewhere, leadership and organization have been important factors in bringing about the conditions of comparative advantage.[1]

To conclude: The extraordinary growth of iron and steel exports since the beginning of the twentieth century seems explicable in the main on the ground of comparative advantage. No doubt, in some branches of trade it has been promoted by dumping. But most of the exports rest on a more solid basis, — effectiveness of labor, cheapness or high quality of the product. That effectiveness of labor, again, rests only in part on the rich natural resources of coal and iron. The most important factors are the qualities of the industrial leaders: mechanical ingenuity, skill in organization and management, the utmost utilization of the advantages of large-scale production.

[1] See the interesting account of the growth of the Steel Corporation's export business given by Mr. Farrell, in his testimony (just cited) in the Government Suit, pp. 3783 *seq.* Cf. his testimony before the Stanley Committee, *Report*, pp. 3748 *seq.* Mr. Farrell had been organizer and president of the Steel Products Co. (the export subsidiary), before being made president of the Steel Corporation itself.

Among the documents introduced by the Steel Corporation in the Government Suit (Defendant's Exhibits, ii, no. 41) is a tabular statement showing for a large list of articles whether export prices were more or less than the domestic. For a considerable number the export prices were not less, but more, — there was no dumping; such were finished structural work, spring steel, steel piling, axles. As a rule export prices were lower. The figures, however, are to be used with caution, since they state merely prices realized f. o. b. at the works, and give no indication whether expenses of transportation to destination were borne by the Steel Corporation (directly or indirectly) or by the purchasers.

PART IV

TEXTILES

CHAPTER XIV

THE GROWTH OF THE AMERICAN SILK MANUFACTURE

THE silk manufacture is in a special sense the child of protection. Hazardous though it always is to undertake to say what would have happened if the conditions had been different, one may venture in this case to assert that if high duties had not been imposed during the civil war there would have been no considerable silk industry in the United States. The situation is different with the other textile manufactures. Cotton and woolen fabrics were made on a large scale under the moderate duties that prevailed for many years before the war; the régime of high duties during the last half-century has simply served to increase the volume and extend the range of industries already established. But the very existence of the silk manufacture is due to protection. To this general statement, it is true, there are some minor exceptions. Certain branches of the industry did develop before the war, — constituting exceptions which, as will appear presently, are instructive. But those parts of the industry which have come to be by far the most important, owe their rise to the tariff.

For other reasons than its origin under the influence of protection the history of the silk manufacture is significant. The industry not only was quite new in the United States, but soon developed along lines of its own. So great has been the transformation in some branches as to suggest at least the possibility of successful application of protection to young industries. Yet a parallel development on the Continent of Europe indicates that forces not peculiar to the United States, but of international scope, have been at work. Something like a belated industrial revolution took place in the industry, greatly altering the relations of the different producing countries. Further, the character and sources of supply for the raw material are unusual. And, finally, less attention has been given in our controversies to this industry than to others stimulated by protection. In many ways the case invites study.

During the civil war, the duty on manufactures of silk, which had before been moderate (25 per cent under the act of 1846, 19 per cent under that of 1857) was raised, and toward the close of the war, in 1864, was fixed at 60 per cent. The increase was solely for revenue, with no trace of that admixture of protectionism which was a factor in so much of the tariff legislation of the period. The 60 per cent rate remained in effect until 1883. In the general revision of that year, one of 50 per cent was substituted. The simple method of imposing a general *ad valorem* duty was retained (with a minor exception, presently to be noted) until 1897.

It is not to be doubted that undervaluation, largely fraudulent, was prevalent throughout this period, and that it caused the effective duty and the rate of protection to be less high than the figure on the statute book would indicate. As the domestic industry developed, those interested in it protested more and more strongly against this state of things and urged the adoption of specific duties. The extraordinary variety of silk fabrics, and the difficulty of grading them by external marks or physical qualities, were long thought to raise insuperable obstacles in the way of specific duties. Yet in 1897 specific rates were devised and applied; anticipated already in 1890 by rates of this kind on one special class of silks, — velvets and other pile fabrics. The elaborate system of specific duties applied in 1897, though advocated chiefly on the ground of checking fraudulent undervaluation, in fact served also the purpose of raising the duties on many goods, and even of making them quite prohibitory on the cheaper grades. A dragnet or stoppage clause was retained by which in any case silks were to be dutiable at a rate at least as high as 50 per cent; and the more expensive grades of silks, on which the specific duties might have been relatively low (such is always the tendency under specific duties), continued to be assessed for duty under this clause. No change in the system was made by the tariff act of 1909; the rates of 1897 were retained; the only change of some moment was that the dragnet or minimum rate became 45 per cent, not 50 per cent.

The revision of 1913 brought less incisive changes in the silk schedule than in almost any other part of the protective system. It is true that the specific duties were entirely swept away. None but *ad valorem* duties remained. But these *ad valorem* duties were left comparatively high, — 45 per cent on most fabrics, 50 per cent on velvets and plushes. These were almost the identical rates previously in force on the more expensive goods. On the cheaper goods, the reduction seemed considerable, yet in fact signified little. As will appear in the course of the discussion, the previous specific duties had been extreme, — above the point of prohibition. The change to the *ad valorem* rate left the tariff so high, even after allowance for probable undervaluation, as still to keep out all imports of the ordinary grades of silks.

Summing up, we may say that the silk manufacture during the half-century that followed the civil war was sheltered by a high barrier on imports. In this case, as in others, duties originally imposed for emergency revenue purposes became protectionist in their effect, and then, with the accentuation and systematization of the protective system, were made more rigorous. Even the supposedly radical revision of 1913 left them little abated.

The growth of the silk industry under this long-maintained régime of high protection was not less extraordinary than that of the iron industry. It doubled in volume almost every decade. The appended tabular statement summarizes the story.[1] The gross value of the domestic silk manufactures increased from an insignificant amount (and almost all of that attributable to a

[1] SILKS (*millions of dollars*)

Census of	Gross Value of Product	Value of Product (Deducting Intermediate Products Counted Twice)	"Value Added by Manufacture" (Deducting Cost of Material)	Imports
1850	1.8*	....	...	17.7
1860	6.6*	....	...	33.0
1870	12.2	....	4.4	24.2
1880	41.0	....	18.6	31.3
1890	87.3	69.2	36.3	37.4
1900	107.2	92.4	44.8	26.8
1905	133.3	118.5	57.4	28.7
1910	196.9	172.2	89.1	33.1

* Chiefly sewing silk, fringes, etc.; see *Census Report of 1860 on Manufactures*, pp. 94–103.

The figures of product are taken from the *Census Reports*, and refer in each case to the year preceding; thus, the census enumeration of 1910 gives the facts for the

single specialty) in 1860, to nearly 200 millions of dollars worth in 1910. It is true that these large figures (given in the first column) need correction. The methods of the industry have undergone a change similar to that in other textile industries, in the direction of specialization. Separate establishments now carry on some processes (*e. g.*, spinning or "throwing") which formerly were combined with other processes (*e. g.*, weaving) in one and the same establishment. Where yarn is made in one mill, and reckoned as its product, and then is used in another mill which reckons the whole value of the woven fabric as *its* product, the same "product" is counted twice; and where a change in the direction of specialization takes place between census periods, there is obviously an exaggeration of the total output in the later period, and a deceptive appearance of rapid growth. Allowance for this sort of exaggeration is made in the second column of the table, in which the corrected product is stated; the census authorities having excluded what was counted twice in the later periods. Even so, the figures show a growth from nearly nothing to 172 millions by 1910. Quite a different qualification is made in the third column, where allowance is made also for the raw material used (chiefly the imported raw silk). The value of the expensive raw material accounts for about half the value of the finished silks; what may be called the separate product of American labor and capital is indicated by the third series.

In striking contrast with the rapid and unceasing increase of the domestic product is the virtually stationary volume of the imports. The figure of imports for 1910 is precisely the same (33 millions) as that for 1860, half a century before. In the intervening years the imports sometimes were considerably larger than this, sometimes considerably smaller; they increased in times of activity, diminished in times of depression. For the

industry as it stood in 1909. The imports are given for the fiscal years ending in the census year; thus, the figure for 1910 is that of the fiscal year 1909–10.

The census figures for the earlier years can make no pretensions to statistical exactness. Beginning with 1890 they can be used with reasonable confidence in their accuracy. They are taken from the *Census Bulletin* of 1910, Statistics of Silk Manufacture.

fifty years as a whole, they show no tendency to rise or fall, fluctuating above or below the same general level. The constituent elements in the imports have indeed changed very much, as will appear presently; but their volume has been virtually constant.

It follows that the imports have formed a steadily decreasing proportion in the total of silks used in the country. The domestic product has formed a larger and larger proportion of the whole. Comparison of the domestic and foreign quotas is not so simple as might appear. The figures to be considered are those in columns 2 and 4; since the imports, as well as the domestic product, are reckoned in these two on the same plan. But the imports, when they reach the purchaser, are weighted with the duties; and in reckoning the share of imports and domestic products in the country's consumption of silk goods, the stated imports must be swelled by the duties. Allowance must also be made for the fact that the imports have been much undervalued at the custom house; the stated value of the imports formed the basis for the imposition of *ad valorem* duties, but sales to purchasers were often on a different and higher basis. For the purposes of a rough comparison (quite sufficient for the present purpose) it will serve to add 60 per cent to the stated imports. So enlarged, the imports will be found to be more than triple the domestic product in 1870, about one and a half times that product in 1880, actually less in amount for the first time in 1890, and then a smaller and smaller proportion, until by 1910 they are but 30 per cent.[1] In 1860 almost all the silk goods used in the country, and quite all of the woven fabrics, were imported; whereas during the last twenty years over two-thirds of the silk goods of all kinds have been supplied by the domestic manufacturers.

So much by way of general survey. We may proceed now to a more detailed consideration of the different branches of the industry.

[1] The comparison would stand thus; the first column giving the " net " domestic product, with deduction for duplication due to increased specialization, *i. e.*, column 2 of the previous table; the second column giving the imports supple-

Raw silk has always been admitted free. In this respect the silk manufacture developed under conditions essentially different from those of the wool manufacture. The application of the protective policy to wool brought in the latter case a complication from which the silk industry was exempt.

This freedom as regards the raw material was not always uncontested. From sundry quarters, at various times, there were suggestions for a duty on raw silk. Both material and finished product have long had a certain fascination: both have been regarded by protectionists as peculiarly enriching, and the acquisition of the industries as peculiarly desirable. For the earlier period (before the industrial revolution of the eighteenth century) this attitude no doubt was explicable on the ground that the high value of silk fabrics for small bulk brought them readily within the range of international dealings, and so made it feasible to apply to them the mercantilist policy. Yet for the earlier periods,

mented by 60 per cent, *i. e.*, the figures in column 4 of the preceding table, with 60 per cent added.

Year	Domestic Product Millions	Imports Millions	Per cent of Imports to Domestic Product
1870	$10.00	$38.7	387%
1880	34.50	50.1	145
1890	69.10	59.9	86
1900	92.40	42.9	46
1905	118.50	45.2	38
1910	171.60	53.0	30

This comparison, needless to say, can make not the slightest pretence to statistical accuracy; but it shows the general trend, and is more accurate than would be one based on the bare Treasury figure for imports.

How far the imports, when compared with the domestic product, should be enlarged by adding the duties, raises some nice questions. Evidently they should be thus weighted if we wish to compare what is paid by consumers for the domestic supply with what is paid by consumers for the imports. It is not so clear that the same correction should be made if we wish merely to compare the quantities supplied. If the prices of domestic goods are raised to the same extent as those of imported goods, — by the full amount of the duties, — the correction must be applied in the same way and to the same extent as in comparing consumers' payments. If the prices of domestic goods are quite unaffected by the duties, then no weighting or correction at all would seem to be called for. Neither extreme, — complete effect of the duties in raising price of the entire domestic output, or complete absence of any effect at all, — is likely to appear in fact. Hence a comparison of the quantitative relation of the imported and domestic quotas can rarely be deduced from the statistics of the money value of the two.

and also for the later stage which set in with the industrial revolution, the predilection for a silk industry has probably been intensified by the supposed preciousness of the product: very much as a gold mine is thought to yield greater riches than a coal mine. During our colonial times there were repeated attempts to foster the cultivation of the mulberry tree, the culture of silk cocoons, the reeling of raw silk; all this being favored, among other reasons, because the industry was one of the then cherished household occupations. In the nineteenth century, there were recurring efforts to promote mulberry growing and silk raising. One curious episode was the furore in the decade 1830–40 concerning a tree, the *morus multicaulis*, which was supposed to be as well adapted for the silk worm as the white mulberry (the "true" mulberry), and which gave rise to a speculative mania comparable to the famed tulip mania.[1]

In 1890, at the time when the McKinley tariff bill stimulated the extension of protection in every direction, there was a movement for a duty on raw silk. It was opposed, of course, by the manufacturers; and, a duty being hopeless, a bounty of one dollar a pound was actually provided for in the bill as passed by the House, but was eventually dropped by the Senate. In later years, our Department of Agriculture, ever awake, under the policy so long dominant, to the possibilities of "acquiring" new industries, made experiments with mulberries and raw silk. Eggs and mulberry seedlings were procured from Italy, and manuals of instruction widely distributed. For a while the Department went so far as to buy cocoons from domestic growers (paying for them at current European prices) and caused the filaments to be reeled from the cocoons by its own employees.[2] Finally Congress wearied of the fruitless efforts, and in 1908 discontinued the appropriation for them; and the country relapsed into un-

[1] Those who may be interested in this little-known episode will find a full account in a volume on *Silk Culture in the United States*, New York, 1844.

[2] The efforts of the Department extended through two periods, one from 1884 to 1891, and another, more important, from 1902 to 1908. They were on a considerable scale; large quantities of cocoons were raised, and thousands of mulberry seedlings planted. See the *Yearbook* of the Department for 1903, and also an article by Dr. L. O. Howard, in the *Cyclopaedia of American Agriculture*, iii, p. 641.

troubled acquiescence with the importation of every ounce of raw silk used by the domestic manufacturers.

The explanation of this complete failure to develop the production of raw silk is to be found in the principle of comparative advantage. The usual statement, especially by protectionists, is that the cheapness of foreign labor makes competition impossible with the countries whence the silk is imported. Here, as in other cases, this statement means simply that we do not find here an advantageous way of applying our labor.

The production of raw silk divides itself into two parts: raising the cocoons, and reeling the filament from them. There is no climatic obstacle to growing mulberry trees in the United States or to raising the cocoons. But the tending of the larvae, worms, and cocoons requires minute attention and wearisome labor. No use of labor-saving implements is feasible. It is carried on, in China, Japan, Italy, in rural districts, largely as an incident to other agricultural occupations.[1] Even more clearly than in the case of the sugar beet,[2] a comparative advantage is lacking. In other agricultural work, the American farmer uses agricultural machinery and those labor-saving devices which are

[1] In Lombardy " the wives of the peasants engage in the business, as the wives of American farmers in their domestic work "; in Japan it is " usually an auxiliary industry of the farmers "; in China, " the vast mass of silk produced comes from China houses where all members of the family take part in the work." I quote from *Sericulture in Italy, Japan and China*, published by the Silk Association of America (1905), pp. 5, 11, 18.

In France, as is well known, bounties have been given since 1892 on raw silk; a compromise between the demands of the producers in the south for protection and those of the manufacturers for cheap material. Because of the method by which it was allotted, the bounty seems to have stood in the way of technical advance in the industry; at all events, the output of raw silk has barely held its own. The bounty was extended in 1909, without change of method, for a twenty-year period, *i. e.*, till 1929. Hungary has also encouraged raw silk production, by supplying eggs gratis, buying and distributing cocoons, and building filatures which are let to reelers on cheap terms. See Antonelli, in *Revue Economique Internationale*, March, 1910.

In Switzerland the production of raw silk has steadily declined since 1870 and now maintains itself only in the Italian cantons. Reichesberg, *Handwörterbuch d. Schweiz. Volkswirtschaft*, p. 962. I have no doubt the explanation is the same as for the American situation: the industry lacks a comparative advantage in Switzerland also.

[2] See the discussion of beet growing, chapter vii, p. 88 and *passim*.

adapted to extensive cultivation. The impracticability of applying them to cocoon raising means that here there is, not indeed a disadvantage, but complete lack of any special advantage.

This is still more the case with reeling. Raw silk differs from all other textile fibres in the length of the fibre unit. From the cocoon a long delicate filament is unwound; a number of filaments are combined into the thread, still delicate, which forms the raw silk of commerce. It comes on the market in a skein very like that of the loose-spun wool or "worsted" which women use for their knitting. The unwinding and combining of the filaments take place in filatures, with use of a reel on which is wound the thread or strand of raw silk. Filatures were long very small household affairs, — adjuncts to peasant agriculture; but in modern times have come to be, in Japan and in those European countries (Italy, for example) which produce raw silk, establishments of some size, with power for moving the reels. But whether small or of comparatively large size, they depend on deft handiwork and meticulous labor. The filament needs to be watched every instant. "In the treatment of the cocoons, the formation of the thread, — in short in the spinning [1] and treatment of the silk itself, — no noteworthy change has been wrought, in spite of incessant study. . . . The winding of the single thread from the cocoon demands such a delicacy of treatment that so far only the manual dexterity and intelligence of the women reelers has (*sic*) been able to cope with it. All mechanical processes proposed in substitution of hand labor have failed." [2]

It is a striking and curious fact that silk reels have been greatly improved by American ingenuity, yet are not used by Americans at all. A type of reel devised by an American mechanic, a foreman in an American silk mill, has made its way all over the world.[3] Yet no reeling is done in the United States. It remains

[1] "Spinning" would seem here to be a misnomer; the term is not usually applied to the process of unwinding from the cocoons, nor even (see p. 228, below) to the subsequent preparation of the raw silk for weaving.

[2] *Sericulture*, p. 9.

[3] The Grant reel, which originated in the well-known Cheney mills. Cf. Mason,

essentially a handicraft operation, precisely of the kind to which American labor does not find it worth while to turn.

It may be noted at this point that the situation is quite different with another grade of silk, — spun silk. "Raw silk" proper is that just described, — the continuous thread reeled from the interior of the cocoon. The exterior hull of the cocoon, however, has broken fibres; in the innermost part of the cocoon, the fibre becomes so attenuated as not to be unwound profitably; and there are also pierced and imperfect cocoons whose filaments are broken. These "waste" fibres, as well as some other "wastes," are used in making spun silk. "In working spun silk there is no effort to use the continuous thread as spun from the silk worm within the cocoon; but the cocoon is treated as a bundle of fibres and spun the same as cotton and wool by special textile machinery, adapted to the characteristics of the particular fibre." Spun silk is more amenable to treatment by fast-moving machinery than reeled silk; and this circumstance, has had important consequences in the development and geographical distribution of the spun silk branch of the manufacture.

Raw silk proper, however, differs essentially from the other textile fibres. The filament from the cocoon, though continuous, is not even. Nature is always irregular, and the silk worm's thread has not the mechanical regularity of man's product. For this reason the silk manufacture retained its ancient characteristics for a century after the other textile industries had been transformed. Raw silk was not so readily amenable to the machine processes. The very fact that cotton and wool have short fibres, and that the fibres must be separated and evened by carding, then twisted together methodically by roving and spinning, makes these materials a ready prey to the machine. The tenuous and comparatively uneven silk fibre long resisted. The main processes in the manipulation of raw silk, — "throwing" (the process corresponding to spinning) and weaving, — remained handicraft and household industries long after power-

The Silk Industry, p. 12. The reels are not manufactured in the United States; the design is simple, and the reels are made in various parts of the world, whereever used.

driven machinery had conquered in the cotton and woolen industries.

For this reason, the industry had no hopeful prospect when introduced into the United States under the stimulus of the war duties. The peculiar qualities of the raw material seemed to make it ill adapted to the prevailing manufacturing methods. Apparently it was likely to be for an indefinitely long period at a comparative disadvantage, and therefore to remain in unceasing dependence on protection. During the early stages of the industry attention was repeatedly called to the special difficulties of the industry by a highly competent observer, Mr. W. C. Wyckoff, the first secretary of the Silk Association of America. The raw material, he pointed out, is uneven and irregular. It is likely to break in the course of weaving, indeed in any of the processes. "A loom may have to be suddenly stopped. It is always the same story, — breakage, stoppage, waste of time (labor) and material. The loss of time when machinery, running at high speed, has to be stopped, becomes a serious matter, from the mere fact that there is no production during the stoppage. 'It costs,' said a manufacturer, 'fully five times as much to tie a knot in this country as in France.'" And again: "it is necessary to have all the threads of warp and woof as perfect as possible, so that there shall be no stoppage of the power loom." In Europe, "the silk manufacturer is a mere contractor. He buys the tram and organzine — *i. e.*, filling and warp — which have been made in a separate factory. He sends this material to another establishment, a dye-house. Finally he puts it out to weavers who have looms in their own homes."[1] This is the familiar domestic system. The American manufacturer, however, was compelled by the social and industrial conditions surrounding him to try to substitute for it concentration in the factory, power-driven machinery, wage labor; yet the nature of the raw material imposed obstacles to carrying out the change with advantage.

[1] See the passages from Wyckoff quoted by me in the *Quarterly Journal of Economics*, iii, pp. 271–273 (1889); also in my *Tariff History of the United States*, 4th edition, pp. 381 *seq.*

Commenting on this situation, I remarked in 1889, in a passage which the subsequent course of events has not contradicted:[1] "A struggle seems to be going on in the silk industry between large factories and machinery, on the one hand, and household industry and manual labor, on the other. . . . The nature of the silk fibre is an obstacle to that extensive use of labor-saving machinery which is characteristic of American industry. The field is not promising for the ingenuity and inventiveness which give American manufactures their distinctive advantages. . . . It may indeed happen that Yankee ingenuity will revolutionize the conditions of this industry. The attempts of the American manufacturers to get a more even supply of raw silk, and to apply machinery to its conversion into silk goods, may prove successful, if not throughout the industry, at least in many parts of it. . . . Should there continue in the future a progress such as has undoubtedly been made in recent years [1880–1888] in the American silk manufacture, it may happen in the end that most sorts of silks will be made here as cheaply as abroad, and that the abolition of protective duties would affect the silk manufacture as little as it would now affect the bulk of the cotton manufacture. If this proves to be the case, we shall have an example, and a striking one, of the successful application of protection to young industries."

These extracts anticipate in part what is to come; but they serve to show what are the special problems in the history of the American silk industry. The nature of these problems will appear more in detail as we proceed to consider step by step the several stages in the manufacturing operations.

After reeling, the next process is throwing. The long filaments of the raw silk, — continuous threads from beginning to end of the skein, — are doubled and tripled, and so given strength and consistency for enabling them to be used in weaving. Thrown silk, the material turned over to the loom, is sometimes called yarn, since it corresponds to cotton or woolen yarn; it is especially so called by Americans in very recent times, because the power-driven machine has succeeded in taking possession of

[1] *Quarterly Journal of Economics*, iii (1889), pp. 273–276.

silk throwing. But the term silk yarn is more commonly used to denote the spun silk which is really spun from the shorter fibres of the cocoon. Thrown silk is quite a different thread, and is generally known by names of its own. That used for weft, which is soft and comparatively open, is called "tram"; that used for warp, more closely twisted, is called organzine.

Silk throwing continued to be a handicraft operation until the latter part of the nineteenth century; just as carding and spinning had so remained until the corresponding part of the eighteenth century. It was carried on in the throwsters' homes, often as an accessory to agriculture or other occupations. Two generations ago the silk throwster was as important and characteristic a figure for this industry as the hand loom weaver was a century ago for the other textile industries. Like the hand loom weaver, he has been displaced by machinery. Not indeed entirely; for in some parts of Europe, and almost throughout the Orient, the silk throwster, like the silk weaver on hand looms, still holds a considerable place. But in the countries of advanced industrial methods, he has quite disappeared; more particularly in the United States and in England.[1]

The significant fact for our inquiry is that the American industry has gone ahead independently, not following the lead of other countries. Newly invented throwing machines came on the market in the United States during the decade 1880–90, — all in the direction of automatic action and great speed. As early as 1890 throwing spindles were operated at a speed no less than that of cotton spindles, 10,000 revolutions per minute; ten years later, by 1900, the number of revolutions had been raised to 11,000 and 12,000. A natural consequence of the perfection of the machines was a change in the character of the persons employed to tend them. The silk throwsters had been men. The

[1] Silk throwing in Italy and France was long carried on in small quasi-handicraft establishments with the aid of water-power; hence called in France "moulinage." It is still in France an industry on a very small scale; petty factories with an average of less than 2,000 spindles, working universally on orders from the manufacturers. Beauquis, *Histoire économique de la soie*, p. 150. In England, though silk throwing has ceased, the Silkthrowsters' Company, established in 1629, still maintains a nominal existence among the Livery Companies of London.

new throwing machines were operated largely by women and children. The change had consequences similar to other historic transitions in textile manufacturing, — from hand loom weaving to power loom weaving, from the power loom to the automatic loom, from mule spinning to ring spinning.[1] In its social aspects, it opened grave questions. But its cheapening effect was great and rapid. The cost of converting raw silk into tram and organzine was lowered to one-quarter and one-fifth of what it had been a generation before.[2]

Similar changes took place in weaving. Silk woven fabrics are divided into two classes, sharply separated as regards manufacture and commercial dealings: dress silks (broad goods) and ribbons (narrow goods). Of these, the latter, the ribbon branch of the industry, has proved the more amenable to the machine processes. The first ribbon looms in the United States were of German or Swiss pattern. In 1889 a high-speed automatic ribbon loom was invented in this country.[3] It proved the beginning in a series of improvements in ribbon weaving. Double-deck looms succeeded single-deck looms. The "weaver" became, as he (or she) inevitably does with a perfected power loom, a mere machine watcher and tender, whose duty is mainly to keep up the supply of spools and tie broken threads. And the same sort of social consequence ensued as in throwing: in larger and larger proportion there was resort to the labor of women.

Similar changes took place in the manufacture of broad goods. Here too, the first looms, brought over from Europe, were soon superseded by looms of American make. As is known to every one conversant with the history of the textile industries of the United States, weaving machinery was from the outset and has remained a peculiarly inviting and fertile field for American ingenuity; and the advances in silk weaving have apparently been no less marked than in other industries. There have not been, indeed,

[1] See below, pp. 270, 273 on the automatic loom and ring spinning.

[2] In the Census of 1900, it is stated in the Report on Silks (p. 218) that the cost of converting one pound of raw silk into organzine was lowered from $4.50 in 1870 to 60 @ 75 cents in 1900. On the employment of women and children, see *ibid.*, p. 209.

[3] Allen, *Silk Industry of the World*, p. 29.

such striking triumphs as those of the automatic loom in the cotton manufacture.[1] But silk looms have been steadily improved in the direction of lightness, simplicity, swiftness of running, steadiness of product. The stage was reached before long where the weaver could be called to tend to more than one loom; a change which, as ever, caused rebellion among the operators, who nevertheless in the end had to accept the inevitable consequences of the march of invention.[2] The rate of progress seems to have been especially rapid for broad looms in the opening years of the present century. Then an exceptional era of general activity and prosperity led to a sharply increased demand for silks, — these being among the articles which are peculiarly subject to fluctuations in demand between good times and bad times. It may be, also, that the high specific duties levied by the tariff act of 1897 added to the demands on the American silk makers, since they served to shut out effectually foreign competition in the grades which were chiefly made at home. The rate of advance hence was extraordinarily rapid in quantity of output; while invention improved both the efficiency of the machinery and the quality of the products.[3]

No change in the silk industry of the United States, nay of any other country or any other industry, has been more striking than the rapid and complete displacement of hand looms. During the decade after the civil war, hand looms and their weavers

[1] See below, p. 273.

[2] The much-discussed strike of 1913 among the Paterson silk operatives, in which the Industrial Workers of the World (I. W. W.) took so active a part, began among the broad silk weavers, in opposition to the introduction of a three loom and four loom weaving system.

[3] The *Silk Association Reports* show that new looms were installed in the United States as follows: —

	Broad Goods	Ribbons
1901	2,328	356
1902	5,500	213
1903	3,797	450
1906	1,268	383

The extraordinarily rapid growth between 1900 and 1905 is shown by the following census figures: —

	No. of Establishments	Capital
1890	472	$51 millions
1900	483	81 "
1905	624	109 "

were brought over from Europe. But the power loom appeared as a rival at once, and the hand loom rapidly disappeared. The contrast with other countries, as will presently appear, is marked: elsewhere the hand loom maintains a place almost equal to that of the power loom. The figures given below tell their own tale for the United States.[1] The difference is strictly analogous to that in other industries, and the explanation is the same. In a country where labor is made effective and wages are kept high through the wide-spread use of labor-saving devices, a strictly handicraft occupation succumbs because it suffers under a comparative disadvantage. The power loom offers at least the chance of a comparative advantage on a par with the rest of the country's occupations.

It has already been pointed out that a natural consequence of these technical advances was a greater employment of women and children. This in turn affected the geographical distribution of the American manufacture. Being able to use in greater degree the labor of women and children, the industry has tended to move to the regions where such labor is easily got and the laws regulating it are loose or loosely enforced. Pennsylvania and New Jersey have the unenviable distinction of having become, partly for this reason, the important silk manufacturing states of the Union. In New Jersey, just one-half (49.6 per cent) of the employees in silk establishments are women; in Pennsylvania, nearly two-thirds (67.8 per cent). In New Jersey, the city of Paterson

[1] The following figures state the number of hand and power looms in the two branches of the industry.

	Broad Goods		Narrow Goods	
	Power	Hand	Power	Hand
1875	1,428	1,005	1,260	809
1880	3,103	1,629	2,218	1,524
1890	14,866	413	5,956	1,334
1900	36,825	164	7,432	9
1905	47,725	0	8,400	0

Allen, *Silk Industry of the World*, p. 31.

The comparatively slow increase in the number of looms for narrow goods between 1890 and 1905 is to be interpreted in the light of the circumstance that each individual loom became larger, quicker, more automatic. The longer persistence of hand looms in this branch of the industry (1,334 such looms as late as 1890) is more apparent than real. These looms were used in 1890 mainly for trimmings, a special and limited branch of the narrow goods trade, — one which proved a decadent part of the silk manufacture. See below, p. 247.

has long been a "silk town," and especially a ribbon center. Here as elsewhere, newly arrived immigrants, eager to swell the family incomes, send their women and children to the mills, where they are able to tend the quasi-automatic machines. In Pennsylvania, oddly enough, the anthracite region formed a favorable field for the silk manufacturers. The miners were mainly foreign born, recently arrived; they were more than willing to send women and children to the mills; labor laws were lax, the conditions of enforcement almost farcical. There could be no better illustration of the need of curbing and bridling the industrial forces of the time. The machine immensely increases the effectiveness of labor; but legislation and a strong conserving standard among the laborers are needed to prevent it from contributing to evil conditions. And yet, so far as the bare matter of advantage in production is under consideration, the case has but one side: perfected machinery, that needs to be tended only by a slip of a girl, means effectiveness and cheapness, and the country in which the greater mechanical perfection is reached has a comparative advantage in the industries where it is found.[1]

Still another consequence of the progress of invention, in quite a different direction, has been a change in the sources of supply for raw silk. Japan has largely supplanted China; and this under the influence chiefly of American demand and American suggestions. The irregularity of the raw silk fibre is, to repeat, an obstacle to its manipulation by power-driven machinery. Spindles and looms can be adjusted to the most tenuous threads, so long as they are homogeneous. No doubt the finer grades of goods always remain less easily subjected to rapid machinery; but as long as the material is even, the possibilities of delicate balance and adjustment are astonishing. Irregularities, however, always mean breakage, stoppage, loss of time, incomplete utilization of plant; they mean, also, greater need of specialized skill on the part of the individual operative. Hence the American manufacturers sought to secure supplies of uniform raw silk. The

[1] On labor conditions, see Mason, *Silk Industry*, pp. 50 *seq.;* and the *Federal Report on Woman and Child Wage-Earners*, 1912, iv; summarized in the *Survey*, May 18, 1912. In Pennsylvania only 9 per cent of those employed in the silk mills of the state are men; 67.8 per cent are women, 23.2 per cent are children.

Chinese, who had long been the main producers and exporters, proved unwilling or unable to supply such raw silk as the Americans wanted; partly perhaps from pervading stolid conservatism, largely because of the impossibility, under existing political and social conditions, of spreading and enforcing the needed instructions. The Japanese rose to the opportunity. There is no more characteristic illustration of the industrial and intellectual uprising of that remarkable people, — the coöperation of a guiding oligarchy with a responsive mass. Instructions on the proper methods of reeling silk were spread through the country by the government and by the leading export firms. Model filatures for reeling were established. The Japanese prepared raw silk such as the American manufacturers could more advantageously use. Their country took the place of China as the main source of supply. Raw silk became a great article of export from Japan, and American supplies came preponderantly from that country.[1]

[1] See on this subject the account in Mason, *Silk Industry*, pp. 15 *seq.* On the continued endeavors of the American manufacturers to improve the quality of Chinese raw silk, see *Thirty-eighth Report of the Silk Association*, pp. 24, 25. "A great proportion of the Canton silks cannot be economically handled by the American manufacturer on account of defective reeling. . . . We suggest that the system which has improved the working qualities of Japan silks, *i. e.*, re-reeling the skeins, if used in Canton, would so vastly enhance the value of Canton filatures that the American buyers would gladly pay such additional price as to more than compensate the reelers." L. Duran, in his trade book on *Raw Silk* (1913), writes: "It is gratifying to see the Japanese reelers doing their utmost to improve the quality of their silks" (p. 114).

CHAPTER XV

THE SILK MANUFACTURE, CONTINUED. EUROPEAN AND AMERICAN CONDITIONS; IMPORTS AND DOMESTIC PRODUCTION

THE principle of which so much has been made in the preceding chapter, — that of comparative advantage, — calls for a consideration not of the American silk industry only, but of that in competing countries as well. And the change from handicraft to machinery did not take place in the United States alone. A belated industrial revolution set in, affecting all the producing countries. But it affected them in different degrees, and with different results for the various branches of the industry. It is instructive to compare the course of development in the several countries.[1]

A general indication of the situation is got by comparing the use of hand looms and power looms. The following figures are given for the year 1900 by a competent authority.[2]

	Power Looms	Hand Looms
France	30,600	60,000
Switzerland	13,300	19,500
Crefeld (Germany)	9,500	6,900
Italy	8,500	11,000

It appears that in each of those countries a large number of hand looms were still in use as late as 1900. The proportion in Germany, or at least in the Crefeld district, was less than in France, Switzerland, Italy; but everywhere hand looms persisted. The contrast is striking with the complete disappearance of hand looms in the United States.

[1] The descriptions of European conditions which follow rest on scattered notes gathered from various sources, and make no pretense of exhaustiveness. So far as I know, this interesting phase of recent industrial history has received scant attention.

[2] Allen, *Silk Industry of the World*, p. 41. The figures for Germany are not for the whole of that country, but only for the district of Crefeld, the chief manufacturing center.

In the Crefeld district of Germany, the most important and highly organized silk center of that country, the transition from household industry to the factory system set in during the last quarter of the nineteenth century. The power loom came into use in the decade 1880–90, and was increasingly used after 1890. It seems to have been perfected earliest for velvet ribbons. An invention of 1887 gave a great impetus to the velvet ribbon industry of the district, and by the beginning of the present century hand looms for these ribbons had almost entirely disappeared. For silks also the power loom made its way rapidly after 1885. Yet hand looms continued to be used for silks, both broad and narrow. Some specialties and goods of unusual pattern, of which but a small quantity of any one kind can be marketed, are still made to most advantage on hand looms. Heavy silks, such as wear long and well, are also so made. But the lighter, less durable fabrics, often made with an admixture of cotton or artificial silk, have come within the domain of the power-driven machine. These differences, as will presently be explained, are of no little significance for the problems of international trade and for the rivalry between the Continent and the United States.[1]

Somewhat similar to Germany is Switzerland, where Basel and Zurich are important silk manufacturing centers. That part of the German industry which is near the Swiss border, toward the south, belongs in reality to the latter country, being mainly conducted by enterprising Switzers who have transferred their establishments across the border because of the German tariff. Basel is a center chiefly for ribbons, Zurich for broad goods. It is in the latter that the machine seems to have conquered most decisively. In general, it is the Swiss and Germans who are the machine-using people of the Continent; and accordingly the power loom and all that goes with it have been introduced furthest in those two countries. But in Switzerland, as in Germany, household production maintains a place. In Basel

[1] On the German transition, see H. Brauns, *Der Uebergang von der Handweberei zum Fabrikbetrieb*, Schmoller's *Forschungen* (1906), pp. 33–37, 44. Cf. Bötzkes, *Seidenwarenproduktion und Seidenwarenhandel* (1909), p. 28.

the ribbon "manufacturers" are largely contractors, who supply material to scattered household weavers and buy from them the ribbons or other woven fabrics. The Swiss peasants, and especially the peasant women, continue to ply the loom during the long winters. This domestic industry holds its own tenaciously. As late as 1905 the number of power looms in Switzerland exceeded but little the number of hand looms.[1]

In France, which had so long been the leading silk manufacturing country, the industry clings even more to the old ways. The number of hand looms is about double the number of power looms; the domestic weaver holds his place. French silks, especially those made for the export trade, are of high quality. They depend for their sustained superiority on excellence of pattern and perfection of make. The cheap everyday silks, turned out in great quantities of one pattern, are characteristic of the machine industry of other countries, especially of the United States. Limited patterns and sterling quality, catering to the well-to-do and the rich, are the typical products of the French industry; and these are precisely the traditional characteristics of the silk manufacture as it was before the machine began to invade it.[2]

[1] In Basel there were in 1908

In household use	4,057 looms
In factories	1,750 "

Three-quarters of the household weaving was done by women; and agriculture was the main occupation of those engaged in weaving. See Thürkauf, *Die Basler Seidenindustrie*, pp. ix, 77, 181. For Switzerland as a whole I find these figures for 1905 (Bötzkes, p. 25): —

Power looms	14,915
Hand looms	13,041

[2] A well-informed American (or Americanized?) observer wrote thus of the French silk industry in 1913: —

"Until 1875 the looms of Lyons were exclusively worked by hand. At present there are yet about 15,000 jacquard hand looms in Lyons and surrounding villages, making special kinds of goods, mostly high-class brocades. In more recent years, especially the last two decades, a number of manufacturers have built large mills in order to weave larger quantities of pile fabrics, but the majority of manufacturers are still placing orders outside 'à façon.' . . .

"How long Lyons will retain her present supremacy over her formidable competitors is a hard thing to guess. Silk manufacturing is growing in such enormous proportions in the United States, Germany, and Switzerland, that perhaps they

An interesting phase of the domestic industry in all the countries of the Continent is the application of electric power to the household loom; or rather, the introduction into domestic industry of a new type of loom driven by electric power. The possibility of dividing and transmitting the electric current makes it feasible to secure, in some degree at least, the advantages of power without the concentration and the large-scale operation which are the inevitable concomitants of the direct use of steam. Electricity has been parcelled out to small users in various branches of industry, — cutlery and other metal trades, and various branches of the textile industries. In silk weaving it has been thus utilized in Switzerland, in Germany, in France. The water power of Switzerland and her winter-bound yet industrious peasantry have led to an extended use of electric household looms, the wires transmitting the water-generated power to the deepest recesses of the mountain valleys.[1] Observers differ on the potentialities of this movement. To some it seems to promise the salvation of the domestic industry, and its maintenance for an indefinite time, — nay, even a reaction against the factory. By others it is thought but a temporary phase, only delaying for a time the inevitable universalization of concentrated large-scale production. Doubtless the factory will prevail eventually in most industries; but in the silk manufacture the nature of the

may manage eventually to put the French out of business through cheaper workmanship and larger output. The economists say that the silk business in Lyons has not progressed during the last decade, but they still recognize that it is in Lyons alone that can be found the highest grades of silks and the most beautiful designs (one has only to pay a visit to the Lyons Art Museum to be convinced of this assertion). The royalties and courts of all nations, for their pageants, cannot find elsewhere silks sold at hundreds of francs per yard and worth it." — L. Duran, *Raw Silk*, pp. 75, 77.

Beauquis, *Histoire économique de la soie*, p. 245, gives the following figures for the Lyons region:

	Hand looms	Power looms
1873	105,000	6,000 (1875)
1888	75,000	19,000
1903	60,000	38,000

[1] See the interesting map prefixed to Thürkauf, *Die Basler Seidenindustrie;* cf. p. 211. See also, on the general possibilities, Brauns, *loc. cit.*, p. 130, and Wilbrandt, *Die Weber in der Gegenwart* (1906), pp. 95, 109.

raw material and the peculiarities of the market seem to give unusual opportunities to household industry fortified by this utilization of electric power.

A peculiar situation has developed in England. The old silk industry has disappeared; but a new one has arisen in its place. Both the disappearance of the old and the emergence of the new are instructive.

The silk manufacture was introduced into England in the sixteenth and seventeenth centuries by Flemish and Huguenot refugees. Carried on as a typical "domestic" industry,[1] it was especially favored by the protective legislation of the succeeding period. Even after the decisive blow had been dealt the protective system through the abolition of the corn laws in 1846, a considerable protecting duty was retained on silks. Not until the Franco-British commercial treaty of 1860 were they admitted free into Great Britain; this being the very last step in carrying into effect the policy of free trade.

The British silk manufacture, as it stood in 1860, succumbed under the new régime. It had been conducted by the same methods as when first introduced from France. It was a handicraft industry, and could not hold its own against the competition of the continental products of the same industrial type. An almost romantic part of it was carried on in the Spitalfields district of London, where the Huguenots had first gathered and where the industry had long been carried on by them and their descendants. The Spitalfields industry was decadent even before 1860; it had been handicapped by the soot and clouds of London

[1] On the eighteenth century, see the memoranda in Held, *Zwei Bücher zur sozialen Geschichte Englands*, p. 560. On the continuance of the "cottage factories" through the middle of the nineteenth century, see the *Report of the* (Chamberlain) *Tariff Commission*, "Evidence on the Silk Industry," paragraph 3390. A former silk manufacturer of Coventry remarked, "The cottage factories were generally built to hold two or three looms, and generally the husband, wife, or eldest son or daughter used to attend the two or three looms. . . . I have seen the High Street in front of our warehouse crowded with carriers' carts [bringing silk goods from the neighboring villages] for several hundred yards up the street." This Tariff Commission, organized under the leadership of Joseph Chamberlain as part of the "tariff reform," *i. e.*, protectionist movement, is not to be confounded with official commissions.

and weakened by the drifting of its workpeople to other industries. After that fatal date, only a few hand loom weavers remained; and these still produce a few specialties for West End retailers, — a contrast to the 50,000 persons once employed in the district.[1] Other places, — Coventry, Macclesfield, Manchester, — also had carried on a considerable silk industry; since 1860 it has shrunk or disappeared. Silk throwing, formerly a trade of importance, has been entirely given up. Most of the hand looms, once thousands in number, have gone. Macclesfield in the old days had 6,000 or 8,000 hand looms; perhaps a 1,000 such remain.[2] In other silk centers of former days, a small industry, in odds and ends for local sales, continues to hold a place.[3] But the remnant is of no considerable industrial importance, and it is dwindling.

A silk industry, however, still remains in England, or rather a congeries of industries. Some are adaptations or growths from the old. Certain specialties continue to be made, more or less after the old methods: rich brocades, heavy damasks for furniture and decorative purposes. Large hand looms, run by skilled men, continue to be used for these goods. Irish poplins also (made of silk and wool mixed) are made on hand looms, and hold their own.[4] But far more important is an industry quite new: the manufacture of spun silk yarns and fabrics. While the making of thrown silk has disappeared from England, — whatever thrown silk the English still use is imported, — that of spun

[1] On the remnant of the Spitalfields industry, see Booth's *Life and Labour in London*, vol. iv, ch. viii (edition of 1897); and an excellent paper by Mr. F. Warner, a silk manufacturer, in the *Journal of the Society of Arts*, 1903–04, pp. 124, 131. Mr. Warner remarks, "In the Spitalfields the weavers, draughtsmen, jacquard machinists, loom builders, card cutters, and other mechanics, possessing a knowledge which had for generations been handed down from father to son . . . were competent and skilful." But he adds that the "manufacturers" were inefficient, and had "no taste, natural or acquired."

[2] See the *Report of the* (Chamberlain) *Tariff Commission*, "Evidence on the Silk Industry," paragraph 3260. The whole of the evidence in this publication is instructive.

[3] For example, the town of Leek; see *Report of the Tariff Commission*, paragraph 3275.

[4] See the *Report of the Tariff Commission*, paragraphs, 3377, 3378, 3396, 3398; Warner's paper, cited above, p. 128.

silks flourishes. As has already been explained, spun silk is made from "waste" silk. As Americans in general do best in weaving, so the English do best in spinning; their special aptitude for this in all textile industries [1] being due in part to climatic advantages, but in large part to causes less easy of discernment. The success of the English in spinning silk is in striking contrast with their abandonment of silk throwing. New machinery has been devised; a great industry has grown up. And not only does the spinning industry hold its own within the country, but exports of silk yarns take place to the Continent and the United States. The case is one among those, puzzling at first, where the same commodity moves two ways, being both imported and exported. The explanation clearly is that the goods which pass in these cross-currents are of different grades and qualities. It is the finest counts of silk yarns that are exported from England, just as are the finest counts of cotton yarns. Thrown silk meanwhile is imported into England. A few woven goods, especially goods of mixed materials, are again exported; so that, while the imports of silk goods into England have greatly increased, the exports of silks have on the whole held their own.[2]

From the protectionist point of view, the decline of the older silk manufacture in England is a clear national misfortune. An industry has gone; so much employment has been lost. In the

[1] Cf. what is said below of cotton and woolen spinning, pp. 290, 357.

[2] Mr. Warner, in the paper already cited, said (pp. 128, 130, 136): "Silk throwing as a separate industry is now but little carried on in this country. . . . Spun silk is a very large industry, and our spinners make the finest qualities and counts in the world, and their products are extensively used in the lace trade of Calais, St. Etienne, Lyons." The growth of the spun silk industry is due largely to the inventive genius of Lister (raised to the peerage, after the British fashion of enoblement, under the title of Lord Masham). The firm, Lister & Co., has a world-wide reputation; it turns out not only spun silk goods, but tapestries, velvets, pile fabrics, for which much reeled silk is used. It not only perfected spinning, but made a patent loom, described as an "automatic" loom, which the Germans are said to have copied when the patent ran out. *Tariff Commission Report*, paragraph 3319. — The head of the firm, Lister, also took a leading part in the development of the British worsted manufacture; see below, p. 339.

Very few fabrics are made entirely of spun silk. The yarns are used mainly as cotton is used in silk manufacturing, — for admixture. They supply the pile for cotton-back pile fabrics; and they are used as warp or as weft (filling) with reeled silk.

evidence gathered by the Chamberlain Tariff Commission, this loss was pointed to as a convincing illustration of the harm caused by the free trade policy. The real question, however, is whether anything was lost which it would have been worth while to retain. England long occupied, in relation to the countries of the Continent, a position similar to that which the United States has occupied in relation to all Europe. She was the country of advanced industry and of general economic effectiveness, and therefore the country of higher wages. Her superiority is not so marked now as it was half a century ago. In comparison with some countries, notably Germany, it seems to be in process of ceasing; but certainly it persisted through the greater part of the period here under review. Silk throwing and silk weaving under the old methods were not industries in which the English excelled; they did excel in other industries; and labor and capital turned to the others, when no longer kept by legislative stimulus in those less adapted to the country's genius. Even before 1860, the older branches of silk manufacturing were declining. Under free trade, they went by the board. Part of the labor formerly occupied in them was turned to the new industry which has sprung up, notably that in spun silk yarns, — an industry based on the traditional excellencies of the British: specialization, effective use of good machinery, sterling quality in the product. But probably the greater part went not to those remaining specialties of the same industry, but to other industries. Thus Coventry, formerly a center for silks and expecially for silk ribbons, is now one for motors and bicycles, and is more prosperous than it was under the old régime. There has been not the net loss which the protectionist bemoans, but an adjustment to new conditions which the free trader may reasonably claim to be advantageous.

Turning now to a comparison between the European and the American silk industries, we find striking resemblances and yet differences equally striking: in some respects a similar course of development, in others a very different one.

An instructive situation is to be found in the manufacture of sewing silk. This is the one branch which is really old in the United States. It goes back to the first half of the nineteenth century. The transition from household industry to machine and factory production here began as early as 1829. Successive improvements in machinery were made from time to time; a great impetus came in the middle of the century from the invention of the sewing machine and the consequent demand for "machine twist," *i. e.*, strands adapted for use on the sewing machine. By 1850 and 1860 the industry had reached dimensions large for those days. It continued to grow steadily in the modern period, mainly in the same localities and even in the same establishments as before the war.[1]

The exceptional position of sewing silk almost tells its own tale. Here is a machine product, peculiarly adapted to American methods of production and also to American needs. The machinery for turning it out is of the automatic type; the minimum of direct labor is required; mechanical ingenuity triumphs. This sort of thing the American can do better than any one else, and he goes ahead indifferent to tariff support. And for the same reasons, the English also have here some comparative advantage. Sewing silks have not disappeared from England under the free trade régime. Like spun silk, they hold their own easily against continental competition.

But as regards reeled silks, — which remain the most important of the silk products, — the resemblance between English and American conditions ceases. They are made in very great quantities in the United States; they are very little made in England. They have been protected in the United States, and left quite without tariff support in England. The march of invention and the conquests of the machine have been noteworthy in the United States, and in Germany also; no such advances in this

[1] For an account of the early history of the sewing silk manufacture, see Wyckoff, *Silk Manufacture in the United States* (1883), pp. 32 *seq.* See also the book of 1844 on *Silk Culture in the United States* (noted above, p. 223) at p. 9. The invention of the first machines began as early as 1828. The Census of 1850 reported sewing silk made to the value of $1,209,000; that of 1860, to the value of $3,600,000. In the Census of 1860 (*Report on Manufactures*, p. xciv), it is said that the chief seat of the industry is Connecticut, "where sewing silk was first made by machinery upwards of twenty-five years ago." An acquaintance whose memory goes back to ante-bellum days has told me of the highly-developed quasi-automatic machinery which he then saw in operation in the sewing silk mills.

branch of the industry have appeared in England. We have here somewhat different questions regarding the influence of protection or free trade, and the causes of the geographical distribution of the industry.

The branch of the silk manufacture which seems to have undergone the greatest changes and shows the greatest contrasts is that of ribbon making. Vast quantities of ribbons, both silk and velvet, are made from start to finish by the power-driven machine; turned out in mass production by the factories of Crefeld and Paterson, the two great seats of the industry in Germany and the United States. They are standardized goods, made for a very wide public; often composed in part of other materials (especially cotton); not articles of luxury, except so far as anything used for adornment may be so regarded. In Great Britain, on the other hand, the ribbon manufacture, which played a considerable part in Coventry and elsewhere before the French treaty, is virtually extinct. Barring a few specialties, silk ribbons, like broad silks, are secured chiefly by importation.[1]

In the United States, again, the domestic manufacture of ribbons has almost complete command of the market. It is true that imports continue; but they are highly specialized imports. A few expensive goods of unusual patterns are alone procured from abroad. They come in partly for sale to the rich and fastidious, partly in order to serve as models for American manufacturers, who still take their cue from the French in matters of fashion. The household loom (hand or electric power), or a slow-moving power loom, can hold its own in making such goods, of which only a small supply can be marketed. Machinery can never be applied to advantage unless large quantities of one particular sort of article are to be produced. But the great mass of standardized ribbons, — by no means necessarily cheap goods,

[1] In the *Tariff Commission Report* (Chamberlain) on the Silk Industry, there are many complaints of the extinction of the Coventry ribbon industry; see paragraphs 3239, 3392, 3511. "Previous to the French treaty there were about seventy rich manufacturers in the ribbon trade; now (1905) there are six very poor ones" (paragraph 3511). "Ribbons and silks are practically all foreign-made now" (paragraph 3471).

but goods not choice, — are made in the United States for domestic sale. Here the household industry has no place whatever; and such of its special products as continue to be in demand are procured by importation.

A position midway between that of France and that of the United States is held by Germany and Switzerland. Crefeld is the seat of a well-developed machine industry. Yet in the environs of Crefeld, and in Elberfeld, still more in southern Germany, there is much household weaving of silk ribbons. So, in Switzerland, the great ribbon industry of Basel is partly factory, partly household.[1] In these two countries, both household and factory industry thus exist side by side. In part, they compete; the victory of the machine is not so assured as in the United States. But in part they tend to turn to the kinds of product to which they are severally adapted. Specialized ribbons, elaborated patterns, expensive grades, tend to be made on the smaller scale, and remain within the domain of household and handicraft production. Fabrics for wide markets and mass consumption are made in the factory.

Velvet ribbons tell a similar tale, though perhaps with a difference of degree in favor of the machine. The older methods of making velvets and pile fabrics were largely displaced in the decade 1880–90, by inventions which seem to have revolutionized this branch of the industry with great rapidity. Here again Crefeld is the seat of a highly developed industry, using much cotton in admixture with silk, and turning out cheaper grades of goods for sale to the masses. It is significant that spun silk (" Schappe ") is largely used, both in the United States and in Germany, in the manufacture of these so-called " popular " fabrics. The machinery was early transferred to the United States, and there seems to have been remodelled and improved. In both countries the steady march of invention has enabled a wider range of goods to be turned out by machine processes than was at first thought possible, — figured goods, more varied patterns. Yet in both it is the standardized articles which are chiefly turned out by the machines. In the United States, velvet ribbons,

[1] Bötzkes, p. 26.

like silk ribbons, are imported only when of special quality or design.[1]

Essentially the same situation appears with broad silks; but here apparently with less decisive conquest by the machine, and with somewhat greater persistence of methods and products of the handicraft type. The silks of half-a-century ago, made from hand thrown tram or organzine on hand looms, had a character and quality of their own, which the machine made article cannot fully rival. For various kinds of textiles, — woolens and linens, as well as silks, — fabrics of a certain solidity and durability do not seem within the competence of rapidly-driven machinery. The "home-spun" goods may lack the sheen and the even finish of the factory article, but their very uneven quality gives them a certain charm. And they "wear like iron." Such were the silks of older days, when a woman kept her best black dress for life. A piece of silk such as is woven on a hand loom in France, or for that matter a Chinese mandarin's similarly woven coat, is an extraordinary product. No wet or wear harms it; it holds its sober gloss year after year, even decade after decade. Such stuffs, too, have a certain touch and appearance never to be found in the factory article. The new types of factory-made broad silks fit in many ways into the whims of the modern woman and into the fast-changing social conditions. If they are cheap, they are dressy. If they wear out in a brief

[1] On pile fabrics in general (velvets, plushes, and the like), I have found it difficult to get satisfactory information. As has already been remarked, these were subjected to high specific duties as early as 1890 (see p. 218, above, and my *Tariff History*, p. 269); one of the provisions in the McKinley tariff which is said to have been a return for heavy contributions by manufacturers to Republican campaign funds. A considerable industry developed in the United States, yet imports continued on a large scale. Rapid changes in fashion here introduce a peculiarly complicating factor. In Europe, the English have the lead in manufacturing plushes, the Germans and French in velvets. In both classes, and especially in velvets, the more expensive qualities tend to be imported into the United States. I have been told by well informed and apparently unbiased observers that the Americans made distinct improvements in the machinery for pile fabrics. What stage in the rivalry between domestic and foreign producers has been reached in this industry it is not easy to make out. Nor is it easy to find indications on the problem more particularly considered in the next following chapter, — the prospects of an eventual surpassing of the foreigners by the developing American industry.

season, so do the current fashions of color and design. Being made in quantities and at comparatively low cost, they can be purveyed to a large constituency. In all the advanced countries, and especially in the United States, the steady democratization of society has caused dress silks as well as silk ribbons to be in wide and growing demand, — a circumstance which in itself tends to give victory to the machine made product.

Imports of broad silks into the United States continue; but, as in the case of ribbons, for specialized fabrics only. France still maintains her place as the country of excellent and expensive silks. Fabrics of high quality or of unusual design, such as are not made in large quantities for any single piece, still come from the looms of Lyons. The circumstance that dress silks give more scope for individuality and variety than ribbons enables the foreigner, and especially the French manufacturer, to hold his own, notwithstanding high duties, in supplying the American women of expensive tastes (no small constituency) with ornate or "distinctive" fabrics. It would seem, too, that broad silks are less successfully handled by the machine than the narrower goods. One reason is that they need more minute inspection, more careful finishing; and these ancillary operations always involve hand labor and minute attention, even where the more essential work has been relegated to the machine. So far as the American output and the continuing imports are concerned, the situation is again the same: the market is mainly supplied by the machine made domestic article, and only special qualities are imported, usually of the kind still made by handicraft or quasi-handicraft methods.

The continuance of imports for still other kinds of silks and the different relation between importation and domestic production[1] for these other goods are explicable on the same principle. Silk laces, for example, are chiefly imported. The situation is

[1] Some figures on the domestic production and the imports of silk laces: —

	Value of Product (Census)	Imports
1880	$433,000	
1890	261,000	
1900	803,000	$3,000,000
1905	745,000	5,000,000

the reverse of that just described for ribbons and broad silks: the domestic production is comparatively small. This, too, notwithstanding the fact that the duty on articles of this class was long kept unusually high; it remained 60 per cent even when the *ad valorem* duty on most silks was reduced (in 1909) to 50 per cent. Silk laces, embroideries, insertions and the like are made by hand, or on hand machines. Some simple patterns are indeed made within the country under the stimulus of the duty; but the tariff, high as it is, has no effect in securing the domestic production of most goods of this class. The comparative disadvantage is too great. A similar case is that of silk trimmings. Dress and cloak trimmings are mainly imported. They are usually made in small quantities and of patterns much varied; consequently it proves not worth while to make them in the United States. And it is characteristic, again, that certain other kinds of silk trimmings, used for upholstery purposes and the like, are made at home, not imported. These are more uniform in pattern, are more in the nature of standardized articles, give an opportunity for machinery and for operations on something approaching large scale: they afford some scope for the American industrial excellencies.

CHAPTER XVI

THE SILK MANUFACTURE — SOME CONCLUSIONS

SUMMARIZING the results of the preceding chapters, we may say that an industry quite new has been brought into being by protection. Imports of great classes of articles have been supplanted almost wholly by domestic products. Not only this; the domestic industry has progressed in technical effectiveness as well. Great advances have been made in its appliances and organization. The further question may now be taken up: has the progress been such as to justify the protectionist policy, not merely on the vulgar mercantilist grounds, but on the more tenable ground that a young industry has been successfully nurtured?

In seeking to answer this question two considerations must be borne in mind. One is that the technical progress in the industry may not have been peculiar to the United States. It may have been,— to some extent beyond doubt it was,— but one phase of a general advance, observable in other countries as well as the United States. So far as the American manufacturers simply adopted those changes which their foreign rivals also were making, they did no more than keep abreast of the times. But to forge ahead is the essential desideratum under the young industries argument. And, second, even if some unusual and unexampled progress was made in the American industry, we must inquire whether it was carried so far as to bring the industry up to the full American standard, — whether it was so great as to enable the industry eventually to hold its own quite without protection. This result has been attained in the iron manufacture; but whether as the consequence of protection or of more general causes, we have found it difficult to determine. If attained at all in the silk manufacture, it is to the protective policy that the result must be fairly credited. Has it been attained to the full? Quite conceivably the technical and industrial improvements, though excelling those in other countries, have brought the industry only to a half-way stage, in which it has risen above the level of effectiveness in rival countries, yet not quite up to the prevailing and dominant level of effectiveness in the United States. It may have reached the stage where it could be maintained with duties lower than those imposed at the outset, yet would succumb to foreign competition if there were no duties at all.

Unfortunately the evidence on these points is far from conclusive; and there is much difficulty in weighing such pertinent evidence as is available. The decisive test of unaided competition with foreign rivals has not been applied; its full application at any early date in the future is beyond the bounds of political probability. On the other hand, the attitude of the American manufacturers, — assumed as a rule without consciousness of its economic significance, — would indicate that no progress whatever had been achieved and that the free traders' goal was not in sight. Not only removal of the duties, but the slightest reduction, is resisted tooth and nail. We are told that the retention of the protective barrier at its original height is indispensable for the very existence of the industry. Every endeavor to lower it is met by declarations that the result must be either a wholesale reduction of operatives' wages or complete abandonment.

Among the things that are clear, however, is the exaggeration in these protests. The case of the protectionists is not so bad as their own spokesmen make it out. As has been already pointed out,[1] opposition of this sort is always offered when reduction of protective duties is suggested. It is due partly to a wish to take no chances, — to "play safe"; partly to mere bluff, with the expectation not so much of preventing reduction as of minimizing it; partly to a vague panicky feeling about the terrors of foreign competition, engendered by the frothy declamation on cheap foreign labor. These same manufacturers, if they are questioned in quiet and give answers without the fear of the terrible free trader on them, will admit that they are not averse

[1] See chapter ii, above, p. 23.

to "scientific" reductions; that many duties could be lowered without harming them; that some articles they really can probably produce as cheaply as the foreigners, at least under the technical conditions existing for the time being (they will usually make reservations as regards the future); and that they simply do not know just how far the process of reduction or removal could be carried without disturbance. They will virtually say, though not using the phraseology of the economists, that there has been after all some approach to the free traders' goal.

Looking for evidence in other directions, I have sought to find facts of significance as regards technical conditions, and have also questioned persons presumably well informed, yet not biased, concerning the general conditions of the competition between domestic and foreign producers. The results so secured are not without haziness, but are not entirely inconclusive.

As regards technical progress, one fact of significance is the source of supply for the machinery. Is it made within the country, or is it imported? Any industry which steadily imports its machinery from other countries makes thereby a confession of the lack of a comparative advantage. Its appliances are *ipso facto* no better than those of its competitors. Not only this, but the appliances are likely to be less effectively utilized. Though machinery imported from elsewhere may be operated as skilfully as in the country of origin, the probability is the other way. The same ingenuity and watchfulness that cause it to be devised in one country cause it also to be worked to best advantage there. On the other hand any industry which in this regard has got quite beyond foreign tutelage, — for which the machinery is of domestic design and make, — can claim at the least full equality. And if the machinery is not only made within the country, but is sought for elsewhere, being exported to other countries or copied there, the claim may be for more than equality: there is evidence of superiority. Every student of economic history knows that such a position of superiority was held by England through the greater part of the nineteenth century. Then foreign manufacturers, and especially those of the Continent, secured their machinery from England, or copied

English models. Yet they were very slow to get the full results from the British machines; and as fast as they did, the British had progressed a stage further, invented or improved still more, and retained their superiority indefinitely. A similar position of sustained excellence is now held by the Americans in the machine tool trades,[1] and in wood working apparatus. How is it with the machinery used in the silk manufacture?

This situation, it appears, is creditable to the American industry, — indicative of real and sustained progress and at least some superiority. As has been noted,[2] the first silk working machinery was imported. The industry began by following the familiar paths. But soon it struck out for itself, and quite left behind the old exemplars. For a decade or two, all the more important silk machinery has been made within the country; only certain specialties, presently to be described, have been imported. This cessation of imports of machinery cannot be ascribed merely to the fact that duties on the machinery itself have been high. True, protection has been applied here also; but by no means with the result of keeping out all machinery of every sort. In other textile industries, and especially in the worsted manufacture, much of the machinery continues to be imported notwithstanding the duties.[3] The fact that it is otherwise for the silk industry, — that most of the equipment of the American mills is of domestic design and construction, — is significant. Still more significant is the exportation of such equipment; or, if not exportation, the copying of American models in foreign countries. Throwing machinery was invented in the United States, following the principle of cotton spinning machin-

[1] See chapter xiii, p. 197, above.

[2] See chapter xiv, p. 230. A Coventry (England) manufacturer said in 1905 that in 1870–80 "a great number of looms and other machinery were sent to America, and at Paterson (N. J.) there are in full operation the very same kinds of looms and other machinery as were used in Coventry thirty and sixty years ago." *Tariff Commission Report*, paragraphs 3275, 3391. It is quite true, I am told, that some old English looms, solidly built, continued to be used thus long, even though it would have paid to substitute new and more efficient looms. The ribbon looms in use at Coventry in 1860 seem to have been made in Basel and exported thence to England. Timmins, *The Resources . . . of Birmingham* (London, 1866), p. 187.

[3] Cf. what is said below, chapter xxi, p. 343, on woolen and worsted machinery.

ery for which also American ingenuity had taken the initiative.[1] It was developed to a high degree of perfection, and American throwing machines were sent to foreign countries, and introduced into the technical schools of England and Switzerland.[2] Ribbon weaving machinery, already mentioned among those improved by Americans, was brought to a high pitch of automatic operation. It too was exported, or manufactured in European countries after American designs.[3] So it was with broad looms. For all the textiles, weaving machinery has been a peculiarly fertile field for American invention. Looms for broad goods as well as for ribbons have been brought to an exceptional pitch of mechanical effectiveness. All thought of importing silk looms has ceased; and broad looms, like ribbon looms, have been exported, or manufactured abroad after American models. They have moreover been operated to best effect within the country. The example of the cotton and worsted industries has been followed: the weaver (in reality a loom tender and watcher) has been called on to take care of several looms, and usually of more looms than are allotted to the weaver of similar fabrics in European countries.

[1] The throwing machine (" spindle ") was an adaptation of the ring spindle which has played so important a part in the American cotton manufacture. " A little after Rabbeth's invention [of a much-improved ring spindle for cotton] Mr. John E. Atwood of Stonington, Conn., made a sleeve whorl spindle in which the bolster and step were made in one piece, and attached ' in a yielding manner ' to the surrounding shell or bolster case. This structure has gone into use to an extent of hundreds of thousands in silk spinning, but not extensively in cotton spinning. . . . In silk spinning . . . the process is entirely different from that necessary in spinning cotton. The silk is spun off the spindle and the cotton is wound upon it." See the historical account of cotton spindles given by W. F. Draper, in *Proceedings*, Twenty-sixth Anniversary Meeting New England Cotton Manufacturers Association, p. 31.

[2] Allen, *Silk Industry of the World*, p. 27. The leading American firm that manufactures this machinery writes me: " For a number of years we have been exporting throwing machinery to various silk producing European and Asiatic countries. It seems to be a constant trade, although not large, but is gradually extending into different fields of silk manufacturing."

[3] For reference to the high-speed automatic ribbon loom, invented in the United States in 1899, see Allen, *Silk Industry*, p. 29, and *Census Report on Manufactures*, 1900, p. 209. A large American firm making ribbon looms writes to me thus (1913): " For a number of years we exported our ribbon looms to Europe — to Switzerland, France, and Germany — but we are now represented in Europe by a large manufacturing concern who build our machinery over there from our models."

Both in construction and in operation there is evidence of superiority, — of a comparative advantage.[1]

It is not inconsistent with this conclusion that certain kinds of machinery are still imported. On the contrary, the continuing partial reliance on foreign makers proves on careful scrutiny to be not inconsistent with a general trend to progress and emancipation. The machinery that continues to be imported is chiefly for finishing purposes. The rapid changes in fashion bring corresponding changes in these devices. An apparatus will be contrived to secure a particular appearance in the fabrics; in a season or two something else comes into fashion; then a new kind of apparatus comes into use. American manufacturers of machinery do not find it worth while to cater to such temporary and sporadic demands. It is a case of "specialties"; and these tend to be imported, whether they are tools or finished

[1] On broad looms, the spokesman of the industry wrote thus in 1900 (Allen, *Silk Industry*, p. 27): "In weaving perhaps there has been more progress in improved machinery the last decade than in the three preceding decades. The improvements have produced a loom of very high efficiency, equipped with mechanical devices designed for saving time, labor, material, such as numerous multipliers, two weave, leno, swivel, embroidery motions, and many others, all arranged to work automatically. Special mention should be made of the improvements by which all classes of taffeta effects, *formerly made on hand looms only, are now made on power looms*" (the italics are mine; the passage deserves emphasis).

Here again I can refer to correspondence (1913) with a great loom making firm. "We commenced exporting silk looms many years ago and as soon as they became established in some of the foreign countries they were copied and are being made there today, exact copies of our machine. The labor cost is so much less there that it is impossible for us to continue to export, although we have sent from time to time quite a lot of machinery into the different countries, but as above stated, as soon as they get well established they get a local maker to manufacture. . . . Were it not for the fact that we have been able, by an enormous expenditure of money and skill to invent improved machinery, we should never have been able to take the position we have amongst the silk manufacturers of this country." It should be added that this firm, like most makers of machinery, expressed its objections to "any appreciable change" in the tariff as it stood in 1912.

Another manufacturer (one making silk fabrics, not machinery) writes me that "in the knitting industry, — silk underwear, hosiery, neckties, — the American machinery is vastly superior to the foreign machinery, against which there is still a considerable prejudice abroad. This prejudice will undoubtedly be broken down within another decade." Here is again the assertion of superiority, and again the fear that it will not be maintained. Cf. the same state of mind among the makers of other machinery, chapter xii, p. 196, above.

products. Such finishing machinery as is continuously used, year after year, is commonly of American make.[1]

Turn now to another kind of evidence. Repeatedly I have asked persons who buy and sell silks,[2] what would happen if there were no duties? Are there any goods which are so cheaply made in the United States that they would in no event be imported? And as regards those which might be imported under free trade, how great is the present difference in price between the European goods and the American? Here, unfortunately, our prohibitive duties so veil the situation that it is difficult to secure satisfactory information. The question, are any silks as cheap in the United States as abroad, is usually answered unhesitatingly: yes, most domestic goods are cheaper than the imported. But a very little further inquiry shows the answer to mean that domestic goods are cheaper than *duty-paid* foreign goods. And when the question is again asked, with careful explanation of its precise bearing; how if the foreign goods were admitted free of duty? — the person in the business hesitates. This question he is not called on to consider in the ordinary course of his dealings. The purchase of most foreign goods, with the duty added, is quite out of the question and the dealer pays no attention to them or their prices. Certain classes of articles, and some specialties, are indeed so much cheaper abroad that they can be imported, even with payment of the duties; and reference is then made to the imported silks described in the pre-

[1] A conversant American dealer writes me: "In the finishing departments . . . a good deal of machinery is imported. This is largely due to the fact that new fabrics are brought out abroad, many of which require special apparatus to produce the desired results in the finishing, and it takes some time before the American producer of finishing machinery begins to manufacture such apparatus. This machinery may be of such limited usefulness that its manufacture is never taken up here at all, and at other times the usefulness of such machinery may be transitory. The ordinary run of finishing machinery, such as spraying machines, paper dryers, can dryers, tentering frames, calenders, singeing machinery . . . are largely made on this side of the water, and there must be few of such machines now (1913) imported." An importer of finishing machinery confirms these statements.

[2] These inquiries have been addressed chiefly to jobbers and to the managers of silk departments in the large retail establishments. Both manufacturers and importers are likely to be biased, even though not consciously; the importers are often the representatives of foreign manufacturers.

ceding chapter. But how much cheaper are the foreign goods which are never imported? are these cheaper at all? One witness who impressed me as well-informed and judicious stated his belief that ribbons and broad silks are, as a rule, somewhat cheaper abroad; perhaps 25 per cent cheaper; yet as regards most goods admitted this to be but a guess. Some goods, he said, are certainly quite as cheap in the United States; such as spun silks and certain smooth-faced satins. And it is significant that another well-informed observer has publicly expressed the opinion that certain standard silk fabrics are so cheaply made that an export trade in them is among the possibilities of the early future.[1]

The fact that the makeup of the American purchasing constituency is different from that of foreign countries adds to the

1 "Where labor enters most largely, we are visibly outclassed. . . . With plain goods, made on a large scale, the unit of labor cost is much decreased. Where a mill is running many hundreds of looms on the same fabric, three or four looms to a weaver, and at high speeds, both the weaving cost and the general expense item fall to a really low figure, and it is in these directions we must look [for possible exports].

"There are many fabrics such as liberty satins, cotton back satins, crêpes de chine, taffetas, etc., that have been so specialized on here as to encourage the belief that their cost is so low that an export business might be done in them." From a chapter on "Finding Foreign Markets" in Chittick, *Silk Manufacturing and its Problems* (1913), p. 324.

The exports of silks, as recorded in the Treasury statistics, were as follows: —

Exports of Silk Manufactures

	To Great Britain	To Canada	Total, to all countries
1909	$13,000	$503,000	$847,000
1910	50,000	722,000	1,097,000
1911	200,000	915,000	1,538,000
1912	210,000	1,159,000	1,993,000
1913	200,000	1,354,000	2,391,000

The only countries besides Great Britain and Canada to which any considerable quantities went, were Cuba and Mexico. The exports to Great Britain were chiefly of knitted silks, for which some newly-devised American machinery had caused a considerable foreign market (cf. p. 254, above). Those to Canada have been explained to me as due largely to mere propinquity; a Canadian merchant whose stock is depleted can send a buyer to New York and get what he wants over night, disregarding for such sporadic purchases a comparatively high price. With all allowance for these exceptional circumstances the recent increase in exports of silks remains striking and apparently significant.

difficulties in comparing domestic silks with the imported. A merchant who had been lifelong in the trade remarked to me that it was almost impossible to compare American ribbons with foreign. The former, of the kind made "for our general trade," are of good quality; better than what is made for mass consumption in Europe, though not so choice as what is there made for the rich and is still exported to the United States for our own rich. The different conditions of the American market, — an enormous number of purchasers who are well-to-do, even though not affluent, and who buy a staple article of good quality, — has caused the American manufacturers to turn out great quantities of ribbons that are not expensive, yet not vilely cheap. These are made on very large looms, twenty or twenty-five feet wide,[1] which are run faster than are looms in European countries, and enable a great yardage to be turned out at low cost per piece. All the witnesses unite in remarking on the great improvements in American silk goods during the last twenty years, the betterment of the quality and taste, the greater variety of goods, the steady lowering of prices.

On the whole, the conclusion seems warranted that there has been at least some approach to a successful application of protection to young industries. How near the approach is to complete success, how good the prospects for such success, would be difficult to say. But it seems beyond question that great advances have been made in the domestic industry, and that both in its technical appliances and in the adaptation of its products to the demands of the domestic market the characteristic American excellencies have been shown. The peculiarities of the raw material and the long-standing traditions of the industry interposed at the outset obstacles which would almost certainly have prevented ventures into this new field but for the stimulus from protection. Competition among the domestic producers stimulated invention, lowered prices, displaced the foreigners in the most important classes of goods, made the burden of the

[1] The ordinary "double deck" loom for ribbons is about 16 feet wide. These wide looms are "single deck." The modern ribbon loom weaves a great number of ribbons side by side in long parallel strips.

duties (so far as a burden remained at all) much less than the nominal rates indicated.[1]

This general conclusion is not weakened by a comparison with the course of development in other countries. The contrast both with England and with Germany and Switzerland is instructive. The older type of silk manufacture succumbed in England under free trade. It was no better adapted to the industrial conditions of England than of the United States; it did not offer the same advantages as other English industries; its disappearance cannot be reasonably a matter for regret. A new silk industry has indeed arisen in England, self-supporting, and profitable alike to the owners and to the country. But it is modest in size, limited in scope, not comparable to the young American giant. Who can say whether a similar great industry would have developed in Great Britain under high protection? Whether innovation, invention, rapid change and improvement, would have been stimulated such as to produce even that success, — still with an uncertain ultimate outcome, — which has been achieved in the United States? Bearing in mind the general character of British industries, their tenacious adherence to ways well-approved, their sustained excellence in the goods of established position, one is led to question whether any prospect existed of eventual gains under protection. The British have doubtless done their best under free trade. On the other hand, the Germans (and apparently the Swiss also) have shown in the silk industry, as elsewhere, a curious juxtaposition of the old industrial régime and the new. The machine has conquered larger and larger sections of the field; yet not to the complete displacement of the handicraft and the household. The quantitative growth of the German silk manufacture has been comparable to that in the United

[1] Notwithstanding occasional suggestions that American silk manufacturers should in some way combine, and cease their "senseless" competition, nothing in the nature of a trust or combination has appeared in the industry. In the *Thirty-ninth Report of the Silk Association*, p. 46, are some expressions of vain longing for a curtailment of competition. In Germany, the Kartel has become, in the silk manufacure as in others, a permanent part of industrial organization; yet, it would seem, mainly as a "condition" Kartel, not one effective in raising prices. Beckerath, *Kartelle der Seidenweberei-industrie*, p. 187 *et passim*.

States; the qualitative advance also has been striking. Here also it would be difficult to say how far the protective policy has contributed to the growth and how far that policy can be justified on the ground of having nurtured the industry to independence. The case would seem less strong in Germany than in the United States. The German industry has old roots; the application of protection was less vigorous and stimulating; the machine has had no such sweeping victory. Yet the problem is part of the larger problem how to explain the extraordinary industrial burst which is transforming the German people. Great political and social forces have been at work. The unbiased historian, when he comes in later times to survey with the needed perspective this marvellous change, will probably conclude that the external commercial policy of the nation was among the least of the impelling causes. A conclusion in general similar is likely to be reached for the United States. Here also the share of protection in causing or even modifying the country's general industrial advance will be found much less than the vehemence of the present controversy would imply. But in the particular case we are here considering, — the American silk manufacture, — a dominant influence from the protective system is not to be gainsaid; nor can it be denied that this influence has shown more potentiality of eventual benefit than the free traders are disposed to admit.

Our survey of the silk industry thus raises more questions than it answers. It appears that protection has caused a great industry to spring up; and there are tenable grounds for maintaining that the growth has been qualitative as well as quantitative, and may illustrate the validity of the argument for protection to young industries. But the protection has been so high and so long-continued that it conceals from view many facts of essential significance. We cannot be sure how great has been the progress of the American silk manufacture. An incisive reduction of duties, — much sharper than that made in the tariff act of 1913, — would show whether its progress toward independence has really been as considerable and as promising as it has been inferred to be, from evidence more or less inconclusive, in the preceding pages. A complete abolition of duties, like that which England made in 1860, would alone show whether the eventual end of protection to young industries has been reached, — complete independence, ability to supply the commodities as cheaply as by importation.

CHAPTER XVII

THE COTTON MANUFACTURE. PROGRESS OF THE DOMESTIC INDUSTRY

THE cotton manufacture has a history very different in some important respects from that of the silk manufacture. It is not a young industry, but an old one. In the United States, as in England, it was the earliest of the textile industries to be reorganized for power-driven machinery, and for the modern factory system; the earliest, indeed, among manufactures of any kind. The epoch-making change was promoted in this case by the even and homogeneous quality of the raw material, as well as by its abundant supply. Cotton was subjected with comparative ease to the machine processes. The same causes which made the industry the first one and the typical one to be affected by the English industrial revolution, facilitated its early growth in the United States. Being preëminently a machine using industry, it was promptly taken up and successfully prosecuted by the Americans, and especially by the New Englanders.

The cotton manufacture grew up, — to recapitulate summarily, — during the period of interrupted foreign trade which preceded the war of 1812 and continued through the war until 1815. It was systematically and successfully developed during the time of the early protective movement which set in with the tariff of 1816; it maintained itself unshaken notwithstanding the gradual reduction of duties carried out in 1833–40 under the provisions of the compromise tariff act of 1833. A marked advance took place in the decade 1840–50, perhaps stimulated by the higher duties of the tariff act of 1842, but at all events not checked by the lower duties of the act of 1846. From 1846 to 1857 cotton goods were subjected to a simple *ad valorem* duty of 25 per cent, and from 1857 to 1861 to one of but 24 per cent. The industry progressed rapidly and grew to large dimensions during this period of moderate duties. Not only did it grow at home, but it reached out to foreign markets. A considerable export trade developed, — conclusive proof, if not of complete independence from protection in every branch, at least of a stage of development to which the young industries argument could no longer apply.[1]

Nevertheless the further growth of the industry since the civil war suggests some questions which are related to the arguments for protection to young industries, and some other questions which bear on the more general problems of the international division of labor. To these attention will be given in this present chapter.

The rates of duty on cotton goods since 1860 tell a somewhat curious story. In the tariff act of 1861, enacted before the war, specific duties were substituted for the *ad valorem* duties of 1846 and 1857; with the declared intention, and in the main probably with the effect, of simply changing the method of levy, not the height of the tariff.[2] But the change to the specific system soon led to unexpected consequences. During the war, the price of raw cotton went up to extraordinary figures. The average price for 1864 was over fifty cents a pound in gold; and for more than ten years after the war it continued to be at a high level. Not until the close of the decade 1870–80 did it fall to something like the normal figures (ten to twelve cents a pound) that had prevailed before 1860. The prices of cotton goods went up correspondingly, the rise being, of course, most marked in the heavier

[1] For an account of this earlier period in somewhat more detail, I refer the reader to my *Tariff History of the United States*, pp. 25–36, 135–142, and to M. T. Copeland, *The Cotton Manufacturing Industry of the United States*, chapter i. I shall have frequent occasion to refer to Dr. Copeland's able volume, which makes it unnecessary to consider in detail some important matters on which he has told the whole story.

In my *Tariff History*, p. 34 and elsewhere, I have stated, with less qualification than I should now make, the conclusion that the duties of 1816 were not clearly needed for protection to the then young industry. As intimated in chapter ii of the present volume (see p. 22), I am disposed to allow a longer time for the trial of protection to young industries, and to admit the probable usefulness not only of the imposition of duties in 1816, but of their retention in 1824, 1828, and 1832.

[2] Such was the opinion, for example, of Samuel Batchelder, the well-known manufacturer and chronicler, expressed in letters written to the Boston *Commercial Advertiser* in 1861.

and cheaper goods for which the raw material was the largest item in the expenses of production. Naturally the specific duties were raised correspondingly. As the prices of cotton and cotton goods had gone up five-fold, so the duties on the goods went up in a similar ratio. On the cheapest grade of unbleached cloth, for example, the rate in 1861 had been one cent per yard; it became five cents per yard in 1864.

The price of cotton began to decline as soon as the war closed; within a year or two it declined greatly. The duties on cotton goods as raised in 1864 became proportionately heavier. Even the rates fixed in 1861 had been prohibitory on the cheap goods; those of 1864 became very heavy, often prohibitory, on goods of medium and finer grades. A reduction was to have been expected; but it was long postponed, and when finally made, still left a high range of rates. Such was the case, as is well-known to all students of our tariff history, with all the protective duties of the war period: it was their prolonged retention, largely through inertia, that caused the protective system to become so extreme. In the case of cottons, the duties, raised to an especially high pitch in 1864, were not overhauled systematically until the general revision of 1883. Even then they were reduced to figures that left them prohibitory for all the cheaper grades of goods. The duty on the lowest class was left at two and one-half cents a yard, amply sufficient to shut out any possibility of importation; and those on most other grades remained correspondingly high. In the protective tariff acts that came after 1883, — those of 1890, 1897, and 1909, — the same process of cautious reduction of the duties on the cheaper grades was continued. By 1897 the duty on the lowest class had gone down to one cent a yard, precisely the figure of 1861. This was still a "safe" rate. So were the corresponding rates on the lower grades generally, — on yarns of the coarser counts, and on the cheap and medium grades of woven fabrics, whether in the gray, or bleached, or printed and dyed.

Meanwhile, as the protective system was extended and stiffened, another movement appeared. The specific duties were differentiated more and more; and side by side with the reduction of the rates on the lower classes of goods, there went a steady increase in those on the dearer goods. In each successive act the same general scheme (that of 1861) was maintained: the specific duties being adjusted first according to the number of threads per square inch of cloth and then according as the cloth was bleached, dyed, printed. In the acts of 1897 and 1909 still another method of differentiation was added, — the number of square yards to the pound, *i. e.*, the weight per square yard; the fabrics within each class being subjected to higher duties as they were lighter in weight. It is not important for the present discussion to follow the changes in detail: it will suffice to indicate the general trend by noting the maximum duties on the finest fabrics. The maximum was in 1883 6 cents a yard; in 1890, 6¾ cents; in 1897, 8 cents; and in 1909, 12½ cents.[1] Part and parcel of the same tendency was the increase in the dragnet rate, — the general *ad valorem* rate on manufactures of cotton not specifically enumerated. The dragnet clause levied, in 1861, a duty of 30 per cent; in 1883, one of 35 per cent; in 1890, 40 per cent; in 1897 and 1909, 45 per cent. The cotton schedule, comparatively simple in 1861, became extremely complex, — so much so that the significance of the rates and gradations of duty was difficult to follow, and the rates became susceptible to the sort of manipulation indicated by the term "joker." The unusually intricate provisions in the cotton schedule of 1909 gave opportunity for veiled and disguised increases of duty which contributed much to the feeling of suspicion and revolt aroused by this last step in the ultra-protectionist series.[2]

[1] The marked increase of the maximum rate in 1909 was due to still another refinement in the elaboration of the specific duties. In previous acts there had been a dragnet clause on cotton cloths: all cloths above a certain value were subjected to one *ad valorem* rate. This *ad valorem* rate had been 25 per cent in 1861, 35 per cent in 1864, 40 per cent in 1883, and again 40 per cent in 1897 and 1909 (45 per cent in 1890). In 1909 it was further provided that the very finest and most expensive goods, if *valued* over 25 cents a yard, should be charged 12½ cents a yard, but in no case less than 40 per cent. — This dragnet clause, or omnibus *ad valorem* duty, on cotton cloths is not to be confounded with the similar dragnet clause on miscellaneous cotton manufactures "not otherwise provided for," to which reference is made in the text.

[2] On the changes of duty in 1909, see an instructive article by S. M. Evans, in the *Journal of Political Economy*, December, 1910, "The Making of a Tariff Law";

The tariff of 1913, it need hardly be said, made a great breach in this huge and complicated structure. It substituted for the mass of intricate and heavy specific duties a simple system of moderate *ad valorem* duties. These were graded, ranging from a minimum of 5 per cent to a maximum of 30 per cent. The lowest rate imposed (5 per cent) was on the coarsest yarns; the highest (30 per cent) was on the finest woven fabrics.[1] The change in the figures of the statute-book was very great. But, as will appear presently, the effect on the cotton manufacture was in most cases negligible. Only on the finer goods was the reduction of real consequence. At the date of writing these pages (1914) it is still uncertain what will be the effects of the changes on the finer goods.

What effects can be traced to the high duties maintained throughout the half-century that followed the civil war? Those

and a careful analysis by M. T. Copeland, in the *Quarterly Journal of Economics*, February, 1910. For an elaborate statement of the duties on cottons from 1890 to 1909, see the *Tariff Board's Report on Cotton Manufacture* (1912), pp. 290 *seq.*

The *Tariff Board Report* gave abundant illustrations of the high range of the duties on cottons until 1913, pointing out that in most cases the duties on cotton cloths were higher than the total "conversion cost" of the goods, — *i. e.*, higher than the total expenses of production over and above the raw material. See the Board's introductory statement or analysis, pp. 10–14, and more detailed statements at pp. 440, 458, 503 *passim.*

[1] The plan on which the duties on cotton goods were fixed in 1913 is indicated by the following tabular statement: —

	Duty on Yarns	Duty on Plain, Unbleached Cloths, Made from Such Yarns	Duty on Cloths that are Bleached, Printed, Dyed, Woven with Figures, Mercerized, etc., Made from Such Yarns
Yarns, numbers 1 to 9 ...	5 per cent	7½ per cent	10 per cent
" " 10 " 39 ...	7½ "	10 "	12½ "
" " 40 " 49 ...	10 "	12½ "	15 "
and so on, until			
Yarns, numbers 80 to 90 ...	22½ "	25 "	27½ "
Yarns above number 100....	25 "	27½ "	30 "

This is a symmetrical arrangement; the duty on plain cloths is always 2½ per cent higher than that on the yarns with which they are woven, and the duty on cloths printed, etc., is always 2½ per cent higher still. The symmetry, however, is more in appearance than in reality. The arrangement left the duties on some cheap cloths in effect higher than on many dear cloths; since raw cotton enters so largely in the price of the former, and causes an *ad valorem* duty to be high in relation to manufacturing (or "conversion") cost.

on fabrics of cheaper grade, — the staple goods of the industry, — were quite prohibitory. Those on finer goods, though not in all cases prohibitory, were put up notch by notch in the successive protectionist acts, with the design of promoting the manufacture of such goods within the country. The free trader might be led to predict that the extreme rates on the ordinary goods, and the exclusion of foreign competition as regards them, would lead to something like stagnation in this part of the domestic industry. On the other hand, the high effective rates on the dearer goods might be expected by the protectionist not only to put an end to their importation and cause domestic goods to be substituted for them, but also to bring about some results of the young industries type, — improvements in the field newly opened for the Americans, and attainment of independence or at least indications of some approach to independence.

First a general survey may be made of the growth of the industry at large. The following figures indicate how steady and great was the increase in domestic production, how comparatively small were the imports.

COTTON GOODS, 1860–1910[1]

Year	No. of Establishments	No. of Spindles (Millions)	Cotton Used (Million Pounds)	Persons Employed	Value of Product (Million Dollars)	Imports (Million Dollars)
1860	1,091	5.2	422.7	122,000	115.7	38.2
1870	956	7.1	398.3	135,000	177.5	23.4
1880	756	10.7	750.3	175,000	192.1	29.9
1890	905	14.2	1,118.0	219,000	268.0	29.9
1900	973	19.0	1,814.0	298,000	332.8	41.3
1910	1,208	27.4	2,332.2	371,000	616.5	66.5

It will be seen that the domestic industry grew rapidly and without check. The best single indication of the extent and growth of such an industry as the cotton manufacture is in the number of spindles; and on this the statistics have been sufficiently accurate. The spindles in 1910 were more than five times

[1] See Copeland, p. 16. These are the census figures, published in the enumerations of the stated years, but referring to the conditions of the years severally preceding (*e. g.*, the figure of 1910 gives information on the industry as it stood in 1909).

as many as in 1860, — twenty-seven millions as compared with about five millions. The same rate of growth is indicated by the consumption of raw cotton; this also increased five-fold. The value of the product (a figure to be used with much more caution) also increased nearly five-fold. The number of persons employed increased distinctly less, about three-fold, — an indication of a growing effectiveness of labor, such as any manufacturing industry may be expected to show. The stationary number of separate establishments is also in accord with the general trend of modern industry; production is on a larger scale, the individual establishment becomes greater, the total number of establishments does not keep pace with the growing volume of production.

The imports, on the other hand, show no considerable change, except in the very last decade. As in the case of silks, they remain not far from constant absolutely, and thus become a steadily diminishing proportion of the total supply. In 1860 they were, in value, still not very far from one-third of the domestic output; in 1910, little more than one-tenth.[1] It will be shown presently that these general figures need much explanation. The continuing imports are in large part specialties; those which really compete with the domestic products are even less considerable than the figures would indicate. It is clear, however, that a very great increase in the cotton industry has taken place within the country. Here also the protective system would seem to have succeeded in attaining at least one object, — a great preponderance of domestic supply, a lessening dependence on imports.

Proceeding now to a more detailed consideration of the several branches of the industry, let attention be given first to the manufacturing of the cheaper grades. This was the earliest to be established, and the only one that flourished before the civil war. As has just been noted, it seems to have already reached in that period the stage of independence. The foreign (British) competitors were not feared, except possibly in times of exceptional

[1] In comparing domestic and foreign supply, attention must be given to the effect of the duties in adding to the price paid by consumers for the foreign goods. How far allowance should be made, and can be made, for this circumstance has been considered in the similar case of silks; see p. 222, note, *supra*.

depression in the foreign markets. Exports on a considerable scale had begun. Even the comparatively moderate duties of 1861 had been virtually prohibitory on the cheaper goods; they were prohibitory beyond doubt through the half-century after the war duties of 1864. The domestic manufacture in this branch has, therefore, gone its own way, quite untroubled by foreign competition.

This part of the cotton manufacture remained, after the war as before, quantitatively by far the most important. In 1905, the census report on the industry stated that "almost three-fourths of all the woven goods reported fall under the classification of coarse or medium counts, — print cloths, sheetings, and shirtings, drills, ticks, denims and stripes, duck and bagging."[1] Over one-half of the yarn spun in American mills was in 1905 and in 1910 of the low counts (1 to 20) used for distinctly coarse goods. Five-sixths of the remainder was of counts still low (20 to 40), — what might be called low-medium counts.[2] In other words, only one-twelfth of the quantitative output (pounds) could be reckoned as spun for the fine or better medium goods. The great growth which has taken place in the industry has therefore been predominantly in that branch already firmly established before the system of high protection was applied.

With this growth in the manufacture of the ordinary (cheaper) goods, a marked change has taken place in geographical distribution. Until 1880, New England and the middle states were almost the sole seats of the industry. After that date a rapid

[1] Quoted by Copeland, p. 21. The situation appeared to be the same in the census figures of 1910, from which I have compiled the following figures (*Bulletin on Cotton Manufactures*, 1910, p. 16): —

	Yards	Value
Total woven cotton goods	6,348 millions	456 million dollars
Of which coarse or medium (as enumerated in the text)	5,436 "	275 " "

[2] Copeland, p. 21. The figures of 1910 (*Census Bulletin*, p. 20), again tell the same story: —

Cotton yarn produced, No. 20 and under	1,014 million lbs.
" " " No. 21 to 40	866 " "
" " " No. 41 and over	157 " "
Total	2,037 " "

The proportion of fine yarns (forty-one and over) was reported even less in 1910 than in 1905.

growth took place in the south (chiefly in South Carolina, North Carolina, and Georgia) until by 1910 this region became comparable in importance with the northern states. The goods made in the south have been almost exclusively of the ordinary grades; and this circumstance has much affected the character of the industry elsewhere. The northern mills, especially those of New England, felt the competition of the south on the cheaper grades and turned more than before to the finer. In the older seats of the industry, therefore, the diversification has been greater than the general figures indicate. The finer goods are made almost exclusively in the north, and chiefly in New England; and hence they form in the last mentioned region a much more important constituent than they do in the country at large. Yet even here much the greater part of the manufacture is still given to the cheaper goods.[1] What causes have influenced the great growth in the south, and the tenacious hold even of the cheaper grades in the north, will be considered as we proceed.

More significant, however, than the volume of growth was the technical development of the cotton manufacture. Both the changes which took place in the American mills and those which failed to take place are instructive. It is chiefly in the manufacture of the cheaper goods that machinery and methods were remodelled; as regards dearer goods there has been least tendency to divergence from the practices of European rivals, especially of Great Britain. It will be convenient to describe briefly the technical changes that most affected the American industry, proceeding then to a consideration of their bearing on the tariff problems.

During the half-century the two fundamental processes in the mills — spinning and weaving — underwent changes almost revolutionary as regards the cheaper goods which constitute the bulk of the American output.

[1] Thus in 1910 the New England states were reported to produce three-quarters of all the fine yarn, and Massachusetts alone over two-fifths (41.5 per cent). Yet in Massachusetts the coarse and medium counts still very greatly exceeded the fine (*Census Bulletin*, p. 20).

Coarse cotton yarn in Massachusetts	(20 and under)	175 million lbs.
Medium " " " "	(21 to 40)	283 " "
Fine " " " "	(41 and over)	65 " "

In spinning, the great change has been the extraordinary growth of ring spinning[1] and the decline of mule spinning. The following figures show what sort of transition has taken place:

Cotton Spindles in the United States (millions)[2]

	1870	1890	1900	1910
Ring	3.7	8.8	13.4	22.7
Mule	3.4	5.4	5.6	4.7
Total	7.1	14.2	19.0	27.4

It will be seen that the number of ring spindles has increased without halt, both absolutely and relatively. The number of mule spindles, on the other hand, has hardly increased at all. Though there was some gain in the twenty years from 1870 to 1890, a loss followed from 1890 to 1910, so that in the last-named year the total of mule spindles exceeded but little that of 1870. At the outset (1870) the two kinds were in use half and half; at the close (1910) the ring spindles had increased nearly ten-fold, and constituted five-sixths of the total.

The mule spindle is in essentials that invented by the English pioneers in the industrial revolution of the eighteenth century. As perfected by Crompton, it involved the placing of a large number of spindles on a single stand or carriage which moves to and fro, spinning on its movement one way only, and getting ready for the next spinning on the return movement. Ring spinning is more recently invented, still more recently of wide use. The essential of the device is a small steel ring, through which passes the roving (the smoothed and partitioned sliver of flimsy cotton) and in passing is given the twist which pulls the fibres together into yarn. Of American invention (1828), it came into extensive use in the United States even before the war. After the war, and particularly in the decade from 1880 to 1890, it was immensely improved by a series of subsidiary changes, and took the commanding place in the industry indicated by the figures just given.[3]

[1] Also designated "frame spinning."

[2] Copeland, p. 70; *Census Bulletin of 1910*, p. 22. No separation of the two kinds of spindles was made in the census of 1880.

[3] A detailed account of the development of ring spinning is in a paper by W. F.

The industrial differences between the two methods of spinning can be stated without entering on the complicated mechanical details. The ring, in brief, is better adapted for coarser yarns, for economy of space, for large-scale operations, for that combination of spinning and weaving in the same establishment which has always been the rule in American mills, and, last but not least, for the utilization of labor little skilled. The ring spins continuously, not intermittently as does the mule; and for this reason, as well as for others, the ring produces more per spindle. The ring puts more strain on the yarn, and hence is available primarily for the coarser yarns; yet the march of improvement has made it available for yarns less coarse than in the earlier stages of its use. It yields yarn comparatively harsh, and not acceptable where a softer quality is needed (*e. g.*, for most hosiery) or where much sizing is to be put into the fabric (as is commonly done in England). The ring winds the yarn on wooden bobbins of appreciable size and weight; and the yarn thus wound and mounted is more expensive to transport than that which comes from the mule. Hence arises an obstacle to specialization between spinning and weaving; ring spinning strengthens the general American practice of combining the two in one establishment.

Perhaps most important of all is the difference in the kind of labor force required. Mule spinning is a trade, and mainly a man's trade. The spinner is a skilled workman, or at least comes close to that grade. In Great Britain the trade is often hereditary. It has been stated to the present writer, by conversant persons, that only a boy who has grown up in a mill can become a good mule spinner. The statement doubtless is exaggerated, but doubtless rests on a basis of fact. Mule spinners have strong unions; they cannot be readily replaced when they strike. They

Draper in *Transactions New England Cotton Manufacturers' Association*, no. 50 (1891). The date of first invention is there given as 1828; other dates near this are also given (cf. Copeland, p. 9). The Draper Company took the lead in manufacturing ring spindles, incorporating improvements of their own into the most promising of previous spindles; and spindles of their make came into use by the million. Compare what is said below (at p. 276) of the same company's primacy in developing the automatic loom.

are often accused by the manufacturers of being a turbulent and unruly set, of clannishly opposing the entrance of recruits into the trade, of having a trade-union monopoly; all of which are indications that, though the degree of skill may be exaggerated, the men must have some of the qualities of the skilled handicraftsman. The ring, on the contrary, is more automatic, needs less continuous and alert watching, can be operated with little need either of strength or skill. Ring spinning has been very greatly improved in the United States during the half-century; and the improvements have taken the direction of making the machinery more self-acting, less in need of skilled attention, less liable to breakdown and repair. Ring spinners are always women and children, who can be easily trained and easily replaced.

The difference in the needed quality of labor goes far to account for the unequal distribution of mule spindles and ring spindles in the various seats of the American industry. Mule spinning in the United States is confined almost entirely to the north. Even there it is overshadowed by its rival; while in the south there is virtually no mule spinning at all. The figures from the Census of 1910 again tell the story.[1]

The progress of invention in ring spinning machinery has been characteristic. A series of Yankee machinists and manufacturers experimented with the various refinements of the device, vied with each other in offering the cotton manufacturers different variants, added improvement to improvement, until by a process of selection and survival the well-nigh perfect machine was developed. The number of revolutions per minute had been 5,500 in 1860, and became 9,000 by 1890. The operation of the spindle was declared by the foremost expert to be "so near absolute perfection that it would seem as though no changes were required."[2]

[1] *Census Bulletin of 1910* on Cotton Manufactures, p. 22.

	Ring Spindles (Millions)	Mule Spindles (Millions)
Massachusetts	7.2	2.1
Rhode Island	2.3	1.4
South Carolina	3.7	.02
North Carolina	2.8	.06
Georgia	1.7	.07

[2] W. F. Draper's paper, p. 38.

Yet after that date the speed of revolution was raised to 10,000 per minute, even to more in some cases; some such figure being apparently the maximum for the device as it now (1910) stands.[1] No more labor, no more power, no more space were required for the improved spindle; the doubling of speed meant a doubling of output.

Even more important than the changes in spinning were those in weaving. As has already been noted, weaving was carried on by Americans with special aptitude and success from the very beginnings of the modern textile industries. The power loom was put into use — nay, virtually invented — in the cotton mills of the United States contemporaneously with its introduction in England.[2] By the first third of the nineteenth century the weaving processes in American mills were found by a skilled observer to be at least equal to those in England, perhaps superior.[3] And in the closing decade of that century a new invention, that of the automatic loom, was perfected in the United States and adopted almost universally for the cheap and medium goods.

The ordinary power loom in a sense is automatic; the weaver is no more than an attendant who simply sees that the machine runs as it should. The degree of attention, however, varies greatly according to the nature of the material turned out. On some goods the power loom weaver can operate but one loom, as did the hand loom weaver before him; and he must have some of the qualities of the skilled artisan. Such is the case with finer woolen and silk fabrics; and, as has already been noted for silks and will be pointed out presently for woolens also,[4] these are the branches of the textile industries which are not easily domiciled in the United States. But on plain cotton goods of the cheaper grades the power loom had long been developed to the point where the mechanism largely took care of itself, and where a weaver could attend to six or eight looms, sometimes even more. One operation, however, had not been subjected to the machine,

[1] Copeland, p. 67.

[2] See my *Tariff History of the United States*, p. 29, and the reference there given.

[3] *Ibid.*, p. 138; Copeland, p. 83; see also James Montgomery, *The Cotton Manufacture of the United States* (Glasgow, 1840), p. 101.

[4] See above, p. 230, on silks, and below, p. 362, on woolens.

and thereby a limitation had remained on its uninterrupted working, — that of replacing the supplies of weft as they were exhausted. The yarn is wound on bobbins; as one bobbin is emptied by the loom, another must be put in its place in the shuttle, and the thread from this other must be attached to the shuttle which moves to and fro in the loom. The chief business of the weaver on the ordinary power loom is to replace bobbins as they are emptied, and to attach the thread of the fresh bobbin to the shuttle. On the average the loom has to be stopped once in eight minutes to accomplish these two closely-related steps. The automatic loom achieved the crowning triumph of carrying out both without the use of the human hand.[1] A magazine is attached to the loom, containing a supply of filled bobbins, which are automatically transferred to the loom shuttle. The shuttle itself is automatically threaded by the motion of the loom; and this takes place whether the bobbin is completely emptied or whether its thread is by accident broken before emptying. In either case the shuttle automatically catches up a thread from a fresh bobbin, and the loom continues to work without interruption. The unhygienic process of attaching the fresh thread to the bobbin by the weaver's sucking it in is done away with.[2] If a warp (not weft) thread breaks, the loom stops automatically, and the weaver ties the broken ends. The weaver now has become more than

1 "In simple terms, these inventions cover a shuttle changing device, a filling hopper from which bobbins or cop spindles containing filling yarn are automatically transferred to the loom shuttle, — a peculiar shuttle which can be threaded automatically by the motion of the loom, — devices that act to stop the loom, or prevent damage in case the shuttle is not in proper position to receive new filling or the hopper is exhausted, and a warp stop motion to prevent the loom from making poor cloth when not watched by the weaver." George O. Draper, "Development of the Northrop Loom," in *Transactions of the New England Cotton Manufacturers' Association*, no. 59, p. 91. Cf. Copeland, pp. 84–88.

2 The weaver's act of thus sucking the thread carries bits of lint and dust into the lungs, and the irritation increases the danger of tuberculosis. "A weaver on eight common looms stands a chance of inhaling cotton fibre about one thousand times a day. It is no wonder they are a shortlived, consumptive class." *Ibid.*, p. 100. The danger, which persists on the ordinary power looms, is real, though often exaggerated. It is in accord with frequent experience in matters of this kind that mechanical devices for threading the shuttles, even when put freely at the weavers' disposal and with urgent advice to use them, are left unused; it is easier and quicker to suck.

ever a mere attendant, keeping an eye on the looms and seeing what is wrong when they are brought to a stop by the automatic devices. The commonest cause of stoppage is the breaking of a thread, and the commonest task of the weaver is to tie a broken thread.

Weaving on the modern power loom, whether of the automatic type or the ordinary type, calls for no strength or special skill. It is not, to be sure, reducible to simple routine as completely as ring spinning. Some alertness is required; and the weaver gets the pay of the average factory worker. But women can be used as well as men, and they seem to be equally efficient. More important, so far as concerns the automatic loom, is the possibility of a more highly developed division of labor. A separate staff (of young persons, boys or girls) can be given the simple task of keeping the magazines charged with bobbins; the weaver can be relieved of this, and called on solely to keep his (or her) eye on the looms. The oiling of the looms and dusting of the floors can be turned over to another set of unskilled persons.[1]

Yet some skilled labor remains indispensable, and on the automatic loom perhaps even more so than on the ordinary loom. The loom fixer, a highly expert mechanic, must be in attendance, to correct any defect in the working of the complicated mechanism or order the transfer of a loom to the repair shop if something serious has happened. The skilled artisan is by no means dispensed with in the modern development of machinery. His sphere of action is merely shifted, and his skill is turned where most needed. This is one of the reasons why machinery which is dubbed "automatic" can never be transported to regions where there is abundance of cheap and unskilled labor, but labor of that kind only. It calls for much more than mere tending and feed-

[1] The practice in mills varies. In one mill which I visited, each weaver was in charge of thirty automatic looms, there being separate staffs of magazine-fillers and oilers. In another, twenty looms were allotted to each weaver, but he (or she) was compelled to see to the charging of the magazines. When the Northrop loom was first put on the market, its makers predicted that a weaver could manage twenty-four looms and also attend to his magazines. Something depends on the character of the fabrics.

A loom fixer can attend to about 150 ordinary looms, 100 automatic looms; this item of expense is higher for the automatics.

ing. It must be supervised and kept in order; there must be intelligent and experienced foremen and superintendents, and a staff of skilled mechanics, such as these very loom fixers. However perfected the machine, — nay, the more it is perfected, — the human hand and the human brain are still indispensable.

The Northrop automatic loom, — so named from one among the inventors by whom it was worked out, — illustrates several matters noteworthy in the history of modern inventions. In the first place, it was deliberately planned, and brought to the point of success after prolonged and expensive experimenting. A number of inventors were kept at work on it for years. Some sixty patents were taken out or applied for in the course of the experiments; and the instance is one among many to show that the patent system, however ill adjusted it may have been in some of its details, serves to stimulate invention and still more to promote investment in inventions calling for long and expensive trial. When finally ready to be put on the market, a demonstration of its efficiency had to be given; and the firm which developed it had to shoulder the additional experiment and investment of equipping a large cotton mill in which the loom was first used in manufacturing on a considerable scale. It required this kind of proof, highly effective, but necessitating a still further commitment of funds, to bring the automatic loom into wide use. Convincing the demonstration was. It became clear that, whereas a weaver could attend to eight ordinary looms, he could look after twenty, twenty-four, even thirty automatic looms. Though the capital outlay was larger (the automatic looms are much more expensive), the saving in current labor was so great that the cost of weaving was cut in two. The use of the loom spread with great rapidity, and soon this process dominated the manufacture of the ordinary grades of plain cotton goods.[1]

[1] The Northrop loom is associated with the name of the Draper Company, whose works are at Hopedale, Mass. The experiments that led to it were spread over a period of seven years. The first loom was ready for trial in 1889. A number were run experimentally at Hopedale in 1893; the demonstration mill referred to in the text was constructed at Burlington, Vt., in 1894. An interesting and authoritative account of the history of the invention was given by Mr. G. O. Draper in the

An instructive aspect of this development is that it has by no means stood alone. The Draper Company had competitors and imitators. A host of inventors and mechanics were vying with them. So it was with the ring spindle just described; there also the leaders did not stand alone, but were spurred on by many keen rivals. So it is, indeed, with every forward movement, whether in literature, in the fine arts, in science, in the mechanic arts. The genius who reaches the crowning achievement is not isolated; he is borne forward by the sweep of a large movement. And every such movement has a character of its own, — the impress of the influences, little understood as regards their relative strength or their channels of operation, of environment, historic growth, the inborn and inherited qualities of a people. So it has been with the various inventions and changes which have marked the industrial growth of the United States throughout its history, and not least during the last half-century.

In the case of the automatic loom — to return to this — rivals and improvers soon appeared. So far as concerned the original field of the Northrop loom, its primacy seems to have been little shaken; there was rivalry, possibly an improvement in one detail or another, but no marked advance. In a neighboring field, however, a striking advance was stimulated by its success. The Northrop loom and its direct rivals were suitable only for plain

paper already referred to in the *Transactions of the New England Cotton Manufacturers' Association*, no. 59.

Both Messrs. W. F. Draper and G. O. Draper, in the two papers quoted, referred to the importance of the patent system in stimulating and sustaining invention. No less than 373 patents for ring spindles were taken out between 1870 and 1903 (so stated by Copeland, in *Quarterly Journal of Economics*, vol. xxiv, p. 127), and 60 for automatic loom devices (Draper, in *Transactions*, no. 59, p. 90).

It is a curious fact that an important part, perhaps the most important, in these inventions was taken by men who had had no previous experience in weaving rooms. "Neither Mr. Northrop, Mr. Roper, or Mr. Stimson [three among the inventors] ever had any practical knowledge of weaving. Mr. Northrop had never examined a loom prior to our [the Draper Company's] start, and Mr. Roper had probably never seen one." G. O. Draper, as cited above, p. 92. Similarly, one of the important improvements in the ring spindle came from a clergyman, the Rev. Mr. Allen. W. F. Draper, in *Transactions New England Cotton Manufacturers*, no. 50, p. 34.

It may be noted also that Cartwright, the inventor of the power loom, "if he had ever seen weaving by hand, had certainly paid no particular attention to the process." *Memoir of Cartwright* (1843), p. 57.

cloth, or goods with the simplest stripe or figure. They were not available for the ginghams and checks in which weft yarns of more than one color are used. Such fabrics were made on the so-called drop-box looms, — a variant of the ordinary power loom. Here again, systematic experimenting, continued over ten years and more, resulted in a further elaboration of the machine's competence, a further extension of the range of automatic action. Another well-known firm [1] put on the market in 1905, a decade after the introduction of the Northrop loom, a gingham loom in which bobbins containing separate colors were held in a magazine and automatically selected for the insertion of the colored threads in the chosen pattern of cloth. Advantages of the same kind as from the Northrop loom, and apparently no less in degree, were secured by this mechanism, when compared with the previous looms for parti-colored fabrics. There was no interruption for putting in fresh bobbins; and the number of looms which one weaver could attend was increased from six to sixteen, — here also more than double. Limitations still remained; the finer and more variegated goods cannot be subjected to this sort of treatment; it was available only for goods of standardized pattern, turned out on a considerable scale. But for the production of quantities of uniform goods on a large scale another striking improvement was achieved.

[1] See the account in Dr. Copeland's article on "Progress of the Automatic Loom," *Quarterly Journal of Economics*, vol. xxv, p. 746 (August, 1911), to which also I refer for the other matters here noted.

CHAPTER XVIII

THE COTTON MANUFACTURE CONTINUED, CONTRASTS WITH OTHER COUNTRIES; THE INFLUENCE OF THE TARIFF

THE consequence of the inventions and improvements described in the preceding chapter was that the cotton goods to which they were applicable came to be produced not only as cheaply in the United States as in Europe, but even more cheaply. The improved devices made their way slowly or not at all in the rival countries; they were adopted promptly and with full effect in this country. It has already been noted that there had not been, even before the war, any inferiority in cost for the American cotton manufacturers, as regards the simplest and cheapest grades of goods. This position of independence was strengthened by the subsequent improvements, and was extended to goods of higher price and quality. The change was greatest in the weaving process. It was here that the comparative advantage of the manufacture as a whole was most securely established; and the special superiority in weaving served to offset any lack of advantage in other processes.

On the general situation, the Report of the Tariff Board, made in 1912, gave invaluable evidence. So far as concerns spinning, it is true, the evidence was not entirely conclusive. The figures secured by the Board indicated that "labor cost," *i. e.*, money expense for labor per unit of output, was slightly greater in the United States than in England. The English labor cost on yarns was found to be lower than American cost, but not much lower, — 78 to 95 per cent of the American.[1] In other words, the effective-

[1] *Tariff Board Report on Cotton Manufactures* (1912), "Letter of Submittal" (Summary), p. 9. Elaborate figures are given elsewhere in the *Report*, pp. 398 *seq.* A chart opposite page 416 shows the differences between "labor costs" and "total conversion costs." The differences become progressively greater as the yarns become finer; they are least on the coarse yarns, greatest on the fine. The phe-

ness of labor in the United States, especially on the lower counts of yarn, was found to be greater, but not quite so great as to offset the difference in money wages. Taken by themselves, the figures would indicate that the comparative advantage of the American cotton spinning industry almost measured up to the country's general standard, yet not quite. The data for the two countries, however, were not comparable without qualification. The English figures were for mule spun yarn, the American for ring spun yarn; and though they were for the same counts (fineness) of yarn, they were not necessarily for the same qualities. A comparison made by an unofficial inquirer seemed to show that, for ring spun yarn in the United States compared with ring spun yarn in Europe, the difference in labor cost was virtually *nil*, — the effectiveness of American labor was so much greater as quite to offset the difference in money wages.[1]

For weaving, however, and for the manufacturing processes as a whole, the Tariff Board's conclusions were unimpeachable. The effectiveness of American industry in weaving was so much greater than that in Europe as not only to offset entirely the difference in weavers' wages, but to leave a margin of superiority which sufficed to offset also various minor items in which there was no marked comparative advantage. The superiority in weaving was due largely to the wide use of the automatic loom; but not solely to this. "In the case of plain looms the English

nomenon is in harmony with the general trend in all these comparisons; it is in the finer and more tenuous qualities that the Americans show no special effectiveness. The comparison between mule spun yarns in England and ring spun yarns in the United States was explained by the Board on the ground that mule spinning was the prevalent method in the former country, ring spinning in the latter; but, as noted in the text, it introduces an element of doubt, making the results not absolutely comparable.

[1] See Copeland, pp. 289, 299. Ring spindles were found to run a trifle faster in the United States than in Europe, — 10,000 revolutions per minute compared to 9,000. A spinner in the United States commonly had in charge 750 to 1,000 spindles; in England 400 to 800; in Germany on the average, 500. There was no more breakage and interruption in the United States. Wages per week were $6.50 to $7.50 in New England, about $6.00 in the South. In England they were $3.75 to $5.50; in Germany, $3.75 to $4.25. Money wages thus seemed to vary almost precisely in proportion to the effectiveness of labor, *i. e.*, to the comparative advantage; the "labor cost" was virtually the same in all three countries.

weaver seldom tends more than four looms, while in this country a weaver rarely tends less than six, and more frequently eight, or even twelve, if equipped with 'warp-stop motions.' . . . Whereas the output per spinner per hour in England is probably as great or greater than in this country,[1] the output per weaver per hour is, upon a large class of plain goods, less, and in the case where automatic looms are used in this country and plain looms in England, very much less." Taking cost of production as a whole, "on many plain fabrics the cost of production [*i. e.*, the money cost] is not greater than in England"; and the American prices of plain goods were in no case much above the English prices, while in the majority of cases they were lower.[2]

Taken as a whole, the result plainly is that, so far as concerns the plain goods and goods of medium quality which constitute the bulk of the output of the American mills, they have a comparative advantage. They pay higher wages than in England, but the effectiveness of the industry as a whole is such that they can yet turn out these goods at as low a price, if not at a lower price. To use the phrase applied elsewhere to this situation, they measure up to the general American standard of effectiveness. In this case, as in others, it must be borne in mind that the effectiveness of the industry depends not mainly, perhaps not at all, on the skill and vigor of the individual workers; not even on those personal qualities in combination with the tools and machines on which the operatives are put to work; it depends on the whole industrial outfit, in which ability for general organization is the greatest factor. As the Tariff Board stated, with reference to weaving, it is a matter not of individual superiority on the part of the American weaver, but of difference in industrial policy.[3]

It goes without saying that goods of the classes to which these inventions and improvements have been applied were quite unaffected by the high duties maintained until 1913. They would

[1] This general statement seems to me not justified by the Board's own figures, as cited earlier in the text. It holds doubtless for some kinds of spinning, and especially for the finer mule spun yarns.

[2] *Report*, "Letter of Submittal," pp. 11, 13. See also pp. 479 *seq*.

[3] *Report*, p. 12.

not have been imported even in the absence of duties. So far from being imported, they have been exported steadily in considerable volume, — sure proof of established independence. The exports of cotton goods began before the civil war, and were even then no negligible item in the total product.[1] The war, with the consequent complete overturn of the industry through a decade or more, put an end to the exports for the time being, and it was not until 1880 that they rose to the volume of the earlier period. They increased rapidly in later years, and in the first decade of the twentieth century ranged from fifty to sixty millions (of dollars). Both unprinted goods and printed figure among the exports. A considerable market is found in the Orient, especially for unbleached heavy fabrics in northern China. The exports show an uneven course, sometimes swelling abruptly and then shrinking as abruptly. They present some curious problems, much debated by those to whom the export trade seems peculiarly precious. For the purposes of the present discussion it suffices to note that the cotton manufacture in its largest branch reached the stage not only of superiority at home, but of aggressiveness abroad.[2]

Still another indication of strength and superiority is found in the conditions of supply for the machinery used. As has been elsewhere stated [3] the source of the machinery is a significant clue to the position of an industry as a whole. If the machinery is not only made within the country, but made on native models and with native improvements; still more, if it has reached that stage of excellence that it is sought for export abroad, — then we have strong evidence of superiority. Precisely this sort of evidence is found for the cotton manufacture. In both of the dominant departments of the manufacture, spinning and weaving, American machinery, as it has been improved for the manufacture of the cheap and medium goods, has come to be exported.

[1] The exports in 1850–60 ranged from $7,000,000 to $10,000,000; the census reported the total value of the domestic product (manufactures of cotton) as $62,000,000 in 1850, $116,000,000 in 1860.

[2] An excellent analysis of the export trade in cotton goods is in Copeland, chapter xii.

[3] In chapter xvi, above, p. 251.

The "Rabbeth" spindle, the most widely used of the American ring spindles, was early sent abroad.[1] The automatic loom has been sent abroad on a considerable scale, and a foreign market for it systematically cultivated. What is not less significant, it has been copied by foreign makers of machinery, especially in Germany; a form of tribute which naturally is irritating to the American pioneers, but is not the less conclusive evidence of their originality and leadership.[2]

The automatic loom, however, has not come into large use either in England or on the Continent. Various causes have prevented its wide adoption; causes partly technical in the strict sense, partly related to the general industrial environment. Among the technical obstacles is the circumstance that in England, still the most important competitor, the automatic loom does not work to full advantage for goods heavily "sized," *i. e.*, much weighted with starch. This heavy weighting, common for the cheap English fabrics made for export to the Orient, has often been condemned as a kind of dishonest adulteration; it seems to be in fact an adaptation of the goods to the preferences and purses of the customers.[3] But it does bring difficulties in the way of using the mechanism of the automatic loom, and thus impedes the spread of that improvement. Among obstacles from the environment, in all European countries, is the absence of that concentration of work on large orders which characterizes American business and gives scope to the special industrial talents of the Americans. The European manufacturer, in England and even more on the Continent, accepts willingly and habitually small or moderate orders, and prefers a system and an equipment which makes it easy to shift from one order to another and different one. The American aims to turn out large quantities of a single product, reducing to a minimum the readjustments of the labor force, and bringing to a maximum the efficiency of all labor-saving devices. The automatic loom fits

[1] W. F. Draper's paper in *Transactions, American Cotton Manufacturers' Association*, no. 50 (1891), p. 41.

[2] For some reference to the German automatic looms, see the article by Dr. Copeland, *Quarterly Journal of Economics*, vol. xxv, p. 747.

[3] See Copeland, p. 79.

into the prevailing American practices; it does not fit into the prevailing European practices.[1]

A different obstacle, the force of which is not easy to estimate, but which beyond question is strong in England, is the attitude of the labor organizations. A well-informed observer has written to me in so many words that "in England the cotton weavers are thoroughly organized, and the union will not permit the English weavers to operate more than four looms each, and will not permit the use of the automatic looms."[2] This perhaps is put too strongly; but it has a large basis of truth. Even for ordinary looms the English weavers oppose rearrangements and reductions in piece rates when improvements make it possible for a weaver to operate with the same effort and attention a larger number of looms. Hence, as was noted a moment ago, the effectiveness of labor is less in England even where power looms of the same general type as in the United States are used. This difficulty is accentuated in the attitude of the English weavers toward the automatic loom. The weavers are afraid of the new device; it threatens to make employment less. They are not disposed to work the looms to their maximum output; they are loth to accept reduced piece-work rates, even though they can earn as much, even more. It is the familiar and almost inevitable disposition to "make work," the hostility to labor-saving appliances. It may not take the form of overt and unqualified refusal (as was stated in the letter just quoted), but it leads to a silent, stolid opposition. Against this the employer cannot make headway without friction and loss, expecially when his power of discharge and his ability to insist on the full productivity of machinery are hampered by a strong labor union. The same situation has already been considered with reference to the iron industry, and

[1] Copeland, pp. 320–326, for some interesting figures and comments. For Switzerland, I find it stated (in 1911) that the "great technical novelty, the Northrop loom, though introduced finds its way into use very slowly . . . it is adapted to the mass production of simple goods, but not to the Swiss industry, which is mobile and subject to great changes in detail; it is least adapted to fine or fancy fabrics." Reichesberg, *Handwörterbuch der Schweizerischen Volkswirtschaft*, vol. iii, p. 895.

[2] I quote from a private letter, written by a person highly conversant with the American industry, who had also made inquiries on the spot in England.

the same perplexities must be admitted.[1] The labor union movement has it good sides and its bad sides. Indispensable as it doubtless is for securing to the workmen a "fair" share in the gains from material progress, the dispassionate observer must face the fact that it leads them often to put checks on that very progress. For all the exaggeration in the statements that English unionism has sounded the death-knell to English industrial leadership, it remains true that the absence of firmly entrenched unions in the cotton and iron manufactures has facilitated the march of improvement in the United States.

The endeavors of the American makers of automatic looms and of other machinery to develop an export business and to secure the adoption of their devices in foreign countries, have led to gloomy forebodings. Similar alarm has been expressed under the analogous conditions in the machine tool trade.[2] What will happen, it is asked, when the foreigners are equipped with our very best machinery, and can still secure operatives at much lower wages to work that very machinery? Will not the American manufacturer, compelled to pay wages at the higher rates of this country, be inevitably forced out of the field? The theoretic aspects of this question have already been considered in the introductory chapters of the present volume.[3] The history of the automatic loom, its rapid adoption in the United States, its slow progress in England and on the Continent, its prompt ultilization to full capacity here, its halting utilization in the rival countries, the restless and unflagging march of improvement in the originating people, — these circumstances all tend to confirm what was there said. The comparative advantage now possessed in the United States does not seem in danger of being lost at any period about which its people need have present concern. What will happen in the more distant future, it would be rash to predict. The time may come when all the advanced civilized countries will have the same equipment in their major manufacturing industries, and the same organization; the same

[1] Cf. what was said in chapter xii, p. 185, of the similar attitude of the English tin plate workers.

[2] See chapter xiii, pp. 197 *seq.*

[3] See chapter iii, pp. 44 *seq.*, above.

enterprise, ingenuity, skill, among both the leaders of business, and the rank and file. Then their social and industrial conditions will be equalized, wages will be on the same plane throughout, and trade between them will be restricted to a much narrower volume than now. But that time, if it ever is to come, is at all events long distant. Such differences as the present case illustrates seem likely to persist for a long time; as long a time as a country need wisely consider in shaping its commercial policy. American enterprise and ingenuity will continue to find opportunities in which these qualities tell to the utmost, a comparative advantage will persist in the congenial industries, the international division of labor will be affected by the same forces that have operated in the past and operate in the present.

One further phase of the American development of machinery has been illustrated in the cotton manufacture as well as in the silk manufacture.[1] I refer to the utilization, — one should hesitate to use the condemnatory term exploitation, — of a great stratum of cheap labor. Not only has the influx of immigrant labor been turned to account in the north, but in the south the supply of cheap native labor. The growth of the cotton manufacture in the south since 1880 has rested chiefly on the discovery of the possibility of using in the mills the ignorant rural whites, previously half-idle. Wages were low at the start and the quality of labor was low; both rose as time went on; yet in neither regard does the northern level seem to have been quite reached. Lamentable as have been some of the concomitants of this development, — long hours, child labor, low wages, — it stands for a stage in progress toward better things; as indeed is the case with the immigrants in the cotton mills of the north. At all events, alike in north and south, the cheap labor was turned to account in those branches of the industry in which machinery had been brought most completely to the automatic stage.[2]

[1] See chapter xiv, pp. 232 *seq.*

[2] A good indication is given by the exclusive use of ring spindles in the south, see the figures given in the preceding chapter. Ring spindles, it will be recalled, can be operated by young girls, mule spindles by men only.

It would not be easy to say which was cause and which effect; whether the character of the labor supply caused the development of machinery adapted to it, or whether the development of the machinery led to the utilization of the labor supply. Probably there was an interaction. The attention of inventors and manufacturers was naturally turned toward adapting the machines to the labor available for this particular industry; at the same time the general industrial trend in the United States was toward automatic labor-saving devices. What would have been the course of invention in the cotton manufacture if the labor supply had been of a different and higher quality must be an open question. In other industries, such as the boot and shoe manufacture and the machine making trades, there has been no lack of advance in machinery adapted to operatives more intelligent and more alert. Given the conditions obtaining in the textile industries, the advances were most striking where profits could be made by utilizing the existing supplies of low-grade labor.

The development of the cotton manufacture, again, illustrates how greatly the effectiveness of industry is influenced by industrial leadership. Repeatedly one hears it stated that the efficiency of labor is no greater in American textile mills than in European; nay, it is said, the European manufacturer has operatives who are more skilful and better trained, not less so. And yet, in such branches of the textile manufacture as have been considered in the preceding pages, the effectiveness of labor as a whole is greater than in Europe. It is greater, not because the operatives are of better quality, but because they are put to work on more highly developed machinery, and are organized and guided better. The cause of superiority is to be found mainly in the inventors and mill managers. Where the machines and tools are the same in the United States as in Europe, there is not necessarily, perhaps not usually, an advantage. When some special sort of artisan's work is required, there may even be a positive inferiority among the Americans. True, barring these cases of special handicraft skill, there is probably some degree of higher efficiency in the United States, due to the general industrial environment. The pace is faster throughout; exertion is more continuous and more strenuous. The American weaver tends more looms even of the ordinary type than the English; the American girl tends more ring spindles than the German. But this sort of efficiency is itself dependent on the management and the oversight of the leaders. It is dependent on the appropriate arrangement of tools and of plant, and it is almost always supplemented by labor-saving machinery. In common pick and shovel work, no one can see the American apparatus for sewer construction or rough railway work without observing the combination of labor-saving plant with management that drives the labor at full speed.

I need hardly repeat what I have already said on the larger social aspects of this problem. Driving at speed has its evil sides as well as its good. The just mean is not easy to strike between the pace that wears the laborer out at fifty and the slack and irritating gait of the work-making trade-unionist; nor is it easy to say which extreme most kills the intrinsic satisfaction from well-directed activity. The ideal doubtless would be alert and strenuous labor for so long a working day as can be steadily maintained without irrecoverable fatigue or a premature old age. A concomitant of the American practice should be a shortening of the working day, and with it the wise restriction of the labor of women and children. In no country is there more solid ground for welcoming the eight-hour system. Oddly enough, the shortened working day obtains much more in Great Britain, where the pace is slacker. These aspects of the question are not to be overlooked, even though they lie apart from the main subjects of the present inquiry.

Compare now the general situation for ordinary cottons, as described in the preceding pages, with that for the more expensive grades. We find a contrast, accentuated as the goods become finer. Imports of these did not cease during the period from 1883 to 1913, notwithstanding the successive increases of duty made in the tariff acts of 1883, 1890, 1897, and 1909. Foreign supplies of fine goods, though checked by the high duties, continued to come in. The domestic manufacturers insisted that they could not turn out these goods unless aided by high duties; and they urged the "acquisition" of the new industries through greater protection. The reduction of duties in the tariff act of 1913, accepted almost with indifference by the makers of the cheaper grades, was the cause of grave forebodings among those of the finer.

One aspect of the contrast between the different branches of the industry appears in the relation between imported and home-made machinery. In the note[1] are given figures collected by the Tariff Board, not indeed for the whole cotton manufacture, but for a number of establishments large enough to indicate the general situation. So far as weaving goes, the situation is obviously one of independence; we have seen that it is even more, — one of superiority. Weaving affords a favorable field for American industrial talent. Not only as regards the new automatic looms, but as regards the older and more familiar power looms, the American has nothing to learn from the foreigner, and usually something to teach. All the ring spindles also are domestic built. The carding machinery is again predominantly domestic; and the same is the case with the "jack" spindles. On the other hand, much the larger part of the mule spindles are imported.

Let it be recalled that mule spindles are adapted for the finer counts of yarn, and are the only ones that can be used for the finest counts. The jack spindles, for which figures are given, serve also for fine yarns. That the mule spindles are chiefly foreign

[1] Per cent of Foreign Built Machinery in American Mills

	Cards		Jack Spindles		Spinning Spindles: Ring		Spinning Spindles: Mule		Looms	
	No.	Per cent	No.	Per cent	No.	Per cent	No.	Per cent	No.	Per cent
Domestic	11,200	83.7	510,000	85.8	4,000,000	99.9	119,000	16.9	127,000	99.7
Foreign	2,182	16.3	84,000	14.2	3,000	.1	584,000	83.1	300	.3

Report of Tariff Board on Cotton Manufactures, p. 473. The figures are for "the mills from which such data were obtained"; by no means all of the American mills, but representative of the whole.

Jack spindles (also called "fine roving spindles") are used where fine yarn is to be spun from sea island and other long fibre cotton; they make the roving (attenuated sliver) fine enough for spinning high counts of yarn. They are roving spindles, not spinning spindles.

built,—which means, British built,—does not necessarily indicate an absolute inferiority in the effectiveness of American industry. It points to the lack of superiority, the lack of a comparative advantage. Using the same machines, and having operatives no more skilful or efficient, — nay, it is stoutly maintained, operatives less skilful, — the American spinners of fine yarns cannot pay higher wages than British competitors and hold their own without tariff support. So far as weaving goes, the makers of fine fabrics would seem at the least to be at no absolute disadvantage. It is true that automatic looms cannot be used for very fine goods; it is true also that even with ordinary looms the weaver cannot take care of so large a number as when coarse goods are made. I judge that, on the whole, there is some superiority in weaving fine goods, though by no means so marked a superiority as in coarse and medium goods.[1] In spinning, however, if the statements of the manufacturers themselves are to be accepted, there is a distinct inferiority; and even if allowance is made for the habitual exaggerations of protected producers, there remains little indication of any comparative advantage. In the manufacture of the expensive cotton fabrics as a whole the characteristic industrial aptitudes of the Yankee find no favorable field.

It is not easy to give a single general reason why the English maintain their undoubted supremacy as manufacturers of the finest yarns, and on the whole of the finest woven fabrics also. Something was due at the outset to the damp and equable climate of Lancashire. This may still be a factor, though in modern times one of much lessened consequence, since ways have been found of humidifying the mills artificially at slight expense. Special skill among the operatives is often alleged. The class of

[1] The Tariff Board (*Report*, p. 11), after explaining that with plain looms, whether ordinary or automatic, the output per weaver per hour is greater in the United States, remarks: "In the case of other methods of weaving, such as dobby, Jacquard, box dobby, box Jacquard, lappet, etc., the difference in output is by no means so great. In the case of dobby looms (without automatic attachment) on some classes of fabric, the American weaver will tend eight or more looms against four in England; but with the more complicated weaves the ratio seems to be nearer that of six to four, and in the case of certain fancy fabrics, where the number of looms tended is necessarily four or less, the output per weaver is about the same in both countries."

factory workpeople in Lancashire is stable. Children succeed their parents in the mills; they do not often strive to rise in the industrial scale, as is commonly the case in the United States. Something like handicraft skill is said to be transmitted from generation to generation.[1] It is probably true that, so far as the spinning staff goes, the American manufacturers are right in maintaining that they have operatives less efficient, not more so. Another factor is the extreme specialization of the cotton industry in Great Britain. Not only are weaving and spinning commonly separated, — to this, as already noted,[2] the technical characteristics of mule spinning contribute, — but the spinning of the different counts, and the various finishing processes, such as bleaching, dyeing and printing, are carried on in independent establishments. With this more highly elaborated partition of labor between establishments goes a great specialization in fabrics. In the nature of the case, the finer goods cannot be produced in great quantities; no large supplies of any one pattern and grade are called for. An industry concentrated in a small district, split up into multitudes of differentiated establishments, with a trained and mobile labor supply, is adapted to such a product. The case is one (in Professor Marshall's phrase) of marked external economies. Not improbably, it is also one of adaptation to national bent and talent. At all events, a superiority in the manufacture of the finer goods, and especially of the finer yarns, Great Britain does possess; as is shown not only by the exports to the United States in face of high duties, but by the continued exports to the Continent. To quote a phrase of Adam Smith's, "whether the advantages which one country has over another be natural or acquired, is in this respect of no consequence. As long as the one country has those advantages, and the other wants them, it will always be more advantageous for the latter, rather to buy of the former than to make."[3] The acquired advantage has persisted long in England for this particular industry and bids fair to persist long in the future.

[1] Cf. the statement regarding mule spinning, quoted in chapter xvii, p. 271.

[2] Chapter xvii, p. 271.

[3] *Wealth of Nations*, Book IV, chapter ii (vol. i, p. 423 of Cannan's edition).

The usual explanation, among manufacturers and technical writers, of the exceptional position of the finer goods, is that the question is simply one of labor. More labor, we are told, is required for the finer goods; the wages bill forms a larger item in the expenses of production, the raw material a smaller one; hence the American producer is handicapped in special degree by the higher scale of wages in the United States. The business men who argue in this way have in mind, as such persons almost always do, the field with which alone they are conversant, and generalize at once from their own experiences. Only in the rarest of instances do they consider the problem as a whole. They do not reflect that in other industries, such as the manufacture of boots and shoes and of machine tools, raw material is no important item in the expenses, direct labor is a great item; yet here the Americans easily hold their own and even export. What remains true throughout is that high wages constitute no insuperable obstacle for the American producer if all the labor is effective, — that applied to the operation of machinery as well as that applied to its construction. It is not the mere use of machines that enables high wages to be paid and a product nevertheless turned out at low cost; it is the fact that the machines are well devised and well run. Wherever there is *no* favorable opportunity for introducing labor-saving methods, high wages cannot be paid unless there be high prices for the goods; and with prices high, foreign competitors who pay low wages cannot be met on even terms. Tariff support is then needed.

Precisely in what industries the favorable opportunity exists cannot safely be predicted in advance. In the case of the silk manufacture an unexpected field was found, or at least seems to be in process of finding. In the case of the finer cottons, — and it will be seen that the case of finer woolens is similar, — no such favoring conditions have yet appeared. And the nature of these branches of industry seems to indicate that they are not likely to appear. A considerable standardization is essential for the successful application of machine methods. The mere fact that raw material is a large item in the expenses of production does not make possible such standardization; it may be feasible where raw material plays a large part, as with ordinary cottons, or where it plays a small part, as with machine tools or sewing machines. But a need of individual attention to each product or pattern, or of handicraft skill trained for the particular trade, constitutes an obstacle for the American employer. Under these conditions he works with no superior effectiveness. The obstacles seem to be found insuperably in the finer grades of all the textile fabrics; they explain the striking contrast between the manufacture of the cheap and medium grades of cotton goods and that of the finer grades.

One topic, referred to in the earlier part of this chapter, remains to be considered. The manufacture of all but the finest grades of cottons has had protection even to the point of prohibition. Is there any indication that this extreme of government support had deadened progress ?

The tale told in the preceding pages gives an unequivocal answer: no. The cotton manufacture, so far from giving any evidence of a slackened pace, has shown striking advances. Whatever may have been the influence of protection, it has not been enfeebling. The case is clear beyond cavil as regards the staple goods which occupy the bulk of the industry. If in the manufacture of finer goods there has been imitation of foreign exemplars and appearance of backwardness, the explanation is to be found not in any lack of enterprise or vigor among the American producers, but in the fact that the field was unfavorable.

To generalize from this instance would be rash. A case of the opposite kind, — lack of progress under a rigid protective system, — seems to be discernible in some branches of the woolen manufacture;[1] and beyond question still others could be adduced. But on the whole the evidence is that, in the United States at least, high protection has not been inconsistent with enterprise, invention, forging ahead. There is ground, on the contrary, for saying that it has in some degree contributed to such progress. What has been set forth in the preceding pages of the development of the iron and silk industries points that way. It would be going quite too far to say that the protective system has been

[1] See chapter xxi, p. 353.

the main cause of the advance in organization and in technical equipment which has appeared in so many American industries and in the cotton manufacture among them. The general sweep of the country's industrial movement, — the vast resources waiting to be exploited by an enterprising people, the keen atmosphere of democracy, the free scope for every talent, the concentration on money making and wealth producing of the enormous influence of social emulation, — here are underlying forces much more powerful. But it is not to be denied that these forces have been directed by protection into some fields which they might not otherwise have touched, and in which they have operated with effects similar to those wrought in American industry at large.

On the other hand, it can hardly be maintained that anything in the nature of protection to young industries has been applied with good effect in the particular case here under consideration, — the cotton manufacture. What has been accomplished for the industry during its stage of trial was accomplished in the first third of the nineteenth century, when the industry was really young. Thereafter, so far as its staple branches were concerned, it grew and prospered without danger from foreign competitors or need of support against them. Even before the civil war, still more after it, whether duties were moderate or were extreme, the development of these branches was affected by the domestic surroundings alone. A field favorable for the talents of the Yankee, a great population ready to purchase staple goods by the million, a labor supply adapted for the utilization of quasi-automatic machines, — here we have the explanation of the progress made in the industry, with no discernible influence either favorable or unfavorable from the tariff system.

Another suggestion has been made: that the manufacture of cotton machinery, both for spinning and weaving, has been promoted by the duties not so much on the goods as on the machinery; with the effects of successful protection to a young industry.[1] The case seems to me at least doubtful. The manu-

[1] This is maintained, — though without the use of the phrase "young industries," — by W. F. Draper, in the paper on the development of spinning machinery already cited; *Transactions New England Cotton Manufacturers' Association*, no. 50.

facture of textile machinery began in the United States as early as the textile industries themselves. Both in spinning and weaving, independent progress was made before the war brought in the régime of extremely high duties. The same general causes which stimulated the invention of labor-saving machinery in other industries brought about their consequences in this field also. The patent system may be adduced among the favoring factors with much more plausibility than the tariff system. The whole spirit of industrial leadership has been toward precisely the sort of mechanical progress which the textile inventions have illustrated. The inventors and business men who ascribe their successes to protection fail to give due credit to themselves.

The general conclusions to be derived from this inquiry on the cotton manufacture have been sufficiently indicated in the preceding pages. In its staple branches the industry possesses advantages; it measures up to the general American standard of effectiveness. It can pay wages higher than those in competitive industries abroad, and yet sell its products as cheaply. It needs no tariff support. But for the finer grades of goods, and for many specialties, the situation is different; here there has not yet been a comparative advantage, nor does there seem to be a prospect of competing with the foreigner on even terms in the future. The staple branches alone seem to offer good opportunities for the characteristic industrial qualities of the American inventor and business man. The course of development in the industry, both in its successes and its failures, serves as an illustration of the principle of comparative effectiveness.

CHAPTER XIX

WOOL

Before proceeding to the woolen manufacture, the third among the great textile industries, something must be said of wool and the duties on wool. The woolen manufacture has differed from that of silks and cottons in at least one important respect: through almost the entire period covered in the present inquiry, its raw material has been subject to duties. The influence of the tariff system on the industry has thus been complicated by the fact that wool itself has been affected. There are independent reasons for examining the development of wool production and imports; the working of the duties here also serves to illustrate general principles. The present chapter accordingly will be given to a consideration of this part of the protective system.[1]

In the tariff acts from 1867 to 1909 (neglecting for a moment the brief period of free admission from 1894 to 1897) wool was divided into three classes: clothing wool, combing wool, carpet wool. For reasons which will be indicated below, the first two classes may be thrown together; though distinguished in the tariff, they are to be treated as one for trade purposes. Moreover, these two classes were subjected to nearly the same rates of duty, and rates which remained nearly constant in the several protectionist tariffs. The details of the changes in the successive acts are of no great moment. Both classes were dutiable throughout at about eleven cents per pound. In relation to the usual foreign price of wool, this was equivalent to something like fifty

[1] The literature on the wool duty is voluminous. Two recent contributions are of signal importance, and supersede those of earlier date: Professor C. W. Wright's *Wool-growing and the Tariff*, in Harvard Economic Studies (1910); and the *Report of the Tariff Board on Wool and Woolens* (1912), vol. ii. To both of these frequent reference will be made. Among the earlier discussions, reference may be made to a frank statement from the wool manufacturers' point of view, by Mr. S. N. D. North, then Secretary of the Wool Manufacturers Association, in the *Bulletin* of that Association, December, 1900.

per cent; the *ad valorem* equivalent of course fluctuated with the ups and downs in price. The specific duties on carpet wool, a much cheaper grade, were always lower than those on the other classes. But for them also the *ad valorem* equivalent was in the neighborhood of fifty per cent.[1] This régime, needless to say, came to an end in 1913, when wool was again put on the free list.

The general relation of imports to domestic production during the thirty odd years of high protection is shown in the chart on page 298. The upper line shows the course of domestic production. The two lower lines show the imports. The imports are separately indicated for two classes, corresponding to the trade differences; clothing and combing wool (classes I and II in the tariff acts) being thrown together as one class; while carpet wool (class III in the tariff) has a separate line.

Looking first at domestic production, it will be seen that during a period of ten or fifteen years after 1870, there was a marked advance. From 1870 to 1885 the wool grown in the United States doubled in amount. But after 1885 the upward movement ceased. There was more or less variation from year to year. The clip diminished considerably under the influence of free trade in

[1] The following tabular statement shows what the wool duties were from 1867. It will be observed that the duties on classes I and II (clothing and combing wools) were split into two, according to the value of the wool, in 1867 and in 1883, but not thereafter. The duties on class III (carpet wool) were similarly split, according to value, throughout; they were *ad valorem* in the act of 1890, but specific in all the other acts.

WOOL DUTIES

Act of	Class I, Clothing Wool	Class II, Combing Wool	Class III, Carpet Wool
1867	Value up to 32c.–10c. per lb., plus 11%	Same duties as on Class I	Value up to 12c.–3c. per lb.
	Value over 32c.–12c. per lb., plus 10%	Same duties as on Class I	Value over 12c.–6c. per lb.
1883	Value up to 30c.–10c. per lb.	Same duties as on Class I	Value up to 12c.–2½c. per lb.
	Value over 30c.–12c. per lb.	Same duties as on Class I	Value over 12c.–5c. per lb.
1890	11c.	12c.	Value up to 13c.–32% *ad valorem*
			Value over 13c.–50% *ad valorem*
1894	Free	Free	Free
1897	11c.	12c.	Value up to 12c.–4c. per lb.
			Value over 12c.–7c. per lb.
1909	Same as 1897	Same as 1897	Same as 1897
1913	Free	Free	Free

CHART VI

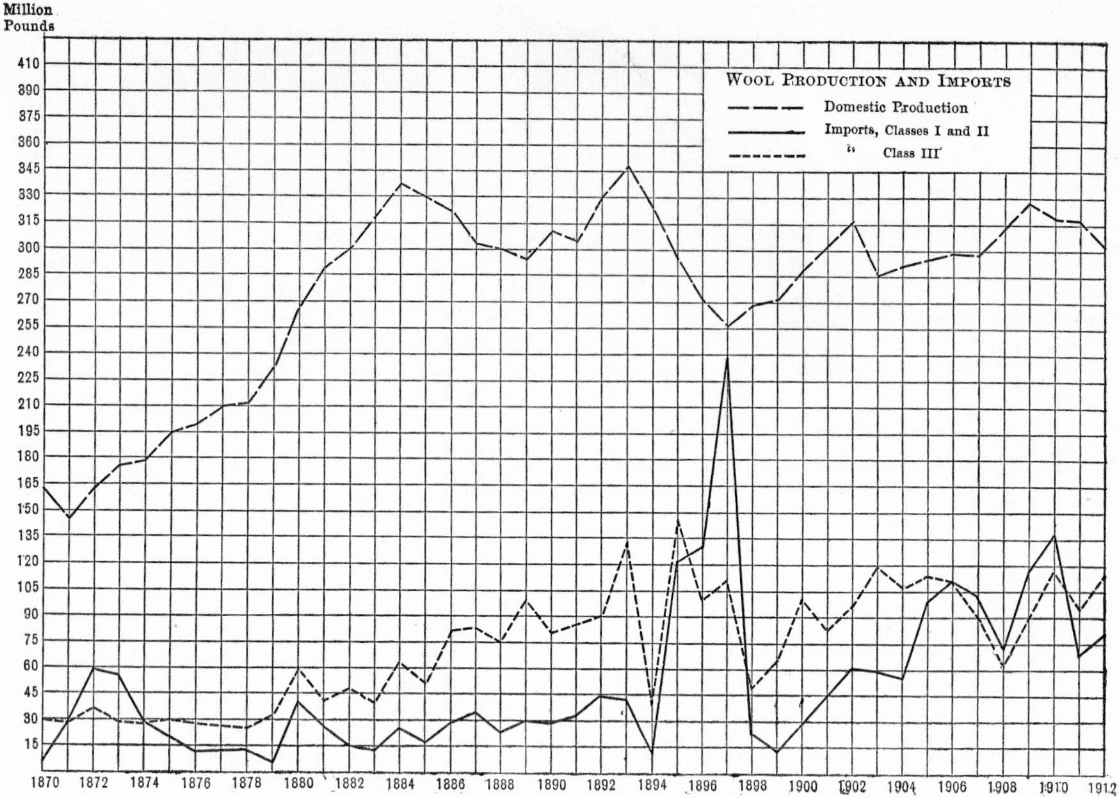
Million Pounds
410
390
375
360
345
330
315
300
285
270
255
240
225
210
195
180
165
150
135
120
105
90
75
60
45
30
15
1870
1872
1874
1876
1878
1880
1882
1884
1886
1888
1890
1892
1894
1896
1898
1900
1902
1904
1906
1908
1910
1912
WOOL PRODUCTION AND IMPORTS
Domestic Production
Imports, Classes I and II
" Class III

wool under the tariff act of 1894; it increased again after 1897; for some of the early years of the present century it attained a figure above that for 1885. But on the whole it remained stationary. Whatever stimulus was given by the duties would appear to have exhausted its effect after the first fifteen years.

The imports, on the other hand, during this period after 1885 show a tendency to increase, especially during the latter part of the period. They never ceased entirely, for any class; and as the years went on, they became larger. Among the extraordinary fluctuations some are obviously accounted for by the tariff changes of 1894–97. The free admission of wool in 1894 and the re-imposition of duties three years later necessarily caused great shifts. In the year just before the act of 1894, when it was almost certain that wool would become free, imports naturally shrank almost to nothing. They then rose abruptly as soon as the abolition of the duty went into effect. Again, after the election of McKinley in the autumn of 1896 it became in turn almost certain that the duty would be restored. Consequently during the fiscal year 1896–1897, imports were rushed in from every possible quarter while wool was still free. They then fell abruptly after the passage of the tariff act of 1897. For several years after 1897 the stocks of wool from these heavy importations weighed on the market, and prevented the price of wool from rising as promptly and fully as had been expected. During the interval imports were naturally small, and confined to special qualities. Not till 1900 were the effects of this abnormal situation out of the way. Then, as the chart shows, imports mounted for all classes. After 1900, — setting aside the changes due to ordinary trade fluctuations, — the general trend was clearly toward an advance in the imports. The larger quantities of wool needed by the growing population came not from increase of the domestic output, but from increase of the foreign supplies.

The simplest case is that of carpet wool. It is simplest because here the entire supply was foreign throughout. Therein carpet wool stands by itself. This absence of any domestic production, notwithstanding long-continued duties of considerable weight, is easily explicable on the principle of comparative advantage.

Carpet wool is of coarse grade, clipped from sheep neglected as to breed or pastured with poor fodder or under harsh climate. It comes to the United States from all parts of the world: from China, India, the interior of Asia, Africa, South America, Russia, Portugal, Spain, even from the Highlands of Scotland. Its coarse quality is usually due to poor care of the sheep and indifference as to breeding. The main sources of supply are the semi-civilized regions, — India, the interior of Asia, China, Asiatic Turkey, southern and southeastern Russia. In other regions, where wool growing is carried on by the highly-civilized races or under their guidance, the poorer grades of sheep are displaced by the better, which yield a fleece commanding a higher price. The careful, intelligent, and well-informed wool grower can produce these better fleeces with the same labor and investment as the inferior grades; he naturally confines himself to the former. Sheep from which carpet wool is clipped are left to the stolid and ignorant Mongolians, Turkomans, Russians; in part also to the growers in mountainous regions (like the Pyrenees and Scotch Highlands) in which the more valuable sheep cannot be sustained.[1]

The American wool grower hence confines himself to the sheep and wools of the better qualities, — clothing and combing wools, — leaving the cheaper grades to be secured by importation. It would not be accurate to say that he has a comparative advantage in the better grades; for, as will appear shortly, there is at least doubt whether the use of the land for sheep is as advantageous as its use for other agricultural or pastoral purposes. But he certainly has a *less disadvantage* in growing clothing and combing wool than in growing carpet wool. The tariff stimulus is sufficient to cause him to produce the former; it would need to be much greater — preposterously greater — to induce him to breed poor sheep and bring carpet wool to market.

The fact that all carpet wool was imported caused the debate on this part of the protective system to take a turn of its own. Why not admit such wool free, since there was no competition

[1] See the account of carpet wools in the *Tariff Board Report on Wool*, pp. 413 *seq.*

with any domestic product? The answer of the wool growers,—who were throughout the most uncompromising and even fanatical among the protectionists,—was that part of this wool in fact did compete with the domestic product. Some fraction was used not for carpets, but for cloths.[1] True, the amount was not considerable; moreover, what was so used was always mixed with other and better wools, chiefly domestic, sometimes also with the various substitutes, such as shoddy or noils or cotton. But even the slightest competition of this sort with the domestic wool growers was regarded as fraudulent, almost criminal. Not only was the repeal of the carpet wool duties steadily resisted, but an increase in them was demanded, and indeed was secured to some degree in the tariff acts of 1890 and 1897. The acrimonious contentions before congressional committees between the wool growers and the carpet makers all rested on a premise which a consistent free trader could not accept,—namely, that so far as the imports in fact did not compete with domestic wool, so far was there a special ground for admitting them free. Precisely no, must the free trader say. A duty of this sort, on a commodity not produced within the country, is a revenue duty. It is not indeed one of the simplest sort or of the best sort, being imposed on a raw material, and hence cumulative in effect as it is eventually paid in the higher price of the finished product. But at least it is not open to the objection that an additional tax is imposed through the higher price of the supply produced at home. The last-named effect does appear as regards wool of the other classes; and if a choice must be made between exempting from duty the carpet wool on the one hand or the clothing and combing wools on the other, the free trader should prefer the latter. It was natural that the protectionists, from their point of view, should think only of admitting free so much of the cheaper wool as was used in fact for carpet making, not the portion used in the manufacturing of cloth. No such discrimination between the two classes, however, was at any time made in the tariff laws enacted by either party. When the opponents of high protection came

[1] On the extent to which carpet wool was used in this way, see *Tariff Board Report on Wool*, pp. 413, 436.

into power, in 1913, as in 1894, wool of every kind was admitted free.[1]

The other classes of wool — clothing and combing — must be considered together. They present some intricate economic problems; they were the occasion of prolonged and bitter controversy. Protection to wool of this sort was the center of the protective system during the greater part of the period covered in the present volume.

Something should first be said on the qualities and uses of the two classes. Clothing wool, as defined in the tariff acts from 1867 to 1913, was wool from sheep of the merino breed, or from sheep having an admixture of this strain. Pure merino wool is short in fibre and fine in quality. Cross-breeding affects the length and quality of the fibre, and hence the textile uses to which it can be put. But the tariff definition and classification throughout regarded every wool with the slightest merino strain as "clothing wool"; even though it was used in the woolen manufacture in a way quite different from that contemplated when the tariff distinctions were first made. What was put in class II, "combing wool," on the other hand, was wool from sheep, pure bred, of the typical English strain: long in fibre, not short like merino wool; coarse in quality, not tenuous and fine; lustrous and somewhat harsh. The differences in the characteristics of these wools bring corresponding differences in the fabrics made from them. Merino wool is used for making "cloths," or "woolen cloths," in which the strands cling to each other as the short fibres touch and interlace; which are compacted and closely woven, often thick and heavy. Cloths have a "nap," or yielding surface, more or less smoothed off in the finishing processes,

[1] In the tariff bills introduced by the Republicans during the 62d Congress (1911–13) it was proposed that the duty on carpet wools should continue to be collected on its importation, but that the carpet manufacturers should get a drawback of the amount paid in duties to the same extent (99 per cent) as if they exported carpets; thus securing virtual exemption for so much of the wool as was actually used in carpet making. This proposal, of course, had no chance of adoption, during the Congress of 1911–13; then the Democrats controlled the House, the Republicans the Senate, and no tariff legislation was possible. But it represented the consistent protectionist policy.

yet giving the fabric a character of its own due to the short fibre of the wool. Combing wool, on the other hand, serves to make "worsteds" and "dress goods," — smooth fabrics, with an even and perhaps glossy surface, usually stiffer than cloths made from merino wool, and usually lighter in weight.

Quite as important as the difference in the fleece of the two kinds of sheep is the difference in their flesh. The English (combing wool) animals are mutton sheep; their meat is excellent; for this primarily they are bred, not for wool. Merino sheep, on the other hand, are scrawny creatures, with a tough and scant covering of flesh; they are bred primarily for their magnificent fleece. The two varieties differ, again, as regards habitat and herding; and these differences also have economic consequences of some importance. The combing wool (mutton) sheep flourish in a cool moist climate like that of England, their country of origin. The merino sheep, of a strain perfected first in Spain, adapt themselves readily to very diverse conditions, yet on the whole do best in a dry, warm climate, and are specially fitted for arid or semi-arid regions.[1] As regards herding, the merino sheep keep together, moving and cropping in bands; whereas the English sheep are apt to stray singly. The former, therefore, are more easily cared for and protected in frontier countries and in regions where lack of sufficient precipitation makes cultivation of the soil impossible.

All these differences, however, are smoothed away, and indeed sometimes quite wiped out, by cross-breeding. Sheep having a strain of either blood show in varying degrees the characteristics of both, according to the preponderance of one or the other strain. The profit through securing from the same animal sale-

[1] "The merino is beyond question the most cosmopolitan of the sheep tribe. No breed has passed into all countries and thriven as the merino, and still further no other breeds have been able to become so closely identified with their environment as to become the progenitors of native families as in the instance of the merino. This would seem to be due to the migrating habits that characterize the merino in Spain, where the flocks are driven towards the north in summer and southward in winter, thus becoming inured to all the variations of a diversified country." Craig, *Sheep-Farming in North America*, p. 34. On the hardiness of the merino and its tendency to herd in large numbers (hence less need of shepherding) see *Tariff Board Report*, pp. 605–607. Cf. the note to p. 315, below.

able mutton and desirable wool has caused growers in most countries, and especially in the United States, to turn to cross-breeding. At the same time improvements in machinery have made it quite feasible to use most cross-bred wool in either of the main manufacturing processes, — for making either cloths or worsteds.[1] Consequently much wool, — probably the larger part, — which was classed by our tariff as "clothing wool" was used in fact for the same purposes as "combing wool." The tariff classification, as has already been said, became quite out of accord with the trade classification, which was based not on blood, but on the industrial uses of the fibre. Both domestic and imported wool was largely cross-bred; and imported wool competed in much the same way with domestic wool, whether classed at the custom houses as clothing or combing. In comparing the imports with the domestic output, the tariff classes I and II may be, therefore, thrown together, — as has been done in constructing the chart.

Comparing now the total imports of wool used for clothing with the domestic production of wool (all used for the same purpose) it is obvious that a substantial contribution to the supply came throughout from the imports. At no time did they cease; as the years went on, they tended to grow.[2] The conclusion would seem warranted that the whole supply, domestic as well as foreign, was raised in price by the full amount of the duty. The proximate economic loss which may be ascribed to a protective tariff seems in this case susceptible of accurate calculation: multiply the domestic output by the rate of the duty.

Some of the qualifications which must be borne in mind when making such calculations do not seem applicable in the case of wool. There were no peculiarities of transportation, no geo-

[1] Cf. what is said below, at p. 327.

[2] The proportion of imports to domestic product is shown summarily by the following figures: —

	Average Imports, Per Year, of Wool, Classes I and II	Average Domestic Product, Per Year
Period 1884–90	26 mill. lbs.	321 mill. lbs.
" 1891–93 (under the McKinley tariff)	45 "	329 "
" 1895–97 (under the Wilson tariff, wool free)	153 "	272 "
" 1900–06 (duty restored)	65 "	297 "
" 1907–12 (duty restored)	95 "	314 "

graphically distinct markets, such as explain the exceptional imports of iron and steel, and show them to be of little significance. Foreign and domestic wools were marketed in the same places, namely, in the large cities of the Atlantic seaboard. Nor were there differences in quality which might require them to be regarded as distinct for industrial purposes. It is true that during the earlier part of our period, say from 1870 to 1885, allowance perhaps would have had to be made for differences in quality. Then the imported quota seems to have been usually of finer grade than the domestic. The latter was then said to be in the main good ordinary merino wool, suited for the medium grades of fabrics chiefly made within the country; while the imported wool was either strictly combing wool or a fine grade of clothing wool. But these differences, if ever they were important, ceased to be so before the close of the period. Domestic wool came to be largely cross-bred; a considerable portion of it was available for all the uses of combing wool; nor was there any marked lack of fine fibres. Wool varies to an extraordinary degree in quality. It is affected not only by the breed of the sheep, but by many and various causes, such as food, climate, shelter, care, and time of shearing.[1] Of all the textile fabrics, it seems least standardizable; and for that reason, it may be remarked, it cannot be made the object of organized speculation. But the gradations were and are very much the same for domestic wool as for imported. Whatever general differences in quality existed in the years 1870–90 ceased to be of much significance during the later period. Though the particular way in which our tariff duties

[1] "The superior purity of the Australian wools, their softness, lightness, and lustre, are attributed to the climatic conditions of that country. . . . Spanish merinos were introduced, and it soon became noticeable that the wool from the Australian flocks was of a finer quality than that grown upon the sheep fed upon the pastures of Spain. Dr. Bowman considers that an even temperature and a certain amount of moisture are necessary for the retention of lustre [that is, for sheep of the English mutton types], and he cites New Zealand wool as illustrative of this relationship. . . . It is known that some soils color wools so that they cannot be washed white. Territory wool has a characteristic bluish tinge that detracts greatly [?] from its market value. Scott asserts that the best wool growing land is generally that on a sandstone foundation, as it gives the wool the quality of being bright and clean, while he considers that volcanic or limestone soils are thought to favor harshness." Craig, *Sheep-Farming in North America*, pp. 38–39.

were assessed (as will presently appear) operated to exclude some sorts of foreign wool, they did not restrict the imports to any one quality or grade, or prevent the imported quotas from being comparable on the whole with the domestic.

In one direction, however, the application of the formula: economic loss = domestic product × rate of duty, must be modified. A point of difference between imported and American wools was that almost all the former were virtually improved in quality, and in that sense graded, by "skirting." A long controversy on skirted wools raged between wool growers and manufacturers. "Skirting" means that some inferior parts of the fleece have been cut off. The better parts are packed separately; a simple and convenient process, the natural result of the different uses of the varying fibres. Skirting is commonly practised in Australia, and the better wool thus differentiated of course commands a somewhat higher price than wool quite unsorted. The tariff acts previous to 1890 had imposed double duties on wool "imported in any other than the ordinary condition"; but in 1890 skirted wool was specifically made subject only to the normal wool duty; and it was similarly treated in 1897 and 1909. American fleeces, on the other hand, were never skirted; all the wool from a sheep was sold (and is) in one batch and at one price. By custom, the process of sorting was left entirely to the dealer or manufacturer.[1] Skirted Australian wool of course commanded a higher price than the unassorted American; and in comparing

[1] On skirted wool, see Wright, pp. 284–286, and *Tariff Report on Wool*, p. 337. It is a curious fact that American wool not only comes to market quite unassorted, but is often fraudulently or carelessly mixed with rubbish, twine and scraps. "Australian and New Zealand wool is packed more honestly than American wool" (I quote from the *Textile World Record*, June, 1908). American cotton is also said to come to market in bad condition. "Poor ginning [of American cotton] injures the staple; baled cotton is left uncovered and is damaged by the weather; the bagging is the heaviest and poorest that ingenuity can devise and it is charged at the same price as cotton. . . . An Egyptian bale is a model of neatness and compactness, with a light and strong covering, held together by proper hoops, and both bagging and hoops are deducted as tare." (From the presidential address of Mr. J. R. MacColl, before the Cotton Manufacturers' Association, April, 1906.) I suspect these defects in both domestic materials are ascribable to the unbridled individualism of the American planter and wool grower. Some form of coöperative organization for sales might bring improvement.

prices, and gauging the effect of the duty, something must be allowed for this circumstance. Competent persons in the trade have concluded that a deduction of about three cents from the stated duty must be made in order to offset the effect of skirting; the duty of eleven cents a pound on skirted wool was equivalent to one of (roughly) eight cents a pound on wool not thus assorted. If all the imported wool had been skirted, the duty of eleven cents would thus have been the same in effect as one of eight cents on wool strictly comparable to the American fleeces. The burden or loss ascribable to the tariff would then be calculated on a basis somewhat lower than that of the full duty.[1]

We may proceed now to a more detailed examination of the history of the domestic production of wool, and more especially of the lessons from the geographical distribution of different periods.

A glance at the table on page 308 will show that the number of sheep (a sufficient indication of the wool clip) in different parts of the country has undergone great and apparently irregular variations. Yet the variations in fact conform to some general tendencies; and these tendencies are instructive.

It will be seen that in the entire region east of the Allegheny mountains there was a marked and uninterrupted decrease in the number of sheep from the middle of the nineteenth century to 1910. The decline is most striking in New England and in New York. It is great also in Pennsylvania, even though, as

[1] Thus for 1912 we should have the following figures: —

Imports (fiscal year, 1911–12): —	
Class I	69,300,000
Class II	10,900,000
Total Imports, clothing wool	80,000,000 lbs.
Domestic Product (calendar year, 1912)	304,000,000 "

Charges on the domestic consumer: —

On 80 million lbs., imported wool, at 11c.	$8,800,000
On 304 million lbs., domestic wool: —	
if reckoned at 11c. lb.	$33,400,000
if reckoned at 8c. lb.	24,300,000

Some figure between the last two would seem to give with a sufficient approach to accuracy the *prima facie* national loss from protection to wool.

From statements made to me by wool dealers I gather that practically all the imported wools of class I (which greatly preponderate in the imports) are skirted.

will appear presently, the tariff has operated in special degree to maintain wool growing in some parts of that state. In the group of states which represent the great northern central region of the country, a somewhat different movement appears. The number of sheep increases from the middle of the nineteenth century until about the year 1880, but thereafter undergoes a progressive decline. Ohio is by far the most important of these states, so far

NUMBER OF SHEEP[1] (*000 omitted*)

	1840	1850	1860	1870	1880	1890	1900	1910
New England........	3,820	2,258	1,780	1,450	1,326	937	563	305
New York	5,119	3,453	2,618	2,182	1,715	1,529	939	605
Pennsylvania	1,768	1,822	1,632	1,794	1,777	1,612	959	637
Ohio	2,028	3,943	3,547	4,929	4,902	4,061	2,648	2,892
Michigan	100	746	1,273	1,986	2,189	2,400	1,626	1,545
Illinois.............	396	894	769	1,568	1,037	923	629	661
California	....	18	1,088	2,768	5,727	3,373	1,725	1,440
Texas	....	105	753	714	3,652	4,264	1,440	1,364
Oregon	....	15	86	318	1,368	1,780	1,961	1,982
Montana...........	....	....	....	2	279	2,353	4,215	4,979
Wyoming	....	....	....	6	450	713	3,327	4,676
Colorado	....	....	....	121	1,091	897	1,353	1,313
New Mexico.........	....	377	830	619	3,939	2,474	3,334	2,931

as wool growing is concerned. Even in Ohio the number of sheep, though it still remained considerable, showed an unmistakable decline after 1890. Turning to the region west of the Missouri river, we find still a different movement. In some states there is an almost continuous increase; in others, fluctuations not dissimilar to those of the eastern region. In California and Texas, for example, during the twenty years from 1860 to 1880, the figures show an extraordinarily rapid increase. But during the next generation the movement is reversed. The

[1] I take these figures from Wright, Appendix Table II. They are derived from Census reports, but no one supposes them to be more than approximations to the truth, especially for the earlier periods. They are sufficient approximations, however, to indicate the general trend.

number of sheep in each of these states declined during the ensuing thirty years, and in 1910 was hardly one-third of what it was in 1880 and 1890. Oregon belongs, on the whole, in the same group. Here, too, there was a rapid increase until 1890; thereafter, the number remained virtually stationary. On the other hand, the characteristic ranching states, like Montana, Colorado, and Wyoming, show an almost continuous growth. Here the number of sheep in 1910 was much greater than it had been twenty years before. New Mexico also holds her own.

The main explanation of these variations is that wool has been and is characteristically a frontier product. It is easily transportable; it is not perishable; sheep raising is a ready and profitable use of the land when land is plenty, population scarce, and transportation expensive. During the earlier stages in the development of New York, Ohio, and Illinois, wool growing was an important industry. As population thickened, other uses of the land became more advantageous, and the pastoral use of the land for sheep was displaced. Precisely the same transition has taken place within the last generation in California and Texas. During the first period of settlement, sheep were herded in these states by the million. As settlement progressed, agriculture took the place of ranching; and sheep and wool declined.[1]

Reference has been made to the rapid and striking increase of the American wool clip which took place during the years from 1870 to 1883. This was a period, as it happened, of unusually rapid extension of the frontier. In 1869, the first transcontinental railway was completed, — the combined Union Pacific-Central Pacific line. During the ensuing decade, several other great systems, the Burlington route, the Northern Pacific, the Atchison, the Southern Pacific, were building rapidly across the western plains. A vast grazing region was opened; the lands upon which the great herds of buffalo had wandered were gradually stocked with sheep. This rapid movement accounts for the growth of

[1] "The decline in the number of sheep with the advent of the farmer is nowhere more noticeable than in California." In 1880 that state had 7,500,000 sheep; in 1910, only 2,250,000. *Tariff Board Report on Wool*, p. 602.

the wool clip. Elsewhere, wool growing was on the decline; it was the rapid growth in the then territories which made up for the loss. After 1885, the decline in the country at large continued, and the growth in the great grazing region, though maintained, was at a slackened rate; consequently, the country's clip as a whole remained stationary.

The great pastoral region west of the Missouri river obviously cannot have the same future as the agricultural region to the eastward. Rainfall becomes progressively less toward the west, until, at about the one hundredth meridian, toward the western edge of Kansas and Nebraska, it becomes insufficient for agriculture. Doubtless it cannot be said just how far the tillable area extends; the methods of "dry farming" may stretch it somewhat farther than was long supposed. But beyond lies the arid and semi-arid country. Patches of it may be reclaimed by irrigation, but patches only. In the main, it must always be a pastoral region. Here sheep herding and wool growing have a chance for permanent lodgment.

The displacement of sheep growing as one of the main uses of the land in the eastern region is simply one further illustration of the working of the principle of comparative advantage. During the frontier stage, this pastoral use of land is advantageous. But as population thickens, settled agriculture becomes unmistakably *more* advantageous, and displaces the other use. Precisely the same movement is taking place the world over. Sheep growing has declined throughout western Europe, — except in England, where some special conditions prevail, sheep being kept primarily for mutton. For wool, the main supply of England as well as of the manufacturing countries of all western Europe comes from various outlying regions, such as Australia, Argentina, South Africa. These correspond for economic purposes to the successive frontier areas of the United States. In Europe, as in the United States, the use of agricultural land for wool growing has given place to other and more advantageous uses.[1]

[1] The history and explanation of the displacement of wool growing by tillage constitute the main theme of Professor Wright's volume, so often referred to in the preceding pages (*Wool-growing and the Tariff*). See particularly, pp. 135 *seq.*,

It would seem that the great arid and semi-arid plains and mountains which stretch from the western edge of the Missouri valley almost to the Pacific coast might become permanent sheep pastures and permanent sources of wool supply. But here once more the principle of comparative advantage comes into play. Use of the land for another pastoral purpose seems likely to displace wool growing. The grazing plains which can support sheep can support cattle also. Meat is in more insistent demand than wool and cattle pay better than sheep. The modern changes in transportation serve to increase the trend toward cattle raising. Cattle as well as meat can be transported with an ease undreamed of a half a century ago. Before the days of highly developed railway transportation, wool was the one product which could be easily carried from the frontier. Now cattle are carried their thousands of miles. The practice of rearing them on the plains, and then transporting them to the corn belt of the Mississippi valley for fattening, has attained great proportions. Wool growing has met in the pastoral region a competitor as formidable as tillage proved to be in the Mississippi valley itself.

Nevertheless, there are considerable parts of the western region which are unavailable for cattle, and which apparently will always be left to the sheep grower. Sheep need less water than cattle, and hence will always retain their place in the drier parts, especially in the southwest. They can be herded in hilly and mountainous regions where cattle cannot be kept; they flourish on herbage which is too scant for the larger animals. Similar causes, it may be remarked, bring about the dominance of sheep growing in Australia. In the vast interior of that continent, precipitation is even less than it is in the greater part of our western region. Moreover the hot and dry climate is better adapted for sheep

on the middle west in 1840–60; pp. 250 *seq.*, on the opening of the far west; and pp. 258 *seq.*, on the general competition between wool growing and other agricultural operations. Instructive maps, showing the westward movement of wool growing, are in a paper by Professor H. C. Taylor, published by the Wisconsin Agricultural Experiment Station, June, 1911.

For some further illustrations of the working of the principle of comparative advantage, — grain and dairying being found more profitable than sheep, — see the *Tariff Board Report on Wool*, pp. 563 (Illinois), 571 (Wisconsin), 581 (Nebraska).

and especially merino sheep, than for cattle. There is a natural division of labor, — natural in the sense of resting on physical causes, — when sheep are herded and wool is produced in the interior of Australia and in the similar parts of our west, while cattle raising dominates those parts of the west where the climate and topography are adapted to them.

There is, however, another and entirely different aspect of wool growing. In the preceding paragraphs regard has been had to those pastoral conditions under which wool growing is the main use of the land. Quite different is the situation when sheep are kept as a by-product of general farming. Sheep in small numbers can probably be kept with profit on almost any farm. They are certainly kept with profit on very many. Their keep costs little; they enrich the soil; and what is got for their wool and mutton is so much extra gain. The gain from keeping a few sheep perhaps becomes greater as farming becomes more intensive; though the circumstance that sheep growing has almost disappeared in the western part of Germany, where cultivation is highly intensive, indicates that generalization on this topic must be guarded.

At all events, in the United States, farmers in considerable number, especially in the northern central region, maintain each a few sheep as a by-product. These are most profitably the cross-breds. Though the pure English strain is not adapted to the food or climate, sheep of mixed breed do well, kept with a view rather to meat than to wool. In the pastoral region of the west the merino strain long predominated. Even there, however, a movement similar to that in cattle growing has taken place; cross-bred sheep are reared on the ranches, and then sent eastward to be fattened in the corn belt. It is in the farming region proper, however, that the keeping of sheep primarily for mutton has most developed. Here the sheep are a by-product of general farming; and the wool itself is a by-product of that by-product.

To the general tendency that wool growing on a large scale tends to disappear from thickly populated countries, being relegated to frontier regions or to those regions whose climatic conditions condemn them to a perpetual frontier state, there are two striking exceptions. One, already referred to, is in England, where more sheep are permanently maintained than in any other thickly settled country. The favoring circumstances are unusual: a great demand for mutton, a climate suited to the mutton breed, soils which seem to benefit unusually by the enrichment from sheep. Wool is much the less important of the chief products. The maintenance of sheep growing in England in face of complete free trade and heavy wool imports indicates that this use of the land is advantageous. The other analogous region is in the northern and eastern part of Ohio, with adjacent districts in Pennsylvania and Michigan. Here also sheep raising remains, not on a small scale as a by-product of general farming, but as an important part, even the most important part, of agricultural operations. Here merino sheep were long maintained; and even though cross-bred sheep kept for mutton have in good part replaced them, wool and the price of wool still bulk large in the farmers' eyes. Here was the main seat of a vehement protectionist feeling. Here lived President McKinley, and here he imbibed that devotion to the principle of protection with which his name is linked in history. The case is unlike the English case, in that the maintenance of wool growing was dependent on protection. It happens that considerable parts of the Ohio area are hilly and easily eroded, and not so advantageous for general agriculture as the typical prairie land of the Mississippi valley. It was natural that wool growing, once established here under frontier conditions, and much promoted by the exceptional need for wool during the civil war period, should be clung to almost with desperation, and should become the basis of an intense and uncompromising demand for protection.

Comparing now the different wool growing regions of the United States, it is clear that the conditions were very diverse in the several seats of the industry. One could hardly find a better illustration of an industry conducted not with constant costs, but with costs greatly varying. On this phase of the wool situation the Tariff Board's inquiries of 1909–12 led to some striking results. The special subject to which the Board directed its attention was the cost of wool within the country and without, — with reference to that principle of "equalizing" costs of production which then played so large a part in the tariff debate. Untenable as is the principle itself, the inquiries to which it gave rise served to supply illustrations on the principles really essential in the controversy.

Wool being a product supplied jointly with mutton, the Board's first task was to demarcate if possible the separate cost of wool. In this task it followed the method approved in economic theory, deducting from the total cost (supply price) of the whole the price obtained (the demand price) for the products other than wool.[1] The total cost of sheep rearing was first ascertained or approximated; then the receipts from products other than wool (chiefly mutton) were deducted; the residue was taken to be the separate cost of wool. Obviously the "cost" of wool, thus made out, was a figure to be used with caution. It was the "derived" cost of wool, not an independent cost. It was directly dependent on the receipts obtained from the mutton; yet none the less, nay, for that very reason, a significant figure. It meant that wherever much was obtained from the sale of mutton, so much less was needed to make it worth while to supply the wool; and conversely that where little was got from mutton, so much more would have to be got from wool in order to make the rearing of sheep worth while.

Calculated in this way, the "cost" of wool showed extraordinary diversities. The summary statement made by the Tariff Board, giving the results in the most general form, ran as follows:[2]

	Number of Sheep	Average "Cost" of Wool
1. Western region (the "Territories")	35,000,000	11 cents
2. Ohio region (merino sheep)	5,000,000	19 cents
3. Cross-bred sheep in other regions east of the Missouri river	10,000 000	*nil*

These figures, however, not only showed an extraordinary range, — from nineteen cents a pound to nothing at all, — but

[1] See the elegant analysis of this case, as well as of the case of joint demand, in Marshall's *Principles of Economics*, Book V, ch. vi, §§ 1, 4 (6th edition).

[2] *Report*, p. 377. Cf. also the Summary, at p. 10.

were themselves averages made up from widely varying figures. Thus, in the most important of the three regions (the western), for which an average cost of eleven cents was given, the individual costs whence the average was deduced varied from a maximum of twenty-four cents a pound to a minimum of four cents. For the Ohio region, the average for the merino sheep there investigated was similarly made up from figures mounting to forty-two cents at the highest and falling to six cents at the lowest.[1] The simple fact is that wool growing in some parts of the United States is carried on under advantageous conditions, — as, for example, in the dry southwestern districts where the climatic conditions are favorable for merino sheep and for nothing else;[2] while in other parts of the country, as for example in the Ohio region, the conditions are distinctly disadvantageous. The lesson even for the staunch protectionists was obvious: the favorite formula of "equalizing cost of production" could not be applied in this case. And the lesson for the staunch free trader was equally obvious: there was no ground for fostering a domestic supply of wool produced at high cost, and no ground for worry about the consequences of abolishing the duty as regards the wool produced at low cost.

The contrast between the last two groups, — the Ohio region with a "cost" of nineteen cents, and other parts of the north central region with a "cost" of nothing at all, — brings out most strikingly the differences. When it was figured out that for cross-bred sheep kept in connection with general farming the wool cost nothing at all, the fact simply was that the proceeds

[1] See the analysis of the Tariff Board's figures made by Mr. W. S. Culbertson (who had been himself a member of the Board) in *American Economic Review*, March, 1913, p. 66. It should be added that for the Ohio region, though the variation from extreme to extreme was great, most of the figures fell within a smaller range (12 to 27 cents). For the western region, however, the varying figures of cost were distributed from highest to lowest without noticeable concentration in a middle range.

[2] "The Southwest is still, as it has always been, the home of the range merino. But little of the mutton blood has been introduced into the flocks of this region, and the indications are that for obvious reasons, — climate, range, etc., — these conditions will continue to exist for many years to come." *Tariff Board Report*, p. 602.

from mutton covered all separable expenses incurred for the sheep, such as feeding, care, and the like. Both wool and sheep were a by-product (joint product) of general farming, and the "cost" of wool was more distinctly a derived cost, and even more elusive, than in the ordinary cases of joint cost. In whatever way calculated, however, it could not be more than nominal. On the other hand, there were in the Ohio region farmers who clung with a certain obstinacy to rearing merino sheep solely for their heavy fleece of short fine wool. Much of the land so used seems to have been not easily available for general agricultural purposes. But much of it was turned to wool growing of this sort through persistent habit, and also, of course, through the influence of the duty on wool. The indications were that where the breeding was chiefly or largely for mutton (cross-breds), even farms on which sheep and wool were the main products were little affected by the price of wool or the wool duty. But as regards farming chiefly for merino wool, it was found that "the highest average cost of production of such wool in the world is in the state of Ohio and contiguous territory"; which from the unflinching protectionist point of view may be a reason for maintaining a high duty on wool, but to the free trader seems a conclusive ground for not endeavoring to stimulate its domestic production at all.[1]

One other phase of the wool situation deserves attention. It was pointed out, in the first part of this chapter, that the orthodox formula (so it may be called) for ascertaining the national

[1] The sentence quoted is from the *Tariff Board Report*, p. 10. On the Ohio situation in general, see pp. 548 *seq*. A certain note of impatience with the merino wool producers of this region is discernible in the *Report*. After pointing out that well-managed sheep farms on which wool was *not* the chief source of income rarely failed to show a profit, the *Report* goes on (p. 548): "Why, then, do not all of the sheep breeders of the Ohio valley follow this system? The answer is that on hill farms especially it is not easy to grow the corn necessary to fatten lambs. Then, the owners of many flocks have not learned to adapt their systems of agriculture to this practice; they have long been accustomed to looking to wool for their chief profit from sheep breeding." The truth seems to be that this sort of wool growing was a survival from the frontier days of Ohio, maintained, precariously and beyond its time, first by the civil war demand for wool and then by the high duties. Cf. Wright, pp. 148, 183, 247.

loss from protection seems in this case applicable; due allowance being made for the complication arising from skirted wool.[1] Imports continue, in quality similar to the domestic product. There are no complications from exceptional conditions of transportation or of geographical distribution. Apply then the formula; multiply the domestic product by the full (effective) rate of duty; and you have the national loss. The assumptions underlying this sort of inference are two: first that the domestic price is in fact raised by the duty, — and this cannot be doubted; second that the foreign price will maintain itself at the same level after abolition of the duty. The second assumption raises a debatable question. It may be asked, will not the foreign price itself be raised, in consequence of the additional pressure on foreign sources of supply due to increased importations into the United States? We may disregard that crude form of the contention which looks simply to temporary results. Whenever a duty is remitted, the immediate effect is greater resort to foreign supplies and some rise in foreign prices. As time goes on, however, foreign prices will ordinarily be reduced to their former level; and *then* the full benefit of remission of taxation will inure to the domestic purchaser. There is the possibility, however, that the enlargement of the foreign supply will take place in the face of obstacles, — with increasing costs, diminishing returns. There may be pressure upon limited sources of supply, resort to less advantageous sources, and consequently some permanent enhancement of price. The case is familiar in economic theory: an increase in demand for a commodity produced under conditions of diminishing returns causes a permanent advance in normal price.

It appears, however, that this result, though quite within the bounds of theoretic possibility, is not likely in fact to ensue; and this because of the expansibility of the supply from the one region which is most important, — Australia. During the last two generations the extraordinary extension of grazing into frontier regions seems to have well-nigh exhausted the other available areas. South Africa, necessarily limited in productive capacity

[1] See p. 306, above.

by an unusually arid climate, apparently has reached its limit. In Argentina a development seems to have taken place essentially similar to that which has already taken place in our Mississippi valley. The plow is displacing the ranch; settled agriculture succeeds grazing. And grazing itself is found more profitable for cattle than for sheep. What with the competition of grain and of cattle, the wool clip of Argentina seems likely to diminish rather than to increase. But in the interior of Australia a large extension of supply may be expected without an increase in cost. Wool production in that vast area is declared by observers who are competent, and who cannot be supposed to have a bias against the maintenance of our wool duties, to be susceptible of very considerable expansion. It would seem that from this region additional quantities can be procured without resort to poorer natural resources, and consequently at costs and prices similar to those which have prevailed in the past. The Australian interior, it is true, is fickle, because of the narrow margin of safety in its precipitation. The rainfall is so scant that a slight deficiency causes immense losses among the sheep. A year or two of drought in Australia affects the wool supply of the whole civilized world, and so the course of wool prices. A conjuncture of Australian drought with the abolition of American wool duty might bring it about that for the time being the American purchaser would experience no lowering of prices. But in the long run, and under the normally prevalent conditions, this combination of circumstances cannot be regarded as probable. The Tariff Board, in the same sentence in which it declared our Ohio region to be the most expensive region in the world for producing wool, declared Australia to be the least expensive in the world; and there appears to be no reason for anticipating that under altered conditions of demand it will cease to be the least expensive source of supply, — that is, the most advantageous.[1]

There is, however, another qualification, of some practical as well as theoretic significance, which must be attached to the

[1] See *Tariff Board Report*, p. 10. The possibilities of increase in foreign supplies are considered in the *Report* at pp. 490, 522 *et passim*. There were in 1910 less than one hundred million sheep in Australia; it is supposed the number can be increased without difficulty to at least one hundred and fifty million (p. 492).

general conclusion concerning the "national loss" ascribable to the wool duty. It results from the great variety in the conditions under which the domestic wool, not the foreign, is grown; it is one which must be borne in mind whenever a raw material, — a commodity belonging to the extractive group, — is subjected to a protective duty. A part of the domestic output of such a commodity is likely to be produced within the protecting country so advantageously that it would hold its place even without the duty. Not the whole output then leans on protection, but only the part which is made under less advantageous conditions. But to this latter part alone can we apply the reasoning about national loss. Here, and here only, is it true that the consumer is taxed, and that the producer yet does not profit; that the extra price which the duty enables the producer to get merely enables him to carry on operations he would not otherwise turn to. As regards the domestic producers who would carry on the same operations in any case, there is nothing in the nature of a national loss; there is merely transfer from one pocket to another. What the consumer pays to them in the way of enhanced price, they really gain. Under these conditions, and to this extent, there is some justification for saying that protection robs Peter to pay Paul. But, by the same token, the free trader is not justified in saying that under these conditions there is wasteful diversion of industry from the more profitable channels into the less. There may be unjustifiable taxing of one set of persons for the advantage of another set, — whether it is deemed unjustifiable must depend on one's convictions regarding the general benefit or lack of benefit from protection. But there is only a transfer from one to another, no net economic loss. In this direction the reasoning about the economic loss from a duty like that on wool must be qualified.[1]

From this sketch of the history and conditions of domestic and foreign production, it will be seen that wool growing in the United States is partly an industry depending upon tariff support, and partly not. The keeping of sheep as a by-product of

[1] Compare what was said in chapter i, pp. 14 *seq.*, on extractive commodities, and in chapter v, p. 63, on the Hawaiian sugar situation.

general farming will be continued whether or no there be a duty upon wool. The trend toward mutton, and the diminution of sheep raising with a view primarily to wool, are inevitable. In the pastoral region of the west, cattle will displace sheep in the long run wherever the climate and the lay of the land make possible the change. Wool growing of the sort which long held its own in the Ohio region was an artificial industry, probably unable to hold its own even against the stress of domestic forces, and almost sure to give way in face of unfettered foreign competition. Yet even under free wool a considerable clip is likely to be forthcoming in the United States. Partly it will be derived from many small flocks of sheep maintained in connection with general farming; supplies of this sort will probably increase as agriculture becomes more intensive. Partly it will come from those regions in the arid west which are not suitable for cattle and can be used for sheep only.

Surveying the situation as a whole, it is difficult to see any ground for the maintenance of duties upon wool, except that of extreme and even fanatical protectionism. The arguments to which economists give a respectful hearing are not applicable. There can be no question of protection to young industries. The physical and industrial obstacles which stand in the way of complete supply of the market from domestic sources are unalterable. It is the steady and growing strength of these forces which explains the increase in the imports of wool after 1900 in face of high duties. Neither do any social or political arguments tell in favor of duties on raw wool. It is, indeed, conceivable that political or social disadvantages may be alleged to ensue from *complete* reliance on foreign sources of supply for this important material. Yet it is striking that even in Germany, where most stress has been laid on considerations of this kind, absolute dependence on imported wool is accepted by all parties with equanimity.[1] So far as the United States are concerned, however, the question is merely one of more or less. Even under

[1] In 1898 Germany imported ten times as much wool as was produced at home (177 mill. kilograms against 17 mill.). Michaelis, in *Handbuch der Wirtschaftskunde Deutschlands*, vol. iii, p. 629.

free wool, the domestic supply will not disappear; it will simply shrink to smaller dimensions. To repeat, the only grounds on which a wool duty can be defended are those of a crass mercantilism: that the international division of labor brings no gain, importation in itself means loss. If foreign supply is admitted ever to be advantageous, it must be so in the case of wool.

CHAPTER XX

THE WOOLEN MANUFACTURE. THE COMPENSATING SYSTEM; WOOLENS AND WORSTEDS

THE main products of the woolen manufacture are woolen and worsted fabrics, and to these attention will be given in the present chapter. To them the much-discussed compensating system was applied, as indeed it was to all woolen products. That system, though initiated as early as 1861, was not fully developed until the passage of the wool and woolens tariff act of 1867. As then elaborated, it remained in operation without essential changes (barring the years 1894–97) until 1913. The questions that arise regarding the effects of protection on the industry cannot be followed without some understanding of the method by which the woolen manufacturers were "compensated" for the charges laid on them through the wool duties. The whole system, be it remembered, was swept away in 1913. The very fact that this episode in protection is closed, at least for the time being, makes its study profitable.[1]

In essence, the system was simple. A duty on wool raises the price of that material for the American manufacturer. He is compelled to pay more for it than is his foreign competitor. To equalize the competition between domestic and foreign manufacturers, a duty should be levied on imported woolens equivalent to the increased price of wool used in making domestic woolens. In the same way, — to state an analogous case, — if an internal tax is put on a commodity, an equal tax should be put on the same commodity when imported; otherwise the importer would be given an advantage, and would undersell the domestic producer. Once a duty was imposed on wool, an equivalent duty was clearly called for on woolens, — known in this case as the compensating duty.

[1] On the history of the compensating system I have summarily repeated here what is said more fully in my *Tariff History of the United States*, where the various modifications of the system are described in detail for the successive tariff acts.

The compensating duty on woolens was fixed, in general, on the supposition that it required four pounds of wool to make one pound of cloth. This large proportion, always surprising to persons not cognizant of the peculiarities of the industry, is due mainly to the amount of fatty matter contained in wool as it comes from the sheep's back. In the scouring process, most wool loses at least one-half of its weight. Often the loss is two-thirds, sometimes even four-fifths; though it is true that there are grades of wool on which the loss is considerably less than half. It is not feasible to take into account the variations in shrinkage by fixing a different compensating duty for each several kind of cloth; some general average, a fair approximation to the usual shrinkage, must be made the basis. The kind of wool most largely used in the United States in 1867, when the system was put in the shape which proved permanent, lost about two-thirds of its weight in scouring; the same was the case with the wool which was then expected to be imported. Further allowance had to be made for some wastage of the fibre in the manufacturing process. The upshot was that four pounds of wool were reckoned to be needed for making one pound of cloth. If, therefore, the duty on wool was eleven cents a pound, a duty on foreign cloths of four times that amount (forty-four cents a pound on the cloth) would put the foreign manufacturer who used four pounds of similar wool in the same position as the domestic manufacturer who also used them and paid duty on them.

A figure not far from this (forty-four cents a pound) appeared as compensating duty on woolen cloths in all the protective tariff acts from 1867 to 1909. Some changes and readjustments were made from time to time. At the very start, in 1867, the compensating figure was swelled, in order to offset some internal taxes then still left over from the civil war levies, though abolished shortly afterwards. In 1883, when the general trend was toward abating somewhat the high range of duties, the figure was reduced to thirty-five cents; the duty on wool itself being also reduced slightly in that year. In 1890, a differentiation was made. Cheap goods, it was admitted, used less wool (some admixture of cotton) and less expensive wool, than dearer goods; the compensating duty was accordingly graded, from thirty-three cents on the cheapest goods to forty-four cents on the dearest. In the tariff acts of 1897 and 1909 no change of note was made in the compensating figures. On the whole, the changes in the several tariffs brought no serious modification of the general system based on the ratio of four to one.

Over and above this compensating duty came the protective duty proper. The former simply put the manufacturer in the same position, relatively to his foreign competitor, as if he, like the foreigner, secured his wool free; it gave him no favor. But the essence of the protective system is to favor the domestic producer. An additional duty was therefore imposed on foreign woolens, which was designed to be the protecting element in the combination, and the sole protecting element. This additional or protecting duty was always *ad valorem*. In 1867, the manufacturers who framed the scheme modestly alleged that they wished a net protection of but 25 per cent; this had been the rate fixed in 1861, just before the civil war. To be sure, the actual duty requested and secured in 1867 was not 25 per cent, but 35 per cent, because allowance was asked here, as in the case of the compensating duty itself, for some additional charges due to the internal taxes of the war. But this moderation soon was forgotten; the supposed standard of a net protection amounting to no more than 25 per cent was early put aside. If one cared to use an analogy from biology, one might say that in the propitious environment a rapid development took place from the original form, until a variety was evolved which, though like its ancestor in structure, quite out-topped it in size. The *ad valorem* or protecting duty not only was retained at 35 per cent long after all the special war charges had disappeared, but was increased (on all but the cheaper goods) to 40 per cent in 1883, to 50 per cent in 1890, and to 55 per cent in 1897 and 1909. The increase and accentuation of protection was nowhere more striking than in the woolens schedule.

In its application to a considerable number of fabrics, the compensating system lost some of that simplicity which it had when both cloth and wool were subjected to specific duties on the same basis, — that is, by the pound. It was not deemed feasible to apply the pound duty to all woolens. Dress goods, — for example, lighter fabrics for women, — were made dutiable by the yard; a fixed sum per yard was calculated which was supposed to be equivalent to the higher price of wool used by the domestic manufacturer in producing a yard of such dress goods. Similarly the compensating duties on carpets were fixed by the yard, not by the pound. These adjustments, already complicated in the tariff act of 1867, became still more so in the later acts; until schedule K became extraordinarily intricate, full of compensations based on approximations twenty or thirty years behind the times, inviting attack, yet difficult to reconstruct without danger of collapse to the entire edifice.[1]

Throughout, in sum, there was the system of double duties: specific duties by the pound (in some cases by the yard) which constituted "compensation" for the effect of the duties on the raw wool; and superimposed on them, *ad valorem* duties, reaching at the maximum 55 per cent, which were alone supposed to give protection. What now was the real weight of the duties, the real outcome of the system? What was the degree of pro-

[1] The development of the system is shown by the following figures, which state the duties on "woolen cloths," the typical class of goods and the one still most important in Schedule K.

Year	Duty on Wool, Per Pound	Duty on Woolen Cloth: Compensating (Specific) Per Pound		Duty on Woolen Cloth: Protective *ad valorem*
1861	3c.		12c.	25%
1864	6c.		24c.	40%
1867	12c.		50c.	35%
1883	10c.	Costing up to 80c. per lb.,	35c.	35%
		" over 80c. "	35c.	40%
1890	11c.	Costing up to 30c. per lb.,	33c.	40%
		" 30 @ 40c. "	38½c.	40%
		" over 40c. "	44c.	50%
1894	Free	No compensating duty		Costing up to 50c. per lb., 40%
				" over 50c. " 50%
1897	11c.	Costing up to 40c. per lb.,	33c.	50%
		" 40 @ 70c. "	44c.	50%
		" over 70c. "	44c.	55%
1909	11c.	Same duties as in 1897		Same duties as in 1897
1913	Free	No compensating duty		35%

The wool duty is here stated approximately; for details see the table given above, p. 297. On the splitting of the compensating duty which begins in 1883 and is maintained until 1913, see p. 330 below.

tection actually given the wool manufacturers? These questions must be answered before proceeding to the further and more important question of the economic consequences.

It is probable that the compensating duties were fixed at the outset in good faith and with sufficient accuracy. The charge was often made, by those free traders who see nothing but robbery and corruption in the protective system, that they were manipulated from the start. No doubt the manufacturers whose calculations were then used made sure that the compensating figures were quite high enough; but there seems to have been no deliberate manipulation on the staple goods, and probably no serious excess.[1] But as time went on, the system got completely out of gear. The compensating duties, so far from being merely sufficient for their avowed purpose, came to be very much more so. In consequence, the duties on woolens as a whole proved to be so much higher than the supposed and avowed rate of protection as to reach the extreme height in the entire tariff system. They became the particular object of attack by its opponents; and they served as still another illustration of the difficulty of ascertaining the real effect of duties that are quite prohibitory to importation.

For this divergence between plan and outcome there were several causes. Attention has already been called to those which must be considered in gauging the effect of the wool duty itself. It did not in fact cause all domestic wool to rise in price by the full amount of the duty. It was quite natural that the framers of the compensating system should have proceeded on the assumption that it would; not only because the assumption underlies the usual discussions of protection, but because the circumstances of the time (1865–70) doubtless warranted it. But, as we have seen, the domestic wool clip grew rapidly during the years 1870–1885, and imports were comparatively small; and

[1] This I judge to have been the case, at all events, as regards woolen cloths of the kind chiefly made at that time within the country. The compensating duties on dress goods (levied by the yard, and not by the pound, and therefore not easily subject to check) seem to have been designedly excessive even from the start. See the *Tariff Board Report*, p. 148. Cf. *ibid.*, p. 184, for a curious manipulation and increase in the duty on rugs in 1897, — fairly to be dubbed a " joker."

during these years there was probably a difference between the quality of the imported wool and most of that grown within the country. And in later years also a difference of the same sort persisted. It is true that after 1890 the domestic supply remained on the whole stationary, while the imports increased; true also that the intrinsic qualities of the two ceased to show considerable differences. But the "skirted wool" complication set in after 1890. Its consequence was, as already noted, that imported wool, in the form in which it came to market, was better in quality than domestic; the latter accordingly did not rise in price by the full amount of the duty on foreign wool.[1] Except for some special wools, used for particular grades of cloth, it was probably never true that the American manufacturer when buying domestic wool (that is, for the great bulk of his purchases) was handicapped as against the foreigner by the wool duty to its full extent.

Even more important, and also of special effect during the later years, was the change in the character of the wool commonly used. This again was a consequence of the great change in the woolen manufacture itself to which attention will presently be given, — the transition from woolens to worsteds. It led to greater use of combing and cross-bred wools, and less use of clothing wools. The latter, it happens, have the highest shrinkage, and alone justify the four-to-one basis of calculation. The strict combing wools, from sheep of the pure English breed, shrink at the most 30 per cent, often as little as 18 or 20; cross-bred wools a little more, but rarely in excess of 33 per cent. Merino wools (clothing wools in the strictest sense) alone shrink as much as 60 per cent; on some of these the scoured wool content goes even as low as 25 per cent, *i. e.*, 75 per cent is lost in scouring.[2] When the compensating system was established, the woolen manufacture was engaged almost exclusively on "cloths," and was

[1] Cf. what was said in the preceding chapter, p. 306.

[2] See the excellent generalized statement in the *Tariff Board Report*, Summary, p. 12. Elsewhere (p. 89) it is remarked that "a fleece from an Angora goat or Lincoln sheep may shrink in scouring only 10 or 20 per cent, leaving 80 or 90 per cent of clean wool; a Cape or Australian merino fleece, on the contrary, may shrink as high as 50 to 70 per cent, yielding only 50 to 30 per cent of clean wool."

using almost exclusively merino wool subject to shrinkage of 60 per cent or more. But in proportion as the worsted branch of the manufacture grew, and the older branch of the industry itself used more and more of cross-bred wool, the computations of the compensating system became quite inapplicable to the prevalent conditions. And yet there remained parts of the woolen industry to which those computations did remain applicable, and for which the four-to-one adjustment was barely sufficient for equalization, occasionally even less than sufficient. Some very fine wools are extremely "heavy," *i. e.*, contain a great proportion of grease; and not only four pounds of such wool, but more, are used in making a pound of (say) fine broadcloth. The rigid simplicity of the compensating was quite out of accord with the great variety and complexity of the industrial conditions.[1]

[1] It was by parading the exceptional cases that the representatives of the woolen manufacturers were able in later years to make a show of validity for the basis of four to one in the compensating system. See, for example, their statement before the Ways and Means Committee in 1909; *Tariff Hearings of 1909*, p. 7257. The stubbornness of the Association of Wool Manufacturers in clinging not only to the principle but the details of the act of 1867 (they interposed a veritable *non possumus* to all proposals for change) must be regarded as a strange piece of political ineptitude. As late as 1911, the President of the American Woolen Company made the following extraordinary statement in an address to his fellow-manufacturers: "Schedule K, much maligned, much misunderstood, if properly understood would be the most appreciated of any schedule in the tariff; and if all schedules in the tariff were as scientifically based and as well poised and balanced as Schedule K, it would be the most remarkable document, next to the Constitution of the United States, that the human mind has ever produced"! I quote from a pamphlet reprint of the address.

I have not referred in the text to another episode which played a considerable part in the attacks on Schedule K. Throughout the period of wool duties, the ordinary or normal duty (about eleven cents a pound) was double on wool which had been washed, and triple on wool scoured. Hence most imports were of unwashed wool. But on combing wool (class II) the duty was the same whether washed or unwashed; though still triple when scoured. Hence wool of class II was almost always imported in the washed state. This exceptional treatment of combing wool was the occasion of not a little controversy. It was sought to be justified on the ground that such wool in fact was almost always washed on the sheep's back, and could not well be imported in any other condition; and also justified frankly on the ground that in 1867, when the exception was instituted, the branch of the manufacture using such wool (the worsted branch) was of small dimensions and in its early stages, and so deserving of special consideration. In any case, the discrimination proved of less importance than might have been expected, because

Another circumstance that contributed much to the misfit was the large use of substitutes or adulterants. This took place more particularly in the woolen branch of the industry. It was in the worsted branch that the low shrinkage of the wool served most to make the compensation excessive; in the other and older branch it was the extensive use of substitutes for wool. Chief among these are shoddy, noils, cheap grades of wool, cotton. Shoddy is the wool fibre got from woolen rags torn to pieces; by no means so worthless as is implied by the familiar connotation of the word, but still poorer and cheaper than wool. Noils are short fibres culled from the longer fibres of combing wool in the process of combing.[1] Different both from shoddy and noils in not being a second-hand or quasi-discarded product, yet of similar significance for the compensating system, are the cheaper grades of wool which the tariff system classed as carpet wool and admitted at rates of duty lower than those on the other wools. Though most of this wool was in fact used in the carpet manufacture, a substantial amount was and is used in making the cheaper grades of woolen cloths. Last but not least among the substitutes is cotton, which forms the warp in many of the cheaper woolens and worsteds.[2]

There was much foolish recrimination between free traders and protectionists concerning these so-called adulterants. The free traders maintained that it was the tariff system which caused them to be resorted to, thus depriving the people of all-wool fabrics; while the protectionists alleged that the foreign manufacturers were the greatest adepts in using shoddy and that the high duties served to keep out flimsy and worthless stuff. The obvious truth was that within the country as well as without the pressure for using any available substitute for the expensive wool

almost all wool actually combed, and actually used in the worsted manufacture, came to be not strict " combing wool " as defined in the tariff, but cross-bred wool classed in the tariff as " clothing wool." Nevertheless some millions of pounds of strict combing wool were imported each year, and in occasional years much more; and as regards this, the compensating arrangement never could pretend to be accurate. — Cf. what is said in the *Tariff Board Report*, p. 89.

[1] Cf. p. 388, below.

[2] The importance of these substitutes or " adulterants " is shown by the fact that little more than half of the woolens made in the country was all wool. The

was enormous, and that every device was tried in order to manufacture presentable fabrics from the cheapest possible material. Probably the tariff, by making wool even dearer than it had to be because of the natural conditions that operate on all animal products, drove American manufacturers to substitute somewhat more than would have been the case under free wool. On the other hand, the very limitations which the wool duty caused in the choice of the various grades may have prevented the domestic makers of woolens from securing as good results as their foreign rivals from the deft mixture of coarse fibres with fine. But the influence of the protective system in these directions was much exaggerated by both sides.

So far as concerns the compensating system, however, the consequences from the use of substitutes were great. Obviously, to the extent they were resorted to, four pounds of wool were not required in order to make one pound of cloth; and the compensating duty based on that assumption, liberal even in the case of most all-wool goods, was grossly excessive on that large portion of the domestic output for which there was use of shoddy, noils, carpet wool, or cotton. A niggardly allowance for this obvious defect in the system was made in the tariff acts passed subsequent

Tariff Board gave the following figures, based on census returns (*Report*, pp. 220, 224, 226, 230): —

	1900	1910
Worsteds:		
Value of total goods	$120.3 mill.	$312.6 mill.
" " all-wool goods	60.5 "	160.9 "
Woolens:		
Value of total goods	118.4 "	107.1 "
" " all-wool goods	57.3 "	60.0 "

The quantity of the various materials used in the woolen branch in 1909 was: —

Wool (in scoured condition)	60	
" (yarn)	8	
	—	68 mill. lbs.
Camel, alpaca, and other hair	18	
Shoddy made from rags in the mill	31	
Shoddy purchased	20	
Noils and waste	24	
Cotton (including cotton yarn)	33	
	—	126 mill. lbs.

I have condensed these figures from the Board's *Report*, p. 228. Between 1900 and 1910 there was a marked increase in proportion of substitutes used; one among the indications that the woolen branch of the industry was in a transitional and perhaps precarious state.

to 1867; woolen goods were graded after 1883 according to the value, and those having the lowest value were subjected to compensating duties based on a proportion of three to one instead of four to one. But the allowance was quite insufficient; the compensating duty remained much higher than would have sufficed for its avowed purpose.[1]

The consequence, to repeat, was that the whole system got out of gear within a few years after its adoption in 1867. At an early date it was easily seen that the apparent simplicity and frankness of schedule K covered a vast amount of complexity and pretense.[2] In its actual working the system was intricate, not simple; the compensating duties did not merely compensate, they added very much to the manufacturers' protection. During the short period of free wool from 1894 to 1897 this fact was brought home to the manufacturers, and then was freely admitted.[3] After 1897, when protectionism revived in full force, and the good old times seemed to have returned without prospect of relapses to tariff reduction, the system in all its details was again accepted as part of the unalterable order of things. But in 1909, in the debates on the tariff act of that year, it was again sharply attacked. The unwillingness of the manufacturers to consider the slightest modification (it will be remembered that in the tariff of 1909 Schedule K was left quite intact) added to the bitterness of the critics. The most important investigation by the Tariff Board was on this schedule; and the conclusions stated in its Report laid bare the anomalies of the compensating system in a way to leave it quite indefensible. The Board un-

[1] See the tabular statement on p. 325. Cf. the *Tariff Board Report*, p. 124.

[2] I said as much in an essay published in 1885; reprinted in my *Tariff History* (pp. 208 *seq.*).

[3] In the spring of 1894, when the tariff bill of that year was being debated and the abolition of the compensating system was impending, the *American Cotton and Wool Reporter* wrote (May 24, 1894): "The specific duty under existing law is more than compensatory. It furnishes a large measure of protection, and in fact is the substance of the protection on medium and low-grade goods. . . . The proper thing to do now for the manufacturers is to confess to a little deception regarding the make-up of the specific duty, admit the truth, and ask for recognition of the actual facts. The protection was needed, and the only sin committed was in the way it was obtained."

equivocally concluded that " the specific duty is more than compensatory for manufacturers using wools of lighter shrinkage "; and in the more detailed portions of the Report the excesses were made clear beyond a shadow of doubt.[1]

The further course of events need not here be recounted in detail. The free admission of wool in the tariff act of 1913 necessarily brought with it the complete abolition of the system. All the specific duties on woolen manufactures were swept away; there was no longer occasion or excuse for compensation. Not only this; the *ad valorem* or protective duty was much reduced. From a range of 50 and 55 per cent it went down to 35 per cent. This simple duty of 35 per cent replaced the previous elaborate compound duties, bringing not only a marked reduction in the nominal protection, but a much greater reduction in the really effective protection. A new chapter was opened in the history of protection and probably in the history of the woolen industry itself.

The outstanding fact in all this tortuous development is that for a long period the duties on most woolens were not only high, but high to the point of prohibition. So far as the range of duties goes, the case is similar to that of cottons; in both instances prohibition on most classes of goods. There is similarity, too, in that the extreme height of the duties was in neither case really designed by the legislators. Those on cottons became undesignedly high because left so long at the figures fixed when the civil war caused the great rise in the price of raw cotton; those on woolens became high because of the unforeseen working of the compensating system. Were the consequences or concomitants of extreme protection similar for the two industries? The answer to this question calls for an examination of the history and characteristics of the woolen manufacture.

[1] See the Summary, p. 13; and such a concise statement as this (p. 125): " If all wools lost 75 per cent from greasy wool to cloth, this four-to-one ratio would be perfect as a basis for compensation, but only in making the best fabrics from heavy-shrinking wools is so much compensation necessary. Cotton-mixed woolens, cotton warp worsteds, in fact the majority of woolen and worsted fabrics made in the United States do not require compensation equal to four times the duty on class I wool."

The growth of the two main branches of the industry — woolens and worsteds — is shown by the appended tabular statement.[1] As regards the relation between domestic production and volume of imports, the figures tell a tale essentially the same as for cottons and silks. The value of the domestic product enormously increased during the half-century; that of the imports at no time showed a substantial increase and in the later years an unmistakable decline. The imports have been a steadily diminishing quota in the total supply, and in recent times an almost negligible fraction. Only certain selected grades have continued to be procured from foreign countries — a few specialties and certain sorts of fine fabrics. Even for these, it may be remarked, the domestic manufacturers have been supplanting their foreign rivals more and more. Concerning the imports which still come in and their significance, more will be said later. It suffices for the present to point out that, if the test of success in a protectionist policy be the mere substitution of domestic products for foreign, almost complete success in this case also has been achieved.

Looking at the figures for domestic production more closely, it will be seen that a marked change took place in the relation

[1] VALUE OF DOMESTIC PRODUCT

(*Millions of Dollars*)

	Woolens	Worsteds	Total Woolens and Worsteds	Total, all Manufactures of Wool	Imports of Manufactures of Wool
1860	$61.9	$3.7	$65.6	$73.4	$43.1
1870	155.4	22.1	177.5	199.3	34.5
1880	160.6	33.5	194.1	238.1	33.9
1890	133.6	79.2	212.8	270.5	56.6
1900	118.4	120.3	238.7	297.0	16.2
1905	142.2	165.7	307.9	381.0	17.9
1910	107.1	312.6	419.7	507.2	23.0

The figures of domestic product in the fourth column are for *all* the manufactures of wool, including carpets, blankets and flannels, and some minor branches, as well as the two leading ones. With these figures (in column four) the imports should be compared, since the figures are for all the imports, not those of worsted and woolens alone. Both in the domestic product and in the imports the woolens and worsteds dominate. — The figures are derived from the *Census Bulletin* of 1910 on the Woolen Manufacture; see also the *Report of the Tariff Board*, pp. 220, 226.

between the two branches. Woolens lost ground, absolutely and still more relatively. Worsteds, comparatively insignificant in 1860, increased with extraordinary rapidity, and came to be by far the most important part of the manufacture as a whole. In the older branch an extraordinary and abnormal growth took place between 1860 and 1870, in consequence of the exceptional demand during the civil war period; and the unusual figure of product which was reached in 1870 was still maintained in 1880. But since the latter year, the output of woolens has declined, while that of worsteds has mounted without interruption.

No doubt the stated figures of value of product somewhat exaggerate the extent of the growth in the worsted branch. As in other cases, allowance must be made for the increase of specialization. A tendency in this direction appeared more especially in the worsted branch. It has become more common than in former times for a worsted mill to buy material in partly-manufactured state, — as tops or as yarn. Then the yarn (say) appears in the census reports as product for the spinning mill, and presently appears again in the value of the cloth turned out by the weaving mill. A curious and unexpected stimulus to specialization was given by the tariff act of 1883, which admitted some yarns (by a miscalculation on the part of those who adjusted the details in the duties) at low rates and tempted domestic mills to buy imported yarns; the practice, once begun, was continued to a large extent even after later tariff acts raised the yarn duties and caused the weaving establishments to turn to domestic spinners. These questions of organization, important and interesting as they are, lie in the main outside the scope of the present inquiry. The extent to which they must be borne in mind when referring to the census figures of "value of product" is indicated by other supplementary figures, such as those for numbers of persons employed, machines, and the like. A glance at such corrective data, given in the note, shows that they lead to no great modification of the general conclusions. It still appears not only that the domestic industry in general has grown greatly, but that the woolen branch has sensibly declined.

For this great shift two explanations have been offered. That which is doubtless most in accord with the facts ascribes it to general industrial causes, — changes both in the demand for goods and in the methods of production.[1] The other ascribes it, at least in large part, to the tariff system, and more particularly to the way in which the duties on wool and woolens were adjusted. Attention may first be given to the latter explanation, since it is closely connected with what has just been said of the compensating system.

The mode in which the duty was levied evidently led the American manufacturers to refrain from buying foreign wools whose shrinkage was high and whose scoured content was low. It proved to be prohibitory on wools whose shrinkage was very high; these could not be profitably imported at all. Now, as has been pointed out, the short fibre wools of the merino type shrink most, and are the wools used by the makers of carded goods, or woolens. These manufacturers were virtually prohibited from using some grades of foreign wool suitable for their branch of the industry.

Not only this: but the compensating system in their case did no more than compensate on the all-wool fabrics, nay, on some grades did not suffice for compensation; whereas on worsteds it quite overshot the mark and gave an additional concealed protection. The cross-bred wools, still more the combing wools, used in the making of worsteds, yielded a larger proportion of scoured wool than was assumed by the four-to-one ratio, and the compensating duties based on this ratio were quite excessive. The real protection to the manufacturers of worsteds was

[1] The best unit of productive capacity is, for woolens, the set of cards; for worsteds, the combing machine. Between 1900 and 1910 the numbers of these were reported as follows: —

	Sets of Cards in Woolen Mfg.	Combing Machines in Worsted Mfg.
1900	6,498	1,317
1905	5,753	1,440
1910	5,079	1,978

The data confirm the conclusion that the woolen branch was virtually stationary till about 1900, and thereafter declined; while the worsted branch grew rapidly and continuously.

much greater than to the manufacturers of the carded woolen goods.[1]

All this is true; but it does not go far toward explaining the differences in the development of the two branches. Beyond question the duty on wool, difficult enough to defend in any case, was made the more indefensible because of the way in which it was levied. Beyond question, too, the compensating system favored the manufacturers of worsteds more than those of woolens. But the long-continued trend toward worsteds cannot be ascribed to these causes alone or to these chiefly. True, it is probable that during the first decade or two after 1867 the excessive duties on worsteds contributed to rapid growth in this branch. It is always during the period just after the establishment of protection that it most serves to give high profits to the domestic producers and most stimulates the growth of the domestic industry. As time goes on, however, competition sets in and unusual profits disappear (barring of course the case of monopoly, which is not found in this instance). The notion that a particularly high duty continues to bring particularly high profits to the protected producers really rests on the other notion that the tariff necessarily causes a rise in domestic price by the full amount of the duty imposed. But where the rate is amply high enough to keep out the foreign rivals, it matters little whether it be 50 or 150 per cent. The domestic price is then determined, under competitive conditions, solely by the domestic conditions of supply and cost. As regards woolens and worsteds, though the duties on the latter were particularly high, the duties on woolens were quite high enough. On them also there was not a little concealed protection in the compensating system; on

[1] The National Association of Wool Manufacturers, the compact and influential organization which represented the industry before Congress and the public, was dominated for many years by the worsted makers. This was natural, not only because of the size and rapid growth of their branch, but because the individual enterprises in it were on a larger scale, and were conducted by the more ambitious and dominating personalities. During the period of general tariff revolt which followed the act of 1909, the manufacturers of carded woolens formed an independent organization of their own, protesting against the favored treatment given to their rivals by the wool duty and the compensating system. See the Statement of the Carded Wool Manufacturers.

them also the rates in general were prohibitory. Exception must doubtless be made for certain classes of woolen goods, particularly for all-wool fabrics made from fine merino wool of heavy shrinkage. On these the compensating duty achieved no more than its avowed purpose, sometimes failed to achieve it fully. Neither was the net protection here pushed to the point of prohibition; some imports continued. But the great bulk of the domestic manufacture of carded woolens was devoted throughout not to these finer goods but to cheaper grades, on which the duties were as prohibitory as they were on most grades of the rival worsteds. If under the circumstances the older branch of the manufacture was surpassed by its younger rival, the explanation must be sought elsewhere than in the peculiarities of the tariff system.

This conclusion is confirmed by the fact that the same general trend appeared in other countries. In free trade England, in protectionist Germany and France, the worsted branch also gained on its rival. Promoted and hastened though the change may have been in the United States by our tariff, it rested on causes of wider operation.

Among these causes, the vagaries of fashion played a large part, and indeed are often declared to have played the leading part. Next to the silk manufacture, that of woolens is most affected, among textiles, by this psychological element. In the last quarter of the nineteenth century fashion turned largely from the close-matted comparatively heavy woolens to the less compacted, lighter, smoother worsteds; and the direction of production necessarily followed the course of demand.[1]

More important, however, and fundamental after all, were changes in the technique of production. These favored the worsted branch both by giving it wider scope and by enabling it to attain in greater degree the advantages of the machine processes, — homogeneity of material and product, standardization, large-scale operation. The changes center about the invention and improvement of the combing machine, from which

[1] See the *Tariff Board Report*, p. 85; cf. Clapham, *The Woolen and Worsted Industries*, pp. 9, 142.

have flown industrial consequences so great as to entitle this to be reckoned among the revolutionary changes in the textile arts. Moreover, they have an important bearing on our tariff problems, and therefore deserve to be considered more fully than would otherwise be pertinent to the present inquiry.

Reverting for a moment to the difference between woolens and worsteds, let it be recalled that in general woolens are made with short staple wool, worsteds with long staple wool. Woolens are carded goods; that is, the fibres of the wool are pulled apart and interlaced by the card, — strips of leather armed with protruding short teeth. The old hand card was succeeded at a comparatively early period in textile development by the machine card, in which the teeth are set on cylinders that revolve at different speeds. In carding, whether of wool or cotton or silk, the aim is to secure a sheet of smoothed, interlacing fibres, ready for the subsequent operation of spinning. The comb also prepares the fibre for spinning, but in a different way and with a somewhat different object. It selects the longer fibres, pulls these out, and arranges them parallel to each other, rejecting the short fibres. The selected long fibres, laid together in a soft, loose, rope-like strand, are called tops; the rejected short fibres are called noils. These noils, it may be noted, are used in the other, rival branch; they are short fibres, such as the carded industry primarily uses; they are a natural substitute, or complementary material, by no means an adulterant, serviceable in making the woolen goods proper.

The machine processes were applied to combing, at a date comparatively recent. The comb remained a hand tool longer than the card. Indeed, the hand card, being simple, and managed with comparative ease, never became the tool of a separate trade. The comb required specialized skill; the wool combers formed a craft, and were important figures in the early history of the worsted manufacture. Like the hand loom weavers, they did not give way to the machine until the middle of the nineteenth century. The fact that machinery triumphed so much later than in carding is in itself an indication of greater complexity in the operation, and so an explanation of the unusual intricacy of the modern combing machine. That machine, or the " comb," as it is now commonly called, was developed by a series of inventors about 1850 and thereafter, exhibiting in its course the characteristic features that appear in the history of most modern inventions. There was a preparatory period of tentative groping, and then an almost simultaneous perfecting of the main processes by several hands; while business shrewdness and enterprise were necessary to bring to full fruition the work of mechanical genius. The main seat of the industry and of the changes in it was Bradford in Yorkshire. As England was the habitat of the long-wool combing breed of sheep, so it was in England that the worsted manufacture began and continued. Bradford was and is still the most important worsted center in the world.[1]

The combing machine greatly changed the worsted industry in two respects. In the first place, it served to standardize the conditions of manufacture and so to stimulate a tendency to large-scale operation. The tops turned out by the comb are a homogeneous material; so much so that they have been systematically dealt with on exchanges, and are often the occasion of contracts for future delivery. They are commonly made in Europe by separate top-makers, who sell to the spinners. Here, as with other processes, specialization in the textile industries is much more marked in Europe than in the United States. The very possession of a homogeneous material facilitates the use of highly-perfected and quasi-automatic machinery in the later manufacturing stages. In all countries the worsted branch of the industry is conducted on a larger scale than the woolen branch; it is more capitalistic, more in line with the general trend of modern industry. Thus in England, there were in 1899

[1] See the excellent account of the inventions in Burnley, *History of Wool and Wool-combing*. Cf. what is said by Clapham, *The Woolen and Worsted Industries*, p. 136. Among the conspicuous inventors were Donisthorpe, Lister, Holden, Heilmann, and Noble, — all English, with the exception of Heilmann (an Alsatian). The start was made by the versatile and indefatigable Cartwright as early as 1790; but it was not until half a century later that machines constructed on his principle were brought to working efficiency. At still later dates various minor improvements were added. Lister (Lord Masham) played in the main the rôle of the business man, appreciating and guiding the inventors, and profiting handsomely. The whole episode is typical of the course of mechanical progress in modern times.

about eighty persons employed in the average woolen mill, but as many as two hundred in the average worsted mill.[1] In the United States, the worsted mills turned out on the average (in 1909) a product more than four times as great per establishment as the woolen mills.[2] This contrast is the more striking because in both countries specialization has gone further in worsteds than in woolens. The typical worsted mill confines itself to a less number of manufacturing operations, and yet is larger in size than the woolen mill whose operations are split up into a greater number.[3] The worsted offers greater opportunities for the economies of large-scale production, and grows at the expense of the branch which offers less opportunities in this direction.

Quite a different consequence of the combing machine was an extension of the range of the industry, both as regards the quality of the wools which could be used and the quality of the fabrics which could be turned out. The hand comb had been available only for wool which is combing wool strictly, — the long staple wool of English sheep. The same was the case with the combing machine when first put into use. But gradual improvement made the machine applicable to wools having fibres not so long. Cross-bred wools could be put through it, their shorter fibres eliminated as noils, their longer fibres laid together as tops. It is for this reason that the classification of wool so long maintained in our tariffs, — "clothing" wool in class I, "combing" wool in class II, — became quite out of accord with the industrial facts. Merino wool proper is still too short to be used in the worsted manufacture. But a large part, probably the larger

[1] Clapham, p. 131.

[2] The *Tariff Board Report* gives the following figures (p. 220): —

AVERAGE VALUE OF PRODUCT

	1899	1909
Worsteds	$647,000	$965,000
Woolens	114,000	182,000

The increase in the average output in woolen mills between 1899 and 1909 is ascribed to the disappearance of a large number of small country mills.

[3] Clapham, pp. 134 *seq.*: "The commonest type of woolen mill . . . combines all processes, from opening the new wool to dyeing, — when it is piece-dyed, — and finishing the cloth." So the Tariff Board reports (p. 220) that "in the woolen industry the typical mill combines all processes from raw wool to finished cloth."

part, of the wool which the tariff classed as clothing wool was in fact put through the combs. The worsted industry thus had at its disposal a very great and varied mass of raw material, and was able to turn out goods resembling closely those of the other branch. The typical worsteds of former days were smooth and lustrous, somewhat harsh in quality. With the improvement in the combing machine softer and suppler goods could be made, having some of the excellences of both kinds. The two in fact came to overlap, and the worsted industry was able to turn out fabrics of much greater variety than in former times.

All these factors were in operation in the United States, and some of them to an exceptional degree. The worsted industry was equipped with machinery at once perfected and expensive, and its material was standardized; so it secured the technological basis for large-scale operations. A wide range of raw material was brought to its disposal. The changes in fashion were toward its products. In the United States an additional factor probably was that the lighter and looser worsteds were better adapted to climate and habit, — a warm summer and in winter houses amply heated. No doubt during the earlier stages the extreme protection which was extended to worsteds under the compensating system gave a special impetus, and caused some manufacturers to reap unusually large profits. But the continued growth and eventual predominance of this branch indicate that, even though stimulated by the tariff and perhaps steadily dependent on the tariff for existence, the protective system alone could not account for its position relatively to the other branch.

CHAPTER XXI

THE WOOLEN MANUFACTURE (*continued*). CHARACTERISTICS OF THE AMERICAN INDUSTRY

HAVING surveyed the growth of the two great branches of the American wool manufacture, we are prepared to consider the more difficult problems concerning the effects of protection: the technical development of the industry in this country and in Europe, the effectiveness of the labor and capital engaged, the prospect of attaining independence of tariff support. Was the growth similar to that in other textile industries? As regards cottons, we have seen that extremely high duties can be fairly said to have been almost without effect either for good or evil: they did not check industrial progress, nor did they serve to promote it. The history of the silk manufacture suggests, even if it does not quite prove, that a newly-established industry may not only grow in size under the influence of protection, but advance in effectiveness. What does the evidence indicate in the case of woolens?

The preceding account of the history and characteristics of the worsted and woolen branches would lead one to surmise that the first named, young though it is, would have proved more likely to give scope to the special industrial excellences of our inventors and business leaders, and more promising as regards eventual independence. The woolen branch, on the other hand, seems to have characteristics that indicate less adaptability to American conditions, a field less favorable for American enterprise. Yet it is not clear that distinctions or conclusions of this sort can be maintained. The course of development in both branches has been different from that in the other textile industries; the situation in many respects is puzzling.

First, as regards worsteds. Here, to repeat, the opportunities for American industrial talent seem promising. Yet it appears that in precisely the direction where one looks for advance by

Americans, — the invention of new machinery or improvement of old, — the worsted manufacture showed least indication of progress or of independence. On the contrary, it seems to have remained under European tutelage, content to import and to use European machinery. This at all events was the case in those departments of the industry which are most distinctive, — combing and the operations closely connected with combing. The facts brought out by the Tariff Board in 1912 were surprising. It appeared that in the worsted mills hardly any machinery, in all the processes up to and including spinning, was of domestic make. Almost all the combing machines were imported, almost all the drawing frames (these begin the manipulation of the tops as delivered from the combs, reducing the tops to a thin sliver ready for spinning), almost all the frame spinning machinery, and absolutely all of the mule spindles. Such small fraction of the combing and spinning machinery as was of American make was a direct copy of that imported. Leadership in the industry was clearly on the other side of the water.[1]

Nor did it appear that there was anything in the organization of the working force or in the efficiency of the individual operatives which gave any advantage to Americans. The evidence on this topic, taken at its face, pointed to but one conclusion. It is true that here, as elsewhere, the turn taken by the protective controversy caused the manufacturers to lay stress on their own disabilities or failings. The notion current among protectionists

[1] The Tariff Board stated in its Summary (p. 16) that "87 per cent of all the machinery [in worsted mills], from the scouring of the raw wool through to the finished yarn, was imported." More in detail (pp. 1026 *seq.*), it appeared that

of the Noble combs (English system)	85%	were imported
" French combs (Continental systems)	100%	" "
" Bradford drawing frames	90%	" "
" French drawing frames	100%	" "
" mule spindles	100%	" "
" frame spindles	92%	" "

In spinning worsted yarn, both mule spindles and "cap" spindles are used; in spinning woolen yarn, mules alone. "Cap" spindles are in principle similar to ring spindles, and like them are often spoken of as "frame spindles." Ring spinning proper has never been found applicable to worsteds, still less to woolens. Cap spindles are largely used in England, and indeed predominate in the English worsted manufacture; whereas the mule alone is used in the French worsted industry. Cf. Barker, *Textiles* (London, 1910), pp. 101, 111.

for many years, that duties should be so levied as to cover higher cost of production in the United States, led their spokesmen to dilate on disadvantages and on the absence of any factors making for advantage or special effectiveness. The mill operatives, it was said, were chiefly of foreign birth, and not of the best foreign birth, — raw agricultural laborers from southern and eastern Europe, suddenly transplanted to factory towns; not equal in steadiness, skill, even tractableness, to the English, German, and French who remained in the competing mills of these several countries.[1] The American mills were said to have the same equipment; the operatives performed the same tasks and performed them no better, nay, not so well; how could the industry possibly maintain itself, paying American rates of wages, without protection? On the principles of protection, the argument was unanswerable; its applicability in this case apparently was beyond cavil. It raised unequivocally the fundamental questions that underlie the whole controversy. Is it worth while to support industries that have no superiority over their foreign competitors, and show no prospect of attaining any? If *all* American industries were in the same state as the worsted manufacture (in the departments here under consideration), — if all machinery were quite the same as in Europe, all workmen no more efficient, all management no better, — could the product of American industry be larger, and *could* wages in general be higher? Was not the industry one in which the effectiveness of industry failed to measure up to the general American standard of effectiveness, which alone makes possible a high general rate of wages?

In some other departments of the manufacture the situation was not so unpromising. As in the textile industries at large, weaving stood in a position apart. Here the conditions as regards domestic and imported machinery were quite reversed. Only one-fifth of the looms were imported; the great majority were of American make.[2] Not only this, but the striking American improvements in weaving had been found applicable, not indeed throughout, but at least in some directions. The auto-

[1] Cf. what is said below, p. 363, note.

[2] *Tariff Board Report*, p. 1042.

matic loom was used in weaving certain kinds of worsteds, and cut down cost, *i. e.*, increased effectiveness, in this part of the manufacturing processes. From the nature of the case it could be used to advantage only where thousands of yards of a single kind of fabric were turned out; such as " blue serges " and the like for women's wear, having a cotton warp, comparatively cheap and sufficiently serviceable, — goods which could be steadily marketed in great quantities.[1] Worsteds and woolens are in general not of uniform pattern or quality, and are much subject to the vagaries of fashion; hence mass production of this sort is not susceptible of the same extension as in the case of cottons. Indeed, as will appear presently, there are peculiarities in woolen weaving which seem to militate against any wide-spread adoption of the methods which have so profoundly affected the cotton manufacture. The apparently exceptional cases in which the automatic loom was used in weaving worsteds served rather to emphasize the contrast between them and the more typical American conditions. It is not to be supposed that this industry was quite outside the main current, and quite uninfluenced by the pervasive tendency in the United States to extend the use of labor-saving devices.[2] Yet the available evidence indicates that,

[1] " In American worsted and woolen mills the weavers, male and female, operate one or two looms as a rule, excepting where worsted dress goods are made with cotton warps. Cotton warp being stronger than woolen or worsted makes it possible to use automatic or weft-replenishing looms, so that one weaver can operate as many as twelve looms in the manufacture of worsted dress goods." *Tariff Board Report*, p. 1045. This has been confirmed to me by conversations with the head of a large company which has put in the automatic looms. I have been told, again by a large manufacturer, that the automatic loom has been used with success for all-wool worsteds also.

[2] Thus the Arlington mills, one of the largest and most conspicuous of the American worsted establishments, has erected a huge and highly efficient plant for saving the grease formerly lost in the process of scouring wool and securing thereby a valuable by-product. The same thing is done in Germany, where wool scouring with utilization of grease is a separate specialized industry. In accord with the American tradition this is done in the Arlington mills as part of great integrated operations, on a larger scale than in Germany, and probably with higher efficiency. It is said also that the labor force necessary for spinning and for tending combs has been cut down in this establishment; but whether in greater degree than in foreign countries does not appear. See a small advertising pamphlet, entitled " Tops," published by the Arlington mills (1898), pp. 56, 96. The Tariff Board con-

as regards machinery, the advances over competing foreigners were less, and surprisingly less, than in other textile industries.

It is possible that forward strides were taken in other directions, — in the more general economies from large-scale operation. In the worsted manufacture, as elsewhere, a contest has been going on between different systems of organization and management, — between the large mill and the very large mill, between integration and specialization, between the single establishment and a combination embracing many establishments. In these respects the American industry shows contrasts both with its European rivals and with other textile industries in the United States.

In the mere fact of a comparatively large scale of production it is not peculiar; worsted mills in Europe also are larger than woolen mills, and as large as cotton and silk mills. But some of the American mills are of such extraordinary size that they may be called giants; they endeavor to secure the advantages of large-scale operations on a scale not elsewhere dreamed of. The much-discussed Wood Mill, erected by the American Woolen Company at Lawrence, Mass., is said to be the largest textile establishment under a single roof in the world. Others, such as the Arlington mills in the same city, are of similar size; there is a well-known list of other great mills. Side by side with them are a number of establishments of more moderate size, comparable with the typical European establishment. It is not certain which type is gaining in the United States; but the huge concern seems at the least to hold its own. Its methods are in accord with those of American industrial triumphs. The worsted industry, or at least some branches of it, may be thought to be on the way to securing a comparative advantage.

Possibilities of the same sort may be considered as regards the effects of integration and combination. The American tendency on the whole is toward integration. Certain it is that specialization is carried less far than in Europe, in the worsted industry

cluded that the cost (in money) of converting wool into tops was nearly twice as great in the United States as in England; in other words, found no indication of special effectiveness in the United States. *Report*, pp. 639 *seq.*

itself as well as in textile industries at large. In some respects there are signs of some reaction toward specialization in the United States; the trend toward integration is by no means without exceptions; but there is nothing like the division of labor between distinct branches, — scouring, combing, dyeing, spinning, weaving, finishing, — which is the established European organization.[1] It remains to be seen in this matter also whether management and organization after the American plan will hold their own, or whether specialization will extend; and further, whether the great integrated establishment will prove to have advantages not only over its specializing competitors at home, but over its competitors of the same character abroad.

So it is with regard to combination. In this industry, as in others, the United States is the scene of a bold experiment in great-scale management. The American Woolen Company is a combination of a number of mills of different character, united under single control, and endeavoring to secure various potential advantages. Among these are economy in the purchase and allotment of materials, standardization of equipment, and specialization among the several establishments, — not specialization of the kind referred to in the preceding paragraph, but in the sense that each mill is confined to one class of goods, operates continuously on its specialty, and makes no endeavor to turn out a " line " of varied products such as the independent manufacturer commonly thinks it necessary to offer. All sorts of mills are combined in this great agglomeration; not only worsted mills, but woolen mills in the narrower sense (carded wool mills); scattered moreover in many far-separated places. The experiment is of no little interest to the economist, quite apart from any bearing it may have on the tariff question. Does this method of organization really conduce to effectiveness in production? It seems to raise no question of monopoly. However important and even dominant is the position of the American Woolen Company, it has not even a quasi-monopolistic control of the industry or of any branch of it. It has to meet competition on every side; the

[1] See Clapham, *The Woolen and Worsted Industries;* and Michaelis, " Die Woll Industrie," in *Handbuch der Wirthschaftskunde Deutschlands,* vol. iii.

contest is a direct uncomplicated one between the single concern and the great combination of similar concerns. The traditional reasoning does not point to any certain or even probable advantage for the latter in this particular case. It is true that large-scale production is growing in the worsted industry; but its advantages are not proved to progress indefinitely with enlarging scale. Integration, though carried on to an unusual extent in American establishments, has to compete with specialization in this country, and even more with the specializing industry of Europe. The goods produced are of great variety, and subject to the whims of fashion; hence standardization of equipment and sweeping application of machine methods cannot be carried as far as, for example, in the manufacture of the ordinary grades of cotton goods. It is to be observed, moreover, that in the two other leading textile industries there has been found no promising field for a great combination: neither for cottons, where mass production has been carried so far, nor for silks, where there are conditions resembling those of woolens as regards variety of goods and irregularity of fashion.[1] It would seem that only certain parts of the woolen manufacture give any prospect of gains from horizontal combination; more particularly those parts of the worsted branch which produce on a large scale great quantities of homogeneous fabrics. But on this subject it is well to refrain from prophecy, perhaps even from speculation. The whole question of the technical and managerial possibilities of combined enterprises awaits solution, and not least so in this industry.

Turn now to the other branch of the woolen industry, that of carded woolen goods. Here the conditions are in many ways different; in some ways they seem more promising for the American producers, in others less so.

This is the older part of the industry, and therefore, it might be supposed, the one less likely to be dependent on the tariff.

[1] There may be an exception in the cotton manufacture as regards the production of yarn, in which the New England Cotton Yarn Company is carrying on an experiment at once in combination and in specialization; and perhaps another exception is the Cotton Duck Consolidation. See Dewing, *Corporate Promotions and Reorganizations*, chs. xii, xiii. On silks, compare what was said above, chapter xv, pp. 246, 254.

The manufacture of worsteds, like that of silks, grew up after the civil war, and was the direct product of high protection. The woolen branch is the oldest of all in the textile group; it goes back to the "domestic" system of colonial days. True, it is younger, as a machine using industry, than the cotton manufacture, since the epoch-making inventions of the eighteenth century were first applied to the latter. But carding, spinning, and weaving machinery was adapted to wool at an early date in the nineteenth century, both in England and the United States. The American tariff controversy of the first half of the nineteenth century was concerned as much with the duties on wool and woolens as with any other single set of duties. The manufacturers were encouraged by high rates during earlier years, and then compelled, after 1846, to adjust themselves to rates decidedly low. Under the tariffs of 1846 and of 1857 the effective duty was less than 25 per cent.[1] Yet the industry did not succumb. Though the imports formed in 1860 a much larger proportion of the total supply than they did in later years, the domestic product even then exceeded the imports, and the manufacturers looked to the future with courage under duties so low that they would be adjudged rank free trade by the modern protectionists.

If this was the situation in the middle of the nineteenth century, it would seem inferable that the degree of dependence on protection would have become less rather than greater after the lapse of another half-century. All manufacturing industries grew and strengthened after the civil war. The textile industries that were well established at the earlier date, as well as other industries then in a firm position, continued to hold their own. The high rates of the later period would seem unnecessary; and

[1] The duty on woolens under the tariff of 1846 was 30 per cent. But wool also was dutiable at 30 per cent, which lessened the net protection for woolens. Just how much net protection remained would be difficult of calculation. In 1857 the rate on woolens was reduced to 24 per cent; but wool having a foreign value of twenty cents or less was admitted free.

The history of the woolen manufacture before the war is little known; it offers a promising field for investigation. Some indications of its position in 1846–60 I have gathered in my *Tariff History*, pp. 144, 159 note. On imports and domestic production in 1860, see the figures given above, p. 333.

the carded woolen manufacture, mature and settled as early as 1860, might be expected to show in 1910 greater independence of tariff support than the newer worsted manufacture which owed its origin to extreme and comparatively recent protection.

Confirmation of this impression would seem to be afforded by a comparison between the two branches as regards one point on which stress has been laid, — namely, the relative use of imported and domestic machinery. The carded woolen branch was found by the Tariff Board to be in a different position from its younger rival, in that it relied but little on imported machinery. Carding is the step in the woolen industry which corresponds to combing in the worsted. The Board's inquiries showed a sharp contrast between the sources of supply for combs and cards. Whereas almost all the combs were imported, the carding machines were preponderantly (92 per cent) of American make. It is noteworthy also that the somewhat modified carding machines used in worsted mills (they prepare wool of comparatively short fibre, such as cross-bred wool, for the combing operation) were also largely of foreign make; here again the worsted branch relied much more on imported equipment. In spinning there was the same contrast. Much the greatest part (85 per cent) of the mule spindles in the woolen mills were made in the United States. But in the worsted mills absolutely every mule spindle was imported. It may be noted also that of the "cap" spindles used in the worsted branch, and there used only (being inapplicable to carded wool), the proportion of American machinery was insignificant, — only 8 per cent, as compared with 92 per cent imported. Here again the worsted branch relied almost exclusively on foreign apparatus.[1]

[1] The figures are as follows (*Tariff Board Report*, p. 1042): —

	Per cent Manufactured in	
	United States	Foreign Countries
Carding machines, woolen	92.2%	7.8%
" " worsted	50.3%	49.7%
Mule spindles, carded wool	85.7%	14.3%
" " combed wool	.0%	100.0%
Spinning frames (cap spindles)	8.4%	91.6%

On combing machines, cf. the figures already given, p. 343, note. On cap spindles, cf. the footnote to p. 343, above.

The significance of this contrast, however, is affected by some other facts brought out in the same investigation. It appeared that the machinery in the worsted mills was the more modern, *i. e.*, had been in use for a shorter period than that in the woolen mills. The cards in the latter were, it is true, of American make; but they were old. Nearly one-half of them (47 per cent) had been in use twenty-five years or more. The cards used by the worsted makers were distinctly more modern, — of foreign manufacture, it is true, but comparatively new. Only 7½ per cent were twenty-five years old or more, as compared with the 47 per cent just stated for the woolen mills. A similar difference, though not so marked, appeared as regards the age of the mule spindles. This part of the equipment of the woolen mills, while chiefly American, was older than the same equipment, all of it imported, in the worsted mills.[1] The combs in the latter, it will be remembered, were almost all of foreign make; but these also were comparatively new. The preponderant use of American machines by the woolen mills might thus be a sign not of progress, but of lack of it. It would be so if the domestic machines were inferior to the foreign, or at least not superior. And similarly the preponderant use of foreign machines by the worsted makers might indicate that they were using the best that was obtainable. This throws the question of the comparative effectiveness of foreign and domestic industry one stage farther back, — to the machine makers who supply the manufacturers. So far as concerns the final outcome, the problem remains the same. Whether an American industry can hold its own against foreign competition depends, to repeat, on the combined effectiveness of *all* the factors, — climate, power resources, and raw material; quality of

[1] The figures for the various machines here mentioned were as follows (*Tariff Board Report*, p. 1042): —

	Manufactured in United States		Manufactured in Foreign Countries		Years in Operation — Per cents			
	Number	Per cent	Number	Per cent	Less than 5 Years	5 @ 15 Years	15 @ 25 Years	Over 25 Years
Carding machines, woolen	399	92.2	34	7.8	9.6	31.0	12 4	47.0
" " worsted	331	50.3	327	49.7	26.3	33.2	32.9	7.6
Mules, carded wool	504	85.7	84	14.3	8.0	59.0	20.2	12.8
Mules, worsted	....	....	370	100.0	24.9	35.9	36.2	3.0
Spinning frames (for cap spindles)	113	8.4	1,233	91.6	20.3	49.6	12.9	17.2

workmen; ability in organization and management; and, finally, the technological equipment. But in comparing the woolen and worsted branches within their own circle of operations, the mere use of domestic machinery by the one, of foreign by the other, does not necessarily measure their relative progress or effectiveness. Apparently the worsted branch, using imported equipment, simply turned to the best that was to be had;[1] while it is conceivable that the domestic equipment used by the woolen branch failed to keep pace with the general American progress in labor-saving devices, perhaps even failed to keep pace with progress in foreign countries.

It must be borne in mind that during the period here under review the woolen branch was virtually at a standstill, while the growth in worsteds was rapid and continuous. The retention of old equipment in the former may seem a natural result of adverse conditions due to shifts in fashion and other extraneous causes. Yet adverse conditions do not necessarily have a deadening effect on industry. It is often said that severe competition and trade crises tend to have the opposite effect, — to compel economies and put every producer to his trumps. In this case, as in the converse case of favoring conditions, there seems to be no *a priori* ground for saying that either progress or stagnation will be promoted. High protection, for example, is said by the free trader to conduce to laxness, by the protectionists to stimulate domestic improvements. Under either set of conditions, — depressing or encouraging, — the only helpful method of inquiry seems to be the examination of the available historical and statistical material, and also of the indications of adaptation, or lack of adaptation, to the country's general industrial environment.

It happens that in this instance there has been some direct testimony to stagnation. It cannot be said that American experi-

[1] "The explanation of the great use of foreign machinery in the mills (in some departments its exclusive use) given by the establishments visited was that while the importation of these machines increased their cost more than 60 per cent above that of their foreign competitors in the woolen and worsted industry, it was necessary to buy abroad, since with the exception of looms and some few other machines American manufacturers had not been able to furnish machines approaching in result the work done by the foreign machines." *Tariff Board Report*, p. 1043.

ence in general verifies the free trader's prediction concerning this sort of consequence from high duties. On the contrary, the history of many industries (such as iron, silks, and cottons) indicates that protection and progress are not incompatible.[1] But there are indications that in the carded woolen branch backward establishments were enabled to hold their own under tariff shelter. The long-continued use of old machinery would seem to point that way. More significant is the fact that the protectionist spokesmen themselves have sounded notes of warning. During the civil war the abrupt increase of demand for woolen cloths inevitably caused all sorts of mills to make profits even with poor equipment and slack management. Notwithstanding a process of weeding out which set in after the war (the wool and woolens act of 1867, with its elaborate compensating system, was in reality an endeavor to stave off the inevitable readjustment) this abnormal stimulus seems to have left its impress on the carded woolen industry throughout the ensuing half-century. During the brief period of free wool and lowered woolen duties under the Wilson tariff act (1894–97) some plain speaking came from the protectionist ranks. It was said that the carded wool branch had been backward, and consequently had been hit by the lowered duties more than the worsted branch. A general overhauling was not to be avoided.[2] This period of low duties

[1] Compare what has been said on this topic in chapter ii, pp. 28, 29.

[2] Mr. S. N. D. North, then Secretary of the National Association of Wool Manufacturers, wrote in 1894: —

"Many manufacturers will find themselves compelled to change altogether the character of their products. . . . At present it seems as though the hardest struggle was before the mills which have been engaged in making the medium cassimeres and similar goods for the masses. These mills have had the American manufacture to themselves and they have been able to determine in large measure the character of the goods made to supply it. That great advantage will no longer be theirs. It follows that radical adjustments will be necessary; much machinery which sufficed for the old conditions of manufacturing will be found to be useless. Many mills will have to be reëquipped throughout; there are many in which it will be found cheaper to abandon them altogether than to incur the expense of a complete overhauling. . . . It has been charged against our manufacturers that they are behind those of other countries in their knowledge and application of modern economies. The charge has been that the high protective tariff has saved them from the necessity of learning those lessons to which the attention of foreigners has

and of stress proved short, — shorter than the protectionists themselves expected; or else such confessions would hardly have been forthcoming. In 1897, the tariff barrier was put up again, high and strong as before; and behind it the industry was enabled to go its way for another long period (from 1897 to 1913) without paying attention to any possibilities of foreign competition.

What now is the explanation of the situation which has come to view in this account of the American woolen manufacture? In general, the tale is one of backwardness; how explain it?

One explanation often given is that all is chargeable to the duties on raw wool. This is the outstanding factor not present in the other textile industries. For silks and cottons the raw materials never were subject to duty. The woolen industry alone labored under the handicap of taxes on its material. The free traders, and especially those who preached the gospel of free materials, laid stress on this circumstance. The wool duty, it was said, handicapped the manufacturers, narrowed the range of the industry, stood in the way of diversification. This explanation was particularly acceptable to the free traders because as a rule they were reluctant to go the full length of their own creed and to admit that the manufacture itself might be in danger if their policy were adopted. No: it was thought that, given free wool, the manufacturing industry would hold its own, and even expand and progress.

But I cannot believe that this tells the whole story. No doubt the wool duty did operate as a handicap on the manufacturing industry. The qualities of wool are extraordinarily diverse; the particular way in which the duty was so long levied served to prohibit many grades, and to hamper the use of others. Probably there was some effect in keeping the manufacture in routine grooves, even in a rut. But the wool duty was so completely offset by the compensating system, and the characteristics of the manufacturing industry appear in so many matters that are little

largely been directed of late years. There is probably some truth in this statement, though not so much as those who make it believe." *Bulletin Wool Manufacturers*, xxiv, p. 258.

related to the duty, that this cannot be judged a decisive or even commanding factor. After all, though the compensating system proved to be ill adjusted, and unequal in its effect on different branches of the industry, the duties on woolens as a whole, — compensating and " protective " taken together, — left a generous margin for protection in almost all cases. Just as the wool duty does not serve to explain the greater growth of the worsted branch as compared with that of carded woolens, so it does not explain the general characteristics of both branches. It has sins enough of its own to answer for, without being held accountable for everything that seemed to go wrong. The question persists: how account for the seeming failure of the woolen manufacture to keep in line with the general march of American industrial effectiveness ?

To this question, as to so many in the field of economics, it is easier to give negative answers than positive; easier to say what was not *the* cause than to say precisely what was. The phenomena are perhaps most puzzling in that the historical sequence in the manufacture seems out of accord with its contemporary position and prospects. The woolen branch (carded woolen) is much the older; apparently it was firmly established at an early date; yet it has been beaten by its younger rival, the worsted branch, not only in size but apparently in adaptability to the general industrial conditions. Yet it is in the last-named circumstance, — adaptability to American conditions in general, — that the solution of the problem is most likely to be found.

The historical anomaly in the carded woolen branch, — its growth and assured position at an early date, contrasting with the more precarious modern stage, — is perhaps to be explained on the ground that in the course of time the industrial environment itself underwent a change. In the United States of the first half of the nineteenth century an industry of small or moderate scale was more likely to hold its own securely than in the United States of the twentieth century. Intelligence and handicraft skill on the part of the individual workmen, which play so marked a part in this branch, had not then found so many other fields for advantageous application. Add to this the circumstance that the industry had traditions and an established basis, inherited from the domestic spinning and weaving of colonial days, with their necessary adjuncts in the fulling and finishing mills, — and it is not so difficult to understand the contrast between the middle of the nineteenth century and the beginning of the twentieth.

The worsted industry, on the other hand, exhibits in all countries the more dominant characteristics of modern industry, — highly-developed and quasi-automatic machinery, standardized material, large plant, a dominance of organization, and (in comparison with the older branch) a lack of individuality. These characteristics appear most sharply in the manufacture of the staple grades of fabrics, turned out in large quantities and at prices low enough to make possible their sale to multitudes of purchasers. It is in accord with the general trend of American industry that our manufacturers should have turned chiefly to goods of this sort, while those calling for more detailed care, more variety, more individual finish continued to be imported even in face of the extremely high duties levied so long. It is in accord, too, with the general international division of labor that the more highly-finished goods should be produced in France more than in Germany, and in Germany more than in England. Thus it would seem that the manufacture of staple worsteds was the most promising part of the industry for the Americans, giving favorable opportunities for the methods and appliances which they have learned to apply better than others. And yet, to repeat, the evidence points little to progress. The record on the whole is one of imitation, not of independent advance, still less of leadership. While the carded woolen branch may be said to have been left behind by the American industrial current, the worsted branch simply kept up with the general European movement, and showed little sign of keeping pace with that in the United States.[1]

[1] This is the general conclusion reached by Mr. T. W. Page, one of the members of the Tariff Board, an able economist quite without bias. In an address reported in the *Wool Manufacturers' Bulletin* (June, 1913, p. 172) he summed up the situation thus: "Some of our industries are more prosperous than others; they afford higher profits and higher wages, and can hold their own in competition with the

In this regard also the technical conditions would seem to be less favorable to the industrial acclimatization of the carded woolen manufacture.

Still another factor works in the same direction. The finishing processes are of the first importance for carded woolen fabrics. They are of great variety, and they are almost decisive as regards the character and saleability of the goods. Typical of the various manipulations is the ancient one of "fulling," — the cloth being passed between rollers and through liquid soap, or soap and water. It is thus shrunk and felted. In essentials, the process remains a handicraft operation, even though no longer carried on, as it was in earlier days, in a separate fulling mill.[1] It is little aided by machinery, and is dependent on the skill and unrelaxing attention of the individual workman. The same is the case with the raising of a surface by teazles, the stretchings and dryings and beatings and ironings. To quote from Professor Clapham's excellent account of the industry in England, where finishing has been carried to greatest elaboration and perfection: "The variety of finishing processes is singularly great. New ones are constantly being devised, many of which are kept more or less secret." But worsteds are much less subject to them than woolens. "Light worsted dress materials are not milled at all. . . . Generally speaking, worsted materials are altered but slightly at this stage. As they appear in the loom, so they appear in the warehouse; colour of course excepted in the case of piece-dyed goods. . . . With woolens, the reverse is often true. Only an expert in these cases, could identify the finished cloth with the loose and altogether different substance that came out of the loom. In one case finishing is a subsidiary, in the other a primary process."[2] And this primary process, it is to be emphasized, is little under the influence of modern machinery and labor-saving devices; in other words it is one in which American industrial talent finds no tempting or remuneratory field.

[1] The small fulling mill of colonial times finished the home-spun and home-woven cloths of the country folk.

[2] Clapham, *The Woolen and Worsted Industries*, p. 74.

In accord with the same general trend, it appears that the finer grades of goods are more likely to be imported, while the cheaper and medium grades are more likely to be made at home; and this, notwithstanding efforts to promote the manufacture of the finer grades by making the duties on them particularly high.[1] The case is alike with all the textiles; the finer goods of all kinds are more apt to be imported. The same explanation is invariably given: they need to be more carefully finished, they call for more labor, and high wages are therefore felt to be an obstacle in particularly great degree. The more fundamental explanation has already been indicated: goods of the most expensive sort fail to be made within the United States because labor is applied to them with less machinery, less of labor-saving devices, less effective organization, — in sum, with less *advantage* than to the cheap and medium grades. So it is with woolens and worsteds. In both branches the protective policy was throughout more effective on the cheaper goods. It is characteristic also that not only the finer fabrics themselves, but the machinery for their manufacture had to be imported, — for carding, combing, and spinning, even for weaving, where the Americans in general are superior. A large German firm, engaged in making fine goods, was tempted by the high duties of 1897 to transfer a plant to the United States. It had to import machinery of every kind; and not only this, but found that the factory labor of this country was also ill adapted to its methods of manufacture. From the then-accepted protectionist point of view, all these disadvantages, and the consequent high expenses of production, should have been offset by correspondingly high duties; the industry was to be " acquired " on any terms necessary to domesticate it. But these special conditions would seem to be in reality but evidences of the unsuitability of this particular branch of textiles to American conditions.[2]

[1] See the sketch of the rates of duty given in chapter xx, p. 325. The *ad valorem* (protective) rate on the dearer goods was pushed up a notch in 1890, and still another in 1897, reaching 55 per cent in the latter year.

[2] The account given by the representative of this firm seems to me so instructive on various aspects of the textile situation that I quote from it with some freedom.
" Many European woolen enterprises have existed for generations, and even

It deserves to be noted that during the last decade of the extreme protective policy there were signs of improvement in the quality of American woolen fabrics, and especially of worsteds. That some change in this direction set in, I am convinced by repeated testimony from all sorts of persons conversant with the trade, — manufacturers, dealers, tailors. Though the bulk of the American woolens remained of medium grade, an increasing proportion, and one not inconsiderable, was of better grade and finish than during the nineteenth century; the improvement being most marked in worsteds. Just what this tendency signi-

those of more recent origin can draw their help from mills which have had such a long existence. The employers, and in very many cases their fathers and grandfathers before them, have been born and brought up in the business; and as a rule the children and grandchildren of the workpeople are also trained to the same trade.

" And what is true of the firms, and the workers and their families, is also true of the communities. The older seats of the woolen industry, like Bradford and Huddersfield in England, parts of the Rhine province, the Lausitz, Silesia and Saxony in Germany, Roubaix, Tourcoing, Elboeuf and Sedan in France, to mention a few of the best known, having gathered about them for centuries a group of trained and efficient workers, possess an inestimable advantage over the centers of the woolen industry in America, the latter being, in comparison with those of Europe above named, themselves still in their childhood and their workers more or less migratory. . . . The operatives in American woolen mills, in spite of the very much higher wages paid, are largely drawn from the ranks of unskilled labor. And whence does this unskilled labor come? There is little of it among native-born Americans. It is taken from the steady flow of immigrants into this country. . . .

" When establishing our enterprise in Passaic, N. J., we were obliged, in order to be able to compete, not only as to price, but also with respect to quality and technical perfection, with the best European mills, to import most of our machinery, because a great deal of American spinning, weaving, dyeing, and finishing machinery is not yet so highly developed as the European. This is especially true of the machinery used in what is known as the French system of worsted spinning, which is being adopted more and more each year. [The French use the mule exclusively, and a drawing system of their own; the whole adapted to making soft fabrics from fine wool of comparatively short fibre. See Barker, *Textiles*, p. 247; *Tariff Board Report*, p. 1031.] Also our entire woolen spinning machinery had to be imported to enable us to compete with the best European manufacturers.

" A great part of our looms could be bought here, while others had to be imported on account of special requirements; but those purchased in this country were nearly as expensive as the imported ones, so that in buying them we had to bear our share of the protection of the textile machinery of this country. Dyeing and finishing machinery used in our mill also had mostly to be imported." From a memorial to Congress, by J. Forstmann, reprinted in *Bulletin Wool Manufacturers*, September, 1911, pp. 416–417.

fied, it would be difficult to say. The obvious explanation would ascribe it simply to extreme protection. Make your duties high enough, and you can bring about the domestic production of anything and everything. The most elaborately finished woolens and silks and cottons will be made within this country if a sufficiently heavy handicap be imposed on foreign producers; even though the outcome may be delayed somewhat by lack of habituation among the manufacturers and by a long-lingering prejudice among consumers in favor of imported fabrics. Presumably the change here noted was the effect of precisely this cause, — extreme protection. But possibly it was due, in part at least, to some beginning in improved processes, better oganization, greater effectiveness. Yet the evidence pointing this way is slight; nor is it on general grounds probable that forward steps by American manufacturers would be first taken in this part of the industry. It is in the production of the standardized fabrics of medium grade that the opportunities are most promising for advances by Americans.[1]

On the whole, the best conclusion I can reach is that the difficulties and the apparent backwardness of the wool manufacture rest partly on the physical characteristics of the raw material and partly on the impossibility of standardizing its fabrics to the same degree as, for example, cotton goods. Both of these circumstances stand in the way of mass production and so of the sweeping use of labor-saving machinery. The silk manufacture long encountered the same obstacles; it has still to face them in a large part of its product; yet, as we have seen, the march of invention appears to be removing the first obstacle, and at all events gives some promise of enabling the American industry to progress to independence. The absence of indications of similar progress in the wool manufacture is not easy to explain. Possibly this is no more than a sporadic episode, standing apart from the general industrial movement. Not everything in economic history can be ascribed to the uniform action of the same causes.

[1] I am glad to record that my general conclusions are similar to those reached by Mr. T. W. Page of the Tariff Board and stated by him in the address already referred to; see *Bulletin Wool Manufacturers*, June, 1913, p. 169.

It remains puzzling why the machine processes were not applied with more decisive success to this material, and why Europeans and not Americans took the lead in the considerable success which was achieved in the worsted branch. Another half-century may bring independent advances in this country; we may still witness considerable changes in the existing relations between the wool manufacturing countries and districts. Possibly free wool will have greater effect in promoting the development of the American manufacturing industry than would be expected in view of the foregoing analysis of the influence exercised by the wool duties in the past. A considerable period must elapse before it will appear how the industry may adjust itself to such new conditions as were established in 1913. The sober-minded investigator will be slow in laying too much stress on single causes, slow in generalization, slowest of all in prediction.

PART V

1910–1930

CHAPTER XXII

SUGAR

1910–1930

THE sugar situation during the twenty years 1910–30 underwent extraordinary changes, and yet, as regards the effects of the import duties and the other fundamental matters considered in Part II, nothing new appeared. The figures changed, but they called for no different interpretation. Prices showed extraordinary fluctuations, and in the later years of the period were abnormally low. Notwithstanding the low prices, production in the world at large persisted at a high level. The amounts contributed by the various regions from which the United States draws its supplies shifted somewhat — greater here, smaller there. More detailed and highly interesting information was collected concerning the costs of production and the relative position of the producers in these widely scattered regions — Cuba, Porto Rico, Hawaii, the Philippines, the beet-sugar states of the west. Import duties were raised in 1921, in 1922, and again in 1930. But there was nothing to raise new questions of principle.

The tariff act of 1913, providing for a reduction in the sugar duty,[1] had as its immediate effect a decrease in the acreage sown with beets. Louisiana, too, made preparations to curtail production, in some cases dismantling sugar mills in expectation of removing the machinery to Cuba. Cuba, on the other hand, anticipating a higher return on her sugar, as well as an increased demand, had produced an enormous crop in 1912–13, — an increase of 1,100 million pounds over the year before, — and followed it in 1913–14 with another 300 million pound increase. Most of the additional output went to the United States, where it completely displaced the already dwindling imports of full-duty paying sugar from the Dutch East Indies and elsewhere, as well as some sugar from domestic sources of supply.

[1] See p. 54 above.

The outbreak of the war completely changed the situation. The world demand and supply of sugar experienced violent disturbances. European beet sugar production, which had been 18 billion pounds in 1913–14, declined to 6 billion in 1919–20, and Europe turned for sugar to Cuba, that is, to the United States, which controlled the Cuban supplies. The opportunity for tracing the effect of a decrease in the duties was thus lost, the increase in Cuban production being absorbed by the new European demand. In any case, the effect of the duty on price was further obscured by the government control of sugar prices and distribution, which lasted from August, 1917 to December, 1919.[1]

The years immediately following the cessation of government control also gave little opportunity for tracing the effect of the tariff. In the early spring of 1920 a fear of shortage, induced by a smaller Cuban crop and by the withdrawal of government control, aroused panic buying and hoarding of sugar. The price soared in a few months to 23 cents a pound (in New York, without duty). The phenomenally high price attracted sugar from all over the world, and for the first time since 1908 imports of full-duty sugar reached important proportions. Almost 2 billion pounds came in from Java, Central America, San Domingo. The drop in price which followed was as precipitous as the rise had been, and continued until the price of sugar reached 3.6 cents in December, 1920. Such wild fluctuations wholly outweighed any possible effect the duty might have had either on prices or on production.

The severe decline in price which continued in the spring of 1921 brought acute financial distress to sugar producers. The domestic producers clamored for relief in the form of increased protection against Cuban sugar, and their plea, like that of other agricultural producers, was answered by an increase in the duty. On Cuban sugar the duty was raised to 1.6 cents (Emergency

[1] For a detailed account of the government control of sugar see J. Bernhardt, "Government Control of Sugar in the United States during the War 1917–18 and the Transition to Competitive Conditions," *Quarterly Journal of Economics*, August, 1919, and August, 1920; "Was Decontrol of Sugar in the United States Advisable," *Journal of Political Economy*, February, 1922; Federal Trade Commission *Report on Sugar Supply and Prices* (Washington, 1920); F. W. Taussig, "Price Fixing as Seen by a Price Fixer," *Quarterly Journal of Economics*, February, 1919.

Tariff Act of 1921). But the increase of the duty did not halt the fall in price. Bumper Cuban and domestic sugar crops, the large unsold Cuban surplus of the previous year, the general depression of business — all caused the price to fall still more. The failure of the increase in duty to bring the desired relief caused domestic producers to demand a further increase in protection against Cuban sugar. Notwithstanding strenuous opposition, the duty was again raised in the general tariff act of September, 1922, from 1.6 cents to 1.7648 cents per pound (on cuban sugar).[1] Finally, in 1930, the duty was raised again, to 2 cents.

The price of sugar during most of the decade following the war remained at its pre-war level [2] — a striking exception to the general maintenance of prices at a level above the pre-war. In 1929 and 1930 the price declined even more, reaching in June, 1930 the lowest price then on record, 3.16 cents duty paid. The low price was caused by the greatly increased world supply of sugar. Cuba and Java, who together produced half the world supply of cane sugar, had doubled their pre-war output; European beet sugar, which from 1913 to 1920 had fallen from 18 to 6 billion pounds, had by 1929 risen to 23 billion. The total world output rose between 1921 and 1930 from 39 billion pounds to 62 billion, an increase of 60 per cent in ten years.

In the United States the consumption of sugar steadily in-

[1] The price of raw sugar rose in 1923 to 8.4 cents. The rise called forth a government inquiry as to the possible relation between high prices and the tariff. The President requested the Tariff Commission to "make an immediate inquiry into the relation of the sugar tariff to the current prices of that commodity." In the communication to the Commission the President stated: "It is difficult to believe that the duty on sugar can have any part in making the abnormal prices which prevail, but if the Commission finds there is any ground for believing the duty to be even partially responsible, I shall be ready to proclaim a reduction in duty as provided by law." The Commission in its answering report to the President concluded that the increase in the price of sugar in 1923 "was due to causes not connected with the American tariff." The report further stated that the evidence indicated that the duty on Cuban sugar was included in the wholesale and retail prices of granulated sugar. See United States Tariff Commission, *The Relation of the Tariff on Sugar to the Rise in Price of February–April, 1923* (Washington, 1923).

[2] Average of Yearly Average Prices. (New York. Wholesale. Raw.)

1909–13	4.064 (including duty of 1.348 cents)
1921–22	4.701 (" " " 1.764 ")
1925–29	4. (" " " 1.764 ")

creased, from 8 billion pounds in 1913 to 12 billion in 1929.[1] Of the 4 billion pound increase, Cuba supplied the largest share and strictly domestic sources the smallest share. Hawaii, the Philippines, and Porto Rico contributed about two-fifths. The domestic sources, both cane and beet, contributed about one-fifth.[2]

Louisiana failed to make any contribution to this huge increase. The importance of that state as a source of sugar supply slowly diminished from 1909 to 1929. During the first decade of the twentieth century she had furnished about ten per cent of the sugar consumed in the United States. After that time her production declined, until by 1929 her output formed only two per cent of the total consumed. The average annual production by periods was as follows:

	Lousiana Production	Proportion of Total Consumed in U. S.
1908–12	700 mill. lbs.	8.7 %
1913–17	600	6.7
1918–22	470	5.0
1923–27	200	1.7
1928–29	300	3.3

The exceptionally low average of the years 1924–28 was due to the spread of the mosaic disease in the cane crop, and was short-lived. New varieties, resistant to the disease, were widely introduced, and a revival set in after 1928. But it is not to be expected that even under favorable crop conditions Louisiana will equal her output of former years. At bottom the climatic conditions are an insuperable obstacle to profitable expansion, even with protection as high as 2 cents per pound. Except during occasional years of favorable weather, the bulk of Louisiana plantations are at a comparative disadvantage in the production of sugar.

1 The per capita consumption increased from 85.4 pounds in 1913 to 108 pounds in 1929. It had reached 110 pounds in 1926.

2 PERCENTAGE OF TOTAL DOMESTIC CONSUMPTION SUPPLIED

	1913	1929
Cuba	53.2%	51.8%
Hawaii	13.5	13.3
Porto Rico	8.8	6.6
Philippines	1.2	10.4
Louisiana	5.5	2.6
Domestic Beet	16.7	14.7

A severe hurricane greatly reduced the crop of Porto Rico in 1929.

The Hawaiian Islands, in contrast with Louisiana, almost doubled their output between 1910–13 and 1927–30. The greater part of the increase came about in the years 1924–28 and was due not to increase of acreage — practically all the land suitable for sugar cane had been under cultivation for many years — but to more intensive cultivation and improved technique. The following figures of the average product per acre clearly show the remarkable increase in yield.[1]

	Cane Tons Harvested per Acre	Sugar Tons Produced per Acre	Total Hawaiian Production (thousands of tons)
1920	40	4.8	555
1921	41	4.5	569
1922	39	4.9	504
1923	38	4.8	537
1924	56	6.1	701
1925	52	6.4	775
1926	53	6.4	789

Better seed selection, control of pests, use of greater quantities of fertilizer, and improvements in the methods of extracting sugar from the cane, all contributed to the increase.[2] Indicative of the progressive methods — progressive, that is, in that there were well planned methods of intensive cultivation — is the maintenance by the Hawaii Sugar Planters' Association of an experiment station with an annual budget of $500,000. The coöperative ownership by Hawaiian sugar planters of one of the largest and most modern refineries in the United States also contributed to the increase in production. It lessened the costs of selling raw sugar, and also, through the close coöperation between sugar planters, mills, and refinery, reduced the cost of refining.[3]

Improved technique and more intensive cultivation, though

[1] These figures are averages for the Hawaiian Islands as a whole. The yields of various districts and plantations differ greatly. The islands of Aahu and Maui depend on irrigation and yield double the amount of sugar per acre that is obtained in the island of Hawaii, which depends almost entirely upon rainfall. See F. Maxwell, *Economic Aspects of Cane Sugar Production*, ch. IV.

[2] In 1924 an average of 1,650 pounds of fertilizer was applied to every acre of sugar cane per crop. It was estimated that ten dollars' worth of fertilizer was used for every ton of sugar produced. — Hawaiian Sugar Planters' Association, *Story of Sugar in Hawaii* (1926).

[3] B. Emmet, *The California and Hawaiian Sugar Refining Corporation* (1928).

similar in that they both result in an increased yield per acre, are very different in their economic significance. Better mechanical technique results in lower cost of production; more intensive cultivation means higher cost for the additional units produced. What has been said in the previous chapter (p. 63 ff.) regarding increases in yield of Hawaiian plantations was no less true for the period after the Great War than for the earlier period. So far as the growing of cane is concerned, the more elaborate and expensive cultivation of each acre meant not more cane at lower cost, but greater effort in wringing more out of the land, not at any lower cost, but on the whole at higher cost for the additional supply. The case, of course, is different as regards economies in refining, selling, transportation. These mean a real decline in the labor and capital needed for a given unit of product. But the highly scientific cultivation meant an endeavor, successful only in part, to offset nature's resistance to increasing output from a given area. The eulogies on the progressive method of the Hawaiian planter involve the familiar fallacy of supposing that high output per acre has the same economic advantage as high output per dollar of expenditure. Hawaiian land watered by expensive irrigation cannot yield sugar so cheaply as Cuban land yields without irrigation costs. High yields per acre in Hawaii result from the refusal of the United States to profit by nature's bounty to Cuba.

In the Philippine Islands the sugar situation underwent radical changes after 1913. Then the restriction on free sugar exports from the Philippines to the United States was removed. Before that time most of the sugar produced in the Philippines was a low grade muscovado sugar, manufactured by small antiquated mills. For this sugar there was little market in the United States, and most of it was exported to China and Japan. From 1910 to 1918 centrifugal sugar began to be produced by a dozen or more small modern mills established by Philippine, American, and Spanish capital. The increase in exports to the United States went on apace as more centrifugal sugar was produced. The increase was checked, however, by the war; Europe became a more favorable market for Philippine sugar. It was not until 1922, following the establishment of numerous large mills, that the sugar exports to the United States became markedly greater. By 1928 the production of centrifugal sugar almost tripled, largely at the expense of muscovado sugar, and exports to the United States reached 1,200 million pounds, practically the entire Philippine output of centrifugal sugar.

The heavy increase in Philippine sugar exports to the United States led domestic sugar producers to demand again a limitation on the amount of sugar that might enter the United States free of duty.[1] Their representatives also spoke in favor of Philippine independence. The grounds for their proposal were frankly selfish; the larger political and international questions played no part. The move was advocated because the grant of independence to the Philippines, by placing the islands on the same footing as foreign countries, would considerably reduce, if not eliminate, Philippine competition.

In Porto Rico as in Hawaii more intensive cultivation and improvements in the technique of production resulted in an increase of sugar output. From 700 million pounds in 1914 it rose to 1,500 million pounds in 1928.[2] Further increase could come only from more intensive cultivation. All of the Porto Rican cane land in use by 1929 had been used for cane growing many years. There was practically no increase in acreage, except for a few thousand acres made available through the completion of an irrigation project. Only this sort of development, necessarily expensive, could bring land under cane cultivation. The case of Porto Rico is thus analogous to that of Hawaii. Porto Rican planters were enabled by the bonus to extend the margin of intensive cultivation far beyond the point that would have been profitable had Porto Rican sugar been subject to the same duty as Cuban.

Cuba continued to hold her position as the greatest sugar pro-

[1] The Timberlake resolution introduced in the House of Representatives in February, 1928, called for a limitation of free Philippine sugar imports to 500,000 long tons, a little less than the amount imported in 1928.

[2] A decline in 1929 to 1,200 million pounds was due to destruction of cane crops by a severe hurricane.

ducing country in the world, and Cuban sugar continued to be the crux of the situation. Throughout the earlier and the later period it constituted one-half of the total United States supply, dominated the market, raised the greatest controversy.

In the years 1913 to 1924 the production of Cuban sugar more than doubled. Most of the enormous increase — not less than 6 billion pounds — came from the development of virgin territory in the eastern part of the island. In the years following, production declined. The decline was the result of a government edict limiting the amount of cane cuttings—a step which was caused by the low price of sugar, and could be carried out only because the low price in itself tended to lower output. The crop of the next three years was curtailed, so that by the third year it was 20 per cent smaller. No move of this kind can bring the desired result unless the total output from *all* sources of supply is curtailed. The other sugar producing countries, however, with the exception of Louisiana, increased their production greatly, and in 1928 the Cuban restriction was removed. In 1928–29 the Cuban crop established a new record.

In spite of great natural advantages for growing cane, and the large capital equipment of Cuba, the prices she received for her raw cane in the years 1927–30 apparently were so low that a large part of the industry could not prosper. In the brief submitted to the Ways and Means Committee of the House of Representatives by the United Sugar Association, representing the mill owners of Cuba, the record of losses of Cuban sugar companies was stated to be as follows:

	Companies and Mills Included	Approximate percentage of Crop	Net Losses for all Companies (thousands of dollars)
1925	124	89.6 %	13.131
1926	128	95.8	29.373
1927	129	93.	8.809
1928	95 [1]	92.7	16.505

Figures for the year 1929 and 1930 are not included, but they probably showed even a greater loss because the average price

[1] Not all the reports received.

Cuba received for her raw sugar in 1929 was, except for 1913, the lowest in twenty-five years.[1]

In view of the losses sustained by Cuban sugar companies, any further extension of cane acreage was scarcely to be expected while sugar prices remained so low. But the possibility of further increase in production was still great, both through more extensive and more intensive cultivation. Much land suitable for cane remained, though probably less fertile, or less favorably situated, than land already in use. And on many active plantations yields could be greatly increased if intensive methods of cultivation, such as were employed in Hawaii and Porto Rico, were resorted to. It was found, for illustration, that in some parts of Cuba irrigation doubled, tripled, and even quadrupled the yield obtained before irrigation. The potential increase of the Cuban sugar supply is great; but what the degree of elasticity is, cannot be readily foretold. Probably some increase would come without higher cost for the additional (marginal) supply; while a considerable further increase could be secured with no great advance in cost. These possibilities and probabilities bear on the effects in the United States of a repeal or marked reduction of the duty, a topic on which more is said below.

The production of beet sugar in the United States maintained its rapid though uneven growth until 1920–21, during which year 2,100 million pounds were produced — an increase of 50 per cent over the 1911–13 average. After that date the domestic production fluctuated between 1,400 and 2,200 million pounds. The major fluctuations can be traced to broad price changes. The year 1914, following the reduction of duty, and the year 1922, following the collapse of sugar prices in 1921, showed considerable decline in the planted beet area. The opposite occurred in 1920, in the spring of which year, it will be remembered, prices soared; and again in 1924, when the high price of sugar prevailing during

[1] In the same brief the earnings of sugar companies in Porto Rico and Hawaii were submitted for comparison. Unfortunately the reported Porto Rican and Hawaiian companies produced only half the crops in each country, and do not therefore give a safe basis of comparison. They did show, however, that many Hawaiian and Porto Rican companies had high earnings in those same years.

most of 1923 extended into 1924. For the rest of the years the areas planted fluctuated little from season to season.

The importance of some of the states as beet sugar producing areas changed during the decade. Colorado, Nebraska, and Montana increased their production, while California greatly decreased hers. The decline in California was due to the increasing value of California land for other crops, and to the ravages of beet pests and disease. The average cost of land per ton of beets (not including capital investments) for the three years 1921–23 was 50 per cent higher in California than in any other beet state, and double the average of all other beet states. The ravages of disease were greater in California in the years 1923–27 than in most other beet states.[1] In 1925, for example, only 72 per cent of the planted area in California was harvested, and the yield on the harvested land was only 6.4 tons per acre. The average yield per acre in the United States was in that year 11.4 tons. The result of this disastrous crop in California was that in the following year the planted area decreased one-half, and rose but little in succeeding years.

The decline in beet sugar production in California was due simply to the fact that other crops — especially fruits and vegetables — could be grown there with a larger return to the same application of labor and capital. It is part of a long-continued, much varied, and almost unique course of development in that region, beginning in the Spanish days with cattle-growing (primarily for the hides), then the gold furore of the fifties and sixties of the nineteenth century, next wheat growing on great ranches

[1] The following table indicates the losses in sugar beet cultivation, chiefly from the ravages of disease, in two of the leading sugar beet states — Colorado and Nebraska — and in California. The figures are for the percentages of the planted crop harvested and for yields of the harvested acres.

	Nebraska		California		Colorado	
	per cent [a]	Yield [b]	per cent [a]	Yield [b]	per cent [a]	Yield [b]
1923	96	11.7	86	9.6	90	12.2
1924	98	11.8	91	9.7	96	11.3
1925	100	15.6	76	6.4	72	12.6
1926	97	15.6	86	8.	99	13.8
1927	99		93		99	

(a) Percentage of planted crop harvested.
(b) Short tons of sugar beet per acre.

(with a small yield per acre but a large yield per man), sugar beets, and finally fruits and vegetables under elaborate irrigation. The story is too long and intricate to be told here. The significant thing for the present subject is that in the last stages the growing of beet sugar had to face competing uses of the land, which became more profitable for the individual farmer, and for the community at large meant a more advantageous use of its resources.

This way of analyzing the situation is in accord with what has already been said about the cultivation of the sugar beet — the larger use of hand labor and the impossibility, or at least failure, of applying agricultural machinery. Beet-sugar culture remained characteristically one of hand labor. As late as 1926, the Tariff Commission, in its elaborate inquiry on the cost of producing sugar beets, still reported that "although some progress has been made in the development of machines for pulling and topping, these have not proved generally practicable, and no machines have as yet been invented for blocking and thinning, or hoeing between plants." [1]

In the labor situation, which thus remained crucial, there was little change. The native American agricultural worker was still averse to the back-breaking toil of the sugar-beet field, and the cultivation of the beet was dependent largely upon foreign labor. In the post-war decade large numbers of Mexicans were brought in to work the beet fields, not only in Colorado, but as far east as Michigan.[2] The employment of women and children continued apparently unabated, and with it the practice of contracting with laborers at so much an acre. The laborers brought their families, who lived in shacks provided by the owners, and the women and children assisted in the fields. As the Tariff Commission said in 1923: "This investigation disclosed convincing and deplorable evidence of child labor in certain sugar-beet regions of the United

[1] *Costs of Producing Sugar-Beets*, Part X, p. 18.

[2] Of the 78,000 contract laborers in sugar-beet cultivation in 1926 the proportions were as follows:

Foreign-born northern Europeans	19%
Japanese	1
Mexicans	31

— *Costs of Producing Sugar-Beets*, p. 17.

States which at present distinctly limits the social value of the domestic sugar industry."[1]

On some important aspects of the sugar situation the literature was much enriched during the post-war period, in the way of theoretic analysis as well as in the quantitative measurement which bears more particularly on the tariff problems.[2] There was new and abundant information on the conditions of supply and cost. When speaking of "cost," we here mean, of course, cost in the business sense — the money costs or expenses of production, not the labor costs or sacrifice costs which we have in mind when considering the principle of comparative cost or comparative advantage. The figures on money cost bear on two subjects: first, on the differences in cost between the United States and Cuba, and between the several domestic regions (domestic in that there is no

[1] Report, p. 89.

[2] Those interested in the details, on both aspects, may turn to the following: H. Schultz, *Statistical Laws of Demand and Supply* (Chicago, 1928); E. W. Gilboy, "Demand Curves in Theory and in Practice," *Quarterly Journal of Economics*, August, 1930; "The Leontief and Schultz Methods of Deriving 'Demand' Curves," *Quarterly Journal of Economics*, February, 1931; H. L. Moore, *Forecasting the Yield and Price of Cotton* (1917), Chap. V; "Elasticity of Demand and Flexibility of Prices," *Journal of the American Statistical Association*, March, 1922; "Partial Elasticity of Demand," *Quarterly Journal of Economics*, May, 1926; H. Working, "Statistical Determination of Demand Curves," *Quarterly Journal of Economics*, August, 1925; E. Working, "What Do Statistical Curves Show?" *Quarterly Journal of Economics*, February, 1927; M. Ezekiel, "Statistical Analysis and the 'Laws' of Price," *Quarterly Journal of Economics*, February, 1928.

The above bear chiefly on the elasticity of demand. As regards theory they are most interesting, but not of much moment on the tariff. The chief thing significant for us is that elasticity of demand for *sugar at the low prices of 1925–30* was very slight; that is, demand was "inelastic," apparently because the point of satiety was being approached.

On the side of supply and cost the following list bears specifically on sugar in relation to the tariff:

Report of the United States Tariff Commission: *Sugar* (1926); *Refined Sugar, Costs, Prices, and Profits* (1920), Tariff Information Series No. 16; *Costs of Production in the Sugar Industry* (1919), Tariff Information Series No. 9; *Costs of Producing Sugar-Beets* (1928), Federal Trade Commission; *Report on the Beet Sugar Industry in the United States* (1917); P. G. Wright, *Sugar in Relation to the Tariff* (Washington, 1924); *The Effect of a Change in the Sugar Tariff* (1929); A. G. Black, "Elasticity of Supply," *Journal of Farm Economics*, April, 1924; "Analysis of Tariff Duties," *Journal of Farm Economics*," January, 1930.

duty on their sugar); second, on the extent to which the supplies, domestic or Cuban, can be increased at the same or higher cost, and hence the ultimate effect on the price of sugar of an increase or reduction of the duty.

Annual data of the costs of producing sugar in the United States — Hawaii and Porto Rico included — and in Cuba have been gathered since 1917 by the United States Tariff Commission. Reference has already been made to the comprehensive investigation of the costs in these areas, the results of which were published in 1926. The data then gathered, as well as the others, much as they add to our information, bring out nothing inconsistent with the conclusions reached in Part II; they serve rather to illustrate and confirm them.

According to the Commission's findings the weighted average costs (f. o. b. mill) of producing sugar were as follows:

	Cents per pound
Cuba	4.4329
Hawaii	4.9372
Porto Rico	5.4983
Beet (United States)	5.8286
Louisiana	6.8437

These figures are the six-year average (weighted arithmetic average) costs, 1917–22.[1] Cuban costs, as would be expected, were lowest and those in Louisiana highest. But the difference between Cuban costs and those of other regions fluctuated widely from year to year. In 1920–21, for illustration, the difference (weighted average) between Cuba and Louisiana was 3.9 cents per pound as against 1.8 cents in the year following. The cost of beet sugar, on the other hand, while lower (on a raw basis) than Cuban cost by 1.11 cents in 1920–21, was higher by 1.34 cents in 1922–23. The figures of annual costs of production clearly indicate that those for any one year cannot be used as a basis for comparing costs in various countries. Only the average costs for the six years may be fairly taken as representative. These indicate beyond question that sugar was produced in Cuba more cheaply than in

[1] *Sugar*, p. 91. A minority report submitted cost figures which made the difference between Cuban costs and domestic costs greater. See *ibid.*, p. 105.

the other territories considered. They indicate also that Louisiana produced sugar under the least advantageous circumstances.

Between Hawaiian costs and Cuban costs the difference was surprisingly small. In the years covered by the studies, a large part of the one cent bonus given to the Hawaiian planters served merely to swell their profits. The same bonus to the beet sugar producers, on the other hand, served for the most part merely to permit the cultivation of sugar beets under conditions so unfavorable as to yield no special profit to the producers. For the Louisiana cane growers the bonus did not cover even half the additional cost necessary to produce sugar there rather than in Cuba. In so far as the bonus to the domestic sugar producers maintained or increased production in those areas, the loss which it represented to the consumer was offset by little or no gain to the producer. The bonus to the Hawaiian planters, on the other hand, although also a loss to the consumer, considerably increased the producer's profits.

If the differences in costs remained as great in the subsequent eight years (1923–29), the profits to Hawaiian planters from the $\frac{3}{4}$ cent increase in duty made in 1922, were very great indeed.[1] Even the beet sugar producers would have retained no inconsiderable part of the bonus. But for the producers of Louisiana the difference between their costs and the Cuban was so great as to render a good part of Louisiana production unprofitable even with the bonus.

The report of 1923 showed not only these (averaged) differences between the regions, but great variations within any one of them. The following table of the costs for 1922–23 illustrates the wide range.

1 The profits made by domestic sugar producers in the years 1925–27, years of low sugar prices, would seem to bear this out. Twelve Hawaiian sugar companies, producing half the crop, earned about 18 per cent annually during those years; three Porto Rican companies, producing almost half, earned 15 per cent; and the San Carlos Milling Co., one of the large mills in the Philippines, paid in dividends an average of 27 per cent in the same period.

	LOWEST QUARTILE 25% at costs less than	HIGHEST QUARTILE 25% at costs between
Cuba	3.578 cents per lb.	4.191– 5.197 cents per lb.
Louisiana	4.691	5.607–10.715
Porto Rico	5.273	6.158– 7.006
Hawaii	4.4179	5.058–10.764
Beet (United States) . .	6.192 [1]	7.078– 8.56

It will be noted that *all* sugar produced in 1922–23 in Cuba was produced at a lower cost than at least 75 per cent of the sugar produced in either Porto Rico or the beet sugar areas. On the other hand, at least 75 per cent of Hawaiian and 25 per cent of Louisiana sugar was produced at costs less than *some* Cuban sugar. Furthermore the report showed that the proportions between the quotas at the several costs varied considerably from year to year. On the basis of the variations found for the years 1920–23, the Commission concluded that "to a considerable extent American sugar production is independent of the tariff. Under a much lower tariff, and apparently even under free trade, a substantial percentage of the industry in all domestic regions (*i. e.*, other than Cuba) would continue."

The other question on which cost inquiries shed light is the degree of accuracy in the measurement of the burden on the consumer. By way of preliminary, we may prepare once again, for a later period, the sort of balance sheet which was made out on page 99 for the year 1916. The following are the figures for 1927.

THE UNITED STATES GOVERNMENT IN ACCOUNT WITH SUGAR CONSUMERS FOR THE CALENDAR YEAR 1927

Dr.[2]	(Mill. dollars)	Cr.	Paid over (mill. dollars) to U. S. Treasury	Paid over (mill. dollars) to Sugar Producers
Taxes collected on 11,846 mill. lbs. of sugar @ 1.898 cents	$224.8	On 15 mill. lbs. of full-duty sugar	$ .4	. . .
Taxes collected on 15 mill. lbs. of sugar @ 2.371 cents	.4	" 6,524 " " " Cuban "	123.9	. . .
		" 86 " " " Louisiana & Texas	. . .	1.6
		" 1,748 " " " U. S. Beet sugar . .	. . .	33.2
		" 1,424 " " " Hawaiian "	. . .	27.0
		" 1,081 " " " Porto Rico "	. . .	20.5
		" 972 " " " Philippine "	. . .	18.4
		" 11 " " " Virgin Is. "	. . .	.2
			$124.3	100.9
	$225.2		$225.2	

[1] As much as 55 per cent was produced at less than this price.

[2] The figures for the two sides of the balance appear in somewhat different ways

The balance indicates that in the year 1927, as a result of the duty of 1.76 cents per pound on Cuban sugar and 2.20 cents per pound on foreign sugar, 125 million dollars were collected as revenue by the government, and approximately 100 million went to sugar producers. Of this 100 million, United States beet sugar producers secured one-third, Hawaiian about one-fourth, and Porto Rican and Philippine one-fifth each. Much of this sum, as already shown, represented extra profit or bonus for the producers.[1] Just how much of the bonus going to domestic producers served to swell profits (*i. e.*, extra or non-competitive profits), how much simply kept them going — this cannot be measured. In any case, to the consumer the tax was a sheer burden. If the profits had been widely diffused, there might be some interest in determining the proportion in which they were divided. But since the burden was borne by 120 million American consumers, and the profits were shared among only a part of the 60 thousand sugar-beet producers in the United States [2] and a smaller number of stockholders in semi-domestic sugar companies, the matter of proportion is of little importance. The significant thing is that

in the sources, and hence have here been adjusted so as to be on a comparable basis. Those for imports and consumption being in terms of refined sugar, those of taxes have been adjusted as if the taxes were collected on refined, not on raw. It takes 107 pounds of raw to make one pound of refined; hence a tax of 1.7648 cents per pound on raw is equivalent to 1.898 cents on refined (including .01 cents per pound for interest on money tied up in duties).

[1] A comparison of the profits *per ton of sugar produced* earned by the three largest Hawaiian and three largest Cuban sugar companies for the crop of 1926–27 suggests that not a small part of the 1.89 cent "tax" on the consumer was retained by Hawaiian producers in the form of extra profits.

Company	Production (thousands of short tons)	Profit per ton
Hawaii		
Ewa Plantation Co.	50	$35.05
Hawaiian Comm. & Agri. Co.	63	28.44
Oahy Sugar Co.	66	19.46
Cuba		
Cuba Am. Sugar Corp.	856	1.02
Cuba Dominican Sugar Corp.	535	.25
Punta Alegre Sugar Co.	301	1.03

[2] The data on profits were obtained from the *Manual of Hawaiian Securities*, published by the Honolulu Stock and Bond Exchange, and from Moody's Manual, *Industrials*. See P. G. Wright, *Effects of a Change in the Sugar Tariff*, pp. 22 ff., on this point.

the consumer was taxed 225 millions, of which the government received only 124 millions.

There is, however, undue simplicity in this calculation. It assumes that the price of sugar was higher by the full amount of the tax than it *would have been* under free sugar. This beyond doubt is not the case for short periods; and for long periods, while the conclusion probably holds, it is affected by some complex conditions and perhaps is open to some qualification.

Under free trade the amount of sugar produced in the domestic areas would decline, because much sugar is produced profitably only because of the duty. Foreign sources of supply would increase their output. They would have to supplement the decreased domestic supply and also satisfy the additional demand for sugar in the United States induced by the lowered price.[1] In order to increase their output, foreign producers would have to resort to less favorable conditions of production. The price, therefore, in the end would rise. Hence abolition of the duty would not reduce the price by the full amount of the duty. The burden to the consumer would be somewhat less than the balance sheet indicates; how much less, would depend upon the ease with which the supply of sugar in the various areas could be increased or decreased, or — to use the technical and more exact terminology — upon the elasticity of supply.

What, now, are the actual probabilities? Just how would a change in tariff affect the production of sugar in Cuba, Hawaii, the Philippines, Porto Rico, Louisiana, and the domestic beet areas?

The elasticity of supply differs according as long-run tendencies or short-time effects are considered. For a given season, over a period less than eight months (the minimum time required to plant and harvest sugar beets, the most flexible part of the supply) the amount of sugar coming into the market, either to

[1] Schultz estimated that a fall in the price of sugar of one cent a pound would have increased the consumption by 952 million pounds in 1914. — H. Schultz, *Statistical Laws of Demand and Supply* (Chicago, 1928), p. 62. The increase in consumption would doubtless be less in 1920 than in 1914. The elasticity of demand becomes less as sugar prices drop and as per capita consumption approaches satiety.

warehouses or to refineries, is fixed. A rise in the price of sugar in the United States would increase the rate at which sugar came out of warehouses or from foreign sources, but the total world supply would remain the same no matter how great the rise. Over a longer period — one of several years, long enough for cane as well as beets to be planted and harvested — production can be easily and considerably increased. Over a still longer period, five years or more, the supply can be increased even more by opening new lands, irrigation, construction of new sugar mills, spread of more scientific methods of cultivation, increased movement of labor to cane fields.

Again: the increased production necessarily comes either from utilization of new land, which is likely to be less fertile or less favorably situated, or from more intensive cultivation of land already devoted to cane or beets. In both cases the cost of additional supply tends to rise. How far this tendency is realized, or how far it goes, is impossible to forecast.[1] But there are marked differences in the several regions from which the sugar supply comes, and from this point of view the probabilities may be gauged.

In Cuba there is a plentiful supply of labor for cane fields, and a great deal of land suitable for cane, though not quite so good as land already in use. There are sugar mills in Cuba with unused capacity, and sugar companies which could easily secure capital with which to build more mills if the demand warrants it. There are also plantations in Cuba whose yield of cane could be increased through irrigation with but slight advance in the unit cost of the additional supply. The indications are that the Cuban output

[1] Professor Schultz has developed a statistical method by which he feels the answers to such problems can be quantitatively measured. In applying the method to the sugar situation in the United States he found that "under such average conditions of demand and supply as had prevailed during the five years before the war, the increase in price due to a tariff on sugar would be approximately 86 per cent of the duty." The same percentage cannot be applied to 1928 because of the difference in height of the tax, as well as the possible differences in elasticity of taxed and untaxed supplies. The method used by Professor Schultz, however, deals only with short-time movements, whereas our main concern is with the long-run tendencies. Even as a means of measuring "short-time" elasticities the method is open to criticism.

could be considerably increased without a rise in cost, and very much increased with but a slight rise. The supply, that is, is very elastic.

In Hawaii the situation is quite different. There all cane land except that of very poor grade is already under cane cultivation. Intensive cultivation, moreover, has already been pushed to the point where further increases in yield could be obtained only at high cost. Labor for cane fields is also scarce in Hawaii and obtainable (from the Philippines) only at high expense. Even a moderate increase in supply could be profitably got only if the rise in price were considerable. The elasticity of supply is slight.

In the Philippines the situation is more like that of Cuba than of Hawaii; in Porto Rico, on the other hand, it resembles that of Hawaii. In the Philippines, cane land and labor are plentiful. Cultivation has not been carried to any high degree of intensiveness. But capital is not easily forthcoming. The uncertainty of the future legal status of the Philippine Islands with regard to the United States, and the Philippine land laws restricting ownership of land by corporations to 2,500 acres, stand in the way of large investment. A rise in the price of sugar would probably not increase the supply of Philippine sugar so much as it would that of Cuban sugar, but more than that of Hawaii. In Porto Rico, while labor is very plentiful, unused cane land is scarce. Irrigation — which means intensive cultivation — has already been carried far, though apparently not so near to the limit as in Hawaii. The elasticity of supply in Porto Rico appears to be somewhat greater than in Hawaii, but less than in the Philippines.

The remaining important source of supply is the beet producing area. The factors making for an increased production of sugar beets are plenty of land upon which beets could be grown,[1] and the fact that beet sugar companies and agricultural departments strongly urge the farmer to plant beets. Against these are necessity for crop rotation when growing beets, lack of available labor, and competing crops.[2] The factors limiting the sugar-beet supply

[1] In 1923 an investigation indicated that the "sugar-beet land capable of being planted in beets on farms investigated without changing greatly the type of farming" equaled 133 per cent of land planted. See *Costs of Producing Sugar-Beets*, p. 98.

[2] *Ibid.*, p. 98.

are shown to be powerful by the fact that notwithstanding a considerable increase in duty the production of beet sugar in the United States was no greater in 1930 than in 1920. In contrast with this were the very marked increases in output in Cuba, the Philippines, Porto Rico, and Hawaii during the same period. The lack of growth in domestic beet sugar production shows the elasticity of supply to be small.

Summing up, it would seem that a great increase in supply could come from Cuba with slight advance in price, from the Philippines a considerable increase, but from Porto Rico, Hawaii and domestic beet areas only a slight increase. The longer the period over which the higher price were sustained, the greater the increase from Cuba and perhaps from the Philippines.

We have so far been discussing the elasticity of an increasing supply. The elasticity of a decreasing supply for these areas depends upon a different factor: namely, the ease of alternative uses for the factors of production. This determines how quickly and to what extent a drop in price will decrease the supply from a given source. At one extreme of elasticity lies Porto Rico; and at the other domestic beet sugar, with Cuba, Hawaii, and the Philippines close behind Porto Rico. Heavy fixed investments, and — for the bulk of cane lands — no closely competing crops, one-crop traditions, and one-crop experience characterize the cane areas of Porto Rico, Cuba, Hawaii, and to a somewhat lesser extent the Philippines. If the decline in sugar prices were to be very severe and protracted over many years, doubtless some cane areas would change to other crops. With a moderate decline any curtailment of output would occur very slowly. There are no alternatives available to the capital invested in cane mills and irrigation works, and the grower must hesitate long before changing to other crops.

As regards sugar beets, the situation is different. Many domestic farmers now raising sugar beets would turn with comparative ease and quickness to other crops if price or profits declined. Witness the decline in sugar-beet area in California following a year of poor yield because of disease, or the decline in area planted in all the states from 882,000 to 606,000 acres immediately after the price decline of 1921. In contrast, Cuba in 1928–29 produced a record crop in spite of the low price and widespread loss prevailing in the previous three years of curtailed production. Cuban supply is easily extended, with difficulty reduced. Domestic sugar-beet crops are extended with difficulty, curtailed easily.

We are now in better position to estimate the effect of an increase or decrease in duties on price and on domestic production. The immediate effect of an increase in the duty on sugar, such as was made for example in the act of 1930, would be a lower price to foreign exporters. But to the domestic producers (Hawaii, Porto Rico, and the Philippines as well as to the beet sugar people) it would mean higher prices only if Cuba decreased her exports to the United States. Such a decrease would set in very slowly, and would not be considerable for several years. Eventually, no doubt, Cuban exports to the United States would decline. The decrease would be made up by increase from the protected regions in proportion to their elasticity of supply. Philippine shipments to the United States would probably show in the long run the greatest increase, beet sugar output the least. The ultimate result would be a higher bonus for all domestic producers who had contributed to the supply before the last increase in duty; while for the marginal product induced by the higher duties, there would be merely the normal profit. The duty would result rather in higher profits for the same number of producers than in normal profits for more producers.

When it comes to the converse case — that of a great reduction or complete removal of the duty, such as was contemplated in 1913 — the outcome is more easily stated. The immediate result would be a drop in the domestic price of sugar. With the duty removed, there would cease to be any difference between the world price (which would be slightly higher) and the domestic price.[1] The lower price received by domestic producers would necessarily

[1] The world price would rise slightly because of the increased consumption of sugar in the United States induced by the lower price and because more sugar would be diverted from other markets to the American market. But the increase in the world price would be slight compared to the drop in domestic price. The elasticity of consumption of sugar is not high in the United States, and it would take a small increase (small, that is, compared with the 50 billion pounds annually consumed in foreign countries) to cause a considerable drop in price.

cause production to decline, and that portion of the supply which had been profitably produced only because of the bonus would eventually disappear. The decline in production would be spread over many years; in areas like Porto Rico and Hawaii five to ten years; in the sugar-beet areas it would be rapid.[1]

Louisiana would doubtless be affected most of all and the Philippines probably least. Beet sugar and Hawaiian production would shrink considerably. In Porto Rico the decline would most likely be slowest and perhaps less than in Hawaii. Cuba's production, on the contrary, would expand, or (if still abnormally swollen, as it was in 1925–30) would fail to contract. The end result — the long-run result — would be that domestic and semi-domestic sources would contribute a much smaller share of domestic consumption, while foreign sources, chiefly Cuba, would contribute a much larger portion. For the consumer the change would result in gain both at once and in the long run, the eventual gain measured by almost the full extent of the reduction in duty.

1 The decline in the growing of sugar beets would be checked by the fact that beet-sugar manufacturers operating in less profitable beet areas would postpone the abandonment of their investment. They would offer the farmer as high a price for beets as they possibly could, leaving themselves little more than just enough to cover operating expenses. For many years a good portion of the decline in the duty would thus be absorbed by beet-sugar companies. The smaller the decline in duties, the longer would beet-sugar companies hang on; but eventually many of them, perhaps most, would have to go. The farmers, on the other hand, having alternate uses for their land, and having very little fixed investment in sugar-beet equipment, would not continue beet raising unless it were profitable.

1929 showed in most cases an increase, in some few a decline. The decline occurred in products least advanced in manufacture: pig-iron, steel ingots, bar iron. Exports of these had never been very large, and now sank to insignificant amounts. Sheets, plates, and structural shapes showed a moderate increase, tin plates a larger increase. The largest gains occurred in such commodities as required the greatest amount of processing: machinery, office appliances, automobiles. Here the exports were striking. Industrial machinery doubled (in value), agricultural machinery and office appliances quadrupled, motor vehicles and parts increased from 30 to 350 million dollars. It is significant that the cost of raw materials in those articles which declined constituted a large proportion of the cost price; whereas in commodities which showed considerable increases of exports, the cost of raw materials formed a very much smaller portion of the total cost. The evidence of the exports appears to substantiate the view expressed earlier that the advantage possessed by American manufacturers rests not so much on the abundance and cheapness of iron ore and coal as on the non-physical factors — the superior mechanical skill, inventiveness, and managerial ability which characterize the American industry. In the manufacture of large quantities of the highly elaborated articles American methods of mass production serve to convert high-wage rates into low-wage costs.

The situation of the special steels and their ores — manganese, tungsten, chrome, silicon, molybdenum, and vanadium — differs, of course, from that of tonnage products. Each of these items presents special problems in regard to the tariff,[1] and much attention has been given them in tariff discussions. But they form a small percentage of the steel produced and used, and are subject to great and rapid shifts with the constant changes in technique;

[1] The forces which developed the fine-steels industries in the United States were quite different from those responsible for the growth of the tonnage-steel industry. The discussion of the effect of the tariff on the iron and steel industry has no bearing on the fine-steels industries. See *The Economic Development of the Fine Steel Industries in the United States*, by S. Stratton (Unpublished Thesis, Harvard University, 1930).

and their history seems to bear little on the larger problems considered in this volume.[1]

We turn to a brief consideration of the possible connection between the tariff and combinations, as illustrated by the tin-plate and steel-rail industries.

The tin plate industry continued its rapid growth in the United States. From 1910 to 1929 domestic production tripled. It constituted two-thirds of the world supply. Imports — even those used for exported commodities and therefore entitled to drawback and not affected by the duty — virtually ceased, while exports increased from 13,000 to 250,000 tons. Before the war the ability of the American manufacturer of tin plate to hold his own without protection had been in doubt. But during the post-war period the situation changed. American manufacturers not only controlled the domestic market, but also competed successfully for foreign markets. Formerly in no small part a hand process, methods of production had improved so much that the industry achieved the level of effectiveness set by the dominant industries, where machine methods and mass production are the characteristic features. Various labor-saving devices were generally adopted, chief amongst them the automatic feeding of plates into tinning machines, the mechanical doubling of the sheet pack during rolling, and steel strip mills. So general was the substitution of machine for hand labor that the yearly output of tin plate per worker rose from 255,000 pounds in 1909 to 825,000 pounds in 1919. Continued mechanization of the industry throughout the next decade increased the output per laborer still further,[2] and caused the export trade to grow in spite of the fact that American hourly earnings in tin plate mills were more than double those of England, her chief competitor. The infant, lusty twenty years before, had now grown to complete maturity.[3]

[1] For a detailed discussion of the relation of special steels to the tariff as it stood in the latter part of the decade 1920–30, see Berglund and Wright, *Tariff on Iron and Steel*, Chap. VII.

[2] Figures of this kind for the years 1919–29 are not available.

[3] The following note appearing in *The Iron Age* of January 26, 1928, suggests that the growing efficiency of the American tin plate producers was setting too swift a pace for the foreign competitor:

"The introduction of steel strip mills in America has revolutionized the tin plate

workers more skilled than that of cottons, and silk mills therefore found it advisable to remain near the centres where there was abundant supply of workers trained "in the silk." [1] The advantages of being near the great silk-goods markets of New York and the dyeing and finishing centres of northern New Jersey also helped to keep the silk mills from following the cotton mills southward.

The expansion of the industry took place behind a barrier of protection that was at least as high as the rates which had fostered its growth in the period before 1910. The act of 1913, it is true, made some reductions in the rates,[2] but any effect that might have come from these was lost amid the violent changes which the war caused in demand, supply, and prices.[3] In the act

[1] In some branches, particularly in full-fashioned hosiery, the union wages were considered so high and union activities so troublesome as to induce many mills to move to North Carolina. The Industrial Bureau of Charlotte, North Carolina, remarked in 1928: "There is absolutely no unionism in the mills in this area, nor have the unionists ever been able to get any kind of foothold in this part of the south." Quoted in G. W. Taylor's *Significant Post-War Changes in the Full-Fashioned Hosiery Industry* (1929), p. 57.

[2] In some years, however, the price of silk goods was so high as to make the *ad valorem* duties under the act of 1913 higher than the specific rates of 1909 would have been.

[3] The only year of normal conditions during which the lower rates applied was that immediately succeeding the passage of the act of 1913. During this year imports of broad silks increased considerably (50 per cent greater than the annual average of 1909–13, and almost double the imports of 1913) and imports of silk ribbons tripled. How much of the increase was due to the lowered duties and how much to the domestic scarcity of silks resulting from a long strike of New Jersey silk workers in 1913, it is difficult to determine. A portion of the increase in imports of broad silks in 1914 consisted of cheap silks (the well-known habutae) from Japan and China. On these the specific duties under the act of 1909 had borne heavily, and the *ad valorem* rate under 1913 in effect made considerable reductions. The bulk of the increase in the imports of broad silks came from France and Switzerland. The duties on those silks had experienced only a moderate decline (from 55–65 per cent to 45 per cent), but the increase in imports was doubtless caused in some part by that decline. On the other hand, the scarcity of domestic silks, and the growing demand for silk goods brought about by the new fashions favoring their use, would have tended to increase imports even if the rates had not been lowered. The fact that increased silk imports began several months before the lower duties of 1913 became effective lends weight to the latter explanation. In any case no great change was going on. The absolute amount of the increase in imports other than habutae was not great enough to indicate that the reduction of duty in 1913 would have had

of 1922, and again in that of 1930, all trace of the reductions contemplated in 1913 disappeared. The act of 1922 increased the *ad valorem* rate on all silk goods. Duties on broad silks were advanced from 45 to 55 per cent; on velvets from 50 to 60 per cent; on spun silk from 35 to 40 per cent and more; and on thrown silk from 15 to 25 per cent and more. On many items the new *ad valorem* rates constituted a higher tax than the specific rates of the act of 1909.[1] The act of 1930 made no marked changes; it raised still further the duties on a few items, lowered them slightly on a few, and left the duties on plain broad silks and knit goods untouched.[2]

All *ad valorem* rates apply, of course, to the value of the finished product. Since raw silk constituted from 50 to 75 per cent of the value, and was imported free of duty, the rates on silk fabrics actually afforded the domestic producer a protection on his manufacturing costs ranging from 100 to 200 per cent. With protection so generous and extended over so long a period, it is not surprising that the expansion of the domestic silk industry kept pace with the growing domestic demand. And not only this: imports of silk goods formed a constantly declining proportion of the total consumption. In 1910, it will be remembered, imports constituted 20 per cent of the value of goods produced at home; by 1929 they had declined to 10 per cent.[3] If silk knit goods were included in this calculation, the decline would be from 20 to 6 per cent. If, further, allowance were made for the fact — to be explained presently — that Oriental habutae (China silk) and pongee, an important part of the imports of 1929, were admitted from 1913 to that date

in the end substantial effect on the proportion of imports to domestic production. The reduced rates still remained mainly prohibitive.

[1] The duties paid on all silk goods under the act of 1909 averaged 52 per cent of the value of imports. Under the act of 1922 the average was 60 per cent. These percentages, it need not be explained, are not accurate comparisons of *ad valorem* rates, as the classes of imports in the two periods were not identical; yet they serve as a rough measure of the height of the two rate schedules.

[2] On jacquard woven fabrics the duty was increased from 55 to 65 per cent; on wearing apparel from 60 to 65 per cent and up; on pile fabrics from 60 to 70 per cent; on umbrella silks from 50 to 60 per cent. The duty on thrown silks was reduced from 25 to 20 per cent.

[3] See p. 219, above.

under duties half as high as those in effect during the earlier period, the decline would be still greater.

The drop in the proportion which imports of silk goods bore to total consumption would seem to indicate that the domestic silk-goods industry had strengthened its competitive position. This decline suggests what the expansion of the industry alone does not: namely, that some further progress had been made toward the successful application of the principle of protection to an infant industry. In certain classes of broad silks, in spun silks, and in silk knit goods, the marked decline of imports supports the view that domestic producers had reached the stage where tariff support was needed to a smaller extent than in 1910, and perhaps was no longer needed at all.

It must be said also that, as regards broad silks in general, the skill of American designers and weavers was steadily improving. By 1929 American manufacturers were successfully producing a far wider range of fabrics and designs than in 1910, and were able to imitate any foreign fabric that acquired sufficient popularity to justify its production on not too small a scale. They were able to supply a large part, perhaps the greater part, of the American demand for the superior silks and the novelty fabrics which before the war had come so largely from Europe. The change was reflected in the imports. By 1929, notwithstanding a greatly increased demand for broad silks, there were fewer yards of high-priced silks imported than in pre-war years.[1]

The meaning of the decline in silk imports becomes greater when an analysis is made of the make-up of those which continued. The imports of broad silks in 1920–30, declining though they were, included a large quantity of silks quite unimportant in 1910: namely, the Japanese habutae and pongee. These, like silks imported from Europe, were fabrics requiring much direct labor in manufacture. Habutae is made of unthrown single-filament silk, of low grade in both warp and filling. The filaments are uneven in strength and size, and cause frequent stoppages in

[1] For a careful and detailed study of the domestic and foreign broad silk manufacturing industry see the excellent report of the United States Tariff Commission on *Broad-Silk Manufacture* prepared by O. B. Ryder and others (1926).

the warping and weaving operations. All-silk pongee is also woven from unthrown silk, not even and easily broken. The wild silk (tussah) used in its manufacture contains more flaws than cultivated silk and is therefore more troublesome to weave. The specific rates which had been applied to these fabrics under the act of 1909 had averaged more than 100 per cent on their value, and as much as 200 per cent on their conversion costs. The imports of these cheap silks hence were kept at a very low level. The *ad valorem* rates of 45 per cent in the act of 1913 and of 55 per cent in the act of 1922 amounted to a reduction in duty to one-half the former height. Imports consequently greatly rose, and constituted a larger fraction of the goods listed as broad silks. In 1927, of the 18 million dollars' worth of broad silks imported, half were Chinese and Japanese pongee. In the production of these cheap silks American mills could not compete. Because of the impossibility of continuous speed in warper and looms, the relatively high wages paid to American weavers[1] could not be translated into low-wage cost per yard of fabric.

[1] COMPARISON OF HOURLY WAGES OF WEAVERS IN THE BROAD SILK INDUSTRY IN THE UNITED STATES AND FOREIGN COUNTRIES

	First Half of 1914	Last Quarter of 1922 [a]	1927
United States (average)	$.2334	$.4950	$.61 [b]
France	.0627	.1072	.11 [c]
Switzerland	.0810	.2324	.16 [d]
Germany	.0919	.0344	.17 [e]
Italy	.0469	.0818	.09 [f]

(*a*) Figures for foreign countries in 1922 are converted at the average rate of exchange prevailing at the time.

(*b*) Average hourly earnings of male skilled and semi-skilled workers in silk manufacturing. Source National Industrial Conference Board, *Wages in the United States, 1914–1927*.

(*c*) Hourly earnings of male weavers in France, 1928. Source: *Bulletin de la Statistique Générale de la France*, Vol. 18.

(*d*) This figure is an estimate. *The International Labor Review* of 1929 contains figures for daily wages of several classes of textile workers which show that wages in 1926 were approximately double those of 1913.

(*e*) Hourly earnings of skilled male workers in the textile industry. Source: *International Labor Review*, 1929, p. 411.

(*f*) Average hourly earnings of all workers in silk weaving, March, 1928. Source: *The Ministry of Labour Gazette*, October, 1928.

No comparable figures for Japanese weavers are available for these years, but in 1919 the wage per hour for female labor was only about $.075. Figures for 1914 and 1922 taken from United States Tariff Commission, *Broad Silk and the Tariff*, pp. 298 and 301. Some figures for the year 1926 are cited in J. E. Orchard, *Japan's Economic Position* (1930, p. 349). The average daily wage (including bonuses and cash allowances) for workers in the textile mills of Japan was (1926) $.78 a day for men and $.45 a day for women.

There is, of course, another side to the case. Other American fabrics — radium silk, imitation pongee,[1] wash satin, woven Jersey, and all-silk foulard, which together constituted about one-fifth of all domestic broad silks — competed for many uses with imported habutae and pongee. At the same price, or even at a somewhat higher price, the domestic goods were usually preferred because of their heavier weight and greater strength. But given a price low enough, the Oriental fabrics would often be preferred. Had they not been burdened by a duty of 55 per cent, they would have supplanted to some extent the better American products; how much, who can say? The same sort of situation doubtless existed where the American silks were not better than the foreign, but poorer. In the production of very fine silks and weaves of unusual design, as in that of very cheap habutae and pongee, America could not have competed with foreign fabrics without high protection. Broad silks of the choicest grades continued to be imported over the tariff barrier, as they had always been; a fact which shows that, had it not been for the duty, many more of the better grade European silks would have supplanted the rival American fabrics. At the two extremes — the manufacture of very expensive and of very cheap silks — domestic mills were still dependent upon high protection.

On the other hand, there is nothing to indicate that the ultimate goal of protection to young industries, domestic production at as low a money cost as in foreign countries, had been reached for broad silks. True, there were exports; but an analysis of them yields no evidence that in neutral markets — that is, in countries giving American goods no preferential rates — American mills were more able to compete with foreign producers in 1929 than in 1910. Exports of broad silks in 1927–29 amounted in all to only 3 million dollars. The bulk of these went to Canada, Cuba, and Mexico. Canada, however, imported only 15 per cent of her broad silks from the United States; in the main, goods de-

[1] Imitation pongee is made in the United States only in part of tussah. Either the warp or the filling is cotton or spun silk, or spun tussah. Similarly with domestic habutae. It is made from a loose-twist tram instead of from unthrown silk, and from medium and coarse silks of good quality. These fabrics can be woven with more speed and fewer stoppages than the imported varieties.

manded for quick delivery. In Cuba, on the other hand, while the value imported from the United States was less than in Canada, American goods did constitute the major part of the total. As with Canada, a large part of these were doubtless caused by the proximity of Cuba to American sources of supply and by the demand for certain special brands and novelties, in the purchase of which price was a minor consideration. In Cuba still another factor entered; American goods entered that country at a preferential rate. Silk goods from America were subject to a duty of only 27 per cent, while those from other countries paid 45 per cent. The exports to Cuba, so far as not explained by proximity and brand, seem to have been due to the preferential rate. American exports of broad silks to Cuba consisted largely of silk and cotton mixed goods and medium-grade, plain, all-silk staples. These were the goods in which the difference between foreign and American costs was smallest. Given a 14 per cent advantage in Cuban duties, American mills appear to have successfully competed with foreign mills. From 1913 to 1926 the proportion of American broad silks in Cuban broad silk imports doubled.[1] The increase may suggest this much, in accord with the general trend: that the range of broad silks in which American mills were becoming progressively less dependent upon high tariff support was enlarging.

Signs of a similar trend are to be found in other directions. The expansion of the broad silk industry was accompanied by mechanical progress in almost every process. Progress in throwing, weaving, and finishing, though not spectacular, was considerable. Particularly was this the case in warping and weaving. Widespread use of automatic stop motion devices for warp and filling, reduction in friction through more accurate adjustments, and smoother acceleration of the harness motion contributed to faster and better weaving. Improved quilling, coping, and finishing machinery, mechanical skein dyers, higher speed warpers, and the automatic "warp let-off" were some of the important new devices. Scarcely a month passed without the issue of a score

[1] During the abnormal years of the war the proportion of American imports to the total rose as high as 85 per cent.

or more patents applying to some phase of broad-silk manufacture. The use of individual motor drives on looms and throwing frames spread rapidly. Automatic looms were successfully developed for the simpler silk weaves; their use, however, was not widespread except on mixed cotton and silk goods. The number of non-automatic looms tended by one weaver increased in many instances from two to four and even six. In mills using automatic looms, one weaver sometimes operated as many as twelve. Winders, too, increased in efficiency. Before the war one winder tended one side of a machine with forty ends of yarn, in later years two sides, and in some mills three. Loom fixers also attended to more looms.

These improvements and refinements resulted in more and better fabrics per worker. Inevitably, they led to readjustments of the labor force, and to labor struggles and disturbances—matters whose consideration would carry us far from our main topic. In 1910, when 105,000 persons were engaged in silk manufacture (not including silk knit goods), the value added by manufacture was 89 million dollars. In 1927 with 127,000 persons (a 20 per cent increase), the value added by manufacture was more than triple (304 millions). Per person the money value increased in the ratio 1 to 3½, which is more than would be in accord with the mere rise in the price level. A comparison even more significant is that in physical terms. In 1910, 64,000 looms produced 185 million yards of broad silk; in 1927, 108,000 looms produced 512 million square yards.[1] The yards per loom increased in the ratio of about 3 to 5. The increase, it may be remarked, was due rather to greater speed and better construction of looms than to changes which would enable each weaver to tend more looms. No figures are available on this latter point for the period after 1919; but from 1910 to 1919 (the last year for which census figures give the number of silk weavers) the number of looms per weaver increased only from 2.25 to 2.27, while the number of yards per weaver increased in much greater proportion, from 6.565 to 8.279. During the period of very intense competition after 1919 there was ad-

[1] The figures in 1910, census for the year 1909, are for linear yards, but the number of square yards would be very nearly the same.

vance in both ways — in the number of looms per weaver and in efficiency in silk mills.

All this, however, must be considered in the light of comparison — the relative positions of American and foreign producers. The technological improvements were not confined to American manufacture; they did not necessarily result in any considerable decrease in the *difference* between domestic and foreign money costs. Furthermore, the relative increase in wages tended to offset whatever advantage accrued to American producers from greater output per worker. In domestic mills money wage rates from 1910 to 1929 rose much higher than in foreign mills. Hence the difference between American and foreign money costs tended to persist. Where the direct labor costs (expenses) constituted a large proportion of the total, the difference tended to persist even more.

In an analysis made by the United States Tariff Commission of the money cost of manufacturing 103 fabrics in the United States, it was found that direct labor costs of weaving varied from 5 per cent (on satins made in part of spun silk) to 22 per cent (on fancy woven fabrics).[1] It is evident, therefore, that in the manufacture of the latter class — fabrics in which the direct labor costs form a large proportion of the total cost, such as fancy woven fabrics habutae, and pongee — the disadvantage to American mills of wage increases in excess of foreign wage increases was felt most. In the production of all-silk fabrics the increases in money wages were less burdensome on the fabrics made with medium and coarse yarns, and it is in this class of the all-silk fabrics that there appears to have been the nearest approach toward independence from tariff support. In the manufacture of mixed silk goods, particularly silk and cotton, the differences between domestic and foreign costs were least. Silk-filled cotton-warp fabrics lend themselves to machine production almost as readily as cotton fabrics, and can therefore be produced at relatively lower labor costs. The fact that a not inconsiderable quantity of these goods was exported — under the classification of cotton goods — suggests that possibly the money costs were even equal.

[1] *Broad-Silk Manufacture*, Table 78 E.